SOUL SEARCHING

SOUL SEARCHING

The Religious and Spiritual Lives

of American Teenagers

CHRISTIAN SMITH

With Melinda Lundquist Denton

OXFORD

UNIVERSITY PRESS

OXFORD
UNIVERSITY PRESS

Oxford University Press, Inc., publishes works that further
Oxford University's objective of excellence
in research, scholarship, and education.

Oxford   New York
Auckland   Cape Town   Dar es Salaam   Hong Kong   Karachi
Kuala Lumpur   Madrid   Melbourne   Mexico City   Nairobi
New Delhi   Shanghai   Taipei   Toronto
With offices in
Argentina   Austria   Brazil   Chile   Czech Republic   France   Greece
Guatemala   Hungary   Italy   Japan   Poland   Portugal   Singapore
South Korea   Switzerland   Thailand   Turkey   Ukraine   Vietnam

Published by Oxford University Press, Inc.
198 Madison Avenue, New York, NY 10016

www.oup.com

First issued as an Oxford University Press paperback, 2009

Oxford is a registered trademark of Oxford University Press

Library of Congress Cataloging-in-Publication Data
Smith, Christian (Christian Stephen), 1960–.
Soul searching : the religious and spiritual lives of American teenagers / Christian Smith
with Melinda Lundquist Denton.
p.   cm.
Includes bibliographical references and index.
ISBN 978-0-19-538477-2 (pbk.)
1. Teenagers—Religious life—United States.   2. Spiritual Life.
I. Denton, Melinda Lundquist.   II. Title.
BL625.47.S63 2005
200'.835'0973—dc22   2004015996

3 5 7 9 8 6 4

Printed in the United States of America
on acid-free paper

For Emily Jean
C.S.S.

For my parents, Gregg and Virginia Lundquist
M.L.D.

Acknowledgments

This project and book would not have been possible without the generous support of Lilly Endowment Inc. Very many heartfelt thanks therefore go especially to Chris Coble and Craig Dykstra for their tremendous support and excellent advice for the National Study of Youth and Religion. Thanks, too, go to Mark Constantine for his early help in mobilizing this research project. Roxann Miller, Debby Pyatt, and Phil Schwadel have all made unique and important contributions to the NSYR, for which we are likewise grateful. Many thanks to staff at the UNC Odum Institute for Research in Social Science for their administrative and logistical support of the NSYR: Ken Bollen, Peter Leousis, and Beverly Wood. We are grateful for the important research contributions of the many graduate students and co-investigators involved in this project: John Bartkowski, Tim Cupery, Kenda Dean, Dan Dehanas, Korie Edwards, Richard Flory, John Hipp, Lindsay Hirschfeld, Younoki Lee, Lisa Pearce, Norm Peart, Darci Powell, Mark Regnerus, Demetrius Semien, David Sikkink, Sondra Smolek, Steve Vaisey, and Eve Veliz. For excellent interview transcription work, thanks to Viviana Calandra, Meredith Conder, Krista Goranson, Laura Hoseley, and Diane Johnson. The NSYR's Public Advisory Board served as a tremendously helpful resource in the development of this project; we are much obliged to Dan Aleshire, Leah Austin, Mary Jo Bane, Dorothy Bass, Brad Braxton, Carmen Cervantes, Gerald Durley, Ian Evison, Robert Franklin, Edwin Hernandez, Rick Lawrence, Sherry Magill, Roland Martinson, Bob McCarty, George Penick, Jonathan Sher, Bill Treanor, and Jonathan Woocher. Thanks to John Blunk and Kathy Holliday for their hard work fielding our survey. For their valuable methodological advice early on, we are grateful to Nancy Ammerman, Peter Bearman, Peter Bensen, Gary Bowen, Don Camburn, Harry Catugno, Shannon Cavanagh, Greg Duncan, Penny Edgell, Glen Elder, Chris Ellison, Michael Emerson, Susan Ennett, Jessica Fields, Frank Furstenberg, Sally Gallagher, John Green, Kathie Harris, Sarah L. Hofferth, Andrea Hussong, Steven Knable, Alma Kuby, Karl Landis, Annette Lareau, Isaac Lipkus, Sara McLanahan, John McNee, Cindy Monteith, Don Richter, Eugene Roehlkepartain, Mark Schulman, Darren Sherkat, Tom Smith, Freya Sonenstein, Julien Teitler, Kathi Harker Tillman, Leah Totten, Chintan Turakhia, Steve Warner, Michael Weeks, and Brad Wilcox. We are also grateful to Howard Aldrich, Jen Ashlock, Kraig Beyerlein, Dean Borgman, Ashley Bowers, Laura Burns, Lynn Clark, Tracy Constantine, Natalia Deeb-Sossa, Elizabeth Earle, Vickie Elmore, Bob Faris, Erin Ferry, Dino Fire, Todd Granger, Sara Haviland, Jim Heft, Pat Hersch, Stewart Hoover, Allen Jackson, Phil Kim, Timothy Kimbrough, Dan Lambert, Erin Lunsford, Carol Lytch, Bill Massey, Linda McDonough, Hannah Meador, Keith Meador, Mark Meares, Don Mikush, Don Miller, Ken Mondragon, Kelly Moore, Evelyn Parker, Clarissa Pinheiro, Robert Shelton, Emily Smith, Dick Soloway, Julien Teitler, Elizabeth Travis, Nicole Tyson, Thomas Tyson, and webslingerZ for so many important and varied contributions to the success of our project. Thanks to John Sanderson of Horizon Designs for the map of interview locations.

We are indebted to the anonymous reviewers of our manuscript for helpful suggestions in strengthening our organization and arguments. Finally, many thanks to the untold number of teenagers and parents who agreed to help us with our focus groups, interview pretests, personal interviews, and survey. We hope and trust that the help and support of all of these good people will result in good things.

Contents

SOUL SEARCHING

Introduction

AMERICAN TEENAGERS CAN embody adults' highest hopes and most gripping fears. They represent a radiant energy that opens doors to the future for families, communities, and society. But they also evoke deep adult anxieties about teen rebellion, trouble, and broken and compromised lives. Parents, teachers, and youth workers behold their teenagers with pride, hope, and enjoyment, but also often worry, distress, and frustration. How are our teenagers doing in life? What is happening to our relationships with them? How will they turn out? Happy and responsible? Troubled and depressed? Or worse? Such personal ambivalent feelings about teenagers are amplified in the discourse and images that animate our culture and institutions. Our youth, it is often said, are the future, our hope for a brighter world. Teenagers are exciting, zany, inventive, fun. We adults love them dearly, we tell ourselves, and would do anything to make their lives happy and full. And yet, adults see and fear in adolescence a dark side as well. Surly indifference and defiance. Dangerous peer pressure. Parties. Foolish choices. Drugs. Drunk driving. Crime. Pregnancy. Abortions. AIDS. Suspensions. School dropouts. School shootings. Suicide. So, many adults worry deeply that, whatever good there is, something may also be profoundly wrong about the lives of American teenagers.

Some adults attempt to respond. Parents make efforts to talk to their kids more often, to be more involved in their lives, to involve them in sports, clubs, camps, and other constructive activities. Communities set up youth centers and organize afterschool programs. School boards incorporate char-

3

acter education and community service into their curricula. And foundations and philanthropies sponsor studies and issue reports and recommendations to improve adolescent well-being. Many of these are worthy efforts, but in all of this there is often a missing element. In many discussions and activities revolving around better understanding and helping teenagers, one aspect of their lives seems frequently to go unnoticed, unconsidered, unexamined. That is their religious and spiritual lives. Very few efforts to better understand American adolescents take seriously their religious faith and spiritual practices. This is a curious neglect. Many teenagers, as this book shows, are very involved in religion. They say on surveys, at least, that their religious beliefs and practices are important parts of their lives. They feel good about the religious congregations they belong to. Many say that faith provides them with guidance and resources for knowing how to live well. To adequately comprehend the lives of American teenagers, it therefore seems important to understand their religious and spiritual beliefs, commitments, practices, experiences, and desires. And yet, so few of us do. In fact, reading many published overview reports on adolescence can leave one with the distinct impression that American youth simply *do not have* religious and spiritual lives.[1]

This book is a response to that situation, intended to help develop a better scholarly and public understanding of the religious and spiritual lives of American adolescents. The following chapters lay out the main survey and interview findings of the National Study of Youth and Religion, a unique research project on the religious and spiritual lives of American adolescents conducted from 2001 to 2005 at the University of North Carolina at Chapel Hill. What follows provides solid answers to questions about the character of teenage religion, the extent of spiritual seeking among youth, how religion affects adolescent moral reasoning and risk behaviors, and much more. We hope that by informing readers about the religious and spiritual lives of American teenagers we will help to foster discussions in families, religious congregations, community organizations, and beyond, not only about the general state of religion in the United States, but also about cultural and institutional practices that may better serve and help to care for America's teens.

The vast majority of research in the sociology of religion in the United States focuses on either religious institutions or on adults, age 18 and older, and many scholars who study adolescents neglect religion in their lives. This inattention to youth religion works to our detriment. American adolescents between the ages of 10 and 19 represent about 14 percent of all Americans, a population deserving the scholarly attention of sociologists of religion as much as any other group. Furthermore, because adolescence represents a crucial developmental transition from childhood to adulthood, research on teens can disclose important knowledge about religious socialization and change in the life course. Adolescents compose a population that many religious organizations, both congregations and parachurch ministries, target to exert influence in their lives. Adolescence and young adulthood are also life stages when religious conversion is likely to take place. Adolescence furthermore provides a unique opportunity to study religious influences on family relationships, peer interactions, risk behaviors, media use, mental and emotional well-being, and many other outcome variables. Finally, adolescence provides an ideal baseline for longitudinal research on religious influences in people's lives. There is thus a great deal of value in pursuing a big-picture, in-depth study of youth religion and spirituality in the United States.

But such a study of the religion and spirituality of youth also affords an important and distinctive window through which to observe and assess American religion as a whole. A variety of recent studies have made diverse claims about the character and transformation of American religion. Some scholars have observed that American religion has recently become profoundly diverse, inundated by waves of new immigrants greatly expanding the demographic pluralism of American faiths.[2] Other scholars suggest that American religion has become culturally individualistic and subjectivistic, driven by religious "seekers" bearing consumerist mentalities about faith.[3] Some writers claim that American youth have become deeply alienated from traditional institutional religion and are either opting out of faith altogether or are on quests to construct more authentic, postmodern versions of faith and spirituality.[4] Along these lines, some suggest that American religion generally is losing the coherence of historical religious traditions, as individuals increasingly create personal, bricolage spiritualities, eclectically mixing and matching spiritual practices from diverse faiths.[5] Some suggest that religion is really a marginal factor in the lives of American teenagers, not central to their real problems and concerns.[6] Yet others observe a growing movement among American youth returning to religious tradition, liturgy, and historical orthodoxy.[7] These are all potentially important observations. But do we really know enough to be sure that these reports accurately describe the character of American religion today?

One way to try to address these issues and questions is through a nationally representative study of American youth. Many of these accounts tell their stories in distinctly generational terms, suggesting that American baby boomers first opened the door to profound religious changes and that younger generations now drive the cutting edge of fundamental religious transformation in America. Of all Americans, youth are often said to be the most intensely exposed to and engaged with the digital and interactive communication technologies that are thought to be transforming American culture.[8] Many claim that youth are particularly influenced by a contemporary postmodern culture that profoundly reconfigures understandings of knowledge, belief, and moral reasoning.[9] Youth are sometimes thought to have the shallowest roots in the substance of their own historical religious traditions, knowing or caring the least about the distinctive content of their own faiths, and so quite open to alternative viewpoints.[10] We also know that they are the target of intense, sophisticated, secular, mass consumer advertising campaigns trying to secure the brand loyalties of a consumer generation with hefty disposable income, and that this significantly shapes their values and assumptions.[11]

For these and other reasons, we might expect American teenagers to serve as excellent indicators of possible developing trends in American religion more broadly. If many of the striking claims noted above are in fact prevalent in the American religious field, we would expect to see them evident among American adolescents. If we do not find them among American adolescents, that might cast some doubt on the claims. This book thus represents in part an attempt to describe and evaluate the shape and texture of American religion broadly by viewing it through the lens of the religious and spiritual practices of religious and nonreligious American youth. The pages that follow do not engage in hypothesis testing per se but seek to use recent claims about profound changes under way in American religion as sensitizing questions and framing devices in our analyses. In this way, we may learn a great deal not only about adolescent religion and spirituality specifically—which is very important in itself—but also about American religion more broadly.

In this book, we report the findings from research conducted by the National Study of Youth and Religion (NSYR; see www.youthandreligion.org). From July 2002 to March 2003, the NSYR conducted a national, random-digit-dial telephone survey of U.S. households containing at least one teenager age 13–17, surveying one household parent for about 30 minutes and one randomly selected household teen for about 50 minutes. Then, in the spring and summer of 2003, 17 trained project researchers conducted 267 in-depth, face-to-face interviews with a subsample of telephone survey respondents in 45 states. The locations of each of these interviews are shown in figure 1.

Figure 1. Locations of NSYR Personal Interviews (N = 267).

These interviews were sampled to capture a broad range of difference among U.S. teens in religion, age, race, sex, socioeconomic status, rural-suburban-urban residence, region of the country, and language spoken (English or Spanish). To our knowledge, this project has been the largest, most comprehensive and detailed study of American teenage religion and spirituality conducted to date (specifics on the NSYR research methods are reported in Appendixes B and C). Altogether, the data collected provide for a dependable, representative description and analysis of the contours and character of adolescent religion and spirituality in the United States today. We address all of the major American religious traditions and two minority religious traditions, Mormonism and Judaism, although the majority traditions receive disproportionate attention in the analysis. Other NSYR researchers will also be publishing books and reports dedicated to better understanding the religious and spiritual lives of U.S. teenagers in minority religious traditions and in specific Protestant denominations.[12]

Here is what to expect in coming chapters and how to read them. Chapter 1 begins laying out some key themes of this book by considering the stories of two Baptist girls whom we personally interviewed. Chapter 2 examines extensive, nationally representative survey findings on the religious and spiritual identities, affiliations, beliefs, experiences, and practices of U.S. adolescents. Chapter 3 focuses on three specific groups of American teenagers—"spiritual seekers" who are "spiritual but not religious," teens who are entirely disengaged from religion, and religiously devoted teenagers—to better understand who these teens are. Chapter 4 explores in much greater depth American adolescents' thoughts, beliefs, and feelings about and experiences of religious faith and spirituality, drawing extensively on our personal interviews. Our purpose in chapter 4 is to elaborate from adolescent discourse many of the central themes and perspectives that define religion and spirituality for the majority of teenagers, while also paying attention to minority and alternative ideas and viewpoints among youth. Chapter 5 explores some of the major social forces and factors that form the lives of U.S. youth, seeking from a sociological perspective to better understand our society's structures and systems that may significantly shape the religious and spiritual lives of teenagers. Chapter 6 zeros in on one religious group of teens, focusing on the question of why U.S. Catholic teenagers as a whole rather consistently score lower on the religiosity measures of this study. Chapter 7 addresses the question of how religious practices associate with different outcomes in adolescents' lives. There we examine evidence suggesting that greater religiosity is significantly associated with more positive adolescent life outcomes and seek to reflect theoretically why and how this is so. The chapters are meant to fit together in order but can also, with the exception of chapters 4 and 5, which depend on each other to portray a bigger picture, be read independently. The conclusion summarizes and elaborates on our findings.

The religious and spiritual lives of U.S. teenagers are complicated. That complication is evident in the general flow of this book, which moves from a fairly positive initial perspective to a more critical tone by its middle and then back to a paradoxically positive viewpoint by its end. We hope our analyses, findings, and stories together provide an understanding of American adolescents more reliable and rich than we have enjoyed to date so as to provoke better-informed conversations among people who care about teenagers' lives in all of their concerns and complexities.

1

Two Baptist Girls

I SAT SLEEPILY in my car waiting in the public library parking lot for 10 A.M. to arrive, the appointed time for my interview with a 16-year-old girl from this small mountain town in a Middle Atlantic state. Her name was Joy, according to my paperwork.[1] I had called her and her parents a few weeks before to ask if she would do a personal interview with me for a large research project I was conducting on American teenagers. They agreed, and we made arrangements to meet at their town's public library. So here I was, quite tired. The previous afternoon and evening I had conducted two interviews with teenagers in two other states, then caught a few hours' sleep at a highway hotel, and in the morning drove a few more hours on winding country roads to this mountain hamlet to meet with Joy. But I was also excited. Both of my interviews had gone very well. When I finished with Joy in a few hours, I had yet another interview scheduled that afternoon a few hours' drive away. Four teen interviews, three states, in 26 hours. Not bad.

Ten minutes before the hour, an old gray sedan pulled into the lot and parked a few spots away from me. Looking discreetly through the car windows between us, I saw what appeared to be an old man and a young girl waiting in their car. I was pretty sure it was my contacts, although not certain. A number of old and young people were also gathering, waiting for the library doors to open. I double-checked to make sure all my digital recording equipment was in order. At 10:00 I got out and locked my doors. The man and girl got out of their car. Our eyes met in the tentative way that strangers who have arranged to meet each other in public often do. "Hello, are you

9

Joy?" I asked. Yes sir, she said. We shook hands, awkwardly. "Thanks so much for agreeing to do this interview. I appreciate your time and help." "Sure thing," Joy said. "Well," Joy's stepfather told me, "I hope your study is gonna help us understand kids better a'cause we got us a problem here. Teens all around here is drinking booze and doin' drugs. It's a real pest." I gave a look of concern. "But my Joy here ain't into that stuff, are you, Joy? At least, you better *not* be, girl," he announced to us both, jokingly. Joy laughed lightly, shaking her head—whether to say "Of course not" or in ridicule of the man I could not tell. Strolling toward the library, I commented on what a nice town theirs was. "Oh, yeah, this a real nice place to live," agreed Joy's stepfather, "though the economy's been on hard times lately." From the parking lot high on a hill, he pointed out below what had been Joy's middle school and on another hill the large garage of a famous NASCAR driver. I had to confess I hadn't heard the racer's name before. "Okay, Joy, you have fun and I'll come back in a few hours to pick you up." I thanked him for his help, then Joy and I disappeared into the library, making our way to the staff meeting room I had reserved for this interview.

JOY, SUFFERING, AND HOPE

Joy sat patiently at the conference table as I set up my recording equipment, smiling as I made small talk. I explained to her the standard ground rules of the interview: there are no right or wrong answers, I only want to have a conversation to better understand her life, all of her answers are confidential, she can refuse to answer any question she's not comfortable with, and so on. No problem, she said. Now, facing Joy, I could see she was not blessed with features reflecting cultural standards of physical beauty: she has bad teeth, impossible hair, and acne. Those kinds of genes can't help any teen, I thought to myself.

We started off talking about her family. Joy lives with her mother and stepfather in her maternal grandmother's house. Grandma owns the place, so there's no rent to pay, but, Joy noted, "what Grandma says, goes." Joy has one brother, two stepbrothers, and five stepsisters, who live all over the East Coast. Her mom, she says, is "not stable enough" to work; she has "a bad problem with keeping concentration." Her stepfather, Rudy, no longer does bricklaying work because of a lung problem that has him on disability. They barely pay bills with Rudy's disability check and some kind of child support from the state. Joy said she wants to get a job to earn some money, but Rudy won't let her: "He wants to do everything himself." Work would also require Joy to get a driver's license, which her parents oppose, " 'Cause they know then I'd never be home. Plus they know I'm probably going to drive pretty wild, they know me that way." Joy tells me she loves her mother and Rudy, but she doesn't feel close to them and they don't get along well. She does not share any personal concerns or feelings with either of them. "Sometimes," she remarks, "when Rudy gets ill about something, he just takes it out on everyone. He gets in a bad mood and goes off in another room and won't speak, and if you try to talk to him he gets ill." Rudy also does not like Joy's real brother, she continues, because he was kicked out of the Army for doing drugs. Doesn't sound like the greatest family situation, I think to myself.

What kinds of people, I ask, is Joy friends with? "I got, I guess you'd say, grungy friends and crazy friends. They like to do wild stuff or whatever." What kind of wild stuff? "Drugs and partying and stuff." What do you mean by "grungy"? "They do drugs and they're sorta, talk about suicide and stuff like that a lot. I try to help them out but some haven't gotten help." What, I ask, does Joy do with her friends? "Go over to their house, just sit around and watch movies or MTV, and if we go out we just go to parties and stuff like that." What they watch, she says, depends partly on what's on the satellite dish. There are no shopping malls or movie theaters in town or nearby. Is there any type of teen, I inquire, that she is not friends with? "People who think they're better than everybody else. I just can't stand that. As long as they respect me, I'll be friends." I ask how well her parents know her friends. They know some of them, but they don't know she has suicidal friends; she keeps them well separated by telling them not to come over to her house. "My parents don't know me that well," Joy explains. "I don't tell them a lot of stuff that I do, like go out and party and do drugs and drink and stuff like that." Did she wish that her parents knew her better? "Not really," she says.

I remark to Joy again about how financially tight their family must be with nobody working. "Well," she notes, "my $757 child support that I was getting from my dad went out, because he died last April." Your dad died last April? Joy explains:

> When I moved here from living with him, a lot of people say he was abusive, and he did hit my mom and my brother but he never hit me, so I can't say nothing bad about him. And when I moved in with my mom and Rudy we went to court over child custody and Dad got custody of my brother and my mom got custody of me, and they asked me if I wanted visitation rights and I said yeah. So, then we had to meet somewhere and then Rudy, I guess he just didn't like it, so I didn't for, it had been probably five or six years since I'd seen my dad. Just never saw him. Then he died.

How, I asked, did that make her feel? "It hurt me because I had to go next state to see him, and his mother told me that all he wanted before he died was to see me. And I couldn't see him." That's very sad, I said. I'm sorry. "Uh-huh. Everybody thought he was a troublemaker so Rudy didn't want him around and told him if he came here and was acting crazy and stuff he'd call the law." She continued: "When my dad died, I just kind of drifted off. I blamed them for a lot of it because they wouldn't let me see him." She's somewhat angry, she explains, but doesn't really hate her parents because she knows they were trying to do what they thought best.

Had there been any other major turning points in her life? "I changed a lot when I went into ninth grade."

'Cause I met one of my little grungy friends that tried to commit suicide all the time. I met him a week before he tried it the first time, before I knew he did anything. I didn't even know he was trying to commit suicide, and a week after I met him he wasn't at school one day and I found out he tried to kill himself. Three weeks later he came back and said that he had been put in the hospital and a mental institution or drug rehab or something. I was like, he'll be all right, and I gave him a hug when he came back and everything. Two days later he tried to commit suicide again and I haven't seen him since. He's in Massachusetts with his dad.

How did that affect you? "It hit me pretty hard. I felt like it was my fault since I didn't do nothing to help him. I felt like I should have talked to him because I had a lot in common with him." What, I questioned, did she have in common? "Because I was suicidal. That's just something I was doing before I met him and then I found out that he tried it, and I felt like I could have related to him a little bit better, but I didn't." Turns out Joy had seen a psychiatrist to whom she was referred by a school guidance counselor, but that, she said, was not helpful. "I just didn't feel like talking about it with him," she said. Joy has a couple of friends who have tried to commit suicide, and she herself has tried many times. "I overdosed on a bunch of stuff once, pills or some prescription of my mom's, I took the whole bottle. It didn't work. I just went to sleep for a long time." Apparently nobody in her family realized anything had happened. "No, they never found out." How did she feel, I asked, trying to kill herself when nobody even knew? "I think," she admitted, "it's pretty pitiful." A few other times she said people knew something was wrong with her and tipped off the school counselor, who notified her parents. What did her parents say? "They're hurt. They think that they're doing something wrong, and it really doesn't have nothing to do with them, it's just me." What does she mean "it's just me"? "A lot of times," she explained matter-of-factly, "I don't feel like I want to be here, here on earth. I get hyper a lot and then it goes straight downhill and I'm depressed. A lot of times I don't feel like I oughta be here, I'm not worth nothing or whatever."

I asked Joy whether she talks to people about her feelings and problems. Her other suicidal friends talk about *their* feelings, she says, but she does not share her own feelings with them. "I hear everybody's problems. But I write poems and short stories and that's how I get it out. I've got probably over 300 of them." Someday, she says, she wants to publish what she has written because it might help other teens: "There's a lot of people out there I know are the same way and feel the same way I do about stuff." But she has never shown her work to any of her teachers. "It's too personal," she says. Anyway, "I just feel if anybody looked at me one way they would know that I was trying to kill myself, just by seeing how I act." But she says she also doesn't want people to know. "I just don't feel like it really applies to them. I don't know." Would she like to change and be a happier person? "I don't care," she replies without feeling.

I ask if she is religious in any way. "I was a Christian for a long time, but right now, I just, I don't believe in nothing right now. I was baptized and pretty much led a Christian life up until ninth grade, when I started doing all that stuff." She says her mom and Rudy consider themselves Christians and attend an independent Baptist church, which Joy also attends about monthly just to keep her parents happy. But she has not told them that she's not a Christian any more. She said she does feel welcomed at church and that the adults there seem pleasant to her. I asked Joy to explain how it was that she decided she was not a Christian. "I don't know, there's just a bunch of different, when I was feeling suicidal and everything, I guess I didn't think God cared that much or it really didn't matter to me if he did, I guess. I just, I'm not, let's see, how I, I don't think I could really lead a Christian life. I'm not strong enough to do that and go out and tell people about that. I can't do that." So, she thinks that being a Christian means behaving in a certain demanding way of life and she realized she couldn't do that? "Yeah, that's pretty much all it was." And it seemed God didn't care for her when she was in trouble? "Well, I think he cared, but it's to the point that I didn't really care whether anybody cared, so." Had she ever felt love from God? "I feel it, it's just I don't want to take part of, I don't know. I think he loves me, but I, I just, it don't really matter to me." Joy then explains that she thinks faith is all about the individual: "People believe what they want to believe and if they get something out of that, then that's what they should believe. That's just not me." She does believe in God, she says: "Just somebody up there watching everything you do." What does God think about her life? "I know he don't like it." Joy also believes God is forgiving. But then she says God is not really a personal being, but more like a cosmic force. It doesn't seem to fit together, I think. Does she feel close to God? "I feel that he's around everybody, but if you choose to block him out, that's your choice, and that's most likely what I do. If I'm drinking or something I push him away. A lot of times I just ignore God."

At this point in the interview, I recalled seeing a locally published Christian newsletter in the funky coffee shop downtown I'd stopped into that morning. One of the newsletter's cover articles, "Are You Lukewarm?," asserted that we are a nation of lukewarm Christians whom, according to the quoted Bible verse, God will "spew out of his mouth." The other cover article's headline, written by someone from Dial-the-Truth Ministries, declared in response to the inquiring letter of an 8-year-old girl named Virginia, "Yes, Virginia, There Is a Hell." The article concluding with the pointed question, "One hundred years from now where will you be?" I started having the feeling, though not the time then to figure it out, that there was some connection between that newsletter's messages and Joy's current spiritual condition.

We moved on. Joy affirmed that she believes in the supernatural and the paranormal. She also has pleasant memories of a week of religious summer camp and of a fun Christian conference or church youth group "lock-in" she had attended. But those were before ninth grade. Now she doesn't read the

Bible or pray or do any other religious practice except occasional church attendance. She has also never heard the phrase "I'm spiritual but not religious." That idea seemed odd to her. One of her best friends since kindergarten, she notes, is a solid Christian. How, I asked, do they relate? "Every once in a while, like if I'm on the phone cussing and stuff, she'll tell me to stop cussing and everything. She doesn't cuss, and she doesn't drink and she doesn't do anything bad, she tries to live a life that God would want her to live or whatever." Another good friend recently converted from Wicca to Christianity but, Joy mentions, she's still having sex with her boyfriend. Joy said there are religious youth groups in the area that she's been invited to attend but does not. "I didn't get along with the people even though they're Christians or whatever, I just didn't get along with them too well. I don't know, I just had differences that they didn't like me for some reason, so, if somebody don't like me, I don't like them, I guess." Again, however, Joy affirmed, "You can believe whatever you want to believe. Like if somebody wanted to be a witch or something, they could study that and decide what they want to do." Joy thinks all religions are true, in the sense that there are people who sincerely believe in them, and that's fine for them. Could someone follow more than one religion? "No, I don't think you could at the same time. You need to research and find what [one] you want to do."

When it comes to morality, Joy thinks people usually know what is right and wrong, they just choose to do what they want to. "A lot of times I know something's wrong but I do it anyway. It's just what I want to do, not 'cause anybody tells me to do it." Joy freely admits lying to her parents, cheating in school, drinking and doing drugs, which she says she knows are wrong. What, I ask, makes them wrong? " 'Cause I get in trouble for it." We go back and forth about morality. She clearly believes certain things are just wrong but cannot explain why they are, what makes them so. It seems in the end the fact that other people think they are wrong is what makes them wrong. Does she ever feel guilty? "Yeah, but most of the time I just ignore it." Her teachers do not closely watch for cheating. "That's school for you," she remarks. And although her parents do get upset when she's caught doing something bad, they are also inconsistent in disciplining her: "They don't follow through and soon I'll go back to what I was doing."

Joy started drinking alcohol at age 14, she said: "First thing I ever drunk was white lightning, it's really hard liquor. I had friends that drunk. It was pretty nasty, but I liked the feeling when I drunk it, so. And then I started drinking beer. I'd much rather drink beer than liquor, 'cause I get sick when I drink liquor." Joy explains, "Alcoholism runs in my family, bad, so I can drink probably a case before I ever got drunk." I ask for a clarification. "Yeah," she explains, "a lot of people have told me that studies or something showed that if it runs in your family you're more likely to either do it or to have a higher toleration." But, I ask, if alcoholism runs in the family, wouldn't she want to avoid drinking? "Nuh-uh, I just don't care about it." What about smoking weed? It turns out, I was astounded to hear, that Joy was introduced to marijuana by her friend's father on the day her own father died: "The first time I smoked weed was, I went over to my friend's house, as soon as I found out my dad had died, and she and her dad knew my dad, so they knew it had hit me pretty hard and they knew I had been wanting to try smoking weed or whatever, so that was the first time I ever did it, the day I found out he died." The fact that her friend's father smokes pot and offered it to help comfort Joy in her grief did not strike her as remarkable. "Oh yeah, just about everybody I know has either tried it or continuously does it." Lately, however, Joy mostly smokes pot at her 23-year-old boyfriend's house. Don't her parents realize she does this stuff? "No, I guess we just, we got ways." To keep it hidden? "Yeah."

So why, I pressed, *does* she drink and smoke? "Just 'cause I feel like it. I like doing it." I was trying to restrain myself from an all-out psychotherapeutic analysis, but it was becoming clear that Joy's problematic life choices had deep and powerful emotional wellsprings. She was obviously depressed. She said she felt bad about herself, that she feels sad "about every other day." She said she often feels invisible and neglected when she's not with her friends, and that she wished she could lose weight. She has few positive adult relationships and discloses few of her bad feelings to anyone other than a few friends' parents—as likely as not the ones who smoke pot with her as an offer of emotional support. Most of all, the recent death of her father seemed to hang about Joy's life like a ball and chain. She feels angry that she was prevented from visiting him for six years. She feels immensely guilty for not having said goodbye to him before he passed away. But she could hardly admit these feelings. So, I asked, what *does* she do when she gets upset or has a problem? "I either sit down and write, or lay down and go to sleep." Sure, I think, for two days with the help of your mother's prescription drugs. And then nobody realizes it.

Joy's boyfriend, Jim, seven years older than she, seemed to be a bright spot in her life, so I asked more about him. He lives an hour's drive away, works in a factory, and comes to see Joy a few times a week. Joy had seriously dated five or so boys before Jim, some of whom did not turn out well. "A couple of relationships I've had, they really hurt me from some of the stuff that happened. One guy just dated me to be dating but didn't really like me, and another guy when I was 14 loved me so much he was like obsessed and stalking me." But Joy seems very happy about Jim. What do they do when they get together? "Well, he'll come up to the house and he'll sit down and watch TV and I'll sit on his lap and watch TV with him. Mostly just cuddling up or whatever. Mm-mm. I love sitting in his lap. I guess I just feel loved when he holds me like that, shows me how much he loves me." So Jim seems to function as Joy's substitute father, an older man unconsciously serving emotionally in place of the one who was never there with Joy to cuddle affectionately on the sofa in front of the television. But Jim isn't the oldest man Joy has dated. She had been dating Jim's older brother before Jim, but when that brother dumped her, Jim asked her out on a date. She accepted, though for a while felt guilty for dating her former boyfriend's brother. But they're all good friends now, she says.

As I moved through my interview questionnaire, the discussion next gravitated toward the subject of sex. Joy stated her basic sexual morality: "If they want to do it they can do it, whenever they feel they are ready, whenever they want to, I don't know." By "ready," she explained when I probed, she means that people should wait until they're at least 14 years old. Joy and Jim are having sex, mostly at his house. Joy's parents know that she sleeps over at his house regularly, but she also said her parents would be upset if they knew she and Jim were having sex. Well, what do they *think* is happening when you sleep over? "I don't know," she says. "I just think they suspect it, probably, but they don't want to say nothing till they catch us or whatever." Joy said she first had sexual intercourse a year before, at age 15, with Jim's brother: "I was at his house one day and we was hanging out and his parents were outside. We were just kissing or whatever and things got carried away, it was real quick. I didn't even think about his parents being right there. I was fine with it, 'cause if I had wanted to stop it, I would have stopped." Joy says she does think about pregnancy and STDs, but concludes, "I make sure whoever is with me has a condom on." Pregnancy is apparently common among her classmates ("Yeah, and the father's usually long gone"), but she herself wants to graduate high school, get a local job, marry Jim, and eventually have children. Joy then told a story about a girl she knows who has lots of sex with many different people who she doesn't have any relationships with. Joy thinks that is wrong because it is just using people for sex. Why, I then ask, does she think her peers are having sex? "I don't know, I guess it just makes them happy." She insists there is no social pressure involved. Joy also reports that many teens, especially boys, view pornography, especially on the Internet, and they brag about it at school. "I just think it's stupid," she says. "It don't make me angry, that's just what they want to do, but I just think it's dumb that they be watching somebody on a video like that."

It was almost noontime and Joy's stomach was growling. We closed with a few questions about the future. She said she does not think about the future much, but when she does it involves "probably getting married and stuff like that." What does she want out of marriage? "I just want to be happy and I guess we'll have kids, but that's later on, down the road." How does she think her life will turn out? "I don't know, I kind of fear it because I don't know what's gonna happen." Neither do I, I think. She just wants to be happy—not too much for a kid to ask for.

We emerge from the library and Rudy is waiting in his car. He had run some errands during the interview and was enjoying the sunshine. He joked that Joy was probably now going to go shopping to spend the $30 incentive I had just paid her for her time and effort to do the interview. Joy grinned slightly. I think: Who knows what she'll save it to spend on later? We say good-bye and part.

During my two-hour drive to my next interview at a Pizza Hut, I decompressed from my interview with Joy. I was grateful that she had honestly shared with me some of the feelings and behaviors that she normally kept so carefully hidden from most adults. I also felt depressed about the many layers of loss and pain and confusion in her life. So sad. I was worried that Joy's boyfriend, Jim, may be less serious about Joy than she was about him. I felt unhappy to be living in a culture that placed such a premium on certain attractive appearances, especially for women, so that Joy, who did not enjoy external beauty, would certainly be disadvantaged in life as a result. As a sociologist of religion, I was also perplexed and confused that a child raised by Christian parents in a Baptist church seemed to have understood so little of the Christian message. Had Joy simply never absorbed the Christian gospel preached in her church? Or was this church not even teaching its own faith tradition's message of God's compassion, grace, and forgiveness, and a calling to become a loved child of God? Driving down more winding roads, I hoped Joy wouldn't run across the newsletter about hell and God spewing out the lukewarm that I had picked up downtown. Mostly, I hoped that someone would come along in Joy's life who could help her deal constructively with her loss, guilt, disappointments, and what seemed to be a desperate yearning to be held tenderly by someone trustworthy, who would assure her that she is indeed much loved and unconditionally embraced. She really needs that, I thought. But I was a sociological researcher, not a counselor or pastor, and I had a Pizza Hut to find.

LOSS AND REDEMPTION

Later that summer, I was again sitting in a car in a parking lot waiting to meet and interview another 16-year-old girl in another public library staff room. Only this time, I was in a medium-size city in a Southwestern state. It was the height of summer, so I squeezed my rental car under the shade of a tree. I was here to interview a girl named Kristen, who proved to have a story quite different from Joy's.

Kristen, her mother, and I met on the sidewalk in front of the library. We went through the introductions routine with which I had become familiar over the course of many interviews that summer. Kristen's mother, like some who came with their teenagers to meet me before interviews, was there in part to make sure I was a bona fide researcher and not a wacko child abductor posing as a sociologist. She wanted to hear a bit more of my story. I showed her my university ID card. She seemed assured, but said she would be staying in the library building, reading.

Kristen and I set up for the interview in the staff meeting room. I gave her the standard ground rules for the interview. Then, just as quickly as in Joy's interview, a sad childhood story began to unfold. When Kristen was 6 years old and living in California, I learned, her father separated from her mother and shortly thereafter committed suicide. Not only that, but it was Kristen and her mother and four brothers and sisters who were the ones who found him dead on a bed with a self-inflicted gunshot wound to the head. Kristen's father had been temporarily staying at a friend's house who was on vacation. One morning when he did not show up for an arranged time to take Kristen and her siblings to an amusement park, Kristen's mother and the kids drove over to where he was staying. Kristen recalled: "The door was open so we went into this room and he looked like he was sleeping, so I asked my mom if I could wake him up and she said okay. So we went over to wake him up and then I saw a phone in the bed with him and my brother saw a gun and my mom saw blood. She told us to get out of the house, so we ran out but I ran back in to get my shoes. I remember going in there. He looked like he was sleeping." Oh, boy, I thought. "It caused us a lot of grief because he did that," Kristen said. "I'm sorry to hear that," I said, thinking that I was in for another case of troubled family, traumatic loss, at-risk child-hood, and bad teen outcomes.

But Kristen's story unfolded quite differently. She explained, "It was some-thing tragic, and now when I look at it I'm just like, 'wow that was pretty bad,' and people were saying like we were going to go off the deep end and that we kids needed counseling. But you know, God used it in a great way and to shape my mom." Although Kristen's family had been Christian all her life, this event seems to have been a religious turning point: "My mom then just really trusted in God and went to the Word [the Bible] and then two years later she took us out of school and home-schooled us for three years and we did some really great curriculum that was just all focused around the Bible. She taught us, you know, God is the father to the fatherless and she didn't let us become depressed and clinging on to what happened. She really kept us going and looking ahead. I think it really helped our family." Every night, Kristen recalled, she and her mother and siblings had family devotions, reading Psalms and Proverbs from the Bible. Her single-mother family did not have much money. But according to Kristen, her mother's faith and de-termination and their family's church involvements made a major difference in her life. And what a life. Kristen was perhaps the most well-adjusted, mature, civically involved, compassionate, and religiously serious teenager I interviewed the entire summer. Throughout the interview, I kept thinking to myself that I must be missing something, that Kristen could simply not be as together a person as she seemed to be, that perhaps Kristen was living in some kind of emotional denial or had been brainwashed into a repressive, straitlaced existence. There might be something like that going on to some extent, but I did not see or hear a trace of it, even as I probed. Although many would not share her conservative religious views, Kristen was none-theless, as far as I could tell, simply a down-to-earth, fun, clear-thinking, religiously committed, generally impressive kid.

How had Kristen's life unfolded? Kristen's mother seems to have taken a strong leadership role in encouraging and guiding her family after her father's death, a major aspect of which was grounding the family in a religious tra-dition and church community. Since the suicide, Kristen's family has been deeply involved in church, Sunday school, Wednesday-night children's church activities, vacation Bible school, and more. Kristen's mother also "decided to put aside traditional dating altogether" and not rush to get remarried, but to focus first on her children's well-being. By Kristen's account, her mother has also effectively combined a close, warm, compassionate relationship with very high expectations and supervision of Kristen's attitudes and behaviors. Kristen says her relationship with her mother is "good, I tell her everything. And we pretty much agree on the same things 'cause she raised me, and on most things I can't find anything to contradict [her on], even though sometimes I try." She laughs. Does she feel close to her mom? "Yeah, I do feel close to her." Isn't there anything, I inquire, that she would not talk with her mother about? "No, not really. I mean, sometimes I think, 'well I'm gonna keep this one secret,' but it all comes out." Kristen also seems to relate well with her siblings: "I get along with them good. I mean, I share with my sister a lot, just like I share with my mom, and I'll bring them to events and stuff that I go to." Kristen says that, overall, her family relationships are "positive and happy."

A few years before our interview, Kristen's mother's brother put Kristen's mother in touch with his own wife's brother, a mail carrier living in a faraway state, whose wife had recently died of cancer. Kristen recalls: "So he gave her a call and they just kept talking on the phone. He came down and visited and we went up and visited, at which point he proposed to her. So she found a guy that had character and was committed to family, you know, and her five kids didn't faze him. And he had been through hard times, too, 'cause his wife had died, and so we became attached to him immediately." And how, I asked, does Kristen get along with her new stepfather? "It's good, I mean I haven't grown up with him but we're good friends and I call him 'Dad' and we joke around. He's adopted us now so we're legally his kids. So that's cool." When I ask Kristen who are the people in the world or in history she most admires, she answers, "I admire my mom for her courage, 'cause I know what she's been through and I was, like, 'wow, you know that can be a lesson.' And I guess I admire my dad, too, because he's been through hardships, losing his wife."

Of her religious faith, Kristen says, "I'm just a Christian, that's it." She and her family are deeply involved in a small Southern Baptist church. What specifically does she believe religiously? "I believe that Jesus is God's Son and that he came and he died for me and for everyone else because we're all sinners and that he didn't stay dead but he rose again and he wants us to come live with him and we just need to admit that we're sinners and believe that he came and died on the cross and rose again and just choose to follow him." Okay. Who or what, I then ask, is God? "He's everything," she replies. "He's a father, like I learned, even though you may not have a dad, he's still a father, he disciplines like a father, he's a good friend, he's a provider, he cares. He is a merciful God, but he is also just." Kristen says she definitely feels close to God: "It's kind of, you know he's there, you know he's watching over you, it's great but you [also] know that there are going to be hard times and that he's still there then." I ask Kristen how she learned all this. "I grew up in a Christian home and my parents, they taught me this, they live it out every day to me in their lives. And watching how God has worked in other people's lives and how he got my mom through stuff. And church and Sunday school and seeing other people there, listening to the pastor's message. And reading his Word, being in it daily and finding out stuff." Her family still has religious devotions together: "Now everyone's running [busy but] we make time for family devotions. Before we go off to school in the mornings, my mom, while we're all sitting at the kitchen table, she'll read a devotional book to us." Kristen also owns her own "chronological Bible," which takes the reader through the entirety of the Scriptures in one year. She reads it every night before going to bed. Kristen seems to love her church youth group, led by a volunteer youth pastor, for its fellowship, sharing, encouragement, and teaching from the Bible. Without youth group, something would definitely feel missing in life, she says. In addition to attending church and reading the Bible, Kristen says she prays daily, takes communion at church, and is involved in numerous Christian ministries.

Kristen believes in divine miracles, the supernatural, angels, and demons, although she has never had a direct experience with any of them. I asked whether she ever has doubts about her faith. "I have," she reported. "I have wondered if I'm really saved and if I died would I go to heaven and is there really a God. But even if there's not, I don't think there's anything else better to believe 'cause then you've lost hope. Sometimes I wonder, there's so many other religions and they all claim to be true and I claim mine to be true and so, you know, what's right? And then I think, whatever it is, [Christianity] is the best that I've heard." Kristen has never heard the phrase "spiritual but not religious" and does not know what it means, but thinks it might have to do with New Age beliefs. She does not believe other religions are true but are, rather, misleading. "Those who trust in Jesus as their personal Lord and Savior will go to heaven when they die and those who don't will go to hell." Kristen also says that it is wrong for Christians to try selectively to customize their own faith: "If you pick and choose you're not being consistent and then who's to say what you pick is true?" She thinks if you're going to be a Christian, you need to believe the whole Christian thing.

Kristen observes that her faith has a real influence on her life, that she is against a compartmentalized religious life. "I don't think it's a separate thing, 'cause I think it should be an everyday thing, an all-the-time thing. It's not like I stop being a Christian." According to Kristen, she is earning all A's at school and her faith affects her attitude about schoolwork: "I care about doing well in school 'cause it gives me something to aim for, gives me goals, now I can practice achieving my goals—you do everything your best for the Lord whether or not it's anything [important]." Faith also affects how she cares for and uses her body, she says: "Our body, if you're saved, we are living examples that you have Christ living in you and so you want to be a good example for that and also our bodies are not our own anymore." Kristen also says religious faith affects her family life: "It has a lot to do with how we treat each other, by forgiving one another and holding each other accountable—that's a big thing in our family—my sisters and I calling each other on weak points but also encouraging each other." I asked for an example. "Yeah, well, like my sister Julia was with this person who was not a very good friend to her and we confronted her on this, 'You know, Julia, this isn't very good, look at how this is going, this is not biblical, it's against God's word.' We didn't all bombard her at the same time, but you know she realized it and now they're not friends anymore." The connection between religious faith and the living of a particular kind of life was also evident in much more of what Kristen had to say. For example, for Kristen, divine revelation and faith define morality. "People know what's right and wrong," she says, "they just choose to do the wrong and then laugh at it like it's a joke." So where, I ask, does morality come from? "God. God's word is truth. In the Bible, I believe that's it." But what if people don't believe in the Bible? "Well, we have law here, too. And I think there's a sense of guiltiness [conscience]." I told Kristen that I had just read in the paper about a man who had tried to kill his pregnant wife because he was afraid she would find out he was addicted to pornography, observing that he didn't seem to have much of a conscience. "No," she replied, "no, they have a conscience, they just choose to ignore it. They've done so many things that I think it's just become hardened." What about the idea that morality is relative? "That's total baloney. There is a moral right and wrong, some people just don't want to have to answer to anyone so that's why they say that—there's no accountability when you have that."

Does Kristen ever do things wrong that make her feel guilty? "I know I've done wrong, I'm not perfect, and I sin, I do bad stuff, but nothing that's outstanding like drugs or something like that. But sometimes I will lie to my parents just to get around things and I know that's wrong." What does Kristen do with her guilty feelings? "I go to my parents and I say, 'Mom and Dad, look, I was wrong about this and I lied to you about this. Will you forgive me?' " Then what happens? "They say, 'all right,' and there's a punishment if there needs to be, like grounding me. Then they'll say, 'thank you, I'll forgive you.' " And the guilt feelings? "It goes away. And I also need to ask God to forgive me, too, 'cause the sin wasn't just against my parents." But why, I press, tell your parents things they don't need to know that will only create trouble? "I don't know, just being in a close relationship with my parents I would tell them." Kristen also thinks dishonesty and cheating are bad because they disrespect authority and lead to bad reputations, whereas honesty "shows [adults] that you can be respected, that you can be trusted."

Kristen has never tried cigarettes, alcohol, or drugs and has no interest in them. "It's bad for you, like brains are fried, plus," she says laughing, "I have asthma so it will just kill me sooner." So why, I ask, do some of her peers do such unhealthy things? "What I hear is it gives you release or peace or whatever. But there's so much better ways to find peace." Like? "Like, um, reading a Bible, finding a good church to go to, I mean, when you have a relationship that's right with God you're gonna find peace." Kristen's beliefs and attitudes themselves also seem to protect her among her peers from information and possible temptations: "People, they tell me, 'ah, she's got a virgin mind so don't tell her anything.' So I know there's stuff that goes on [among peers] that I don't know about." Kristen goes out to parties, but she first has to call and confirm for her parents that other parents will be home while the party is on. She goes out to and rents movies, but not R-rated ones. And she can stay out late, past her parents' bedtime, and spend the night at a friend's house, but she says she always (eventually) tells the truth about what she did and when she finally came home.

Kristen attends a large Christian school that enrolls Christian and non-Christian students. Her family does not have much money, but they scrape together what they need to pay the tuition. Some of Kristen's church friends attend the same school, so her important social relationships involve a relatively high degree of institutional overlap. Most of her friends are Christians, so they talk about faith matters, such as what different Bible verses mean. Through these church and school connections, Kristen reports, her parents also know most of her friends' parents: "Very well, really well. My dad knew some of my friends' parents even before I moved here. We go to school sports and my dad's a big sports fan so he'll discuss sports with all the dads. And through church, too, they know some of my good friends' parents through church." Through all of these overlapping network ties, Kristen agrees, her parents are able to keep fairly good tabs on what she and her friends are up to. "I know they trust me," Kristen says, "but they [also] keep track of my behavior and [say], 'no, you can't do that' and I'm like, 'why?' and they're like, ' 'cause your attitude isn't right.' And I'm like, 'how did they know that?' If I was involved in something that was bad, they would know it, they would ask me about it." Kristen says she also knows her teachers and adults at church well: "I'm good friends with my teachers, I really like being around them. And at church I'm good friends with the parents there. They're an encouragement, I just talk to them and be friendly." She says if she were in a crisis she would definitely feel comfortable calling on adults at her church for help.

Kristen says she thinks a lot of teenagers these days are "just dumb. A lot of them don't listen to their parents and a lot don't have parents they can listen to that are gonna give good advice either. They're in dumb dating relationships and do and say dumb things." She says she knows of teens whose parents trust them with whatever they do, but in fact the parents actually simply don't care whether they're drinking, doing drugs, and hanging out with their girlfriends in the middle of the night. "These kids wouldn't be doing this if they had parents like mine, but not everyone's like my parents." Kristen says her parents prevent her from doing certain things that she does want to do, like hang out with certain friends, but "if my parents don't want me hanging out with them then it's probably a good thing." But doesn't she ever feel rebellious or want to be wild or free, to break out and assert herself? "Not really. Sometimes I tell my parents that they never let me do anything I want to do. And they say, 'Okay, Kristen, [do] whatever you want to do that we haven't let you.' And then I think about it and whatever comes to mind is something that I hear about later wasn't good anyway."

Many of Kristen's views have a conservative edge that many people would think prudish. For instance, she seems much concerned about the "bad language" some of her peers use. She is bothered by other girls who dress like boys, in baggy jeans and chains: "I'm just like, 'be feminine! You're not a guy, get over it.' " She does not want to start dating until she is ready to get married. She believes in trusting in and submitting to her parents: "I'm pretty much looking at their perspective. I've been trying to do that lately, seeing how they would feel and how I would if I had a daughter." And she likes classical music, watches Shirley Temple and other classic movies, and frequents a video shop called Clean Flicks that carries a line of videos that has edited out bad language, violence, and sex scenes from otherwise good movies. But she says that, for herself, she feels not the least bit odd or left out of mainstream American youth culture. "I think *they're* the ones missing out," she exclaims, laughing. "I don't think what I'm doing is wrong." At the very least, I think to myself, she's not insecure.

The number of organized and volunteer activities in which Kristen is involved is astonishing. She runs on the school track team. She is involved in Honor Society at school. She participates in the local 4-H Club. She is involved in her church's youth group, which studies the Bible and has fun but also volunteers to cook at the local soup kitchen. She has also gone on mission trips organized by her youth pastor to far-away cities to volunteer to sort donated clothes for the homeless and to help in soup kitchens. She plays piano at church. She teaches summer vacation Bible school with her friends at church. And she helps do a child evangelism fellowship program with her older sister. During the summer she also runs Five-Day-Clubs: "It's like VBS [vacation Bible school] in someone's backyard, like with people from another church or in [Mexican farmworker] migrant housing; you meet one kid and get a bunch of kids together to do it. I like doing that during the summer." She's also involved in a "water bottle ministry": "During sports, after our home varsity games, we go and hand out water bottles to the other team with Bible verses on the bottle of water." And she is involved in a school-based program called Teen Coalition, which advocates against early teen involvement in drugs and sex. Despite the fact that Teen Coalition encourages teen abstinence from sex and drugs only "until teens are 'ready' or 'can handle it' "—which Kristen thinks is "dumb" in its vagueness about boundaries—she still actively promotes the program as well intentioned and worth supporting even if not perfect or fully Christian. So why is Kristen so involved in so many organizations and programs? "I think it's something that a lot of people should do," she explains. "You're kind of obliged to do it because where would you be if you didn't have any help either? Helping one another, I mean, it's biblical, how can it not be? And so it's not just like, 'Oh, if it feels good, do it.' "

It is clear that Kristen is no angel, but a normal, imperfect teen in various ways. She says she whines a lot to try to get her way. She struggles with obeying her parents. She would rather be out playing with her friends than unloading the dishwasher. She thinks (without reason) that she's somewhat overweight but struggles to articulate why that bothers her: "Sometimes I wish that I looked better or were skinnier, because when you see other girls and stuff and they can wear like really short shorts. I mean not that I have a desire to wear short shorts around to show off my body, but just because I would feel good about myself. Yeah, I think I just [would] have more self-esteem, but not that I'm lacking in self-esteem right now. I just, I think what the goal is, is to be in shape, so that's pretty much it. I'm exercising less this year so I'm worried I'm gonna be totally out of shape." And sometimes she gets tired of helping other people through her volunteering. But she recurrently comes back to her commitment to live out the life she believes is right. What, I ask, does she do when she gets upset or has a problem? "I usually think it through, think about why I'm upset about it, is there any point to being upset. Or I like go talk to my mom or one of my sisters or brothers. Sometimes I'll tell my friends."

Kristen has no desire to date at this point. "I know I'm not mature enough to handle it," she says. "I've seen it happen, people think they're perfect for each other and three months later they don't work out, so it's a dumb thing to do right now." Her view on not dating until she's ready to get married seems influenced in part by her mother's example, but also by an older sister who was once hurt badly in a dating relationship. Kristen elaborated, "You kind of leave a piece of yourself with everyone you date, you give away something of yourself or share with them a lot of stuff. And then you marry someone else, maybe someone from school after dating like 13 other people in the same school who everyone involved knows, it's kind of weird." I asked Kristen if she had read *I Kissed Dating Goodbye*, a controversial evangelical book advocating abstaining from dating and a return to older models of courtship. "Right, I read that, and I didn't really agree with a lot of things in it." Well, I thought, at least she's not swallowing any ideology uncritically. Kristen then went on to tell me about a friend of hers who is not dating anyone because she shares Kristen's views, but whose *parents* are actually pressuring her to date. I asked her if dating was perhaps valuable for helping to figure out who you are, what you like, who would be good to marry, as a learning experience. "Um, I think you can find out who you are without finding a guy," she replied.

Predictably, by this point, when it came to sex, Kristen's view was "no sex before marriage." This, she said, is simply Christian teaching on the matter. "Marriage and sex is a great gift God gave us," she explained, "so I think [sex] should only be used then, when you're married." We discussed what physical intimacies might or might not be appropriate before marriage, and she emphasized her belief in the importance of clear boundaries: "Boundaries should be set because if you don't have boundaries, if you don't set goals then there's nothing to achieve and you will just fall. I think I might be interested in doing what my older sister did, she set certain guidelines, she sat down with her guy and they wrote stuff out that they could only go so far. I don't know if they even hold hands but they do give each other side hugs." What should people do, then, I probed, about the physical desires they have before marriage? "I don't think it's a sin to like others, that's how God made us, you know, you're gonna have those emotions, it's what you choose to do with them [that matters]." Kristen said she didn't think she would want even to get into heavy kissing before marriage.

When it comes to media consumption, Kristen says she does not watch a lot of television, "just 'cause so much of it is perverted and the commercials are perverted, just gross, nasty, like the innuendos. And I have younger sisters and brothers and I think it would be a bad example for them, and I could probably be doing better things." She reports that her parents are strict in monitoring their kids' television watching, and that they do not subscribe to cable, so only receive about six channels to watch anyway. Kristen listens to contemporary Christian music on the radio, and composes her own songs to sing on the piano. She also has her own cell phone, but mostly, she says, for safety reasons, because she gets lost a lot while driving. Her family's dial-up Internet service is slow, so she doesn't use it a lot. She writes just as many letters to friends as she does e-mails, she says. As to pornography, "I don't think that's something we should be into, I don't agree with it, it's like fantasizing."

By this time, we're coming down the homestretch of the interview. Kristen tells me that even if she could change her life she would keep it just as it is, " 'cause even the bad things that may have happened they're used [by God] to shape my life." What, I ask, is the meaning or purpose of life? "I think we're here because God put us here and our ultimate goal I think is to tell other people about God." And what does she want to do with her life? "I think I might want to be a teacher, I don't know, I really want to impact [other people's] lives, but I'm not really knowing how yet." Does she want to get married? "It would be something good to do, not that I'm dependent on another person, because I think it's a good thing to be able to survive on your own without another person, but to have someone that I could work with and enjoy." How does she feel about the future? "I'm not really worried, I just think about finishing my junior year, then my senior year, then I'll think about college." And what does she hope to be like religiously when she's 25 years old? "Um, I hope to be still growing and learning stuff and [relating to] God everyday and still just progressing."

We wrapped up the interview, I packed up my recording equipment, and we went to find Kristen's mother. I thanked Kristen and her mother again for their help and wished Kristen all the best.

Two nights later, just before it was time for me to head back to North Carolina, I caught the opening night of the big rodeo that had come to town. The cowgirl show, calf roping, bucking broncos, and bull riding were a great ending to an intense but successful interview trip out West. The crowd was having a great time and so was I. Halfway through the evening, my eye caught sight of someone who looked familiar, coming up my aisle. Ah. It was Kristen, wearing a green 4-H volunteer's apron and lugging a large tray of soft drinks she was selling to raise money for 4-H. I said "Hi" and bought a Coke. She smiled, blushing somewhat. But we said nothing more. Sociologists have got to protect their interviewees' confidentiality, after all.

REAL TEENS AND MAJOR THEMES

Neither Joy nor Kristen are "typical" American teenagers, whatever that might mean. No two teenage girls ever could be, of course. Joy and Kristen are simply two white 16-year-old Baptist girls from meager backgrounds who have both lost their fathers and who also are situated at opposite sides of a complicated field of teenage religiosity and life outcomes. Joy is a closet unbeliever who is struggling in life, Kristen a committed religious believer whose life seems to be going well. We recount these two stories here not because Joy and Kristen somehow represent all American teens. They don't. The nationally representative picture of U.S. teenagers comes in later chapters. Neither do we tell these stories together to suggest that all religious teens are doing well in life and all nonreligious teens are not. It is not that simple. We recount their stories, rather, for two reasons. First, they help to put a human face on this book's statistics. The big picture this book seeks to portray relies heavily on survey numbers to summarize proportions and differences on many variables in the lives of American teens. Such statistics are helpful and important, but they can also inadvertently suggest that teenagers' lives amount to so many abstractions and aggregations. Far from it. Each American teenager is, let us remind ourselves, a specific human person with very real feelings and desires, problems and accomplishments, unchangeable histories and unknown futures. Behind the numbers in this book's tables, we must always remember, lie the very real struggles, enthusiasms, sufferings, and hopes of this country's Joys, Kristens, and other teens.

The second reason we recount Joy and Kristen's stories are because, even in all of the particularity of their lives, their stories do highlight many of the central themes that emerged from our interviews with all kinds of American teenagers, which we develop further in this book. Already in these two girls' lives, we can observe certain ideas and influences that emerged out of our national study of American teens that we came to believe are important on a broader scale. We unpack and elaborate such themes in various chapters of this book, but the following are worth noting briefly even here:

❧ American adolescents as a whole experience and represent in their lives an immense variety of religious and spiritual beliefs, practices, experiences, identities, and attitudes. We see this clearly with Joy and Kristen, who are both tied to the same religious tradition but are religiously very dissimilar. There is no one way to summarize the religious and spiritual lives of American teenagers as a whole because they encompass a sweeping range on a variety of religious variables—from total religious obliviousness and indifference to intense religious passion and commitment. Religiously, American teens are complicated and "all over the map." Among other things, this means that a balanced view of the religious lives of teenagers includes strengths and weaknesses, apathy and investment—all of which comes out in different ways in this book's chapters.

✺ By logical implication of the theme just noted, there are a significant number of adolescents in the United States for whom religion and spirituality are important if not defining features of their lives. Millions of different kinds of American teenagers embrace particular religious beliefs and engage in deliberate practices of faith that seem to significantly affect their lives. Any adequate understanding of American adolescents must recognize and account for these religious and spiritual realities in many of their lives.

✺ Among the more religiously serious American teenagers, religious *practices* appear to play an important role in their faith lives. For the committed adolescent, religion is not simply a matter of general identity or affiliation or cognitive belief. Faith for these teenagers is also *activated, practiced, and formed* through specific religious and spiritual practices. For such teens, faith involves their intentionally engaging in regularly enacted religious habits and works that have theological, spiritual, or moral meanings that form their lives, such as habitually worshiping with other believers, reading scriptures, praying regularly, practicing confession and forgiveness and reconciliation, engaging in service to others, using and not using one's body in particular ways, tuning into religious music and other religious art forms, and engaging in regular faith education and formation. Religious practices, in short, seem crucial to vibrant religious faith among American teens.

✺ Very, very few American adolescents appear to be caught up in the much-discussed phenomenon of "spiritual seeking" by "spiritual but not religious" seekers on a quest for higher meaning. Neither Joy nor Kristen, nor most teens we interviewed, had even heard of the expression "spiritual but not religious," much less knew what it meant. Contrary to popular perceptions, the vast majority of American adolescents are not spiritual seekers or questers of the type often described by journalists and some scholars, but are instead mostly oriented toward and engaged in conventional religious traditions and communities.

✺ In her understanding of the beliefs and culture of her own religious tradition, Joy came across in her interview as rather inarticulate and confused. This is not surprising, because she had abandoned her faith and attends church only sporadically. But Joy was hardly the only teen we interviewed who struggled with inarticulacy and confusion when it came to religion. If there is indeed a significant number of American teens who are serious and lucid about their religious faith, there is also a much larger number who are remarkably inarticulate and befuddled about religion. Interviewing teens, one finds little evidence that the agents of religious socialization in this country are being highly effective and successful with the majority of their young people.

❧ Religious faith and practice in American teenagers' lives operate in a social and institutional environment that is highly competitive for time, attention, and energy. Religious interests and values in teens' lives typically compete against those of school, homework, television, other media, sports, romantic relationships, paid work, and more. Indeed, in many adolescents' lives, religion occupies a quite weak and often losing position among these competing influences. Those teenagers for whom religious faith and practice are important tend to have religious lives constructed relationally and institutionally to intersect and overlap with other important aspects of their lives. In Kristen's life, for example, church, family, school, friendships, and volunteer and social activities hang together in a fairly integrated whole. By contrast, for Joy, religion is something she does only a few hours on Sunday morning every three or four weeks. For American adolescents more broadly, the structure of relational networks and institutional ties of both teens and their parents seems significantly correlated with the character of their religious faith and practice.

❧ Even though agents of religious socialization do not appear to be wildly successful in fostering clarity and articulacy about faith among teens, it remains true nevertheless that parents and other adults exert huge influences in the lives of American adolescents—whether for good or ill, and whether adults can perceive it or not—when it comes to religious faith and most other areas of teens' lives. The influence of adults in Joy and Kristen's lives are only two examples of this larger reality. Some observers suggest that American teenagers have outgrown the influence of their parents and other adults, are shaped primarily by their peers, and, in the name of independence, are best set free of adult oversight and support to find their own individual ways. Such views, our observations suggest, are badly misguided.[2] Adults inescapably exercise immense influence in the lives of teens—positive and negative, passive and active. The question therefore is not whether adults exert influence, but what kinds of influence they exert.

❧ Despite their frequent confusion and inarticulacy about religion, American adolescents as a whole exhibit a positive association between greater teen religious involvement and more positive outcomes in life. In general, for whatever reasons and whatever the causal directions, more highly religiously active teenagers are doing significantly better in life on a variety of important outcomes than are less religiously active teens. Joy and Kristen are not proof of this association—most U.S. teenagers' stories are more complex and muddled than theirs appear when placed side by side—but they do illustrate it. More systematic evidence of this relationship is examined in chapter 7.

These are by no means the only analytic themes that this book examines, but they are important ones and good for getting started. The chapters that follow draw on both survey and interview data from the NSYR to map out a nationally representative big picture of the religious and spiritual lives of

American teenagers and to interpret some of the meanings, processes, and complexities involved in various key aspects of that big picture. Between the statistics and the stories, we hope to elaborate a much fuller and richer understanding of this important and interesting dimension of adolescent and American life.

2

Mapping the Big Picture

MAPS ARE GREAT for providing a big picture sense of the proportions and contours of the spaces that we occupy. Maps help us to understand the geography through which we move, so that we know where we stand in the world and what the world is like beyond our immediate field of vision. Maps do this by simplifying relevant features of the actual world we live in with visual symbols, such as lines, colors, dots, and shapes depicting roads, rivers, cities, and altitudes. Sociological research can also descriptively map the contours and proportions of social life by simplifying features of the social world relevant to a particular interest and representing them with symbols. But instead of using lines, colors, and dots for its symbolic representations, sociological research often uses numbers—such as frequencies, percentages, averages—to represent through numeric abstraction the social world's dimensions and qualities. All such descriptions oversimplify the complexity of the real social world in which we live. And maps as abstractions are never as interesting as, say, personal stories. But, as with maps generally, such simplified descriptions can help to provide an overarching sense of our social world, where we stand within it, and what it looks like beyond our immediate field of vision.

In this chapter, we descriptively map the world of contemporary U.S. adolescent religion and spirituality by presenting statistical findings from the National Survey of Youth and Religion. Following chapters explore some of the cultural meanings, textures, and complexities of U.S. adolescent faith. But before getting to such meanings and complexities, we outline some of the major dimensions of adolescent religion and spirituality to build a general framework of knowledge about the proportions and distributions of the matter in question. This chapter is full of numbers and percentages, which take some effort to digest. But working through the abstract statistics pays off in providing us with a clear overview of the religious and spiritual lives of U.S. teenagers.[1] Even so, those who are less interested in detailed statistics but are intrigued by the cultural meanings of religion can easily skim this chapter, read its conclusion, and come back to the details later.

RELIGIOUS AFFILIATIONS AND IDENTITIES

We begin with some basic statistics about U.S. adolescent religious affiliations and identities. What kind of religious people do U.S. teens consider themselves to be? In which religious denominations are they located? According to NSYR data presented in table 1, three quarters of U.S. teens between 13 and 17 years old are Christians. About one-half of teens are Protestant and one-quarter are Catholic. Christianity, in other words, still very much dominates American religion numerically at the level of teenage affiliation. The next largest group is the 16 percent of U.S. teens who consider themselves to be not religious. Note that not all of this 16 percent *acts* not religious. As we will see in the next chapter, many nonreligious U.S. teens believe in God, attend church, and pray; thus, there must be something in the way they understand the term "religious" that causes them to identify themselves as not

Table 1. Religious Affiliations of U.S. Adolescents, Ages 13–17 (Percentages)

	U.S.
Teen religious affiliation	
Protestant	52
Catholic	23
Mormon	2.5
Jewish	1.5
Jehovah's Witness	0.6
Muslim	0.5
Eastern Orthodox	0.3
Buddhist	0.3
Pagan or Wiccan	0.3
Hindu	0.1
Christian Science	0.1
Native American	0.1
Unitarian Universalist	0.1
Miscellaneous other	0.2
Don't know/refused	1.8
Teen not religious	16
Teen affiliates with two different faiths	2.8

Source: National Survey of Youth and Religion, 2002–3.

Note: Percentages may not add to 100 due to rounding.

religious on surveys. Seven percent of U.S. teens affiliate with one of the many minority U.S. religions, particularly Mormonism (2.5 percent) and Judaism (1.5 percent). Finally, nearly 2 percent do not know what their religion is or refused to answer the question.

Some interesting findings are immediately apparent in table 1. First, U.S. youth are not flocking in droves to "alternative" religions and spiritualities such as paganism and Wicca. Teenagers who are pagan or Wiccan represent fewer than one-third of 1 percent of U.S. teens. There are thus twice the number of Jehovah's Witness teens as there are pagan and Wiccan teens. Second, it does not appear that American religion, at the adolescent level at least, is being profoundly diversified by new immigrant groups. Harvard's Diana Eck asserts that the United States is the most religiously diverse nation in the world.[2] That simply is not true. The vast majority of U.S. teens (like adults) are Christian or not religious. The so-called new immigrant religions are tiny fractions of adolescent religion. Muslim teens represent one-half of 1 percent of U.S. teens, Buddhists less than one-third of 1 percent, and Hindu a mere one-tenth of 1 percent.[3] For every one Muslim teen in the United States there are five in the home-grown American religion of Mormonism.[4] For every Buddhist teen there are five Jewish teens. The case for rapid numeric diversification and pluralization of U.S. religions seems to have been overstated. The country has indeed seen a great deal of immigration in recent decades, but many of those immigrants came to the United States as Christians, such as Catholic Latinos from Mexico, the Caribbean, and Central America, and Christian believers from a variety of non-Christian nations seeking refuge from anti-Christian persecution in their home countries. In addition, some immigrant youth become Christians in the process of assimilating to U.S. culture.

The third finding worth noting in table 1 is that relatively few U.S. teens (2.8 percent) affiliate with more than one religion. Numerous scholarly and journalistic voices have recently called attention to an alleged rise in an eclectic, mix-and-match approach to religion among youth. We do not find evidence for this in our data. Nearly all U.S. teens affiliate with one religion or no religion. Very few adhere to two religions, and that small minority apparently does so not because they are on some syncretistic spiritual quest, but because their parents affiliate with two different religions which they wish to honor. Even more telling, only *one* of our 3,290 survey respondents (0.0003 percent of all U.S. teens) professed to affiliate with three religions, in this case, Catholicism, Judaism, and Buddhism. U.S. teenagers as a whole are thus not religiously promiscuous faith mixers. Almost all stick with one religious faith, if any.

Table 2 unpacks the 52 percent of Protestants seen in table 1, specifying the various denominational families and traditions that teens call their religious homes.[5] The proportions seen in table 2 roughly mirror the distribution of U.S. adults into these groups. Clearly, the Baptists have the largest proportion of teens here (17.3 percent), followed by other traditions with notable numbers, including Methodists (4.7 percent), Lutherans (3.5 percent), and

Table 2. Protestant Denominations of the Congregations Teens Attend, Protestant U.S. Adolescents, Ages 13–17 (Percentages)

Adventist	0.43	Free Methodist Church	0.03
Assemblies of God	0.71	Friends/Quaker	0.11
Baptist	17.3	Holiness	0.34
Bible Church	0.22	Independent/Nondenominational	3.02
Brethren	0.21	Lutheran	3.54
Charismatic	0.04	Mennonite	0.12
Christian and Missionary Alliance	0.03	Methodist	4.74
Church of Christ	1.21	Missionary Church	0.04
Church of God	0.46	Nazarene, Church of the	0.09
Calvary Chapel	0.02	Pentecostal	1.82
Congregationalist	0.2	Presbyterian/Reformed	1.83
Disciples of Christ	0.06	United Church of Christ	0.09
Episcopalian	0.82	Vineyard Fellowship	0.02
Evangelical, Independent	0.31	Wesleyan Church	0.16
Evangelical Covenant	0.02	Just Protestant	0.18
Evangelical Free Church	0.07	Just Christian	12.58
Four Square	0.08	Don't know/refused	3.01

Source: National Survey of Youth and Religion, 2002–3.

Note: Percentages may not add to 100 due to rounding.

nondenominational churches (3 percent). Most of the remainder are scattered across the vast variety of denominations and traditions that constitute U.S. Protestantism. Note, however, that nearly 16 percent of youth do not appear familiar enough with any specific group they may be affiliated with and so answer this question as "Just Christian," "Just Protestant," or "Don't know" or refused to answer the question.

Another way of understanding the location of different Americans within various available religious traditions is by asking with which tradition they self-identify. Table 3 shows the distributions of key self-identifications for Protestant, Catholic, and Jewish parents of teenagers. Among Protestants, parents of teens are evenly split at 19 percent between fundamentalist/evangelical and mainline/liberal Protestant. Catholic parents are also evenly spread across traditional, moderate, and liberal Catholicism. The majority of Jewish parents identify with Reform Judaism; fewer identify with Conservative and Orthodox Judaism. Ten percent of parents of U.S. teens consider themselves charismatic Christians, and 14 percent identify as Pentecostal Christians (only 5 percent identify as both). How do these parents distribute on a general scale of religious liberalism-conservativism? According to findings in table 3, nearly 3 in 10 parents have not even thought enough about the issue to give an answer. Among those who offered an answer, we see a great deal of variance, although the numbers do tip toward the conservative side: 28 percent said they were religiously conservative or very conservative, and 18 percent said they were liberal or very liberal. Altogether, the findings of table 3 add to the observation that there exists a great deal of religious variation among Christian and Jewish families of U.S. teenagers when it comes to iden-

Table 3. Religious Self-identities of Parents of U.S.
Adolescents, Ages 13–17 (Percentages)

	All U.S. Parents
Protestant tradition identity	
Fundamentalist	9
Evangelical	10
Mainline	8
Theologically liberal	11
Other Protestant identity	6
Catholic tradition identity	
Traditional Catholic	8
Moderate Catholic	8
Liberal Catholic	9
Other Catholic identity	1
Jewish tradition identity	
Orthodox Jew	0.08
Conservative Jew	0.35
Reform Jew	1.16
Other Jewish identity	0.1
Parent is a Charismatic Christian	10
Parent is a Pentecostal Christian	14
Compared to other religious Americans, parent views self as religiously	
Very conservative	7
Conservative	21
Moderate	17
Liberal	13
Very liberal	5
Has not thought much about this	29
Don't know/refused/not religious	7

Source: National Survey of Youth and Religion, 2002–3.

Note: Percentages may not add to full amount due to rounding and unreported don't know and refused answers.

tification with alternative traditions in their religions and among all U.S. parents of teens with regard to their position on a liberal-conservative spectrum.

How similar to or different from their parents are U.S. religious teens? One popular stereotype of American youth casts them as religious dissidents who find their parents' religious beliefs and practices old and meaningless and want to have little to do with any of it. Is this so? According to NSYR data shown in table 4, about three in four religious teens in the United States consider their own religious beliefs somewhat or very similar to their parents; they are more similar to mother's than to father's beliefs (teen similarity to parent religion for nonreligious teens is examined in chapter 3). Only 6 percent of teens consider their religious beliefs very different from that of their mother and 11 percent very different from that of their father. And not all who reported "very different" for this question are rebellious, antireligious teens of religiously devout parents. Fully 37 percent of teens whose beliefs

Table 4. Belief Similarity of Religious U.S. Adolescents, Ages 13–17,
to Mother and Father (Percentages)

	U.S. Religious Teens	Teen Religious Tradition					
		CP	MP	BP	RC	J	LDS
Religious belief similarity to mother's							
Very similar	41	48	36	39	33	41	73
Somewhat similar	37	34	43	37	41	27	18
Somewhat different	15	12	14	15	20	24	5
Very different	6	5	6	7	6	8	4
Religious belief similarity to father's							
Very similar	36	42	30	32	31	38	75
Somewhat similar	36	34	40	34	39	22	17
Somewhat different	16	15	19	20	17	35	4
Very different	11	8	9	13	13	5	4

Source: National Survey of Youth and Religion, 2002–3.

Notes: Percentages may not add to 100 due to rounding and unreported don't know and refused answers. Jewish respondents include only religiously Jewish, not culturally Jewish only respondents.

are very different from their mother's and 45 percent whose beliefs are very different from their father's report on another question that their own religious faith is very or extremely important to them in their daily lives. They appear to hold firm to their own faith but apparently simply don't agree with their parents on most religious matters.

Religious similarity to parents varies somewhat by the religious tradition the teen belongs to, as do many of the other religion variables we examine in this chapter. Therefore, table 4 and most of the tables below split out all U.S. teens for comparisons into six religious traditions by the denominations with which they affiliate (Appendix D explains the methods used to categorize teens into these groups by religious denomination):

- Conservative Protestant (CP)
- Mainline Protestant (MP)
- Black Protestant (BP)
- Catholic (RC)
- Jewish (J)
- Mormon/Latter-day Saint (LDS)

Here we see that Mormon teens are the most likely among all U.S. teens to hold religious beliefs similar to their parents', followed by conservative Protestant, mainline Protestant, Catholic, and black Protestant teens. Jewish teens are comparatively the least likely to say they share the beliefs of their parents, although, to keep it in perspective, still an impressive majority of them do. If anything, then, U.S. teens lean strongly toward similarity with their parents in religious belief.

This, however, raises the question of whether, regardless of their own personal religious beliefs, American teens affiliate themselves with the same religious traditions of their parents or are drifting or converting to other religious traditions. Table 5 examines the distribution of teens (in rows) by the religious traditions of their parents (in columns). Three new categories have been added: other religion (OR), not religious (NR), and indeterminate (IND) for uninterpretable survey responses.[6] The diagonal line of large numbers from upper left to lower right shows the percentages of teens who share the religious tradition of their parents. Conceived as a matter of retention of youth, conservative Protestant and Mormon parents are doing the best job, retaining 86 percent of their teens each, followed by Catholics at 83 percent, black Protestants at 81 percent, and Jewish parents at 75 percent. Only 68 percent of mainline Protestant parents' teens are mainline Protestant themselves. Parents of other religions—a conglomeration of Jehovah's Witness, Hindu, pagan, Buddhist, Unitarian, and so on—are doing considerably worse than the Mormon, Christian, and Jewish parents in retaining (at 57 percent) their youth in any of these other religions. Nonreligious parents at 63 percent are faring relatively poorly at retaining their youth as nonreligious.

Viewed from a different angle, table 5 tells us which religious traditions of parents are more or less susceptible to "losing" teens to other religious traditions or to no religion at all. Most striking are the relatively low numbers on religious switching generally. Seven and 5 percent of mainline Protestant parents have, respectively, conservative Protestant and Catholic teens. We also see the notable percentages of conservative Protestant and Catholic teens of nonreligious parents (12 and 16 percent, respectively). All other combinations of religious switching in this table, besides teens becoming nonreligious, involve a mere 3 percent or fewer of teens of different kinds of religious parents. There appears to be, in other words, relatively little switching of teens away from their parents' religion into other religious traditions. Significant percentages of teens with religious parents, however, consider themselves nonreligious. About one-third of teens of "other religion" parents are not religious; 17 percent of teens of mainline and black Protestant parents and 18 percent of teens of Jewish parents are not religious. Mormon and Catholic

Table 5. Current Religious Tradition of U.S. Adolescents, Ages 13–17, by Parent Religious Traditions (Column percentages)

Teen current religious tradition	Parent Religious Tradition								
	CP	MP	BP	RC	J	LDS	OR	NR	IND
CP	86	7	~	2	~	1	2	12	8
MP	~	68	~	~	3	~	2	1	~
BP	~	~	81	~	~	~	~	~	~
RC	3	5	2	83	2	~	2	16	10
J	~	~	~	~	75	~	~	1	~
LDS	~	1	~	~	~	86	~	~	2
OR	~	1	1	1	3	~	57	2	3
NR	10	17	17	12	18	13	35	63	32
IND	1	~	~	2	~	~	6	5	45

Source: National Survey of Youth and Religion, 2002–3.

Note: Percentages may not add to 100 due to rounding; cells of <1 are reported as ~.

parents follow at 13 and 12 percent, respectively. Conservative Protestant parents show the lowest levels of teens deserting their faiths for nonreligious identities, at 10 percent. Simple religious minority status alone cannot be the explanation for these differences, because Mormons and "other religions" are both minority religions in the United States, yet they are at the far extremes in their teens becoming not religious. Such tradition-specific differences in the chance of teens becoming not religious are explored further in the next chapter. For now, we do well simply to note these differences and keep them in mind.

RELIGIOUS SERVICE ATTENDANCE

Aside from the religious backgrounds of U.S. youth, how frequently do teenagers attend religious services and with whom do they attend? According to data in table 6, 40 percent of all surveyed U.S. teens report attending religious services once a week or more, and 19 percent report attending one to three times per month; 22 percent report attending religious services a few or many times a year, and 18 percent report never attending religious services. Again,

Table 6. Religious Service Attendance of U.S. Adolescents, Ages 13–17 (Percentages)

	U.S.	Religious Tradition						
		CP	MP	BP	RC	J	LDS	NR
Religious service attendance								
More than once a week	16	29	13	24	6	~	28	~
Once a week	24	26	31	17	34	8	43	~
2–3 times a month	12	15	16	18	12	10	5	~
Once a month	7	7	9	4	8	11	6	~
Many times a year	8	7	10	19	8	13	6	1
A few times a year	14	13	12	11	21	36	8	4
Never	18	4	9	7	11	22	4	95
Would attend if totally up to teen								
More than once a week	17	33	15	21	6	2	22	4
Once a week	28	30	32	27	34	9	47	8
2–3 times a month	15	14	20	16	17	8	10	7
Once a month	7	4	10	6	8	22	1	9
Many times a year	7	7	5	20	7	9	1	2
A few times a year	12	6	11	6	14	28	6	29
Never	13	6	7	4	14	23	13	40
Attends more than one religious congregation	16	18	22	28	14	26	3	~
Attends with								
Both parents	45	58	53	36	53	44	66	~
Only one parent	21	20	24	46	20	23	19	~
Neither parent	10	14	9	10	7	5	5	2
Doesn't attend/Other	24	9	14	8	20	30	10	98

Source: National Survey of Youth and Religion, 2002–3.

Note: Percentages may not add to 100 due to rounding and unreported don't know and refused answers; cells of <1 are reported as ~.

religious service attendance varies greatly by religious tradition of the teen. Seventy-one percent of Mormon teens and 55 percent of conservative Protestant teens attend weekly or more; on the other hand, 58 percent of Jewish teens, for whom religious service attendance often means something different than for Christian teens, and 31 percent of Catholic teens attend religious services only a few times a year or never. Almost all of the nonreligious teens never attend religious services. Mainline and black Protestant teens fall in their frequency of church attendance between the extremes. Still, in all of the religious traditions (not including the nonreligious), there is notable variance in religious service attendance, with teens falling all along the spectrum.

Some observers suggest and some assume that youth attend religious services mostly because their parents make them attend, but would not attend if it were their own choice. To examine this possibility, the NSYR included the question "If it were totally up to you, how often would you attend religious services?" Perhaps surprisingly, table 6 shows that U.S. teens as a whole report that they would like to attend religious services even *more* than they currently do. Fully 5 percent *more* than those who report actually attending services once a week or more say that they would like to attend weekly or more (45 compared to 40 percent). And 7 percent *fewer* than those who attend only a few times a year or never say they would like to attend religious services that infrequently (32 compared to 25 percent). In other words, U.S. teens as a group profess to want to attend religious services not less, but actually more than they currently do. Some of this difference may be mere wishful thinking, with the effect of making the teens feel better about themselves more than actually motivating them to attend religious services more often. On the other hand, at least some of the teens we interviewed did report uncooperative parents and transportation problems preventing them from attending religious services more often than they did. In any case, these findings provide no evidence supporting the belief that significant numbers of teens would like to stop attending religious service and are only doing otherwise because their parents are forcing them to attend.

Table 6 also shows that, although most U.S. teens seem content adhering to only one religion, significant numbers of them attend services at more than one religious congregation. Black Protestant, Jewish, and mainline Protestant teens range on the high end, in the 20 percent range. Conservative Protestant and Catholic teens attend more than one church at 18 and 14 percent, respectively. Mormon teens are the only group that clearly attend only one congregation (or ward), with few exceptions. Thus, although U.S. youth are generally not mixing and matching different religious faiths, significant proportions of them appear to be involved with different churches or other religious congregations.

With whom do U.S. teenagers attend? Slightly fewer than half attend with both parents, 21 percent attend with only one parent, and 10 percent attend with neither parent. The last group may attend with a friend, with another family relative such as an aunt or grandparent, or by themselves. Again, almost one in four never attend. More than half of Mormon, conservative Protestant, mainline Protestant, and Catholic teens attend religious services with both of their parents. Jewish teens attend with both parents at a rate about the national norm. Black Protestant teens are much more likely than all other groups to attend with only one parent, probably in part because black teens are more likely to come from single-parent families. Nearly all nonreligious teens do not attend or do not have parents with whom they might attend.

FEATURES OF FAITH

What does the NSYR tell us about the character of faith of U.S. adolescents? Aside from organizational participation, what might we learn about teens' subjective experience of religious belief? According to table 7, an impressive proportion of U.S. teens profess that religious faith is important in their lives, both in shaping daily life and in making major life decisions. On both measures, about half of teens said that faith is very or extremely important in their lives; only about 8 percent said faith was not important at all. To simplify matters a bit, we believe that the most important dividing line separating these answer categories is between the "very" and "somewhat" important answers, a distinct impression formed through our hundreds of hours of monitoring actual telephone surveys and by conducting in-depth interviews around the country. For teens to say that faith is "very important" to them is to take a fairly strong stand on the matter. But for them to say that faith is "somewhat important" can describe some fairly inconsequential experiences of religious belief when the teens may not feel comfortable saying on a survey that "faith doesn't matter much." If so, then table 7 tells us, in rough terms, that faith is an important matter for about half of U.S. teens and not particularly important for the other half.

Table 7 also reports on how close to God U.S. teens say they feel. Thirty-six percent report that they feel very or extremely close to God; 35 percent report feeling somewhat close to God; 25 percent feel some degree of distance from God; and 3 percent do not believe in any God to feel either close to or distant from. To the extent that survey answers provide reliable measures, then, we can conclude that slightly more than one-third of U.S. teens experience an intimate relationship with God, another third feel something in the middle, neither intimate nor distant, and almost one-third either feel distant from or do not believe in God. This variance is impressive, and differs again by religious tradition. This time, however, Mormon teens do not top the charts. Rather, black Protestants and conservative Protestants rank highest on closeness to God, with nearly 50 percent of each reporting that they feel very or extremely close to God. Forty-four percent of Mormon, 40 percent of mainline Protestant, and 31 percent of Catholic teens say they feel very or extremely close to God. Only 10 percent of Jewish teens—whose traditions, note, may or may not place God at the center of Judaism—report the same,

Table 7. Characteristics of Religious Faith of U.S. Adolescents, Ages 13–17
(Percentages)

	U.S.	Religious Tradition						
		CP	MP	BP	RC	J	LDS	NR
Importance of religious faith shaping daily life								
Extremely important	20	29	20	31	10	8	43	4
Very important	31	38	30	42	31	5	25	10
Somewhat important	31	25	34	22	41	51	16	29
Not very important	11	6	10	3	13	24	10	24
Not important at all	7	1	6	2	5	13	5	33
Importance of faith shaping major life decisions								
Extremely important	20	28	19	31	11	7	52	7
Very important	29	37	34	35	30	9	14	12
Somewhat important	31	28	30	27	41	29	21	22
Not very important	11	6	11	3	12	31	9	23
Not important at all	8	2	6	3	6	24	4	35
How close teen feels to God								
Extremely close	11	15	7	22	9	3	20	2
Very close	25	33	33	27	22	7	24	7
Somewhat close	35	33	34	35	43	25	39	26
Somewhat distant	17	15	18	11	20	38	11	22
Very distant	5	3	4	3	3	12	4	13
Extremely distant	3	1	2	2	2	9	2	11
Does not believe in God	3	1	2	~	1	5	~	17
Believers' doubts about religious beliefs in prior year								
Many doubts	5	4	6	6	5	3	4	—
Some doubts	14	14	10	15	16	19	4	—
A few doubts	32	30	36	26	35	30	40	—
No doubts	48	51	48	52	44	45	51	—
Refused	~	~	~	~	~	4	~	—

Source: National Survey of Youth and Religion, 2002–3.

Note: Percentages may not add to 100 due to rounding and unreported don't know and refused answers; cells of <1 are reported as ~; doubts about religion findings for nonreligious teens are reported in table 26.

a mere 1 percent more than the report of nonreligious youth. Viewed from the other direction, 64 percent of Jewish and 63 percent of nonreligious teens either feel distant from or do not believe in God; about one in four Catholic and mainline Protestant youth feel distant from or do not believe in God; between one in six and one in four Mormon and black and conservative Protestant teens feel the same. Once again, U.S. teens of all major traditions are spread across the spectrum of closeness to God, although with a few exceptions, more say they feel close to God than distant.

Finally, how many doubts about their religious beliefs do religious U.S. adolescents have? According to table 7, relatively few. Nearly half of religious teens report having no doubts at all in the prior year; another one-third had a few doubts. Only one in 20 religious teens reported dealing with many doubts about their faith in the previous year. Furthermore, compared to the other faith variables in table 7, the doubts answers varied less by religious traditions. While Mormon teens had somewhat fewer doubts and Jewish teens somewhat more, the differences are not major. In general, U.S. religious teens do not appear to struggle a great deal with doubt about their faith.

RELIGIOUS AND SPIRITUAL BELIEFS AND EXPERIENCES

What do U.S. teenagers actually believe religiously? According to table 8, more than 80 percent do believe in God, slightly more than 10 percent are unsure about their belief in God, and, as we saw above, only 3 percent definitely do not believe in God. But what is the God that most teens believe in? About two-thirds of teens say they believe in God as a personal being involved in the lives of people today; 13 percent profess something like a deist's view of God as having created the world but not being involved in it now; and 14 percent take a more New Age approach to God as an impersonal, cosmic life force. Five percent simply do not know or refuse to answer the question.

These findings are striking in different ways, depending on what one might have been expecting. Two out of three teens profess to believe in something like the Bible's personal, historically active God. On the other hand, more than 30 percent hold a deistic, New Age, or simply uncertain picture of God. Those who assume U.S. youth have been largely secularized might

Table 8. Beliefs of U.S. Adolescents about God, Ages 13–17 (Percentages)

	U.S.	Religious Tradition						
		CP	MP	BP	RC	J	LDS	NR
Belief in God								
Believes in God	84	94	86	97	85	72	84	49
Is unsure in belief about God	12	5	13	2	14	23	13	34
Does not believe in God	3	1	2	~	1	5	~	17
Views of God								
A personal being involved in the lives of people today	65	77	69	74	64	44	76	30
Created the world, but is not involved in world today	13	10	13	13	17	12	7	15
Not personal, something like a cosmic life force	14	8	13	7	14	33	9	31
Don't know/refused/none of these views	5	4	3	5	4	5	8	7
Does not believe in God	3	1	2	~	1	5	~	17
Believes in a judgment day when God will reward some and punish others								
Yes	71	88	63	91	67	25	85	33
No	22	10	31	7	28	67	5	43
Don't know/refused	4	2	5	2	5	4	9	7
Does not believe in God	3	1	2	~	1	5	~	17

Source: National Survey of Youth and Religion, 2002–3.

Note: Percentages may not add to 100 due to rounding and unreported don't know and refused answers; cells of <1 are reported as ~.

be surprised by the first finding. Those who assume U.S. youth are continuing on with a biblically traditional or orthodox view of God should be surprised by the second finding. Complicating the matter is the apparent logical inconsistency of some teens in relating to God; for example, while teens who embrace a personal view of God are *much* more likely than others to also say they feel close to God, 22 percent of teen "deists" in our survey reported feeling very or extremely close to God (the God they believe is not involved in the world today). Go figure. The bottom line is, when it comes to their religious belief about God, U.S. teens reflect a great deal of variance on the matter, and perhaps in some cases more than a little conceptual confusion. All of this calls for in-depth interviews with teens, which we also conducted, to delve deeper into the content and possible complexities of their beliefs; many of those findings are reported in chapter 4.

In the meantime, it is useful to probe teens with more specific survey questions about religious beliefs. The bottom of table 8, for instance, tells us that more than 7 in 10 U.S. teens profess to belief in a coming judgment day when God will reward some and punish others. The vast majority of teens maintain that at least some people will have some divine consequences, good and bad, for their faith or actions. On the other hand, about one-quarter of U.S. teens—a sizable proportion—do not believe or do not know if they believe in a divine judgment day. Our analysis of interviews in chapter 4 will also help to inform this finding.

As with most other NSYR measures, all of these belief-in-God measures show notable variance across the religious traditions analyzed. Black and conservative Protestant teens, for example, stand out for their relatively high rates of definite belief in God. Among religious youth, Jewish, Catholic, Mormon, and mainline Protestant teens are relatively likely to not be sure whether they believe in God. On the other hand, about half of nonreligious teens profess to believe in God and another third are open to the possibility; only 17 percent of them say they simply do not believe in God. Likewise, about three-quarters of Mormon and black and conservative Protestant teens believe in a personal God whom they can know, while Jewish and nonreligious teens are comparatively more likely to gravitate toward a New Age version of God. This kind of variance is even more pronounced for the question about a judgment day, which Mormon and black and conservative Protestant teens are very likely to believe in, Catholic and mainline Protestant teens are somewhat likely to believe in, and Jewish and nonreligious teens are quite unlikely to believe in.

The meaning of all of this again depends largely on what one expects and hopes for. If one's baseline assumption is the widespread loss of religious belief among youth, then U.S. teens look awfully religious by these measures. Then again, there may be more than a few Catholic and Mormon leaders who may be justifiably concerned that roughly one in every seven of their teenagers are not even convinced that God exists, or conservative Protestant pastors who are startled to learn that 10 and 8 percent of their teens hold deistic and New Age views of God, respectively, while another 5 percent are confused, silent, or atheistic on the matter. In any case, table 8 reveals both a great deal of religious belief and a great deal of variance among teens in religious belief.

Table 9 further explores a variety of specific religious belief items—including traditionally Christian, non-Christian, and "paranormal" beliefs—for all religious types analyzed here. The items are ranked from top to bottom in order of most to least believed in. Perhaps not surprisingly, the majority of U.S. teens are confident in their belief in the existence of angels. Almost

Table 9. Religious, Spiritual, and Paranormal Beliefs of U.S. Adolescents, Ages 13–17 (Percentages)

	U.S.	Religious Tradition						
		CP	MP	BP	RC	J	LDS	NR
Believes in existence of angels								
Definitely	63	79	59	76	58	30	80	33
Maybe	29	18	36	19	35	50	20	42
Not at all	8	3	5	5	7	20	1	25
Believes in divine miracles from God								
Definitely	61	77	59	76	55	21	73	26
Maybe	30	20	33	19	38	59	21	45
Not at all	9	3	8	4	7	20	3	29
Believes there is life after death								
Definitely	49	62	51	50	45	23	76	24
Maybe	37	26	40	31	44	60	19	57
Not at all	13	12	10	19	11	16	2	19
Believes in existence of demons or evil spirits								
Definitely	41	58	37	48	28	17	69	22
Maybe	34	26	39	27	44	46	19	39
Not at all	25	16	24	25	27	37	12	39
Believes in reincarnation								
Definitely	13	7	11	12	13	24	11	21
Maybe	36	26	33	40	41	35	15	48
Not at all	51	66	55	48	47	42	71	31
Believes in astrology								
Definitely	9	6	7	12	11	8	1	13
Maybe	31	27	30	33	35	47	16	35
Not at all	59	67	63	54	54	45	83	52
Believes in communicating with the dead								
Definitely	9	7	6	10	9	15	9	11
Maybe	30	24	33	26	39	43	26	33
Not at all	60	69	61	64	52	43	66	56
Believes in psychics and fortune-tellers								
Definitely	6	5	4	5	6	3	~	10
Maybe	21	16	22	16	26	24	12	28
Not at all	73	79	74	79	68	74	85	62

Source: National Survey of Youth and Religion, 2002–3.

Note: Percentages may not add to 100 due to rounding and unreported refused answers (don't know included in "maybe"); cells of <1 are reported as ~.

as many also believe in divine miracles from God. About half definitely be-lieve there is life after death, and four out of ten believe in demons or evil spirits. From there, the numbers believing drop off precipitously. Only small minorities of U.S. teens definitely believe in reincarnation, astrology, com-municating with the dead, and psychics and fortune-tellers—although roughly one-third are open to the possibilities that these things may be real. Once again, the general pattern across religious traditions that is by now becoming familiar is evident in this table, too. Mormon and black and con-servative Protestant teens are the most likely to hold traditional, biblical re-ligious beliefs, such as in angels, demons, and miracles, and the least likely to hold non-Christian, paranormal, or occultic beliefs. Jewish and nonreli-gious teens tend toward the opposite, and mainline Protestant and Catholic youth generally fall between those sets of groups.

Aside from these broad generalizations about tradition-specific differ-ences, many observers should be interested in the results of the "maybe" answers in table 9, which give hints of significant slippage in the religious education of youth. When combined with the "not at all" answers, large segments of Catholic youth, for example, are far from convinced about the existence of angels (42 percent report maybe or not at all), miracles (45 per-cent), life after death (55 percent), or the existence of evil spirits (71 percent report maybe or not at all). On the other hand, 57 percent of Catholic youth maybe or definitely believe in reincarnation, 46 percent in astrology, 48 per-cent in communicating with the dead, and 32 percent in psychics and fortune-tellers. There is an immense amount of slippage here between the official Catholic catechism and the actual professed beliefs of Catholic teenagers. Likewise, significant portions of conservative Protestant youth are not assured about the existence of angels (21 percent report maybe or not at all), miracles (23 percent), life after death (38 percent), or the existence of evil spirits (42 percent report maybe or not at all). On the other hand, 33 percent of con-servative Protestant youth maybe or definitely believe in reincarnation, 33 percent in astrology, 31 percent in communicating with the dead, and 21 percent in psychics and fortune-tellers. For a tradition that has so strongly emphasized the infallibility or inerrancy of the Bible, the exclusive claims of conservative Christianity, and the need for a personal commitment of one's life to God, some of these numbers are astounding. Even the conservative Protestants evince a great deal of slippage in the effectiveness of the Christian education of their youth. At the same time, large proportions of the self-identified nonreligious teens either definitely believe in or are open to the possibility of believing in all eight of these religious and magical ideas. Dis-missive of the existence of a possible spiritual world America's professed non-religious teens are not.

Table 10 examines various personal religious experiences of U.S. teen-agers, in which we see that roughly half report having had each of a variety of religious experiences. Further analysis (not shown in the table) reveals that only 20 percent of all U.S. teenagers report not having had any of these four religious experiences. Twenty percent of teens report having experienced all

Table 10. Religious Experiences of U.S. Adolescents, Ages 13–17 (Percentages)

	U.S.	Religious Tradition						
		CP	MP	BP	RC	J	LDS	NR
Has made a personal commitment to live life for God	55	79	60	74	41	21	69	13
Has ever had an experience of spiritual worship that was very moving and powerful	51	70	64	59	37	45	76	11
Has ever experienced a definite answer to prayer or specific guidance from God	50	65	53	61	42	34	67	18
Has ever witnessed or experienced what teen believed was a miracle from God	46	60	37	68	38	41	47	22

Source: National Survey of Youth and Religion, 2002–3.

four, another 20 percent have experienced three of the four, 18 percent have experienced two, and 17 percent have had one of these four religious experiences (the remaining 5 percent involve don't know and refused answers). The vast majority of U.S. religious teens and minorities of nonreligious teens, then, report having had one or more significant religious experiences.

The likelihood of a teen having had one of these religious experiences varies significantly by religious tradition. Following the general pattern observed in previous tables, conservative Protestant, black Protestant, and Mormon teens are the most likely to have had these religious experiences; nonreligious teens are the least likely; and Jewish, Catholic, and mainline Protestant teens fall somewhere between those groups, depending on the specific question. Jewish teens, for example, are not big on making personal commitments to live for God,[7] but are ahead of the Catholics on experiences of powerful worship and ahead of the mainline Protestants on having witnessed a miracle. Altogether, however, we can repeat our observation that U.S. teens of almost any religious tradition are not deprived of significant religious experiences.

PERSONAL RELIGIOUS PRACTICES

Yet another important dimension of religious life worth examining is religious practices: specific actions in which religious believers engage over time that embody spiritual meaning and foster personal formation toward excellence in religious faith and works. Religious practices are spiritually significant habits intentionally engaged in for the purpose of being shaped by them toward the good as known by a religious faith. Prayer, scripture reading, meditation, and tithing are well-known religious practices, but there are many other possibilities.[8] Not all religious traditions encourage or require observing the same religious practices, obviously, but the NSYR survey asked all teens about many practices anyway, simply to map out proportions. Inclusion in table 11, however, does not imply that all teens should be engaging all of these practices. In any case, table 11 shows their reported engagement in a great

Table 11. Personal Religious Practices of U.S. Adolescents, Ages 13–17
(Percentages)

	U.S.	Religious Tradition						
		CP	MP	BP	RC	J	LDS	NR
In prior year, teen:								
Practiced religious or spiritual meditation not including prayer	10	8	10	7	10	7	9	11
Served as an acolyte or altar server	11	7	25	10	16	1	13	—
Been part of a religious support of evangelism or prayer group that meets at school	15	25	17	17	8	7	17	—
Taught a Sunday School or religious education class	20	28	26	22	15	16	42	—
Burned candles or incense that had religious or spiritual meaning	21	14	24	12	35	43	7	11
Fasted or denied self something as spiritual discipline	24	22	25	20	29	49	68	4
Been part of any other scripture study or prayer group	27	42	31	35	17	26	50	—
Played or sang in a religious music group or choir	28	37	35	52	18	14	49	—
Read a devotional, religious, or spiritual book other than the scriptures	30	45	28	29	22	28	68	—
Spoke publicly about own faith in a religious service or meeting (not including bar/bat mitzvah)	30	42	33	34	20	21	65	—
Tried to practice a weekly day of rest or Sabbath	31	40	27	35	30	25	67	5
Attended a religious music concert	34	51	51	41	20	16	42	9
Chose to wear jewelry or clothing expressing religious or spiritual meaning	41	49	47	41	42	37	37	15
Shared own religious faith with someone not of faith	43	56	51	41	37	58	72	—
Listened to religious radio programs, or CDs or tapes by a religious music group	51	70	52	79	35	18	59	20
Worked hard to reconcile a broken relationship	59	61	63	50	61	57	55	53
Frequency of teen praying alone								
Many times a day	16	22	13	30	10	1	33	4
About once a day	22	27	19	25	23	8	24	7
A few times a week	15	18	18	14	16	4	11	8
About once a week	12	11	16	13	13	7	7	8
1–2 times a month	13	12	14	10	16	28	4	10
Less than once a month	7	5	8	3	9	18	9	10
Never	15	5	11	5	13	34	12	51
Public professions of faith								
Of all Christians: been confirmed or baptized as public affirmation of faith (not infant baptism)	46	54	59	53	41	—	—	—
Of all Jewish: had a bar or bat mitzvah						73		
Of all Mormons: been confirmed or baptized as public affirmation of faith (not infant baptism)							79	
Of all other religions: done any religious rite of passage or public affirmation of religious faith: 15 percent								

Source: National Survey of Youth and Religion, 2002–3.

Note: Percentages may not add to 100 due to rounding and unreported don't know and refused answers; cells of <1 are reported as ~.

variety of religious practices, with the first cluster of measures listed in order of participation, from least to greatest. What we see is that significant minorities of U.S. teenagers report having engaged in most of a long list of religious practices in the previous year. Fewer than 20 percent have meditated, served as acolytes, or participated in a religious group meeting at school. Between 20 and 29 percent have taught Sunday school, burned candles or incense for religious reasons, engaged in the spiritual disciplines of fasting or self-denial, and participated in a scripture study or prayer or religious music group. About one-third of teens report having read a religious book, spoken at a religious service, practiced a religious day of rest, and attended a religious music concert, and nearly half have worn clothing or jewelry with religious meaning, shared their faith with another person, and listened to religious music outside of a concert. (Nearly 60 percent of teens report having worked toward relational reconciliation, although whether or not this was religiously motivated was not specified by the survey question.)

Differences across religious traditions for many of these practices are notable, although not consistent across them all. Mormon teens, for instance, are strong on sharing their faith and teaching Sunday school, among other practices, but seem to avoid burning candles and incense and are less likely than other groups to wear jewelry or clothing that expresses spiritual meaning. Black Protestant teens are big on playing or singing in religious music groups and choirs but come out on the lower end on spiritual meditation. Similar comparative observations could be made for teens in other religious traditions, although space does not allow for specific mention of all interesting differences, which readers will have to study in greater depth. Suffice it to say here that significant minorities of U.S. teens of all religious traditions examined profess in their survey answers to have in the previous year engaged in nearly all of the different religious practices we asked about. Furthermore, although the NSYR did not ask all religious practice questions of nonreligious teens, for obvious reasons, more than trivial numbers of them report having engaged in the previous year in most of the religious practices about which the survey did ask. Twenty percent of nonreligious teens, for instance, listen to religious music, 15 percent wore religious jewelry or clothing, 11 percent burned candles or incense for spiritual reasons, 11 percent practiced spiritual meditation, and 9 percent attended a religious music concert. Thus, while the majority of nonreligious U.S. teenagers refrain from religious practices, not all do.

Table 11 also explores the reported personal prayer practices of U.S. teens. Nearly 40 percent report that they pray daily or more often; nearly 30 percent pray once or a few times a week; 20 percent pray more sporadically than that; and 15 percent of U.S. teens never pray. Again, the variance in frequency of personal prayer across all U.S. teens is impressive. Mormon teens appear to pray the most often, followed by black Protestant and conservative Protestant teens. Catholics and mainline Protestants pray alone with comparative moderate frequency. Jewish and nonreligious teens are the least likely to engage in the regular practice of personal prayer. At 51 percent, the nonreligious

are the most likely never to pray, but they are also slightly more likely than
Jewish youth to pray once a week or more. Social location in a particular
U.S. religious tradition thus strongly influences the likelihood of teens engag-
ing in the practice of personal prayer.

The NSYR also asked teens of different religious groups whether they
have ever completed the religious rite of passage or public affirmation of faith
appropriate to their tradition (table 11). On the high end, 79 percent of
Mormon teens had been baptized. Fewer than half of all Christian teens
together (46 percent) had been confirmed or baptized as youth, with the
spread among those traditions ranging from 59 percent of mainline Protestant
teens to 41 percent of Catholic teens on the high and low ends, respectively.
Only 15 percent of teens in other religions (not Christian, Jewish, or Mormon) appear to have performed a religious rite of passage or public affirmation of faith.

Because some religious practices are tradition-specific, the NSYR asked
certain questions of U.S. teens in particular religious groups. The survey asked
U.S. teenagers who either identified themselves as Catholic or who had a
Catholic parent—whom we here refer to as "Catholic teens"—for instance,
about six specific Catholic practices. According to table 12, 71 percent of
those Catholic teens have taken First Communion, nearly half have religious
altars in their homes, and 44 percent prayed the rosary, Novenas, or to a
special saint in the previous year. Forty percent of U.S. Catholic teenagers
had participated in a confession or a reconciliation liturgy and 19 percent in
a religious pilgrimage, procession, or way of the cross in the previous year.
Celebrating the Virgin of Guadalupe or a Virgin of another country of origin
is a popular religious practice among many Hispanic Catholics in the United
States; fully 61 percent (this question was only asked of Hispanic Catholics)
do so, according to findings in table 12. Because some Catholics are practic-

Table 12. Faith Tradition-specific Religious Practices of U.S. Catholic Adolescents,
Ages 13–17 (Percentages) (N=906)

	All	Attends 2–3 Times a Month or More Often (51%)	Attends Once a Month or Less Often (48%)
Taken First Communion	71	84	57
Has sacred altars or images in home	49	53	44
Prayed the rosary, Novenas, or to special saints in the prior year	44	57	31
Been to a confession or reconciliation liturgy in the prior year	40	55	26
Participated in a religious pilgrimage, procession, way of the cross, or other similar practice	19	27	12
Celebrates the Virgin of Guadalupe or Virgin of country of origin (Hispanic Catholics only, N=231)	61	66	57

Source: National Survey of Youth and Religion, 2002–3.

ing Catholics and others are nominally Catholic, table 12 divides the NSYR Catholic teen sample into those who attend church services two to three times a month or more often and those who attend church once a month or less often.[9] As we would expect, we see that the regularly attending Catholic teens engage in all of the religious practices at noticeably higher rates, in some cases at about double the rate of the lower-attending Catholic teens. Even so, significant proportions of regularly attending Catholic teenagers do not engage in various Catholic religious practices; 45 percent of them, for instance, have not been to confession or a reconciliation liturgy in the prior year. All told, the U.S. Catholic Church could be doing better at engaging its teenagers in its religious practices, though our findings hardly suggest that overall it is entirely failing to do so.

The NSYR asked another tradition-specific set of religious practices of its 72 Jewish teen respondents. These 72 either identified their first or second religion as Jewish or had a Jewish parent respondent. This sample represents a modest but nevertheless respectable number for a national sample of such a relatively small religious minority. Because there are different kinds of these Jewish teens in the United States, we broke the sample down into three groups: teens who consider themselves "religiously Jewish" (22 percent of the sample), those who consider themselves mostly "culturally Jewish" (42 percent), and those who do not identify themselves as Jewish but have at least one Jewish parent and so may engage in some Jewish observances despite their personal lack of Jewish identity (31 percent of the sample; 5 percent responded "don't know"). Those three groups are broken out into three columns in table 13, along with all 72 sampled teens totaled together on the far left. There we see, first, that there are large differences between the three types of Jewish teenagers. As we might expect, the religiously Jewish teens

Table 13. Religious Observances of U.S. Jewish Adolescents, Ages 13–17 (Percentages) (N=72)

	All: Teen Is Jewish or Has a Jewish Parent	Teen Identifies Self as Religiously Jewish	Teen Identifies Self as Culturally Jewish	Teen Not Self-identified as Jewish but Has a Jewish Parent
Regularly practices Jewish traditions observing the Sabbath	32	74	22	19
Have taken classes to study Hebrew, Jewish history, traditions, or modern Jewish life in prior two years	40	100	24	21
Celebrated Hanukkah last year	93	100	100	80
Celebrated Passover last year	85	100	96	67
Celebrated Rosh Hashanah last year	69	85	79	46
Celebrated Yom Kippur last year	72	85	87	44
Celebrated Sukkot last year	38	78	35	19
Celebrated Simkhat Torah last year	30	70	23	17

Source: National Survey of Youth and Religion, 2002–3.

say they observe most Jewish holidays and practices at much higher rates than the culturally Jewish teens, who themselves appear to be observant at generally higher rates than the non-Jewish teens with Jewish parents. Somewhere between three-quarters and all self-described religiously Jewish teenagers report observing the Sabbath and major holidays and engage in Jewish education. Significant numbers of "culturally Jewish" teenagers are also observant of many Jewish holidays and practices. Even among the non-Jewish teens with Jewish parents, notable proportions report celebrating Hanukkah, Passover, Rosh Hashanah, and Yom Kippur, and approximately 20 percent observe the Sabbath, engage in Jewish education, and celebrate Sukkot and Simkhat Torah. When grouped together, between 33 and about 90 percent of this sample of Jewish teenagers observe these various Jewish holidays and practices. These findings comport with our understanding of contemporary American Judaism as centered more on family and community observance of rituals and holidays than on commitment to specific cognitive beliefs and doctrines. Measured in these specific terms, U.S. Jewish teenagers are doing fairly well in practicing their religious faith, at least no less well than teens in many Christian traditions.

News from studies and projections about the future of the Jewish community in the United States often convey dismal messages about the effects of high rates of marriage to non-Jews as well as other social processes and factors that appear to be eroding Jewish community boundaries and identities. There is no doubt that many social changes in recent decades are raising real challenges for the continuation of a distinct, coherent religioethnic Judaism in the United States. Yet the findings of table 13 should also be accounted for in considering American Judaism's future. Whatever theological beliefs Jewish teenagers embrace and however subjectively important Jewish faith and identity may or may not be to them, we at least still find notable levels of traditional Jewish observances not only among "religiously Jewish" teenagers, as we would expect, but also among the "culturally Jewish." Even teens who do not consider themselves Jewish but have Jewish parents appear to be drawn into many Jewish observances in significant numbers. The future of American Judaism is a complex and challenging subject, which we do not want naïvely to oversimplify here. But we do think these findings on U.S. Jewish teenagers may contribute another important piece of the larger puzzle well worth trying to fit into the bigger picture.[10]

RELIGIOUS GROUP ACTIVITIES

For many American teenagers, religious involvement means more than simply attending church, synagogue, mosque, or temple. A variety of other religious activities are often also available for their participation. Table 14 begins our examination of these activities by focusing in depth on U.S. teens' involvement in religious youth groups. According to NSYR data, 38 percent of all U.S. teenagers are currently involved in a religious youth group, and 69 percent are now or previously have been involved in a religious youth group.

Table 14. Religious Youth Group Experiences of U.S. Adolescents, Ages 13–17
(Percentages)

	U.S.	Religious Tradition						
		CP	MP	BP	RC	J	LDS	NR
Currently involved in a religious youth group	38	56	55	38	24	27	72	1
Ever in life involved in a religious youth group	69	86	86	76	59	58	87	31
Involved in a congregation with a youth group (of religious service–attending teens: 85 percent)	69	86	84	81	67	63	90	—
Youth group participation rate (currently involved in YG/YG available in congregation)	52	64	64	44	32	41	75	—
Congregation has a designated youth minister								
Full-time	30	44	37	41	21	21	7	—
Part-time	9	8	12	11	11	10	2	—
Volunteer	20	18	17	21	23	12	85	—
Don't know	5	4	2	7	8	5	1	—
Not attending congregation or no youth minister	36	26	32	20	37	52	5	—
Youth group teen is involved with is								
Part of teen's religious congregation	32	49	49	32	20	22	66	—
Part of another religious congregation	4	6	5	5	3	4	5	—
Of another religious faith	0.4	0.5	0.5	0.4	0.5	~	~	—
Teen not in youth group	62	43	45	62	76	73	28	—
Frequency of current youth group attendance								
More than once a week	8	14	9	8	2	1	24	1
About once a week	18	29	26	15	11	11	33	~
2–3 times a month	6	7	11	7	4	5	6	~
About once a month	4	4	6	3	4	8	6	~
A few times a year	2	3	3	4	3	2	3	~
Never	62	44	45	62	76	73	28	99
Number of years currently involved teen in youth group								
8–10	5	7	4	9	4	4	15	~
5–7	7	11	13	8	3	2	15	~
2–4	19	30	32	14	11	17	42	1
1	5	7	5	5	5	4	~	~
<1	1	1	1	1	1	~	~	~
Zero	62	44	45	62	76	73	28	99
Type of youth group involvement								
Teen is a leader	13	19	19	15	5	7	36	~
Teen is just a participant	24	35	35	22	18	19	35	~
Both (leader and participant)	1	2	2	~	~	~	1	~
Not involved	62	44	45	62	76	73	28	99

Source: National Survey of Youth and Religion, 2002–3.

Note: Percentages may not add to 100 due to rounding and unreported don't know and refused answers; cells of <1 are reported as ~.

The lives of the majority of young Americans, then, connect to religious youth groups at some time during the teenage years. Nearly 70 percent of all teens attend a religious congregation that also sponsors a youth group; fully 85 percent of teens who attend religious services belong to congregations with youth groups. The vast majority of religious congregations with teens present, then, appear to offer youth groups for their teenagers. Furthermore, 30 percent of all teens have available to them youth group programs overseen by full-time youth ministers (whether or not the teens participate in them), according to teen reports, and nearly the same number have youth groups with part-time or volunteer youth ministers (again, whether or not they participate). Slightly more than one-third of U.S. teens (36 percent) either do not attend services at a religious congregation where they might encounter a youth group or do attend a congregation that does not sponsor any youth group. Of teens involved in religious youth groups, the vast majority (32 percent of all teens, 84 percent of youth group–involved teens) participate in a youth group from their own religious congregation. Only 4 percent of all teens participating in a youth group attend youth groups at religious congregations other than their own, and fewer than one-half of 1 percent participate in religious youth groups from another religious faith altogether.

Teen involvement with religious youth groups is highly variable by tradition. The majority of Mormon and conservative and mainline Protestant teens are currently involved in youth groups. But only about one-quarter of Catholic and Jewish youth participate in religious youth groups. Nearly one-third of currently nonreligious teens were once involved in a religious youth group, but all but 1 percent have dropped that involvement, presumably in the process of having become not religious. By dividing the percentage of teens currently involved in a religious youth group by the percentage attending congregations sponsoring youth groups, we can estimate the youth group participation rate of teens in various traditions. Mormons have the highest participation rate (75 percent), followed by mainline and conservative Protestants (64 percent each). Black Protestant and Jewish teens have participation rates of 44 and 41 percent, respectively (in many black churches, participation in youth choir functions as the equivalent of involvement in a religious youth group, about which see table 11). Of all the religious groups examined, Catholic teens have the lowest youth group participation rate, thus calculated, at 32 percent; in other words, two-thirds of Catholic teens who attend churches that sponsor youth groups do not participate in them.

But how deeply are U.S. teens involved in religious youth groups? According to table 14, nearly one-third of all teens (32 percent) report attending youth group two to three times a month or more often. Only a handful attend more sporadically. The remaining teens simply do not attend. Youth group attendance thus appears to be something teens do regularly or not do at all. Youth group attendance varies by religious tradition as well. Fifty-seven percent of Mormon teens, 43 percent of conservative Protestant teens, and 35 percent of mainline Protestant teens attend youth group weekly or more often. By contrast, only 13 percent of Catholic and 12 percent of Jewish teens attend youth group weekly or more often, and about three-quarters of those groups never attend youth group, a number surpassed only by the 99 percent of nonreligious teens who also never attend. As to years spent in youth groups, of those teens participating in religious youth groups, the majority have been involved for more than one year, with 31 percent of all U.S. teens involved for two or more years. Mormon teens tend to have been involved in youth group for more years, as have conservative and mainline Protestant teens, compared to black Protestant, Catholic, and Jewish teens. Finally, overall, one in three teens in youth groups appear to think of themselves as leaders and not merely participants. Mormon youth are the most likely to claim to be leaders in their youth groups and Catholic youth the least likely.

Table 15 examines U.S. teens' participation in a number of other kinds

Table 15. Religious Group Activities of U.S. Adolescents, Ages 13–17 (Percentages)

	U.S.	Religious Tradition						
		CP	MP	BP	RC	J	LDS	NR
Frequency of religious Sunday School or CCD attendance								
More than once a week	7	12	7	9	2	3	35	1
Once a week	18	24	18	18	17	19	27	1
Almost every week	11	15	17	14	9	5	11	1
A few times a month	10	12	9	20	10	9	5	1
Once a month	6	8	10	4	3	10	2	2
A few times a year	18	15	19	22	19	16	8	19
Never	29	13	19	12	40	35	9	74
Number of religious youth retreats, conferences, rallies, or congresses participated in								
0	55	42	39	57	63	59	24	85
1	12	13	14	11	13	11	11	7
2–4	19	22	28	18	18	15	22	5
5–7	6	10	10	7	3	7	17	2
8+	6	10	8	6	2	8	26	1
Number of times attended religious summer camp as a camper								
0	61	44	47	67	76	50	18	87
1	13	17	18	12	11	14	13	7
2–4	17	25	23	15	10	25	43	5
5–7	6	8	9	4	3	5	17	2
8+	3	4	3	2	1	7	8	~
Number of times gone on a religious missions team or service project								
0	70	65	55	70	77	74	30	92
1	11	13	18	10	9	8	9	4
2–4	13	16	19	13	12	3	22	2
5–7	2	2	2	2	1	6	10	~
8+	3	2	3	3	1	5	29	~

Source: National Survey of Youth and Religion, 2002–3.

Note: Percentages may not add to 100 due to rounding and unreported don't know and refused answers.

of organized religious group activities. Here we see, first, that 36 percent of U.S. teenagers report attending Sunday school or CCD (Confraternity of Christian Doctrine) classes almost every week or more often; 34 percent attend sporadically, between a few times a year and a few times a month; and 29 percent never attend Sunday school or CCD. Again, the variance across all U.S. teens is great. Mormon and conservative Protestant teens attend such religious education classes the most, and nonreligious and Catholic teens attend the least.

Nearly half (45 percent) of U.S. teens have attended religious youth retreats, conferences, rallies, or congresses; 39 percent have attended religious summer camps as campers; and 30 percent have participated in a religious missions team or service project. Substantial numbers of U.S. teenagers, in other words, have at least been exposed to if not significantly involved in a variety of youth-oriented religious group learning and service activities beyond religious service attendance and religious education classes. Indeed, when answers for these three questions are combined, 60 percent of all U.S. teens have participated in at least one of these religious group activities at least once; only 40 percent have done none of these activities. Mormon and conservative and mainline Protestant teens were much more likely than the average teen to be involved in youth retreats, camps, and missions and service projects; while nonreligious and Catholic youth were much less likely than the average. Even so, fully 24 percent of nonreligious teens have participated in at least one of these religious group activities. Jewish teens are somewhat less likely than the average teen to be involved in religious retreats and missions and service projects, but they are also more likely to have attended a religious summer camp as a camper. Taken altogether, the numbers in table 15 suggest that the means by which U.S. teenagers connect to religion through organized group activities are many and significant, even if the effects of such involvements remain to be explored.

RELIGION IN RELATIONSHIPS: FAMILY, FRIENDS, SCHOOL, AND OTHER ADULTS

Religious faith and spiritual practice are not simply matters of individual experience and institutional involvements. They are also embedded in and sometimes draw much of their life from personal relationships in families, with friends, at school, and with other adults. The NSYR asked its sample of U.S. teenagers how religion connected through and interacted with these kinds of personal social ties. Table 16 examines religious expression and interaction in the teens' families. There we see that about one-third of families (34 percent) talk together about God, the scriptures, prayer, or other religious or spiritual matters a few times a week or more; 28 percent talk about these matters a few times a month or weekly; and 38 percent a few times a year or never. Thus, in their family conversations about matters of faith, U.S. families of teenagers are split roughly into thirds between high, medium, and low levels of discussion. Families of Mormon teens appear to talk about

Table 16. Religious Life in Families of U.S. Adolescents, Ages 13–17 (Percentages)

	U.S.	Religious Tradition						
		CP	MP	BP	RC	J	LDS	NR
Family talks about God, the scriptures, prayer, or other religious or spiritual things together								
Every day	14	19	8	27	6	~	50	4
A few times a week	20	27	15	29	18	9	24	5
About once a week	11	14	11	12	10	8	6	5
A few times a month	17	16	26	17	22	16	3	10
A few times a year	19	14	19	10	25	22	5	26
Never	19	10	20	5	19	44	11	48
Family gives thanks before or after mealtimes	54	67	54	79	45	13	84	18
Teen prays out loud or silently with one or both parents, other than at mealtimes or religious services	41	53	35	56	36	22	79	11

Source: National Survey of Youth and Religion, 2002–3.

Note: Percentages may not add to 100 due to rounding and unreported don't know and refused answers; cells of <1 are reported as ~.

religious and spiritual matters the most, followed next in frequency by families of black and conservative Protestant teens. Families of nonreligious and Jewish teens talk about religion the least, with only 9 percent each talking a few times a week or more often. Families of mainline Protestant and Catholic teenagers fall between those groups. Overall, however, it is a minority of every type of household that never talks about religious or spiritual matters.

A slight majority of all U.S. families with teenagers (54 percent) is reported by teens as regularly praying to give thanks before or after mealtimes. Families of Mormon, black Protestant, and conservative Protestant teens are more likely than the average family with teens to pray to give thanks at meals. They are followed in frequency by Catholic (45 percent) and nonreligious teen families (18 percent). Jewish teen families are, at 13 percent, the least likely to give thanks at meals, which, like some of the other measures in this chapter, is not an expected or required religious observance for Jews anyway. Mainline Protestant teen families pray at meals at the national average. But praying to give thanks at family mealtimes, one might think, is a rather easy and costless habit that can be as perfunctory and rote as sincere and meaningful. What about more obviously significant family religious practices? Table 16 also presents the percentage of teens whose parents in the previous year prayed together with them, out loud or silently, at times other than at meals or religious services. Forty-one percent of all teenagers report praying in this way with their parents in the previous year. Again, Mormon, black Protestant, and conservative Protestant teens are most likely to pray with their parents, and nonreligious, Jewish, mainline Protestant, and Catholic teens are less likely than the national average to pray with their parents. The overall large minorities and sometimes majorities of teens across the religious groups whose parents pray together with them other than at mealtimes or religious services is notable and perhaps even surprising, given the intimacy that can be involved in such experiences. More generally, table 16 tells us that for a significant number of U.S. teens, religion and spirituality are not simply compartmentalized in church, synagogue, mosque, or temple, but are also expressed and shared in the family life of the home.

One of the key themes of this book is that parents are normally very important in shaping the religious and spiritual lives of their teenage children, even though they may not realize it. It seems that many parents of teens rely primarily on the immediate evidence of the overt attitudes, statements, and sometimes behaviors that their teenage children dole out to them on a daily basis in order to estimate their current level of parental influence. Many of the attitudes and statements that teenagers communicate to their parents do not exactly express great admiration and gratitude for and readiness to listen to, emulate, or freely obey their parents. Many parents therefore appear to come to the conclusion that they have lost their influence in shaping the lives of their teenage children, that they no longer make any significant difference. But for most, this conclusion is mistaken. Teenagers' attitudes, verbal utterances, and immediate behaviors are often not the best evidence with which to estimate parental influence in their lives. For better or worse, most parents in fact still do profoundly influence their adolescents—often more than do their peers—their children's apparent resistance and lack of appreciation notwithstanding. This influence often also includes parental influence in adolescents' religious and spiritual lives. Simply by living and interacting with their children, most parents establish expectations, define normalcy, model life practices, set boundaries, and make demands—all of which cannot help but influence teenagers, for good or ill. Most teenagers and their parents may not realize it, but a lot of research in the sociology of religion suggests that the most important social influence in shaping young people's religious lives is the religious life modeled and taught to them by their parents.[11]

These findings in prior research are also evident in NSYR data. Take, for instance, the figures presented in table 17, which cross-tabulates differences

Table 17. Association of the Importance of Faith in Daily Life for U.S. Parents of Teenagers and of Their Adolescent Children, Ages 13–17 (Row percentages)

Parent importance of faith	Teen Importance of Faith					
	Extremely	Very	Somewhat	Not Very	Not at All	Percent Total
Extremely important	30	37	24	5	3	100
Very important	14	32	36	12	5	100
Fairly important	7	23	38	21	10	100
Somewhat important	8	15	41	20	16	100
Not very important	3	11	37	22	26	100
Not important at all	2	15	37	19	28	100

Source: National Survey of Youth and Religion, 2002–3.

Note: Percentages may not add to 100 due to rounding and unreported don't know and refused answers.

in the importance of faith in the daily life of U.S. teenagers (in columns) by the importance of faith for their parents (in rows). Table 17 shows clearly that the importance of faith for teenagers fairly closely tracks the importance of faith for their parents. Parents for whom religious faith is quite important are thus likely to be raising teenagers for whom faith is quite important, while parents whose faith is not important are likely to be raising teenagers for whom faith is also not important. The fit is not perfect. None of this is guaranteed or determined, and sometimes, in specific instances, things turn out otherwise. But the overall positive association is clear. Hence, of parents who report that their faith is extremely important in their daily lives, 67 percent of their teens report that faith is extremely or very important in their daily lives; only 8 percent of those parents' teens report that faith is not very or not at all important in their lives. Likewise, of parents for whom faith is somewhat important in their daily lives, 61 percent of their teens also report that faith is somewhat or not very important in their daily lives; only 8 percent of those parents' teens report that faith is extremely important in their lives. Finally, of parents for whom faith is not at all important in their daily lives, 47 percent of their teens also report that religious faith is not at all or not very important in their lives; only 2 percent report that faith is extremely important in their lives. In sum, therefore, we think that the best general rule of thumb that parents might use to reckon their children's most likely religious outcomes is this: "We'll get what we are." By normal processes of socialization, and unless other significant forces intervene, more than what parents might *say* they *want* as religious outcomes in their children, most parents most likely will end up getting religiously of their children what they themselves *are*. This observation we will make again in different ways in later chapters.

Other influences in the lives of many U.S. adolescents are friends and peers. Table 18 presents findings on the religious characteristics of the sampled teens' five closest friends. An average of about one-half (2.6) of all teens' five closest friends hold religious beliefs similar to those of the teens. This varies only slightly between the religious groups, with the exception of Jewish

Table 18. Religious Characteristics of Five Closest Friends of U.S. Adolescents, Ages 13–17 (Average number out of 5)

	U.S.	Religious Tradition						
Number out of 5 closest friends who		CP	MP	BP	RC	J	LDS	NR
Hold similar religious beliefs as teen does	2.6	3	3	2.9	2.9	1.5	2.7	—
Are involved in same religious group as teen	1.2	1.5	1.2	1.4	1.2	0.7	2.1	—
Are not religious	0.3	0.4	0.3	0.2	0.3	0.7	0.3	—
Are religious	—	—	—	—	—	—	—	1.1
Are involved in any religious youth group	1.4	2.1	1.8	1.3	0.9	1.2	2.7	0.5
Teen talks to about religious beliefs and experiences	1.8	2.1	2.0	1.8	1.4	1.4	3.1	1.2
Are bad moral influences on teen	0.3	0.3	0.3	0.3	0.4	0.4	0.2	0.3

Source: National Survey of Youth and Religion, 2002–3.

teens, who have a lower proportion of best friends who share their faith.[12] An average of slightly more than one out of five (1.2) of teens' five closest friends are involved in any of the same religious groups in which the teens are involved. Mormon and black and conservative Protestant teens have somewhat higher proportions of friends involved in their own religious groups, and Jewish teens have notably lower proportions. All but the Jewish religious teens have among their five best friends roughly the national average for religious teens of 0.3 friends who are not religious; Jewish teens have almost double that rate at 0.7. By comparison, nonreligious teens have an average of 1.1 of their five best friends who are religious. In other words, religious teenagers tend to make most of their best friendships with other religious teens, and nonreligious teenagers tend to make most of their friendships with nonreligious teens. Religious and nonreligious identities thus tend to cluster around and be reinforced by close friendship networks.

Religious American teens have averages of between one and almost three of their five best friends involved in some religious youth group. Mormon teens take the high end, with 2.7 friends, followed by conservative Protestants (2.1 friends) and mainline Protestants (1.8 friends). Nonreligious, Catholic, and Jewish teens fall below the national average. Even so, on average, one out of two nonreligious teens has one of their five best friends who is involved in a religious youth group. U.S. teenagers are slightly more likely to have friends with whom they talk about religious beliefs and experiences (1.8 out of five best friends). The same groups come out as comparatively more and less likely to have best friends with whom they talk about religion: Mormons and conservative and mainline Protestants have more, and nonreligious, Jewish, and Catholic teens have fewer. Finally, U.S. teens of all types have about the same number among their best friends who they report are bad moral influences on them, about 0.3 of five best friends, with deviations from the national average ranging no more than 0.1 in either direction. From one perspective, U.S. teenagers of all religious and nonreligious kinds appear unwilling or unable to tolerate more than an average of about one out of 17 friends (= 0.3/5) who are a bad moral influence on them. Read from another perspective, as we will see in chapter 4, U.S. teens generally do not believe that anything or anybody directly influences them, but that they are self-directed; thus, they may be significantly underestimating negative moral peer influences in this survey question. In general, however, we see in table 18 that, almost by mathematical inevitabilities, U.S. teens have significant relational network ties that link them to religious resources and likely help to reinforce their religious beliefs and commitments, such as they are. Again, religion in the lives of teenagers appears to be not simply restricted to time spent in religious congregations, but also flows in various ways and to different degrees into and through teens' relational networks.

What about religion at school? Is religious faith openly expressed by teenagers at school? What is the atmosphere in schools for religious teens? According to table 19, the great majority of religious U.S. teens openly express their faith at school in quite limited ways; 65 percent do so only some or a

Table 19. Experiences of School-attending U.S. Adolescents among Peers and at School, Ages 13–17 (Percentages)

	U.S.	Religious Tradition						
		CP	MP	BP	RC	J	LDS	NR
Openly expresses faith at school (religious teens)								
A lot	12	15	11	15	6	12	23	—
Some	36	41	32	41	30	24	35	—
A little	29	29	33	23	30	17	33	—
None	23	15	24	20	33	47	10	—
Other students at school generally look down on teens who are openly religious	18	20	19	17	18	34	13	13
Feel pressured or made fun of because of their religious beliefs and practices (religious teens)								
A lot	2	3	1	2	1	7	4	—
Some	7	9	4	4	4	13	20	—
A little	13	17	11	8	8	36	20	—
None	78	72	84	86	87	44	56	—

Source: National Survey of Youth and Religion, 2002–3.

Note: Percentages may not add to 100 due to rounding and unreported don't know and refused answers.

little. Only 12 percent of religious teens report expressing their faith a lot at school; 23 percent do not express their faith at school at all. Mormon teens (23 percent) are most likely to express their faith a lot at school, followed by conservative and black Protestant teens (15 percent each). On the other hand, nearly half of Jewish teens and about one-third of Catholic teens never express their faith openly at school. These numbers suggest that for the vast majority of U.S. teens expressions of religious faith at school are kept to a minimum. Only fairly small minorities from each religious group—Mormons being an exception—express their religious faith at school a lot.

According to NSYR teen respondents, however, this is not because schools are perceived by teens to be especially hostile places to students who are openly religious. On average, fewer than one in five U.S. teens reports that other students at school generally look down on teens who are openly religious, although more Jewish teens (34 percent) and fewer Mormon and nonreligious teens (13 percent each) report perceptions of such antireligious condescension among students at school. Furthermore, only a minority of religious teens from all traditions report that they themselves have been pressured or made fun of because of their religious beliefs and practices; overall, 2 percent report a lot and 7 percent some pressure. Religious minority teens, Jewish and Mormon, however, do report noticeably higher levels of pressure and teasing than do religious majority (Christian) teens, perhaps for such behaviors as wearing yarmulkes, keeping Kosher, and observing Sabbath. Still, the great majority of religious teens of all groups report only a little or no pressure or teasing. The generally limited expression of faith by teens at school observed above, therefore, likely has other causes than fear of persecution.

Finally, we examine in this section the extent and nature of the relational ties that U.S. teenagers attending religious services may have with adults other than their family members in their religious congregations. What kind of relational links do religious service–attending teenagers have with fellow-believing, nonfamilial adults? According to table 20, large majorities of teens from all religious traditions report having nonfamily adults in their religious congregations whom they enjoy talking to and who give them lots of encouragement. Jewish teens report the highest percentage (92 percent) and Catholic teens the lowest (68 percent). Religious American teens thus do not appear to be entirely relationally isolated from other adults in their congregations. Moreover, even more teenagers would like to have significant relationships with adults in their congregations. The majority of teens who do *not* have such enjoyable and encouraging adult ties in their congregations—between 56 percent of those Catholic and 100 percent of those Jewish

Table 20. Relationships with Adults in Religious Congregations of Religious Service–attending U.S. Adolescents, Ages 13–17 (Percentages)

	U.S. Attending	Religious Tradition					
		CP	MP	BP	RC	J	LDS
Teens have adults in congregation, other than family members, whom they enjoy talking with and who give lots of encouragement (Of all U.S. teens: 53 percent)	79	84	84	78	68	92	90
Teens would like to have adults in congregation whom teen enjoys talking to (asked only of teens without adult in congregation to talk to)	61	61	67	75	56	100	77
Most adults in congregation for getting to know							
Very easy to talk with	38	42	35	41	29	48	52
Somewhat easy to talk with	41	40	45	39	43	36	39
Neither	7	6	6	7	9	3	3
Somewhat hard to talk with	9	8	10	8	12	14	1
Very hard to talk with	4	3	3	4	4	~	5
Percentage of teens who have adults in life to turn to for support, advice, and help who are part of teen's religious congregation or youth group (Of all U.S. teens: 54 percent)	61	65	65	68	53	28	73
Number of adults in a religious congregation or religious youth group attending teens can turn to for support, advice, and help (not including parents)							
0	39	35	35	32	47	72	27
1–2	27	26	35	30	27	23	22
3–4	13	16	11	15	11	2	12
5–6	10	11	10	11	8	~	17
7–9	3	3	4	4	3	2	3
10+	8	9	7	8	4	2	20

Source: National Survey of Youth and Religion, 2002–3.

Note: Percentages may not add to 100 due to rounding and unreported don't know and refused answers; cells of <1 are reported as ~.

teens[13]—say that they wish they did. Nevertheless, the vast majority of religious teenagers from all of the traditions compared also report that most adults in their religious congregations are either somewhat or very easy to talk with and get to know. Only between 6 percent (of Mormons) and 16 percent (of Catholics) report that most adults in their congregations are somewhat or very hard to talk with and get to know.

Approached from another angle, we might ask what percentage of U.S. teenagers have adults in their lives, other than their parents, whom they can turn to when they need support, advice, or help and who are part of their religious congregations or other religious groups in which they are involved. According to NSYR data, 54 percent of all U.S. teens and 61 percent of U.S. teens who attend religious services enjoy those kinds of supportive relationships. This is noticeably higher for Mormon and lower for Jewish and Catholic youth. Yet overall, we can conclude that the majority of religious U.S. teens have nonparental adult relationships with fellow religious congregants whom they can rely on for help in life. And, according to the findings at the bottom of table 20, the majority of U.S. teens attending religious services actually have at least one potentially helpful adult in their lives, and 34 percent have three or more. Religious organizations thus appear to help foster cross-generational relational ties for large numbers of U.S. teenagers, ties we would expect to help legitimize and reinforce the religious faith and practices of those teens.

TEENS' EVALUATIONS OF RELIGIOUS CONGREGATIONS

To complete this chapter's number-filled, big-picture, descriptive overview of the religious and spiritual lives of U.S. teenagers, we consider evidence concerning teens' evaluations, according to a variety of standards, of the appeal and effectiveness of their own religious congregations. Do teens think well of their churches, synagogues, mosques, and temples? Are they happy with their experiences with them? Table 21 begins this consideration with data on various features of their congregations' general environments. There we see that the majority of all service-attending teens say that their congregation usually makes them think about important things, although Jewish teens appear more split on this question than the other teens. Furthermore, relatively few teens complain that their congregation is usually boring. The most typical response is that congregations are sometimes boring, although our in-depth interviews with teens clearly suggested that they are realistic—probably well trained by school—in expecting a certain amount of life to be boring and so are not particularly put off by religious services being boring sometimes. Table 21 also shows that the vast majority of teens find their religious congregation to be a warm and welcoming place for youth. Only small minorities rarely or never find their congregation to be warm and welcoming. If such reports tell us anything at all, then, they suggest that most U.S. teens who attend religious services feel relatively positive about the general environment of their congregation. This observation calls into question popular stereotypes assuming

Table 21. Evaluations of Own Religious Congregation's Environment by Religious Service–attending U.S. Adolescents, Ages 13–17 (Percentages)

	U.S. Attending	Religious Tradition					
		CP	MP	BP	RC	J	LDS
Makes teen think about important things							
Usually	62	70	58	63	52	59	81
Sometimes	27	23	33	27	33	5	11
Rarely	7	4	5	7	9	24	6
Never	3	2	4	3	4	12	2
Is boring to teen							
Usually	15	10	16	14	20	30	14
Sometimes	38	35	40	39	41	44	32
Rarely	23	26	26	13	21	19	30
Never	24	29	18	34	18	7	24
Is a warm and welcoming place for teen							
Usually	75	80	82	74	66	85	85
Sometimes	19	15	14	21	26	4	10
Rarely	3	2	4	2	5	3	1
Never	2	2	~	2	2	8	4
Regular opportunities exist to get involved in services, such as reading or praying aloud	82	84	82	85	76	83	96
Teenagers in congregation who are hypocrites							
All	2	2	3	5	2	~	~
Most	8	8	9	10	8	3	5
Some	25	22	26	27	29	33	16
A few	31	33	31	24	30	31	51
None	32	34	29	33	30	33	28
Don't know	1	1	2	2	2	~	~
Evaluation of youth group (asked of youth group–attenders only)							
Likes it very much	56	63	50	53	45	51	53
Likes it somewhat	34	29	34	39	43	49	33
Doesn't feel either way	5	4	4	5	8	~	7
Dislikes it somewhat	4	3	11	2	3	~	7
Dislikes it very much	1	1	1	~	1	~	~

Source: National Survey of Youth and Religion, 2002–3.

Note: Percentages may not add to 100 due to rounding and unreported don't know and refused answers; cells of <1 are reported as ~; evaluation of youth group is only by respondents involved in a youth group.

and some published accounts claiming that many or most religious U.S. teens think their congregation is irrelevant, tedious, cold, and off-putting. Quite the contrary, it appears.

Table 21 also shows that the large majority of U.S. teens attending religious services belong to congregations in which there are regular opportunities for youth to get actively involved in the services, such as by reading scripture or praying out loud—but not including participation in a bar or bat mitzvah. The lowest among all groups are teens in Catholic churches, but even they report opportunities for participation at 76 percent. What about attending teens' assessments of the integrity of other teens in their congregations? Do they see much hypocrisy among their attending peers that might make them feel put off by their congregations? Apparently not. Only a small minority, 10 percent for the whole, say that most or all other teens in their congregation are hypocrites; more than three times that number say none of the teens are hypocrites. There appears little basis, then, for many attending teenagers to become alienated from their congregation by the perception of widespread hypocrisy among other religious youth. Finally, the NSYR asked teens who participate in a religious youth group how much they like or dislike it. Their responses show that the vast majority do like their youth groups. On average, only 5 percent of teens do not like them. Literally all sampled Jewish teens involved in youth groups like them, and, among the rest, only mainline Protestant teens stand out (at 12 percent) as disliking their youth groups either somewhat or very much. Of course, teens who did not like their youth groups probably have mostly dropped out, accounting, in part, for the 31 percent of U.S. teens in table 14 who once had been involved in a religious youth group but currently are not. Most youth unhappy with youth groups likely vote with their feet. And the somewhat higher percentage of mainline Protestant teens who dislike their youth groups (12 percent) may simply reflect a greater number of mainline parents who require their teens to attend youth groups, and not less appealing youth group programs per se. In any event, it does not appear to be the case that religious youth groups are peppered with teens who are unhappy with them. Most who are involved seem to like their youth groups very much.

How do teens who attend religious services evaluate the adults in their congregations? A certain conventional wisdom expects that teenagers view church adults as clueless, square, phony, or remote—something like a cross between the old *Saturday Night Live* church lady and Sinclair Lewis's Elmer Gantry. Table 22 suggests a rather different picture, however. U.S. teens who attend religious services are, for example, even less likely to view adults in their congregation as hypocrites than they are to view other teens as hypocrites. Overall, seven out of ten say that only a few or none of the adults in their congregation are hypocrites; only handfuls in each tradition say that all or most adults are hypocrites. Not many attending teens, then, seem suspicious of the integrity of the adults in their congregation. Furthermore, when asked specifically about their experiences in talking with a minister at their congregation about a personal question or problem, almost none of the 19 percent of teens who had done so reported that this had been a bad or even ambiguous experience; on the contrary, nearly all reported it as a good experience. To be clear, most service-attending teens have not approached a minister in their congregation with a personal question or problem; still, perhaps no fewer teens than adults have done so and, considering the potential vulnerability involved in such a personal talk with a local religious leader, perhaps 19 percent is not too surprising. In any case, there is no evidence that teens who do have such personal talks with adult ministers find them to be unsatisfying or alienating. Again, when asked, teens attending religious

Table 22. Evaluations of Adults in and Support of Religious Congregations by U.S. Adolescents, Ages 13–17, and Parents Attending Religious Congregations (Percentages)

	U.S. Attending	Religious Tradition of Teen and Parent					
		CP	MP	BP	RC	J	LDS
Adults in congregation who are hypocrites (teen report)							
All	2	1	2	3	3	~	~
Most	6	5	7	6	5	7	5
Some	21	15	19	29	26	3	22
A few	34	37	36	29	32	53	37
None	37	40	35	31	34	37	36
Don't know/refused	1	2	1	2	1	~	~
Experience talking with adult youth minister or religious youth leader about a personal question or problem (teen report)							
Good	19	30	32	16	9	6	48
Mixed, good and bad	~	1	~	~	~	~	~
Bad	~	1	1	~	~	~	~
Have not talked with a youth minister	81	69	68	84	91	95	52
Perceived priority of congregational ministry to teens (parent report)							
A very important priority	65	75	56	80	47	32	96
A fairly important priority	14	11	20	8	17	24	1
A somewhat important priority	14	9	14	9	23	18	2
A low priority	4	3	5	2	6	18	~
Is not a priority at all	2	1	2	~	4	~	1
Don't know/refused	2	1	2	1	3	8	~
Supportiveness and helpfulness of church for parent in trying to raise teen (parent report)							
Extremely supportive and helpful	22	26	14	26	13	8	65
Very supportive and helpful	33	38	34	39	27	21	22
Somewhat supportive and helpful	23	20	24	19	31	42	4
A little supportive and helpful	10	8	13	8	15	20	5
Not supportive and helpful	8	7	10	5	11	4	3
Don't know/refused	3	2	5	4	2	6	1

Source: National Survey of Youth and Religion, 2002–3.

Note: Percentages may not add to 100 due to rounding; cells of <1 are reported as ~; parent report variables rely on parent, not teen, religious tradition classification.

services generally give high evaluation marks to the adults, both laity and ministers, in their congregations.

The NSYR also asked religious service–attending parents of teens to evaluate their congregation both for the priority their congregation places on ministering to teens and for their congregation's helpfulness to them as parents raising teens. Though not representing the viewpoint of youth, parents' answers to these questions, shown in the bottom half of table 22, do contribute to our larger understanding of the role of religious congregations in the lives of U.S. teenagers. There we find that the majority of most groups of parents see ministry to teens as a very important priority in their congregation, Jewish and Catholic parents being the exceptions at 32 and 47 percent, respectively. Particularly in Mormon and conservative and black Protestant churches, ministry to youth is quite an important priority, according to attending parents. Again, with the exception of Jewish parents, few attending parents report that ministry to teens is a low or nonexistent priority, probably in part because many parents with teens actively seek out or gravitate toward congregations that prioritize ministry to teens. The numbers on the supportiveness and helpfulness of congregations to parents in raising teens are more mixed: 18 percent report that their congregation is only a little or not at all supportive and helpful; nearly one-quarter say their congregation is somewhat helpful; and more than half say their congregation is very or extremely helpful. More Mormon and black and conservative Protestant parents report their congregation as helpful, compared to the average. Jewish parents in particular tend to say their congregation is not particularly helpful to parents raising teens. Still, on balance, attending parents of U.S. teenagers give quite positive evaluations of their congregations as places in which to raise teenagers in their religious faiths.

Finally, we examine teens' evaluations of their congregations' pastoral and teaching effectiveness. The survey question asked: Do teenagers think that their own religious congregation is a good or not good place for them to go "to talk about serious issues like family problems, alcohol, or troubles at school?" According to the data presented in table 23, most attending teens (70 percent) rate their congregation as a very good or fairly good place to talk about such serious issues. Relatively few teens panned their congregation as a context in which to address serious issues. Only among Jewish teens was there a substantial minority giving their congregation bad marks on this question. The NSYR also asked specifically what kind of job their congregation has done in helping them better understand their own sexuality and sexual morality. Fifteen percent of all attending teens said their congregation has done nothing to help them understand sex; Jewish and mainline Protestant teens reported this well above the average for all attending teens, at 41 and 21 percent, respectively. Otherwise, the majority of attending teens gave their congregation quite high ratings on this question. Eighty-four percent of Mormon teens report that their congregation has done a fairly good or excellent job in helping them understand sex, and 67 percent of conservative Protestant, 60 percent of black Protestant, and 53 percent of mainline Protestant teens report the same. Catholic teens find their congregation somewhat more lacking on this issue. Still, the overall marks are fairly positive.

Likewise, attending teenagers rate their religious congregation with high marks for teaching them what they want to know about their faith. Overall, one out of five attending teens has no interest in learning more about their own religion; presumably, most of these are not teens who know so much that they do not need to know any more, but simply do not care to know much in the first place. Catholic and Jewish teens tend to score relatively high on lack of interest; for these uninterested teens, this question is irrelevant.

Table 23. Evaluation of Religious Congregation's Teaching Effectiveness by Religious Service–attending U.S. Adolescents, Ages 13–17 (Percentages)

	U.S. Attending	Religious Tradition					
		CP	MP	BP	RC	J	LDS
How good congregation is for talking about serious issues, problems, and troubles							
A very good place	45	52	38	48	33	40	65
A fairly good place	25	26	32	21	27	12	16
An okay place	21	16	21	25	28	15	13
Not a good place	6	3	6	4	9	25	4
A bad place	2	2	2	1	1	8	3
Don't know/refused	1	1	~	1	2	~	~
Job congregation has done helping better understand own sexuality and sexual morality							
An excellent job	30	35	22	35	18	21	66
A fairly good job	30	32	31	25	31	16	18
An okay job	21	19	19	21	26	3	8
Not a good job	4	2	4	2	6	7	3
Has done nothing for understanding sexuality	15	9	21	14	17	41	3
Don't know/refuse	2	2	2	2	2	11	2
Job congregation has done helping teach what teen wants to learn about own religion							
An excellent job	27	31	24	35	17	26	47
A fairly good job	33	37	33	34	29	25	32
An okay job	18	16	18	18	21	16	1
Not a good job	2	1	2	~	2	1	~
A bad job	1	~	1	1	1	1	2
Teen not interested in learning about own religion	20	14	21	11	29	29	19
Kind of congregation teen anticipates attending when 25 years old							
Kind of congregation teen goes to now	77	80	79	74	73	51	83
A different kind of congregation	14	13	14	21	14	8	2
Will not attend anywhere	7	5	4	3	10	30	10
Don't know/refused	2	1	3	1	3	11	5

Source: National Survey of Youth and Religion, 2002–3.

Note: Percentages may not add to 100 due to rounding; cells of <1 are reported as ~.

But for those teens who do have some interest in learning about their faith, the majority report that their congregation does a fairly good or excellent job at teaching them what they want to learn. A significant minority of all but Mormon teens give the lukewarm answer that their congregation does only an "okay job." Very few attending teens give their congregation more critical ratings than that. Most teens who care about learning more about their own religious faith, then, tend to view their congregation as doing an adequate if not quite a good job in teaching.

Finally, the NSYR asked attending teenagers what kind of religious congregation, if any, they think they will attend when they are 25 years old. We interpret their answers as indirect evaluations of their current religious congregation, insofar as dissatisfied customers will presumably stop returning when the choice is fully theirs. In fact, 77 percent of all attending teens said that they expect at age 25 to attend the same kind of congregation they attend now; 14 percent said they anticipate attending a different kind of congregation; only 7 percent said they do not think they will be attending anywhere at all, which closely fits with the 9 percent of currently attending teens who said they would never attend if the choice were entirely up to them whether and how much to attend religious services. Mormon and conservative and mainline Protestant teens were the most likely to say they expect to attend the same kind of church they currently attend, at 83, 80, and 79 percent, respectively. Yet Mormon teens were also relatively more likely to say they expect not to attend services at all (10 percent) or to refuse to answer or say that they did not know the answer (5 percent). Jewish teens were the most likely by far to say they did not expect to be attending religious services at age 25 (30 percent) and to refuse to answer or say "don't know" (11 percent). Nevertheless, overall, attending U.S. teens did not offer a clearly negative judgment on their religious congregations by suggesting in response to this question that they look forward to doing something very different or to entirely dropping out of religious attendance when they are older. For most traditions, the vast majority expect to keep attending religious services that are similar to those they attend at present.

CONCLUSION

Surveys cannot tell us everything or perhaps even the most important and interesting things there are to know about people and their lives. Surveys do have real limits in the insights they can render about the social world and personal experiences, perhaps especially about the lives of adolescents and perhaps especially about faith and spiritual practices. All of this is important to bear in mind. Nevertheless, survey research findings can provide an important, general starting point for further understanding of what we want to know about people's lives. We began this chapter by suggesting that, although survey data may oversimplify the complexity of the real social world, they can also help to draw a kind of map that provides an overarching sense of our social world, where we stand within it, and what it looks like beyond our immediate field of vision. We believe the NSYR findings presented in this chapter have done precisely this. Having ploughed through and begun to digest the multitude of numbers in this chapter, we can now proceed forward with a big picture in our minds of the rough proportions and contours describing the religious and spiritual lives of U.S. teenagers. In the following chapters, with other data, we confirm or question some of what we learned in this chapter. We also add complexity and specify our findings. In some cases, we reinterpret the meaning of some of the numbers reviewed here. By chapters 4 and 5 we will come to see many of these numbers in a considerably more critical light. But this chapter's survey findings provide an important, sound, and fairly comprehensive starting point for further investigations in following chapters.

All of the findings in the 23 tables presented above and their implications for various academic scholars, faith communities, and secular organizations are too numerous to highlight and summarize in this conclusion. Readers will have to draw from this chapter what is most relevant for them and their communities. But an attempt to briefly summarize some of this chapter's major observations and conclusions seems warranted, as incomplete or tentative as they may be. We believe these observations include the following:

☙ The vast majority of U.S. teenagers identify themselves as Christian, either among the broad array of American Protestant denominations or as Catholic (tables 1 and 2). Significant minorities of other U.S. adolescents are nonreligious, Mormon, and Jewish. The percentage of other minority faiths that often draw a great deal of public attention—paganism, Wicca, Buddhism, Muslim, and so on—remains at the start of the twenty-first century very small. Few U.S. teens appear to be dabbling with, much less switching to, such alternative faiths.

☙ The majority of U.S. teenagers tend to be quite like their parents when it comes to religion. They tend to share similar beliefs (table 4), tend to be situated in the same general religious traditions (table 5), and tend to attend religious services with one or both of their parents (table 6).

☙ A substantial minority of U.S. teenagers regularly practice religious faith. Four out of ten say they attend religious services weekly or more often (table 6), pray daily or more often (table 11), and are currently involved in a religious youth group (table 14). Between one-quarter and one-half report engaging in a broad variety of other religious practices in the previous year (table 11). This means, of course, that the majority of U.S. teenagers practice religious faith only sporadically or not at all.

☙ About half of U.S. teenagers report in their survey answers strong subjective importance and experiences of religious faith in their own lives, measured as importance of faith, closeness to God, commitment of life to God, experience of powerful worship, answer to prayer, lack of religious doubts, and receiving guidance from God (tables 7 and 10). This means that the other half of U.S. teenagers express weak or no subjective attachment to religion and have fewer or no religious experiences. (More critical chapters ahead also examine in greater depth the actual substantive character of the religious faith and view of God that most U.S. teens profess to hold.)

☙ The vast majority of U.S. teenagers profess to be theists and to believe in divine judgment (table 8). Between four and six out of ten U.S. teens also say they believe in angels, demons, divine miracles, and life after death, though many fewer believe in reincarnation, astrology, communicating with the dead, and fortune-telling (table 9). In these ways, many U.S. teenagers appear quite conventional in following many of the traditional beliefs of the Jewish, Christian, and Mormon heritages. At the same time, significant proportions of other teens express uncertainty about these beliefs. Furthermore, when probed about their more precise images of God, about one-third of teens do not believe that God is personal and involved in the lives of people today (table 8). Broadly speaking, then, as far as survey answers can tell, most U.S. teens appear to embrace rather conventional, apparently traditional beliefs about religion and the supernatural; still, we have some reason to critically probe further into the more specific content and texture of teens' beliefs, to see just how traditional they may be after all.

❧ Religious youth groups seem to be an important part of the religious and spiritual experiences of a substantial minority of U.S. adolescents (table 14). Nearly four in ten U.S. teens are involved in a religious youth group and have been for multiple years. About seven in ten have been involved in a religious youth group at some time in their lives. Most of those currently involved belong to youth groups sponsored by their own religious congregation. As to frequency of involvement, one-quarter of all U.S. teens report attending religious youth group weekly or more often; more than one in three youth group–attending teens sees him or herself functioning in a leadership role in their youth group. Viewed from the other direction, however, all of this also means that the majority of U.S. teenagers are not involved in a religious youth group, and nearly half of U.S. teens who at one time did participate in a religious youth group no longer do so.

❧ Large numbers of U.S. teenagers have been or are currently involved in a variety of other organized religious activities (table 15). About half attend Sunday school monthly or more often and have participated in at least one religious youth retreat, conference, rally, or congress. Nearly four in ten U.S. teens have attended a religious summer camp as a camper, and nearly three in ten have participated in a religious missions team or service project. Of course, this also means that substantial majorities of U.S. teenagers have never been involved in such religious camps, conferences, retreats, and projects.

❧ Religious congregations appear to be important sites for U.S. teenagers to make significant contact with adults other than family members. Most attending U.S. teens have adults in their congregation whom they enjoy talking to and who encourage them, and the majority who do not have such adults wish that they did. Most also report that adults in their congregation are rather easy to talk to and get to know and that they believe they can turn to these adults for support, advice, and help in life (table 20).

❧ Religion and spirituality for the majority of U.S. teenagers find some expression in the life of their families. Many U.S. families with teenagers appear to talk together about God, the scriptures, prayer, or other matters of faith. More than half pray to give thanks at mealtimes, and four in ten U.S. teens say they have prayed with one or both of their parents other than at mealtimes in the previous year. Most parents normally exert significant influence in forming the religious and spiritual lives of their adolescent children (table 17).

🥢 When it comes to U.S. teenagers' close friendships and school experiences, however, religion seems somewhat more remote than in their families and religious congregations. On average, half of their closest friends do not share their religious beliefs, and the majority of their closest friends are not involved in any of their own religious groups. U.S. teens are more likely than not to have close friends with whom they never talk about religious matters (table 18). Furthermore, although most U.S. teenagers report that schools are not hostile to teens who are seriously religious, only about one in ten teens expresses their religious faith at school a lot (table 19). Thus, the visibility and perhaps significance of religious faith and practice for U.S. teens seem to drop off markedly in spheres outside of religious congregation and family.

🥢 Most U.S. teenagers seem to hold rather positive general attitudes about religion and their own congregation. More than six in ten say they would attend religious services regularly (two to three times a month or more often) if it were entirely up to them (table 6). Of religious service–attending U.S. teenagers, most report that their religious congregation is relationally warm and intellectually stimulating, provides opportunities for youth to get involved in services, offers youth groups which they like very much, and provides a good context for learning about faith and talking about serious life issues (tables 21 and 23). Nearly eight in ten attending U.S. teens say that they expect to attend the same congregation they are currently involved with when they are 25 years old (table 23). Very few attending teens say that many teens or adults in their congregation are hypocrites, and almost none report having had bad experiences interacting with their clergy or youth leaders (table 22). It is difficult to tease out from these survey statistics exactly how positively enthusiastic and committed U.S. teenagers are about and to their religious congregations, and what exactly that means and reflects. But at the very least we can observe that relatively few teens appear to be actively negative about or hostile toward their religious congregations.

🥢 Comparisons of the many religion measures across the religious traditions examined in this chapter reveal a noticeable pattern of religiosity, ranging from Mormons at the high end, to conservative and black Protestants, further down to mainline Protestant and Catholic teens, and then to Jewish and nonreligious teens on the lower end. This book does not seek to explain this larger pattern; we simply note it here. Explanations, however, would likely appeal to strictness or subcultural identity theories to help make sense of these across-tradition differences.[14]

This is a good start. But we have to do much more digging to fill in details and to explore the more complex meanings of and feelings about such religious and spiritual matters among U.S. teenagers. By chapters 4 and 5 we will have significantly qualified the initial view developed here. Before diving headlong into interpreting the data and findings from our 267 personal interviews with teenagers in 45 states around the country, however, the next chapter focuses on better understanding three specific religious groups of U.S. teens: the few "spiritual but not religious" teens who are often thought of as "spiritual seekers," teens who appear entirely disengaged from American religion, and teens who are highly devoted religiously. Better comprehending these three types of teenagers will provide important depth to the picture that this chapter begins to sketch.

3

Spiritual Seekers, the Disengaged, and Religiously Devoted Teens

THE PREVIOUS CHAPTER used NSYR survey data to provide an overview of the religious and spiritual lives of American adolescents. Its approach was to examine answers to survey questions by U.S. teenagers age 13 to 17 and by the teens as grouped into six religious traditions and one nonreligious category. This chapter extends that investigation by focusing on three different populations of American teens, seeking to understand more clearly their composition and defining features. First, we explore the extent and characteristics of adolescent "religious seekers" and teens who claim to be "spiritual but not religious," approaches to faith often said to be popular and widespread among American youth. Next, we examine American teenagers who identify themselves as nonreligious and who never attend religious services. Finally, we analyze American teens who are religiously highly active and devoted and attempt to identify the features that define them as a particular group of youth. All three are categories of teens that many religion observers are interested in better understanding. Furthermore, examining these types of teens in greater depth provides helpful windows into some of the key features defining and shaping the religious and spiritual lives of U.S. teenagers broadly. Finally, the findings of this chapter help to put some of the previous chapter's survey findings into clearer perspective.

A GENERATION OF TEENAGE SPIRITUAL SEEKERS?

Scholars and journalists have been writing prolifically about a purportedly widespread and growing contemporary phenomenon of "spiritual seeking" by people who think of themselves as "spiritual but not religious." Seekers are described as people who have an interest in spiritual matters but who are not devoted to one particular historical faith or denomination and in fact may be hostile to traditional or organized religion per se. Such spiritual seekers are reported to be exploring the world's storehouse of faiths and spiritualities for a variety of meaning systems and practices with which to experiment in order to find some that work for them, that meet their needs. They are dispositionally open to a multiplicity of truths, willing eclectically and selectively to mix and match traditionally distinct religious beliefs and practices, and suspicious of commitment to a single religious congregation. They tend to eschew religious proselytizing as paternalistic and coercive. And they operate, whether self-consciously or not, as religious and spiritual consumers by defining themselves as individual seekers, the authoritative judges of truth and relevance in faith according to how things subjectively feel to them. Such consuming seekers are not religiously rooted or settled but are spiritual nomads on a perpetual quest for greater insight and more authentic and fulfilling experiences.[1]

Baby boomers, who grew up through a series of cultural revolutions and liberations from traditional American ways of life, are often said to be the original and quintessential spiritual seekers in America.[2] They pioneered and popularized contemporary spiritual seeking in the form of Zen meditation centers, evangelical megachurches, and more. Recently, however, some observers have suggested that the phenomenon of spiritual seeking is moving down the generational food chain and being adopted increasingly by younger Americans, including those currently in college and even teenagers.[3] If this is the case, then it signals a potentially even more profound transformation of American religious culture than perhaps even some prior observers of spiritual seeking have realized. The question then is, Is this really so?

Very little reliable empirical research on the extent and characteristics of spiritual seeking among American adolescents has been conducted. Much of what informs popular stereotypes on the matter is anecdotal and impressionistic. In what follows, by contrast, we examine NSYR survey and interview data on the issue of spiritual seeking among American teenagers to provide a reliable, nationally representative picture. By so doing, we may learn not only about adolescent religion and spirituality specifically, but also about religious cultural change in the United States more broadly.

Seeker Attitudes

We begin by examining a set of American teenagers' beliefs and attitudes that together represent key indicators of possible resonance with spiritual seeking—as opposed to particularistic religious faith set in historical religious traditions.[4] Do American teens reflect the attitudinal features of typical spiritual seekers? The findings of table 24 offer some evidence of this. Consider, for example, teens' beliefs about religion and truth. Fewer than one-third of teens (29 percent) report that they believe that only one religion is true. The majority of teens (60 percent) say they believe that many religions may be

Table 24. Religious Particularity and Individualism among U.S. Adolescents, Ages 13–17 (Percentages)

	U.S.	Religious Tradition						
		CP	MP	BP	RC	J	LDS	NR
Beliefs about religion's truth								
Only one religion is true	29	46	26	31	19	9	67	5
Many religions may be true	60	48	67	63	71	79	23	62
There is very little truth in any religion	9	4	5	4	9	12	5	27
Don't know/refused	2	2	2	2	1	~	5	6
Beliefs about religious particularity								
People should practice only one faith	46	59	38	57	40	21	59	25
It is okay to practice religions besides own	51	36	59	40	58	78	36	70
Don't know/refused	3	4	3	3	2	1	5	5
Beliefs about religious conversion attempts								
Okay for religious people to try to convert others	54	70	58	54	43	18	83	32
Everyone should leave everyone else alone	43	27	39	42	55	75	15	66
Don't know/refused	3	3	3	4	2	8	2	3
Okay to pick and choose religious beliefs without having to accept teachings of faith as a whole								
Agree	46	36	53	34	54	71	31	62
Disagree	52	61	46	64	45	29	69	35
Don't know/refused	2	3	1	1	1	~	~	4
For believers to be truly religious and spiritual, they need to be involved in a religious congregation								
Agree	32	35	27	45	32	20	60	14
Disagree	67	64	72	54	67	80	40	84
Don't know/refused	1	1	1	1	1	~	~	2

Source: National Survey of Youth and Religion, 2002–3.

Note: Percentages may not add to 100 due to rounding; cells of <1 are reported as ~.

true. Only 9 percent say there is very little truth in any religion. What is clear is that most American teens believe that religion or religions possess and offer reliable truth claims. But most American teens appear to take a fairly inclusive and pluralistic position about the truth that different religions claim to possess. A substantial minority of teens do take a more exclusive or particularistic approach to truth in religion, but 29 percent is still a clear minority. To be sure, affirming that "many religions may be true" can indicate a broad range of ideas on the matter. Some of the 60 percent of teens choosing this survey answer may believe something like, "All religions are equally true," "All religions share the same vision of truth underneath," or "Different religions grasp different parts of a larger truth." These respondents fall on the more inclusive or religiously relativistic side of this answer. Others among this 60 percent may think, essentially, "I don't really know, but 'One religion is true' sounds awfully hard-line, so I'll say many *may* be true." This is more of a safe default answer than a positive commitment to pluralism. And yet others among the 60 percent affirming this response may be thinking something more like, "My religion is the one true religion, but other religions can reflect fragments of my true religion in their own religious teachings, and in that sense many religions may be 'true.' " This response falls closer to the exclusive side on the pluralistic spectrum. Nevertheless, whatever the answer "many religions may be true" exactly represents among our teens, it remains clear that those respondents did not choose the sharper, more particular answer "Only one religion is true." American teenagers, then, as a group seem to lean toward an open and inclusive religious pluralism on the matter of religions' truth claims.

Regardless of their views of religion and truth, what do American teens think about the appropriateness of people actually practicing one versus more than one religious faith? On this question teens are more evenly split. About half (51 percent) say they think it is okay for people of one religious faith to also practice other faiths, that is, to practice multiple faiths simultaneously. However, nearly another half say that people should practice only one faith. Once again, it is only a large minority of American teens who advocate the exclusive practicing of particular faiths. A slightly larger number than those are okay with people practicing more than one faith. This may or may not indicate a positive interest in spiritual seeking, but in any case, we do see here that at least half of American teens hold an attitude about religious exclusivity that potentially lends itself to the seeker orientation.

Table 24 also examines teenagers' views about the legitimacy of religious believers attempting to convert others to their faith, which seekers are typically thought to find disagreeable. According to the seeker viewpoint, each individual must follow his or her own quest in spirituality, and not have to be confronted and perhaps pressured by others to adopt their faith. According to the findings in table 24, the slight majority of American teens, 54 percent, disagree with that position; they believe it is okay for people to try to convert others. A large minority of teens, by comparison, 43 percent, believe that when it comes to proselytizing, everyone should just leave everyone else alone. Thus, although the vast majority of teens have not adopted a "right not to be proselytized" attitude, a very large portion of teens, nearly half, do lean toward a live-and-let-live approach to faith in which believers should not try to convert others to their faith. Again, this does not itself make these teens spiritual seekers, but the attitude lends itself to that approach.

Another aspect of the spiritual seeker mentality is thought to be a readiness to selectively choose which beliefs from a religious tradition one wants to believe and which beliefs one may disregard. In contrast to more historically traditional notions of religious faith—which tend to view beliefs as hanging together in larger, coherent, interdependent systems of authoritative thought and commitment that should be embraced by faith as wholes—spiritual seekers are more prepared to customize and personally design their own faith systems from bits of belief pulled out of those larger systems. Put another way, spiritual seekers do not hesitate to discount and ignore teachings of a religious tradition that do not seem right to them. They thus act as their own spiritual authorities, adjudicating religious beliefs based primarily on their personal experiences, rather than as followers being formed by the teachings and directives of larger, coherent, authoritative faith traditions. So, where do American teenagers come down on this question? They are nearly split down the middle: 52 percent say that people should not pick and choose their religious beliefs but should accept the teachings of their faith as a whole; 46 percent believe the opposite, that it is okay to pick and choose, that one does not have to accept all the teachings of a faith. Thus, neither side claims a clear majority.

Finally, the NSYR asked teens whether religious believers need to be involved in a religious congregation to be truly religious and spiritual, as opposed to being freelance believers unattached to any specific congregation of adherents. Here the majority of American teens swings back to the more individualistic position: two-thirds say believers do not need to be involved in congregations to be religious and spiritual; only one-third say that they do. Again, the difference is not enormous but clearly leans toward an attitude amenable to that of the spiritual seeker. None of this establishes that any of these teens are *actually themselves* spiritual seekers, but if an opportunity and advocate for seeking did come along, a large proportion of them do appear to have the attitudinal predilection compatible with seeking. At the very least, theoretically up to half of American teenagers appear to be a potential market for a seeking spirituality.

What about differences between religious traditions? Are some types of religious teens more disposed to religious seeking attitudes than others? The evidence in table 24 shows that some clearly are. Following the general pattern of answers across religious traditions in the previous chapter, table 24 suggests that Mormon teens tend to hold the most particularistic and exclusive views of religion and tend to be the least individualistic about faith and belief. They are typically followed by conservative Protestants, who are also generally less individualistic and more exclusive about faith than most other comparison groups. Black Protestant teens then follow as the next most particularistic and least individualistic religious group, typically being distinctly different from the average American teen in these regards. Mainline Protestant answers tend to come in fairly close to the national average, reflecting a middle position. Catholic youth move relatively further toward pluralistic and individualistic approaches to faith. Nonreligious teens are in their attitudes and beliefs relatively very individualistic and inclusive when it comes to religion and faith, but not more so than Jewish teens, who on most counts are the most individualistic and inclusive about faith and belief of all of the groups compared. The vast majority of Jewish teenagers in the NSYR sample believe that many religions may be true, that it is okay to practice more than one faith, that people should not try to convert others, that people can pick and choose their religious beliefs, and that it is not necessary for a truly religious and spiritual person to be involved in a religious congregation. The propensity toward spiritual seeker attitudes, then, is not evenly distributed across all American teens: some religious groups of teens are much friendlier to seeker attitudes than others.

Some of the religious traditions considered here may, in light of their own commitments, find cause for concern in table 24. Consider conservative Protestants, for example. About half of their teens say that many religions may be true; more than one-third say it is okay to practice multiple religions; more than one-quarter believe people should not try to evangelize others; more than one-third say it is okay to pick and choose one's religious beliefs and not accept the teachings of one's faith as a whole; and nearly two-thirds say a person can be truly religious and spiritual without being involved in a church. It appears that these conservative Protestant youth have not been very successfully inducted into their tradition's distinctive commitment to Christian particularity, evangelism, the need to accept all that the Bible teaches, and serious church involvement. Whether this represents a decline over time in commitment among youth to these conservative Protestant distinctives and commitments we cannot say, as we do not have comparable data from earlier eras. But it certainly does appear to represent a large current-day gap between what most conservative Protestant pastors and leaders want their teens to assume and believe and what many conservative Protestant teens actually do assume and believe. The same kinds of observations might be offered for other religious groups compared in this table, perhaps especially for the Catholic youth whose religious tradition also emphasizes the uniqueness of the Catholic faith, the importance of correct Church teaching, and the centrality of the Church as an institution of faith practice.

In their attitudes expressed on the NSYR survey, then, very many teens seem quite friendly with the spiritual seeker's view of the world. But these, let us remember, are merely agreeable attitudes in response to survey questions, not necessarily actual identities and actions. Do we have evidence that American teens not only share various key attitudes with seekers but actually think of themselves as and act like spiritual seekers? We turn next to trying to answer that question.

"Spiritual but not Religious"

First, we consider to what extent American teenagers embrace the most popular slogan, perhaps even common creed, of contemporary spiritual seekers, namely, that they are "spiritual but not religious." Numerous writers identify this as the emblematic identity of seekers. Do teens identify with it themselves? According to data in table 25, only 8 percent of American teens say it is very true that they are "spiritual but not religious," 46 percent say it is somewhat true, and 43 percent say it is not true of them at all. Teens from other religions (at 17 percent) followed by nonreligious (at 13 percent) and black Protestant teens (at 12 percent) were the most likely to say this was very true of them. Teens from the remaining religious traditions were less likely than the national average to say this identity was very true of them. About half of Mormon and conservative and mainline Protestant teenagers said it was not true of them at all.

How do we interpret these numbers? Much hangs on the meaning of the "somewhat true" answers, which represent 46 percent of all teens. If these in fact are youth who are significantly starting to get into spiritual seeking,

Table 25. Spiritual Seeking and Syncretistic Religious Practices among U.S. Adolescents, Ages 13–17 (Percentages)

	U.S.	Religious Tradition							
		CP	MP	BP	RC	J	LDS	OR	NR
Teen considers self "spiritual but not religious"									
Very true	8	8	6	12	6	~	5	17	13
Somewhat true	46	40	45	47	52	57	41	50	49
Not true at all	43	49	47	40	41	39	53	31	35
Don't know/refused	2	3	3	1	1	3	~	2	3
Teen tries to include in own spirituality any practices from (not asked of own religion)									
Christianity	37	—	—	—	—	18	—	32	44
Buddhism, Hinduism, Zen, or other Asian religion	4	2	4	2	5	5	~	19	4
Wicca, witchcraft, or other pagan religion	3	2	3	1	3	7	2	5	4
Judaism	2	3	3	1	2	—	~	12	2
Islam	1	~	1	3	1	7	~	6	1

Source: National Survey of Youth and Religion, 2002–3.

Note: Percentages may not add to 100 due to rounding and unreported don't know and refused answers; cells of <1 are reported as ~; OR = Other Religion (not Christian, Jewish, or LDS).

then American teenagers indeed seem to be converting in great numbers to this alternative style of spirituality and questing. If, however, the "somewhat true" teens are instead representing in that answer something other than a partial and growing embrace of spiritual seeking, then spiritual seekers are likely only a small minority of American teens after all.

We are completely convinced by the latter interpretation and firmly believe that spiritual seeking as described above exists among only a very small fraction of American teenagers and that its influence on teens has been greatly overstated. Our reason for thinking this comes primarily from our experience personally interviewing hundreds of teenagers across the United States. Whatever their answers were to the survey question, when we came to interview questions about being "spiritual but not religious," as we will see below, the majority of all of the teenagers we interviewed said that they had never heard this phrase before, and the vast majority, even if they had heard this phrase, said that they had no clue what it meant. Most teens literally did not understand what it was we were asking about. Some struggled to provide answers because they seemed to think that they should know what we were asking about. But most simply said, "No, I haven't really heard that" and "I guess I really don't know what it means." Thus, although the slogan "spiritual but not religious" can be seen on many bookshelves, read in many newspapers, and heard on many talk shows, very few American teenagers have heard of it, much less learned to what beliefs and lifestyles it refers. We are thus persuaded that the vast majority of teen survey respondents who said it was "somewhat true" that they are spiritual but not religious meant by this answer to say, essentially, "Well, let's see, in some ways I think I am somewhat spiritual—I do pray and go to church sometimes—but I'm really not entirely *not* religious, so it is neither very true nor not true at all, so I guess it must be the other answer: somewhat true." Which is to say they should have answered "Don't know" or, had they actually understood the spiritual seeking phenomenon the question was attempting to measure but which they are not actually a part of, "Not true at all." In which case, as our personal interviews clearly indicated, commitment to the kind of spiritual seeking that multiple writers have highlighted in recent years exists among only a small minority of American teenagers.

In fact, we strongly suspect that many of the 8 percent of American teens who reported that it is "very true" that they are spiritual but not religious are themselves not even spiritual seekers of the kind described above. Much of mainstream American Christianity inherits strong anti-institutional tendencies with historical roots as far back as at least the Revolutionary era.[5] This individualistic, antiestablishment proclivity lives, ironically, in the heart of much of American institutional religion itself. And it has helped to form an important popular cultural distinction between an "authentic faith"— which is personally chosen, regularly practiced, and spiritually meaningful— and an "empty faith," which is ritualistically rote, spiritually dry, and invested more in organizational associations than "real," personal experience. Hence the very popular evangelical book authored by Fritz Ridenour, first published in 1967 and still in print today: *How to Be a Christian without Being Religious*.[6] Importantly, however, such "authentic" and "truly spiritual" faith does not reject institutional commitment and involvement. Indeed, regularly attending churchgoers might hear the "be truly spiritual and not merely religious" message preached from hundreds of church pulpits on any given week. Serious church involvement is actually important in the believer's life, from this perspective; it simply can't displace or substitute for an accompanying personal, authentic faith and meaningful spirituality. We strongly suspect that most of the teen respondents in the Christian traditions who answered "very true" that they are spiritual but not religious meant their answer in precisely this way: that in their mind and self-image institutional trappings have not displaced their personal, spiritual faith. This interpretation is corroborated by the fact that 58 percent of those who answered "very true" also attend religious services many times a year or more often, and the Christians among them, at least, are not statistically significantly more likely to say that truly religious and spiritual believers do not need to be involved in a religious congregation. Based on our experience talking through these issues face-to-face with teens around the country, we estimate that no more than *2 to 3 percent* of American teens are serious spiritual seekers of the kind described above: self-directing and self-authenticating individuals pursuing an experimental and eclectic quest for personal spiritual meaning outside of historical religious traditions.

Again, our personal interviews with teenagers around the country, when examined in greater detail, confirm this interpretation of the numbers. For starters, half of the teens who the NYSR personally interviewed who had answered on the telephone survey that it was "very true" that they were "spiritual but not religious" said in their interviews later that they actually did not see any distinction between religion and spirituality. It is hard to explain their apparently inaccurate survey answers; perhaps they had a change of thinking or misunderstood the survey question. Perhaps lack of familiarity with the term resulted in less reliable answers. In any case, the "spiritual versus religious" distinction clearly was not an important conceptual or experiential difference shaping their ongoing thinking or identities. Many of them said that they had never actually heard the phrase before. And those who had often had only the vaguest notions about what "spiritual but not religious" might mean. One white nominally Catholic boy from Wisconsin who considered himself to be nonreligious, for example, said, "What comes to mind is like weirdos, you know, like hippies and stuff like that, but I don't really care to think about it." Another white boy from New York with Catholic background but currently weakly affiliated with Ba'hai said, "It's sort of semantics, I guess." A few, such as this nonattending Lutheran girl from Nevada who had never heard the phrase before, guessed that what other people mean by this distinction is simply that "they don't go to church but they still believe in God."

Even some of the teens who did say in their interviews that they think of themselves as spiritual but not religious were vague about what that meant. One Jewish girl from New York, for example, explained, "I guess spirituality is just your connections and religion is more like, um, I don't know, like what you believe, like the bigger picture. I'm not sure, I don't know how to describe it." When asked specifically about the phrase "spiritual but not religious," she said it applied to herself "sort of, in a way, I'm not so much, like more towards that than anything else I guess, maybe I'm more spiritual because I don't follow my religion too much, but I don't know, I like believe in God, I mean, I think I do, but I'm not sure." One white nonreligious boy from California pointed to a nebulous distinction between the specific and the general: "Religion is a specific religion, spiritual is more of a general thing, spiritual is kind of your own thing." And one nominal Christian girl from Arizona explained somewhat unclearly, "Being religious is being set on something. Being spiritual doesn't necessarily mean you're set on something, it just means you need something to believe in, something to, for your mind. It's just what comes with the owning of your belief, you know what I mean?"

Some of the interviewed teens who *did* see a distinction between religious and spiritual, whether or not they said it applied to themselves, were somewhat more clear on what the phrase might mean. One white Presbyterian boy from Southern California, for instance, focused on individual versus organized faith, explaining, "Being spiritual is more of an individual type of thing, less an organized." For himself, he noted, "I'm more spiritual than religious because I don't get caught up in a lot of [church controversies], like this and that thing is happening and you can't wear hats in church." Likewise, this black Baptist boy from South Carolina, who says he feels close to God but attends church rarely, observed, "When I think about 'religion' I think of going to church. But 'spiritual' I would say is having a relationship with God like praying and anything like that. Religion is just the Bible and church. And spiritual is just your relationship with God." And one West Coast, non-religious boy raised in a Muslim family said simply that "religion" is believing in the Bible, while "spiritual" is believing in the paranormal. Thus, while some of these teens have somewhat more articulate views on the matter, it is far from clear that they share a common view. But generally, the phrase "spiritual but not religious" seems to denote something like a personal openness to or interest in the divine or the spiritual but a lack of certainty about or commitment to regular, visible religious practices and affiliations.

However, also in the group of self-identified "spiritual but not religious" teenagers, another quite different voice emerged in the interviews. We spoke with one Protestant Hispanic girl from Florida, for instance, who told us, "I just don't like religion, so I'd rather be spiritual." What did she actually mean by this? To be spiritual, in her view, is to "have an intimate relationship with God" when you "pray and really mean it, not like do it out of habit," whereas being religious means when "you don't really have an intimate [relationship with God]" and when things like praying are "all like very routine." This girl in fact attends church more than once a week. What she means by being spiritual but not religious is not being distant from church, but rather not being distant from God in the context of church, not having a habitualized or routinized faith. Fritz Ridenour strikes again. Similarly, this white Baptist boy from Ohio who attends church regularly explained, " 'Religion' is basically going to church, knowing God like 'book smart' and stuff; whereas a 'spiritual' relationship would be more like speaking to him daily and really feeling like you know him and you can talk to him, feeling him as a friend and more being spiritual." About himself, he said, "I feel like I can talk to Jesus and stuff but I also go to church and know the Bible decently well, so I would say I have both. But if I could pick the most important, I'd pick 'spiritual.' " Thus, some spiritual but not religious teens use these categories not to disparage or distance themselves from organized religion per se, but to emphasize the importance of personally meaningful faith *that is practiced in the context of organized religion*. Theirs is a critique, not of traditional religion itself, which they actually practice happily, but merely of the prospect of an empty, habitual, ritualistic faith. For them, "spiritual but not religious" is not the rejection of traditional religion but a reminder to sustain spiritual vitality within traditional religion.

Spiritual Syncretism and Experimentation

Our estimate of 2 to 3 percent of true spiritual seekers is also confirmed by the other findings presented in table 25 on teens' actual seeker-like behaviors, specifically whether teens include in their own spirituality any practices from religious and spiritual traditions not their own. Their answers are instructive. One percent of non-Muslim American teens try to include spiritual practices from Islam in their own spirituality; 2 percent of non-Jewish American teens try to include spiritual practices from Judaism in their own spirituality; 3

percent of nonpagan American teens try to include spiritual practices from Wicca, witchcraft, or any pagan religion in their own spirituality; and 4 percent of American teens not affiliated with an Asian religion—such as Buddhism, Hinduism, or Zen—try to include spiritual practices from such religions in their own spirituality. Yet fully 37 percent of non-Christian and non-Mormon American teens try to include spiritual practices from Christianity in their own spirituality! In comparing across the religious traditions, we see that the teenagers most likely to be incorporating spiritual practices from other faiths and spiritualities are Jewish teens and those in the "other religion" category, that is, non-Mormon religious minorities and nonreligious teens. By comparison, only a few percent of the Christian teens are trying to incorporate non-Christian religious practices in their own spiritualities.

Three important general observations here suggest themselves. First, exceedingly few teenagers from the dominant religion in America, Christianity (about 2 to 3 percent on average) are spiritually seeking, if by that we mean personally experimenting with religious or spiritual practices from other faiths. Second, the most likely seekers, thus defined, are by far non-Mormon religious minorities, those whose primary religious affiliations are Buddhism, Islam, Judaism, Hinduism, Unitarianism, Christian Science, Wicca, and so on. Third, in the U.S. marketplace of spiritual practices, the religious option that is actually having the greatest influence on teen experimenters with other faiths is not an "exotic" faith or spirituality, but Christianity, the dominant American faith. Much higher proportions of non-Christian and non-Mormon teens are incorporating Christian practices into their own spiritualities—18 percent of Jewish teens, 32 percent of "other religion" teens, and 44 percent of nonreligious teens—than Christian and Mormon teens are incorporating non-Christian practices into their spiritualities. If these data suggest any observable direction of teenage spiritual seeking in the United States, such as it is, it is of non-Christian teens seeking out Christianity, not the reverse. While this counters the conventional wisdom about spiritual seeking and may challenge normative advocates of religious pluralism, it should not be surprising. The laws of mathematics almost determine that minorities surrounded by a dominant majority will be more influenced by the ever-present majority than the dominant majority will be influenced by the relatively scattered minorities. That is simply the normal outcome of a statistical property of a certain structure of social distributions and relations. Furthermore, standard processes of immigrant and ethnic cultural assimilation into the dominant society also mean that non-Christians in the United States are much more likely to be influenced by Christianity than Christians are to be influenced by minority non-Christian faiths. And that is exactly what appears to be happening among American teenagers of different faiths.

Overall, therefore, our general conclusion based on these data remains the same: the phenomenon of spiritual seeking recently discussed by many observers of American religion is, according to the best available nationally representative evidence—and, we will see below, our interview data as well—very limited in the extent of its influence among American teenagers. There clearly are some teenagers who think of themselves as spiritual but not religious and who behave in various ways like the new spiritual seekers that writers have discussed in recent years. But they appear to be a very small percentage of all U.S. teens. And even among them, it is not easy to find one who is clear and articulate about what it all means. It appears to be much more an amorphous feeling or sensibility than a specific idea or experience catalyzing a significant cultural or religious movement.

Who Are the Seekers?

Are we able to say what kinds of teenagers, few though they may be, tend to think of themselves as spiritual but not religious or incorporate spiritual practices from other faiths into their own spiritualities? Statistical regression techniques enable us to test for associations between these spiritual seeker indicators and many other social, personal, and religious factors to see if the correlations are strong enough, given the size of the groups involved, to be considered statistically significant. By testing for a variety of factors at one time, these regression techniques compute complicated equations allowing us to isolate the possible association of each separate factor while controlling for the influences of all of the other factors simultaneously for all factors tested. This enables us to sort through the great variety of variables to identify those with the clearest and strongest associations with spiritual seeking independent of the effects of any other tested variable. What follows are the results of the analyses we ran for the two seeking variables examined above.

First, we ran logistic regression analyses identifying factors associated with teens saying that it is definitely true that they are spiritual but not religious, as distinct from saying that this is either somewhat or not true. Results reveal the following variables are statistically significantly associated with definitely being spiritual but not religious while controlling for the effects of all of the other control variables:

❧ *Religious tradition*: Teens from minority religions (other than Judaism and Mormonism) and nonreligious teens are more likely than are mainline Protestants (the reference category) to be definitely spiritual but not religious.

❧ *Religious service attendance*: Teens who attend religious services less often are more likely than teens who attend more often to be definitely spiritual but not religious.

❧ *Lower desired attendance*: Teens who themselves would like to attend religious services less often than they do are more likely than those who would like to attend more often to be definitely spiritual but not religious.

❧ *Close friends*: Teens with fewer close friends involved in a religious youth group or any other religious group they themselves are involved in are more likely than teens with more friends in religious groups to be definitely spiritual but not religious.

✒ *Parent religiosity*: Teens with parents who attend religious services less often and for whom faith is of low importance are more likely than teens with more religious parents to be definitely spiritual but not religious.

✒ *Relationship with parents*: Teens who say their parents do not understand, love, or pay attention to them are more likely than teens who say that their parents do understand, love, and pay enough attention to them to be definitely spiritual but not religious.[7]

What do we learn from this analysis? It appears that the relatively small percentage of serious spiritual but not religious adolescents in the United States are those who are located on the culture's religious periphery, who are marginal to mainstream religious institutions. They tend disproportionately to come from (non-Jewish and non-Mormon) religious minorities—Unitarians, Muslims, pagans, Buddhists, Satanists, Taoists, Christian Scientists—all teens on the fringe of U.S. religious culture, or to identify themselves as not religious. They are likely to attend religious services infrequently or never and to want to participate in religious services even less than they already do. America's spiritual but not religious adolescents also tend to make friends with other teens who are not in the same religious organizations. They are more likely to have parents who attend religious services infrequently or never and for whom faith is of low importance in their lives. They are also teens who are less likely to feel that their parents love, understand, and pay attention to them, which is itself also a significant predictor variable of youth distance from mainstream religion. In at least these six important, distinct ways, then, spiritual but not religious adolescents are teenagers who have very weak ties to and perhaps feel outright alienation from mainstream, institutional religion. By saying that they are spiritual but not religious, these teens are likely both distancing themselves from what they consider to be religious while simultaneously maintaining a spiritual identity which, in contemporary culture, indicates that they are not hard-core, secular, atheistic materialists.

What about those relatively few teenagers who incorporate into their own spirituality practices from some other religious faith? What social or religious factors set them apart from those who engage only in the spiritual practices of their own religion? Logistic regression analyses show these variables to be statistically significantly associated with teens including into their own spirituality one or more practices from a religion not their own while controlling for the effects of all of the other control variables:

✒ *Religious tradition*: Jewish teens and teens from other non-Christian minority religions are more likely than are mainline Protestants to incorporate other spiritual practices, while evangelical Protestant and Mormon teens are less likely.

✒ *Lower desired attendance*: Teens who themselves would like to attend religious services less often than they do are more likely than those who would like to attend more often to incorporate other spiritual practices.

👄 *Close friends*: Teens with fewer close friends involved in a religious youth group or any other religious group they themselves are involved in are more likely than teens with more friends in religious groups to incorporate other spiritual practices.

👄 *Relationship with parents*: Teens who say their parents do not understand, love, or pay attention to them are more likely than teens who say their parents do understand, love, and pay attention to them to incorporate other spiritual practices.

👄 *Parental marital status*: Teens with divorced parents are more likely than teens with married parents to incorporate other spiritual practices.

👄 *Urban residence*: Urban residents are more likely than rural residents to incorporate other spiritual practices.

👄 *Family income*: Teens from families with higher incomes are more likely than those with lower incomes to incorporate other spiritual practices.

👄 *Parent education*: Teens with more highly educated parents are more likely than teens with less educated parents to incorporate other spiritual practices.

We see again that teens from minority religions, who are surrounded by a dominant religious faith not their own (Christianity), are more likely to incorporate the spiritualities of other religions into their own practices. Teens with weak social ties to mainstream American religion—low-attending teens and those with fewer close friends in religious organizations—are also more likely to experiment with or practice the spiritualities of religions other than their own. These adolescent spiritual seekers thus again appear to be socially located on the culture's religious periphery. Second, it appears that teens in family situations involving greater distance and freedom from parents—teens who feel relatively unloved, not understood, and not paid attention to by their parents, and teens with divorced parents—are more likely to experiment with or practice the spiritualities of religions other than their own. When teens' close ties to both parents break down, it seems, they are more likely to experiment with spiritual practices of faiths other than the one in which they were raised. Finally, we can see a third theme in these findings: those teens more likely to experiment with or practice the spiritualities of other religions also appear socially located in ways that make them more likely to be exposed to and have the resources to appropriate culturally different practices: they tend to live in the cities, their parents are more highly educated, and they tend to come from families with higher incomes. There thus also appear to be social class and cosmopolitanism effects at work in this version of adolescent spiritual experimentation and eclecticism, which facilitate teens' appropriations of spiritualities from other faith traditions.

Having explored spiritual seeking among U.S. teenagers, we turn now to examine U.S. teens who are entirely disengaged from American religion. Who are the American teenagers who are simply disengaged from religious beliefs, practices, and institutions? What do we know about their numbers and characteristics? And how did they come to be religiously disengaged?

RELIGIOUSLY DISENGAGED TEENAGERS

The NSYR investigated not only religious teens, but also American teenagers who never attend religious services and who self-identify as nonreligious. Here we review these populations of teens to better understand their social locations and experiences.

Nonreligious Teens

The category "not religious" can include a variety of kinds of people. To explore these differences, the NSYR asked teens who identified themselves as not religious whether they considered themselves atheists, agnostics, just not religious, or something else. According to the data presented in table 26, 8 percent of nonreligious American teens (1.4 percent of all teens) consider themselves atheists. The same number consider themselves agnostics. This is roughly the same proportion as American adults (about 2 percent) who identify explicitly as atheist or agnostic. More than half (54 percent) of nonreligious teens do not accept those labels, but consider themselves "just not religious." Twenty-one percent don't know what kind of not-religious person they are or refused to answer the question. Nine percent said "something

Table 26. Identities and Beliefs of Nonreligious U.S. Adolescents, Ages 13–17 (Percentages)

	Nonreligious Teens	All U.S. Teens
Nonreligious teen considers self		
Atheist	8	1.4
Agnostic	8	1.4
Just not religious	54	9.6
"Religious" nonreligious	9	1.8
Don't know/refused	21	4
Believes in God	52	—
Prays alone a few times a week or more often	24	—
Reads the Bible a few times a week or more often	7	—
Teen atheists who once did believe in God	66	—
Doubts about being nonreligious		
Many doubts	8	—
Some doubts	15	—
A few doubts	27	—
No doubts	50	—
Don't know/refused	1	—

Source: National Survey of Youth and Religion, 2002–3.

Note: Percentages may not add to 100 due to rounding.

else" and then gave a verbatim answer suggesting some link to a religious identity; most likely these teens think of themselves personally as not religious, yet are connected, perhaps by family affiliation, to some religious tradition, such as Catholic, Baptist, or Lutheran. We see, then, that nonreligious American teens encompass a variety of identities, including some that seem confused and even connected somehow to religion. Viewed from a different angle, American teens professing a nonreligious identity are not "not religious" on all measures of religiosity. Table 26, for example, also shows that 52 percent of nonreligious American teenagers believe in God, 24 percent pray alone a few times a week or more often, and 7 percent read the Bible a few times a week or more often. Self-identified nonreligious teenagers are far from entirely secular in beliefs and practices.

The NSYR also asked the 3 percent of U.S. teens who reported that they do not believe in God whether they ever once in their lives *had* believed in God. Sixty-six percent of them said that at one time they had believed in God; 31 percent (fewer than one-half of 1 percent of all American teens) say they never in their lives believed in God. Most of the very few teenage atheists thus at one point in their lives lost a previous faith they had held in God.

Religious believers can have doubts about their faith. In theory, nonreligious people might also have doubts about being not religious, perhaps questioning whether they really ought instead to have religious faith. Do they? According to the findings in table 26, half of all nonreligious teens have no doubts about being nonreligious; about one quarter (27 percent) have only a few doubts; and nearly one-quarter (23 percent) have some or many doubts about being nonreligious. Comparing these results to those for religious believers in table 7, we see that nonreligious teens have just as many doubts about being not religious—perhaps even slightly more—than religious teens have about their religious beliefs. Clearly, while the majority of both types doubt little or not at all, we see that teenage nonreligiosity is subject to just as much doubt as is teenage religious belief.

From what religious backgrounds do self-identified nonreligious American teens come? We know from table 5 in the previous chapter that currently nonreligious teens have parents that represent a variety of religious traditions, particularly minority religions and mainline Protestantism. The majority of nonreligious teens' parents, however, are also not religious. But the religion of a survey respondent parent may not be the same as the religion a nonreligious teen was raised in as a child. Is it possible to say with more precision in what religious traditions youth were raised who as teens came to think of themselves as not religious? According to table 27, 22 percent reported that they were raised Catholic, 22 percent Protestant of various sorts, 20 percent "just Christian" (suggesting a nominal family religious identity or low involvement in church), 14 percent were raised in nonreligious families, 3 percent Mormon, 2 percent Jewish, and 1 percent or fewer were raised in a variety of other minority religious traditions. Fifteen percent did not know in what religion they were raised or refused to answer the question. The 20

Table 27. Religion in Which Currently Nonreligious U.S. Adolescents Were
Raised, Ages 13–17 (Percentages)

Catholic	22	No religion	14
Protestant	22	Mormon	3
Baptist	9	Jewish	2
Lutheran	4	Jehovah's Witness	1
Methodist	2	Eastern Orthodox	0.4
Pentecostal	2	Native American	0.4
Episcopalian	1	Muslim	0.3
Presbyterian	1	General theist	0.3
Just Protestant	1	Buddhist	0.3
Holiness	0.4	Hindu	0.2
Nondenominational	0.4	Unitarian-Universalist	0.2
Church of God	0.3	Christian Science	0.2
Evangelical	0.1	Other	0.1
Church of Christ	0.1	Don't know/refused	15
Just Christian	20		

Source: National Survey of Youth and Religion, 2002–3.

Note: Percentages may not add to 100 due to rounding.

percent "just Christian" and 15 percent "don't know/refused" add some in-terpretive ambiguity to these findings.

What seems evident in table 27, when compared to tables 1 and 2 of the prior chapter, is that no one religious group is especially overrepresented as the religious tradition out of which nonreligious American teenagers come. In other words, no one religious group appears to be disproportionately likely to have their youth become nonreligious in their teenage years. All religious groups seem at risk of losing teens to nonreligious identities in roughly the same proportion to their share of the teenage population. For instance, 1.5 percent of American teens are Jewish, and 2 percent of nonreligious teens were raised Jewish; 23 percent of American teens are Catholic, and 22 percent of nonreligious teens (plus some unknown percentage of the "just Christian" and "don't know" teens) were raised Catholic. Less clear is the differential probability of fundamentalist and evangelical versus mainline and liberal Protestant youth in becoming nonreligious, because Lutheran, Methodist, Presbyterian, and even Baptist congregations can be either indistinguishably conservative or liberal Protestant without more specific information. Non-religious teens raised Episcopalian, however, are roughly the same proportion as currently Episcopalian teens (about 1 percent for both). The same parallel holds for Pentecostal, Church of God, and Church of Christ teenagers. If the majority of the 35 percent of "just Christian" and "don't know" respondents were raised Protestant, therefore, the chances of becoming nonreligious as teens appears to be equal among all religious traditions in which the youth were raised. If, however, the majority of those 35 percent were not raised Protestant but, say, Catholic or some minority religion, then Protestants, per-haps especially conservative Protestants, are less likely than some other group or groups to have their teenagers become nonreligious. The findings of table

5 seem to confirm this latter interpretation. But the 35 percent of nonreligious teenagers' inability to remember the exact kind of religion (or nonreligion) in which they were raised makes it difficult to determine this precisely.

The NSYR asked all nonreligious teenagers who said they were raised in a religion *why* it was that they became nonreligious. Why did they fall away from the faith in which they were raised? This was asked as an open-ended question to which teens' answers were recorded verbatim and coded into general categories, as reported in table 28. The most common answer for becoming nonreligious (32 percent) was some version of intellectual skepticism or disbelief. These answers included teens who said, "It didn't make any sense anymore," "Some stuff is too far-fetched for me to believe," "I think scientifically and there is no real proof," and "Too many questions that can't be answered." Twenty-two percent merely said they do not know why they became nonreligious; they simply had no particular reason to offer for their apparent loss of faith. Thirteen percent referred to a general lack of interest in religion, saying things like, "It never seemed that interesting to me," "It got kind of boring," and "I just drifted away, I guess." Twelve percent of teens who had been raised in a religion explained their becoming nonreligious as simply having stopped attending religious services. Being raised religious, apparently, simply meant attending church, synagogue, mosque, temple, and so on such that when they stopped attending they were, by definition, not religious. Ten percent of nonreligious teens raised in a religion pointed to various life disruptions and troubles, such as deaths, divorces, and disappointments, as explanations for becoming nonreligious; they said things like, "My sister got sick and died," "My parents divorced," and "Just a lot of things happened in my life that proved God didn't really help whatsoever." Seven percent conveyed not so much a disbelief or disinterest in religion, but actually a strong dislike for religion, reporting explanations like, "The people at temple were not nice," "The lie the church has," "It didn't accept everybody's viewpoints." One percent suggested that their parents did not support their possible interest in religion, usually due to being too busy with work. Finally, 2 percent gave vague reasons or asked to skip the question.

So what does this tell us? Half of American nonreligious teens who were

Table 28. Reasons Nonreligious U.S. Adolescents Raised in a Religion Became Nonreligious, Ages 13–17 (Percentages)

Intellectual skepticism and disbelief	32
Don't know why	22
Lack of interest	13
Just stopped attending services	12
Life disruptions and troubles	10
Dislikes religion	7
Lacked parental support	1
Vague or no reason	2

Source: National Survey of Youth and Religion, 2002–3.

Note: Percentages may not add to 100 due to rounding.

raised in a religion apparently lost their faith or dropped out of religion for fairly passive reasons: for lack of interest, for reasons unknown or vague, because they "just stopped" attending religious services, for lack of parental support, and so on. On the other hand, nearly 40 percent of these teens expressed more substantive reasons, such as intellectual disbelief and skepticism or some kind of active dislike of their church or religion. Ten percent seem to have dropped out of religion or lost their faith because disruptive or troubling events left them feeling that religious faith was deficient. Thus, half of nonreligious teens who leave the faith in which they were raised do so for seemingly significant emotional and intellectual reasons, and half drop out or lose their faith for what sound like rather unremarkable reasons. The former were positively incredulous, upset, or disillusioned, while the latter seemed to have simply drifted away. So we again see significant variance in teenagers' experiences with and perceptions of religion.

What is it like being nonreligious in a culture where most peers claim a religious affiliation or identity? Do nonreligious teens make an issue of their beliefs? And how are they treated perhaps as a result? Table 29 examines the responses of nonreligious American teenagers to two questions about their experiences among their peers at school. According to these findings, the large majority (64 percent) of nonreligious teens never speak out openly against religion at school. That is simply an issue they do not engage in their school settings. Sixteen percent speak out openly against religion at school only a little, and 12 percent some. Only 7 percent of nonreligious teens (about 1 percent of all teens) speak out openly against religion at school a lot. The vast majority of nonreligious teens thus appear to keep their views about religion to themselves. Comparing these figures against those of table 19 in the prior chapter, we see that religious teens are somewhat more likely to openly express their faith at school than nonreligious teens are to speak out against religion.

How much are nonreligious teens made fun of or pressured by others for being nonreligious? According to their answers in table 29, not much: 85 percent are not pressured or made fun of at all, 13 percent only some or a little, and only 2 percent are made fun of or pressured a lot for not being religious. Comparing these answers to those of the religious teens in table 19, we see that religious teens are somewhat more likely to be made fun of or pressured by others for their religious faith than nonreligious teens are for being nonreligious. In sum, few nonreligious American teenagers are being bothered by others for their lack of religious faith, even fewer than the small minority of religious believers who are teased and pressured by others for being religious. Religion and nonreligion simply do not appear to be issues around which teens square off against each other. For most American teens, who have been well socialized into a culture of tolerance and acceptance of all cultural identity differences, as we will see in chapter 4, religion simply does not seem to matter enough to wrangle over.

Can we say with any more precision who are the American teenagers that identify as not religious? To answer this, we ran logistic regression analyses,

Table 29. Experiences of Nonreligious U.S. Adolescents among
Peers and at School, Ages 13–17 (Percentages)

	U.S. Nonreligious
Nonreligious teens speak out openly against religion at school	
A lot	7
Some	12
A little	16
None	64
Pressured or made fun of for being nonreligious	
A lot	2
Some	4
A little	9
None	85

Source: National Survey of Youth and Religion, 2002–3.

Note: Percentages may not add to 100 due to rounding and unreported don't know and refused answers.

as we did with the spiritual seekers above, examining a variety of social and religious variables to see which are statistically significantly associated with teens being nonreligious. Results of our analyses show the following variables to be significantly associated, while controlling for the effects of other variables, with American teens' self-identifying as not religious:

❧ *Parent religiosity*: Teens with parents who attend religious services less often and for whom faith is less important are more likely to be nonreligious than teens whose parents attend more often and for whom faith is more important.

❧ *Parental marital status*: Teens with divorced parents are more likely to be nonreligious than teens with married parents.

❧ *Relationship with parents*: Teens who say their parents do not understand, love, or pay attention to them are more likely to be nonreligious than teens who say their parents do understand, love, and pay attention to them.

❧ *Age*: Older teens are more likely to be nonreligious than younger teens.

❧ *Lower desired attendance*: Teens who themselves would like to attend religious services less often than they do are more likely to be nonreligious than those who would like to attend more often.

❧ *Close friends*: Teens with fewer close friends involved in a religious youth group or any other religious group they themselves may be involved in are more likely to be nonreligious than teens with more friends in religious groups.

➤ *Negative peer influences*: Teens whose parents say their friends have a negative influence on their teens' lives are more likely to be nonreligious than teens whose parents say they have a positive influence.

➤ *Organized activities*: Teen involved in fewer programs, clubs, hobby groups, sports, or other organized activities are more likely to be nonreligious than teens in more organized activities.

Multiple parental influences appear to be important in differentiating non-religious from religious teens in the United States. Self-identifying nonreligious teenagers are more likely to have parents who themselves reflect low levels of religiosity, who are divorced, and who their teens say give them not enough attention, love, and understanding. Stated differently, teenagers with parents who are more religious, who are married, and who are perceived as expressing more love for, attention to, and understanding of their adolescent are more likely to embrace some religious identity. U.S. teens who are not religious also tend to be older and so likely enjoy greater personal freedom from their parents and over their own identity. Their parents are also more apt to say that their friends are a bad influence in their teens' lives, another sign of strained relationships between parents and teens. Furthermore, non-religious teens are, as we might expect, less likely to have friends involved in religious groups and to want to attend religious services. Finally, they tend to be generally less involved in all types of organized activities, groups, and programs, and not merely religious organizations.

Two Nonreligious Baltimore Boys

No two teenagers could possibly represent all nonreligious teens in the United States. Any such grouping of American adolescents comprises a great deal of diversity in background, experience, and life outcomes. Here we portray two nonreligious boys from Baltimore, Maryland, not because they are somehow typical of all nonreligious adolescents—they are neither typical nor atypical— but simply to help put faces on the numbers, to convey some of the personal specifics and complexities of individual teenage cases. Such cases cannot truly represent a group, but they may illustrate certain larger points. One of the boys, Steve, who simply has no interest in organized religion, has in past years struggled with problems in life but now appears to be doing much better. The second boy, Raymond, who is currently in serious trouble, con-siders himself nonreligious, yet is finding himself hesitantly attracted to a church he has stumbled upon.

Steve showed up early for his interview on a sunny morning at the public library decently dressed and with great enthusiasm and courtesy. He was, it was clear, a really nice 17-year-old, middle-class, white kid. He lives in a decent city neighborhood with his parents, works part time at a pizza shop, and generally enjoys school, where he is, he says, "a socialite, drama buff, and video enthusiast." Early in the interview Steve makes clear that he doesn't drink much, doesn't smoke or do drugs, and isn't having sex with his girl-friend, Amy, with whom he is clearly madly in love. Steve says his parents love him very much. They also trust him, and rightfully so, he says, because he is a trustworthy person. He enjoys making pizzas, mountain biking, and playing "Dungeons and Dragons" with an organized game club comprised of older friends. But most of all, he likes making videos at school, where he enjoys the support of a very friendly media teacher. He is keen to buy his own digital video camera and is thinking of studying video production in college. Throughout the interview, Steve showed himself to be an earnest, caring, hard-working, affable adolescent, the kind most adults would enjoy and admire. Indeed, Steve observes about himself, "I like pleasing people."

At the same time, however, in the course of the interview it becomes clear that Steve has also struggled with his share of problems. For starters, he describes his father as a "hard ass" who in past years "worked so much I hardly ever saw him." Steve elaborates: "I don't feel like I know him well as a person, he's always been a mystery to me. I don't know much about his life or even his family. I love spending time with him but I wish we were closer. I'm closer to him now than when I was little. But it almost seems like it's too little, too late, like investing so much now, it would just almost hurt more when I have to leave."

Steve describes his mother as "really New Age-y, into a lot of weird, crazy things. She always has something new just about every week, which I love about her but at the same time it makes it kind of hard for me to relate to her. She's not a hippie but really darn close, she's a flake, but like in the best possible way." Steve's maternal grandfather, he explains, was for many years a hard-core alcoholic, mean and abusive, even to Steve—at least until he had a heart attack, which dramatically changed him into the kind person Steve now likes. Observing his grandfather's drinking, however, turned Steve off alcohol, and seeing his cousins and his older brother's friends smoke too much marijuana and some even ruin their lives on cocaine has also soured him on experimenting with drugs. In all of this, Steve is quite self-aware and self-reflective, more so than most boys we interviewed. In fact, he is able to explain that he knows that he struggles generally with emotional attachment and independence. When he was young, he recounts, an older male friend of the family named Vinny took to Steve and, by all accounts, served somewhat as a father figure. But, Steve explains, Vinny was "kinda spacey, he would always say he was going to come over, gonna do something, and he would just never show up. It was very disappointing." Steve says his mom's current "flakiness" now "kinda retriggers that" in him.

A few years before our interview, Steve also had another problem: a nasty relationship with a girlfriend that he says drove him to attempt suicide. When Steve was 13, he began a two-year-long romantic relationship with a girl he says was anorexic and self-hating and who emotionally abused him. "I went head over heels for this girl and she was really horrible to me, and my grades were going down and I couldn't take it any more. It was a horrible, horrible year." Steve said he stuck with her for two years because he thought he could rescue her. Complicating that situation, he says, was his ninth-grade English teacher, who was "a heinous, heinous woman. She had such a negative outlook on life and thought all teens were horrible people. She would degrade kids in class. My friend and I were the brunt of her jokes, she really would just degrade our work in front of the class and make fun of us and call us idiots." In ninth grade, Steve twice tried cutting himself, he says, in order to die. Then a friend told on him to a school counselor and his parents found out. He then went to therapy, which he says helped him a lot. "It did improve things," Steve remembers. "It was really hard for about a year after that. My parents were really hard on me and I was hard on them. We struggled, but through it we came to a closer point." Still, Steve says that he has not forgiven his former girlfriend "for anything" and that he feels guilty for trying to commit suicide, because it made his parents doubt themselves and think they had done something wrong, when, he says, they did not. He was just looking for attention in the wrong way. What does he do with his guilt? "I kind of dismiss it, kinda just deal with it. I live with it. But I feel like I have atoned for it in the last year, kind of made up for it." But it is clear in the interview that his attempts at suicide still embarrass and bother him.

Moving on to the topic of religion, Steve says: "I really can't buy into the organized religions. I'm kind of agnostic really. I don't know what I believe in. Something. I don't believe there's nothing. There's definitely a force at work. There's gotta be something. I like the idea that I've got some higher meaning, that there's some greater thing out there than the prime material right here in front of us." But what that something is, Steve doesn't know. He sees a lot of "coincidences" in life that may point to something spiritual. But then again, he says, they may just be mere coincidences. In any case, "Religion is just something I've never quite been able to get behind." Steve was raised Catholic but says that at 6 years old he decided that he wanted nothing to do with it: "I hated going to church and I hated Sunday School. Everything seemed so hokey to me as a kid. It was like, 'What are you talking about? There's all kinds of great things about the world.' I felt they were trying to sell me something almost. And I still feel that way."

Steve described three childhood memories that seemed to connect to his rejection of religion. His mother, who apparently had religious questions herself, had never had Steve baptized, and her Catholic parents "chastised her for a long time" about that, worried that their grandchild would go to hell. Also, one of Steve's Sunday School classes did a taste test once between identical-looking ground-up chocolate and coffee grounds, to demonstrate, he says, that looks can be deceiving. "I got the coffee grounds and was just pissed off. That's one of the things I remember most, is the deception." Finally, he recounts, "My best friend in kindergarten, Daniel Langdon, his mom said I couldn't hang out with him anymore 'cause I wasn't a Mormon. I often see people get stuck into trying to find the truth in religion and they shut out the world around them."

Still, Steve balances any hostility toward religion with a sense of appreciation. "It's a great guideline for people that need the guideline. I just have never felt like I need the guidelines. Religion gives people good moral foundations, it's a great foundation for people who don't have that." He has friends involved in church youth groups and in the evangelical high school group, Young Life. "They love it, think it's the greatest thing in the world. I've been invited, but I'm not really interested. I've got enough going on for me. If it works for them, fantastic, I'm happy for them." He says that whether or not there is an afterlife, "I'll be happy with whatever it is, if it's there, [good], if it's not, I'll be happy with that too. Why can't you [simply] know the end of your life is the end of your life and that's it?" But he understands other people's "need for continuance, for self-preservation, for self-importance" that he thinks gives rise to belief in life after death. Steve has never been to a religious summer camp, missions trip, or youth retreat. And he says his current girlfriend is "more hard-core not-religious than I am." Steve, at least, says that he is "spiritual" and prays, which he describes as "a kind of a more inner feeling, like an inner communication for hoping somebody's betterment." He also thinks bad people, like Hitler, should be punished for their wrongs after they die "if they're not willing to let go or admit they're wrong, I think absolutely he should be punished." But he's not sure there is any kind of actual hell. Overall, he wishes people would just get along, which affects his views of religion. "I really do. I think the search for truth through organized religion is what causes conflict lots of times. It does separate people." Like your friend from kindergarten? I asked. "Yeah," Steve says.

When it comes to moral reasoning, Steve is fun to talk with, but he seems to lack solid grounding for his ideas and beliefs. He says some things are universally right and wrong and that he knows what they are. "There are fewer [moral truths] than some people would make. I wouldn't draw as many lines as some people would, but there are definite rights and wrongs: you don't steal, you don't kill, you don't cheat people in any way." But when it comes to explaining *why* such things are wrong, he struggles. He first says things are wrong that make people unhappy, that "ruin their day," but he cannot explain why anyone should be morally committed to other people's happiness. He then says wrong behavior has "bad consequences, it'll catch up to you," but also cannot say why one should not act immorally in cases when one knows one will never get caught. He also says that it is wrong to kill because "human life is precious and has dignity because every person is here for a reason and you shouldn't shorten their life." But he can't explain or describe where that life-dignifying reason comes from. "Maybe it's just to work at McDonalds and serve food," he offers. When asked about the idea that some people in the world do not seem to believe that each human life is precious, Steve replies, "I don't know, let each person decide for themselves, that's what everybody has to do." He says he himself doesn't feel any moral obligation to help other people by volunteering for community organizations, "I feel like if I do, it's great, if I don't, all right." Steve says he does believe in basic, intrinsic human rights, but that he thinks they are merely "an unwritten code, really a human invention"—which, if you think about it, he says, could probably be "un-invented." What about people who are economic drains, who do not promote human evolution? Would society be justified in exterminating them? "That's not even a question about morals, it's a question of survival, which I think is above and beyond morals," Steve reasons. "It may be the most horrible thing to exterminate people just for the sake of genes, but it would be the correct thing to do for survival. I don't think it would ever make it okay, but I think it would make it situationally justified. Which is odd." Steve explains that evolution involves self-preservation, which in theory could wipe out contemporary humanistic notions of morality from the universe, "which is a sad thing, really. I wish it didn't have to be that way." But, he says, he does not find such thoughts depressing, but rather "fun to think about and kind of interesting, 'cause, I don't know, I don't really let it bother me." In all of this—lacking recourse to grounding his moral commitments in, say, divine command or natural law—Steve finds himself in the common, intellectually sticky position of many of his teenage and adult contemporaries: asserting high moral standards (e.g., belief in human rights, equality, dignity of life) while possessing few coherent, rational grounds for explaining, justifying, and defending those standards. Thus, Steve began by asserting universal moral facts and human dignity, then quickly shifted to arbitrary individualism ("let each person decide for themselves"), and ended up conceding the rational justification for exterminating entire groups of humans and the extinction of traditional humanistic morality in the name of evolutionary species survival. Of course, nobody expects a 17-year-old to be an articulate moral philosopher. But the apparent lack of clear bearings or firm anchors in Steve's moral reasoning are conspicuous and perhaps worrisome.

More generally, Steve's case highlights some larger themes that emerged in teen interviews. For one, the capacity of adults both to harm and to help adolescents is obvious in Steve's story. American teenagers' own individualism and assertions of autonomy notwithstanding, parents, grandparents, teachers, older friends, family relations, and parents of friends inevitably and profoundly form the lives of the youth they touch—for better and for worse. Adults simply matter tremendously in the lives of teens, both in general and specifically when it comes to religion. Steve's personal rejection of religion, note, is set against the backdrop of an abusive alcoholic grandfather whom Steve describes as "a hard-core Catholic"; a Catholic mother who had had enough religious doubts to not have Steve baptized and who herself later switched into "flakey" New Age experimentation; and a distant, overworked father who seems to have played no religious role in Steve's life. Steve casts the matter of religion in epistemological terms, as an inability to know. But it also appears that for Steve the issue of religious faith and practice is fraught with powerful *emotional* energy that is rooted in problematic relationships. Given his past experiences, it is no wonder sociologically that Steve is not religious. Furthermore, he uses the structure of his current social relations— his antireligious girlfriend, his sustained distance from his Young Life friends' activities, his immersion in his "Dungeons and Dragons" game club—to sustain his nonreligious position. At the same time, Steve is no aggressively iconoclastic agnostic. If other people feel the need to be religious, that's great. If religious beliefs turn out to be true, he's fine with that. If there's a God who stands behind the coincidences, he's open to that possibility. Religion, in Steve's view, can be a help, can provide useful guidelines, can provide people an important foundation. He just does not need that for himself. At the same time, however, when it comes to articulating the guidelines and foundations of his own moral beliefs Steve is rather at sea. He wants to defend a core of traditional, humanistic morality, but he seems to have few resources or reference points for explaining his moral beliefs and so easily gravitates to very different moral ideas. All in all, however, Steve is a very nice kid who has survived some personal griefs and mistakes and is now moving forward into what seems will be a happy, nonreligious young adult life.

Raymond, a fairly scrawny 18-year-old, nonreligious, Native American boy also originally from a middle-class household in the Baltimore area, is in many ways a more religiously open nonreligious teen than Steve is, but, by contrast, is not likely facing such a happy future. I had a very difficult time scheduling Raymond's interview, as he had recently become a transient, living in various friends' houses. When finally arranged, he showed up on time at the public library for his interview—along with four of his buddies, who I then had to inform were not invited to participate in the interview. Raymond struck me in many ways as a good-hearted, likeable kid. But he was also clearly in trouble. A 17-year-old friend, the son of his best friend's mother's boyfriend, started him smoking marijuana at the end of seventh grade. Two years later, Raymond started dealing drugs himself, buying and selling and taking cuts of his own. "A lot of stuff we got right now is from New Hampshire. The guy actually drives it down here and delivers it, there's a whole network set up," he explains. For a while, Raymond was doing crystal meth but realized that that was messing him up, so he quit, limiting himself to smoking pot, drinking hard liquor (beer makes him sick), and smoking cigarettes. Raymond says now he does drugs in moderation: "When I first left home, for the first two months I smoked weed every single day, I was addicted. Then I stopped for two weeks and I was like shaking, getting withdrawals, I'd get pissed off easily, you know, I wouldn't talk to nobody. Then I really wanted to smoke some bud, so my friends would get it and then I'd be happy, you know. But I've tried to cut down a lot on that, too. We can actually have fun being sober, you know." What, I asked, does he like about drugs? "Every time I get high, I'm always happy, I just get in a good mood, just sit there, yeah, talk to my friends, sometimes drive around. It's just hanging out and feeling good, it's a release from everything, you know, from like all the problems I have every day, the daily problems of life."

Raymond was expelled from high school for absenteeism and then dropped out of a special remedial school because he said they were not teaching him anything he didn't already know. "I was like, 'Go to hell you guys, I'm gonna go get my G.E.D.' " At 15, Raymond, high on pot, starting taking his mother's car on joyrides against her will and without a driver's license. His mother eventually called the police and Raymond was arrested, put in jail, and later put on probation. "I didn't know what the heck probation was and I didn't care either. You know really, to be honest, I just kept smoking weed." Raymond has had a hard time landing a job. He has filled out many applications at restaurants and stores, but he does not understand why nobody calls him for an interview. Meanwhile, most of his current friends are school dropouts and also do drugs. At least one, he says, is in "juvie" (Juvenile Detention). The rest have fun hanging out together, cruising in cars downtown, and watching DVDs. Raymond likes to listen to heavy metal music, particularly his favorite band, Metallica. He also watches certain kinds of porn videos. "Porno is stupid shit, gay," he says. "I don't know why people watch it when it's guys having sex with girls. I'll have a picture of girls on my wall or I would watch girls going at it, like just girls, lesbian and stuff, I have videos of that, I like that, but only girls, not with guys, that's stupid, you know. Why would you want to watch that?"

Many of Raymond's troubles seem connected to his anger at his mother and his separation from his father. Raymond was adopted as a baby by parents in a troubled marriage. "I don't know why my mom and dad got married in the first place," Raymond shook his head, " 'cause they don't have anything in common." According to Raymond, when he was 14 years old, his mother decided unilaterally to divorce his father without telling anyone, mailing his father the divorce papers at work. "It sucked. My dad was crying when he told me about it, you know, and it really pissed me off at my mom." Raymond clearly cannot stand his mother, but he adores his father. Unfortunately, his father has moved to Nebraska and Raymond rarely sees him. After the divorce, Raymond fought continually with his mother, whom he viewed as being too strict, and finally she kicked him out of the house. "Her discipline was not effective, 'cause, you know, if I want to do it I'm gonna do it." Raymond's 13-year-old brother and 16-year-old sister have also both run away from home and are on probation after run-ins with the law. Of his sister, he says, "She hates my mom 'cause of the divorce. She'd never come back if she could." Raymond's father, by contrast, is not strict. He is a biker who drinks and sends Raymond soft-porn backgrounds for his computer desktop; his current one, he tells me, is eight topless women in bikini bottoms with hunting rifles slung over their shoulders. When Raymond told his father that he was dealing drugs, Raymond says, "He wasn't pissed. But he was like, 'You better watch out. If you get caught you're going to jail for a long time.' " His dad bought him a Van Halen album when he was 8 years old, which is what originally got him into heavy metal music; his mom's attempt to replace that album with one by Michael Jackson was ineffective. Some of his friends' parents also do not seem to be encouraging him in good directions. A few nights before our interview, for example, Raymond said he had gotten drunk on vodka that a friend's mother, whom he considers a friend and counselor, gave to him.

Raymond did express some regrets for the course his life has taken. "When I first went to high school my understanding was like, 'Wow, this is the time to party, it's high school, everybody's supposed to party in high school.' I don't know, I wish I wouldn't have that thought that, I wish I could have hung out with better people, I kind of wish I would have listened to my mom, like taken her advice." Even now, Raymond says he hopes to sober up and settle down soon. "I've tried to quit dealing 'cause I know I'm gonna get caught if I don't quit. I'm not gonna smoke weed forever. I want to sober up and get my G.E.D." After that, he explains, he wants to join the Army: "I think about my future a few times a week, like, 'Damn, what do I want to do with my life? Do I want to sit around and be a pothead all my life?' Hell no. Sometimes in bad moods or on bad days I just won't care, like I'll sit here and smoke weed forever. Then I'll wake up next morning and think, 'That was dumb.' " Why, I asked, doesn't he simply decide to sober up now? "I don't know," he replied. "I've thought about it, but I kind of look at this as the summer to have fun and party, 'cause I'm 18 years old and I don't have to worry about living under my mom's roof, I can be out as long as I want. So I'm like, 'This will be a summer for fun, I'm gonna party and have fun this summer.' Then after that I just want to sober up and be clean and get my life together and straighten up. But I don't want the future to get here too quick, I want to be able to live life and still have fun, you know."

Raymond considers himself neither a religious nor a spiritual person. His mother has long been a regular churchgoer and he has no interest in following her path. At the same time, he is intrigued by religious questions and struggles to come up with convincing answers for himself. About "that Jesus thing, you know, whether he was actually here or not," Raymond says: "I'll just sit there and think about it and, you know, I can't convince myself of one thing and can't be for sure and it pisses me off 'cause I don't like it. If I don't know something, I don't like it. But I think about this stuff all the time. I just sometimes sit and think about it for hours and hours and [eventually] fall asleep and wake up the next morning. I don't know." About the existence of God, he says, "I believe in God and everything. I don't know if it's God but something that created everything, something higher than all of us. I used to believe in the Big Bang when I was getting stoned, but when I sobered up I knew that was a bunch of crap, I was like, 'that's stupid,' you know, all of a sudden it explodes and here's everything? No, I don't think so." When asked about what God is like, he says he suspects God is something more like a higher power or life force, then adds that he and his friends were just talking the other night about whether God was more forgiving or more judging. "I think it's messed up, some of the things we do. Like we'll sin, then ask him forgiveness and he will forgive, you know, that's what I think. I don't know, I, I don't know." So, Raymond thinks people are sinful? "Yeah, all the time," he says. In general, he thinks religion is a good thing: "You gotta have something to believe in, I mean, where would we be? I think it is pretty good 'cause why would God just create the world and not let us know he's there, you know?" Raymond does not read the Bible but he does pray before meals. "If I'm lucky enough to have food then obviously somebody's watching over me," he observes. He thinks he believes in angels, demons, heaven, hell, but is not entirely sure. He has no interest in any other religions besides Christianity, except for an intellectual interest in ancient Egyptian culture. And psychics and fortune-tellers, he says, are "a bunch of shit, they're full of crap." Raymond also seems to detest Mormon missionaries and violent Muslim extremists. Still, he says, "I'm not gonna go up and tell them that I think it's wrong."

During the interview, it came out that Raymond had recently been sporadically attending a Nazarene church in the area for a few months. A sister of one of his friends, it turns out, is a regular there and invited him to come along with her. Raymond actually seems to like it a great deal. "It's cool," he reports: "It's more structured than my mom's church and they got more things to do. They have teen nights, Wednesday night services, Sunday night church, and that's pretty cool. They have youth group and Sunday school. They have a first service, then Sunday school, then some kind of breakfast thing where kids talk and then get together and discuss what they talked about. It's pretty cool, I like it." In fact, he has invited one of his ex-girlfriends to attend this church with him when she told him that she was interested in going to church somewhere: "I was like, 'All right, I'll take you sometime,' and she's like, 'All right, that will be cool.' " But, he says, his living situation and transportation problems have prevented that from happening yet. Recently, however, he ran into the church's Sunday School director at the mall and had a pleasant conversation with him. "He's cool, yeah, he's cool just to talk to about whatever, you know, ask advice." I asked Raymond whether he actually understood what the Nazarene church was teaching or whether he was mostly there to have a good time. "Yeah," he said, "I understand," explaining: "The last thing they talked about was, what was it? They talked about like when you prune a tree, you know? Like that's what you have to do through life, you have to take the bad things out or whatever. I can't remember exactly what they said, but it made sense, I know. That's what I like about this church, what they say actually makes sense. Unlike my mom's dumb church that talked about the same freaking thing all the time, the same freaking thing, that's what pissed me off. I was like, 'This is dumb.' " Raymond thinks he'll probably continue going to this church. "I've been actually thinking about asking Rich [his friend] if he wanted to start going again with his sister and her friend 'cause they go every Sunday and Wednesday. I know they'd let me go with them. I just don't know, it's just, if I want to, you know. But I've been thinking about that." What exactly, I pressed further, did he find appealing about this church? "It's good people, you know. And not only that, I also actually learn, 'cause like I said I'm not even sure about this stuff and I want to learn more. Like whether you have to go to church to get into heaven or if you can just pray and be a God-fearing person and go to heaven or whatever, you know?" In fact, Raymond has been working on specific questions to which he wants to get answers from church: "I don't know who goes to heaven and hell. Like people that do drugs, I don't know, or like if I were a bum, would a bum go to hell just 'cause he lives on the streets and drinks all the time? I've actually thought of asking some people from that church but I never have gotten around to it, so I don't actually know."

In all of this, Raymond struck me as a confused but sincere person who was at least in part wrestling with questions of truth and goodness. It was clear he had spent time thinking about moral boundaries and the nature of a good life. For instance, he says he attempts somewhat to watch his language: "I try to do good—I don't use the Lord's name in vain or whatever, I know that's a sin. Whether I believe in it or not, I'm not gonna do that, you know, I'll substitute some other word for it." Also, Raymond has volunteered at a local nursing home, doing arts and crafts and puzzles with the elderly residents. "I think it's right," he explains, "it's only fair, 'cause they were here before us and they took care of us so we might as well take care of them." Furthermore, he says he remained a virgin until he was 17 years old. At that point, however, "I tried sex then 'cause people were making fun of me 'cause I was still a virgin at 17." His first sexual intercourse was with a girl he met when he was visiting his father in Nebraska. Since then he's had sex with numerous girls but, he says, he is not like a lot of guys who will have sex with someone right away; he really believes in getting to know someone first, waiting at least two, three, or maybe four months. One of his friends just got a girl pregnant, he said, and when he found out, "I didn't know whether to say 'Congratulations!' or 'I'm sorry,' you know?" Raymond himself is adamant about using condoms to avoid pregnancy and STDs.

In these and many other specific ways, then, Raymond seems always to keep one eye on some kind of moral compass. But he also has little compelling language to draw on to explain *why* he thinks things are right and wrong. For the most part, he simply praises and condemns people and actions as "cool," "stupid," "messed up," "dumb," and as making him "pissed off." His other noticeable approach to moral reasoning is purely consequential: certain things are wrong because they will hurt you if you get caught. "It's gonna come back and kick you in the ass later," he said about why cheating in school (which he did) is wrong. "I don't want to do drugs for the rest of my life, don't want to end up like some people I know," he said in reflecting on what is wrong with doing drugs. In part, Raymond's inarticulacy about morality seems connected to his general inability to see life within any larger meaningful framework. When asked about life's possible larger purpose, about what people are ultimately on earth for, Raymond responded: "Actually, I don't even know, I've thought about it once in a while. I actually don't think there is a point. I think this is hell right now. I guess you just have to live it out to the fullest, you know. It can be a bitch sometimes, it can be cool sometimes." He then mentioned the possibility of some kind of life after death, that "after you pass this then it gets better afterwards." But exactly how or why he's not sure. He summarized his view of life's purpose this way: "Make life good for yourself, you know?"

As to his own life, Raymond hopes someday to own a BMW dealership. "I love cars and BMWs are my favorite car," he explained. "I want to have enough money just to do what I want and have a nice car, like a nice BMW, so I can drive around, and have a fairly nice house that I don't have to make payments on." Raymond subscribes to *Dupont Registry*, a magazine about luxury cars, houses, and boats—something that seems to help keep his dreams alive. He seems unaware, however, that the facts that he has no specific plan for reaching these goals and cannot even get the local Chinese restaurant to hire him as a busboy pose obstacles to the reaching of his career and financial goals. Raymond also says he wants someday to settle down with a woman he can "take care of." But, he explained, he probably does not want to get married, primarily because if he splits up with his woman he would be pissed if she got to take half of his BMW dealership after the divorce. So he and she will probably just live together. Finally, as to his religious future, Raymond says, "I'll probably end up going to church, yeah, probably."

Again, Raymond is not representative of nonreligious U.S. teenagers, any more than is Steve. Yet his story highlights certain themes well worth noting about nonreligious youth. As with the lives of so many other adolescents, the role of the adults has been powerful in shaping Raymond's life generally and his religious and spiritual life specifically. His mother, father, friends' parents, and teachers have profoundly formed his outlook on life and faith. In this process, emotions generated out of positive and negative relationships seem to have played at least as important a role as cognitive beliefs. Raymond's story also illustrates another important theme that emerged from our data: the lives of self-described nonreligious teenagers actually often contain at least some religious interests, questions, practices, ethics, and values. Even a religious faith rejected can exercise a grip on the thoughts, feelings, and desires of youth. This observation connects to yet another theme: the majority of nonreligious U.S. adolescents are not particularly antireligious. Most are fairly appreciative of religion's value, even if they do not wish to appropriate it for themselves, and hold very little animosity against religion per se. Raymond hated his mother's church, but that did not make him globally antireligious. Indeed, he was quite willing to try a new church recommended by a friend's sister, which he found, upon attending, was quite intriguing. Our interviews in general suggest that this is not unusual. It could be that many U.S. adolescents currently disengaged from organized religion could be drawn through the attention and invitations of relationships into the life of religious communities with good programs for teenagers—perhaps just as readily as similar and other forces pull teens away from religious communities. Many American youth may be more receptive to the invitations and teachings of communities of faith than many such communities likely realize.

A final notable theme that Raymond's story, like Steve's, illustrates is the difficulty that many teens, but especially nonreligious teens, have in understanding and articulating what it is exactly that makes right and wrong right and wrong. The vocabulary and ideas on which Raymond draws to make sense of moral thought and behavior are impoverished. As such, in navigating the troubled waters of his own life, he seems able to express only subjective, rather arbitrary feelings and reactions to explain his own moral experience and sensibilities. Overall, he seems to be a disarranged young man lacking helpful adult guidance in his life. His circumstances and choices have placed him in a difficult position in life with fairly bleak prospects for the future. Even so, Raymond is hearing messages that intrigue him about the need to prune bad parts from trees so they will produce good fruit. Whether he draws closer to the source of those messages, however, remains to be seen.

Nonattending Teens

Not all religiously disengaged American teenagers think of themselves in identity terms as not religious. Another type of religiously disengaged youth consists of those who never attend religious services, whether or not they hold some nominal religious identity as, say, Catholic or Jewish or just Christian. What do the 18 percent of American teens who never attend religious services look like? Who are these teens who never darken the door of a church, synagogue, mosque, or temple? According to the findings in table 30, a full 43 percent of them think of themselves as part of a religious denomination or tradition. Thus, never attending religious services does not equate in the minds of many teens with being nonreligious. Or, stated differently, and as we saw in table 24 earlier, most teenagers do not think that being religious means that one has to attend religious services. For many, being religious and attending services are often disconnected matters.

Do teenagers who never attend *want* to attend religious services, or are they happy never to attend? According to table 30, nearly one-quarter of never-attending teens report that if it were totally up to them they would like to attend religious services regularly, that is, two or three times a month or more often. Another 10 percent say they would like to attend once a month. Sixty-one percent say they would like to attend only a few times a year or never. If we believe these reports, it appears that a substantial minority of teens who never attend services would actually like to attend religious services regularly: 34 percent say once a month or more often. Moreover, when asked whether they expect to attend religious services when they are 25 years old, a strong majority of never-attending teens (63 percent) say yes or maybe. Only 37 percent say definitely no.

So why do they not attend more? Nearly two-thirds of American teens who never attend services have been invited by someone to attend religious services in the prior two years. There appears to be no correlation (analysis not shown) between wanting to attend religious services more often than never and having been invited to attend religious services in the previous two years: those who want to attend services a lot more but do not are just as likely to get invited as not. Thus, nonattenders' never attending services cannot be fully explained by nobody reaching out and inviting them. Nor can it be entirely explained by unsupportive parents, as 24 percent of survey respondent parents of nonattending teens say that they attend religious services themselves once a month or more (unless, of course, some of these parents are overreporting their attendance). Nor can it be explained by a lack of experiential familiarity with religious service attendance. According to their retrospective accounts, shown in table 30, fully 27 percent of nonattending teens have regularly attended religious services for one or two years since they were 6 years old, and another 50 percent regularly attended services for three years or more since they were 6. Only 8 percent of nonattenders have

Table 30. Characteristics of U.S. Adolescents, Ages 13–17,
Not Currently Attending Religious Services (Percentages)

Nonattenders who still think of themselves as part of a religion, denomination, or church	43
How often nonattenders would attend religious services if totally up to them	
More than once a week	4
Once a week	11
2–3 times a month	9
Once a month	10
Many times a year	4
A few times a year	31
Never	30
Expects to attend services regularly at age 25	
Yes	16
Maybe	47
No	37
Invited to attend a religious service in prior 2 years	63
Parent attends monthly or more often	24
Years regularly attended religious services since age 6	
0	8
1	10
2	17
3	15
4	15
5	9
6	10
7+	11
Don't know/refused	5
Feelings about religion in the United States	
Very positive	12
Somewhat positive	37
Neither positive nor negative	32
Somewhat negative	11
Very negative	6
Don't know/refused	2

Source: National Survey of Youth and Religion, 2002–3.

Note: Percentages may not add to 100 due to rounding.

never regularly attended religious services since they were 6. Nonattending teenagers are thus not a people devoid of experience attending religious services. So why do they not attend more regularly? Is it because they harbor negative feelings toward religion in general? No. When asked about their personal feelings toward religion in the United States, nonattending teens were generally positive, as shown in table 30. About half (49 percent) of nonattending teens feel very or somewhat positive about religion in the United States; about one-third feel neutral; and 17 percent feel negative about American religion, and of those, 6 percent feel very negative. Thus, a prevailing hostility against religion generally does not explain these teens' lack of religious service attendance.

So, again, if many nonattenders profess to want to attend religious services more often, why don't they? The NSYR asked them directly: we asked religious teens who in earlier years had attended religious services more often than a few times a year but who at the time of the survey were not attending services regularly, "Is there any particular reason why you stopped attending religious services regularly?" Their answers, combined with those of the nonreligious teens represented in table 28—who were not asked this question because their answers were anticipated to be "Because I became not religious"—are presented in table 31. There we find relatively few teens offering substantive antireligious reasons for declining religious service attendance. Forty-one percent simply could think of no reason why they stopped attending religious services as much as they had been attending, and 17 percent said they were simply disinterested or bored. Thirteen percent attributed their declining attendance to life transitions and disruptions—mostly moving to new locations or parents divorcing; 5 percent said their parents stopped taking them to religious services; and 4 percent reported availability problems, such as lack of transportation. Three percent said they simply felt no religious needs. Only 17 percent of these teens (about 3 percent of all teens) reported a religiously skeptical or hostile reason for reducing their service attendance to a few times a year or less often: 11 percent said they stopped believing or had never believed the teachings of their congregation, and 6 percent reported some bad experience or personal dislike for religion generally as their explanation for stopping attending religious services regularly.

We cannot be certain that these accounts represent the "true" reasons behind these teens' declining religious service attendance. But insofar as they are roughly valid and reliable, we can conclude that only a small minority of American teens who have gone from being at least somewhat regular religious service attenders to attending only a few times a year or never have been motivated to do so by an active hostility toward, skepticism of, or negative

Table 31. Reasons Nonattending U.S. Adolescents, Ages 13–17, Who Once Attended Religious Services Stopped Attending (Percentages)

No reason or don't know	41
Disinterest	17
Life transition or disruption	13
Teen disbelief	11
Bad experience with or dislikes religion	6
Parental nonsupport	5
Availability problem	4
No felt religious need	3

Source: National Survey of Youth and Religion, 2002–3.

Note: Percentages may not add to 100 due to rounding.

experience with church, synagogue, mosque, or temple. The great majority instead either have no apparent reason, are just not interested, have been dislodged from regular attendance by some other life disruption, have some availability or transportation problem, or just feel no need for religious meetings—all fairly nonchalant motivations for religious disengagement. Again, we see relatively little active rebellion or animosity directed toward religious practice by even religiously disengaged teenagers. Instead, they appear rather passively to see religion as simply not that important or much of a priority. They seem to find little that is attractive or compelling about practicing a religious faith in a congregation.

Can we specify more clearly the social locations of low-attending and nonattending teens? Results of regression analyses show the following variables to be significantly associated, while controlling for the effects of other variables, with American teens attending religious services only rarely or never:

☙ *Parent religiosity*: Teens with parents who attend religious services less often and for whom faith is less important are more likely than teens whose parents attend more often and for whom faith is more important to attend religious services only rarely or never.

☙ *Relationship with parents*: Teens who say their parents do not understand, love, or pay attention to them are more likely than teens who say their parents do understand, love, and pay attention to them to attend religious services only rarely or never.

☙ *Parent education*: Teens with less educated parents are more likely than teens with more educated parents to attend religious services only rarely or never.

☙ *Age*: Older teens are more likely than younger teens to attend religious services only rarely or never.

☙ *Organized activities*: Teens involved in fewer programs, clubs, hobby groups, sports, or other organized activities are more likely than teens in more organized activities to attend religious services only rarely or never.

☙ *Negative peer influences*: Teens whose parents say their friends have a negative influence on their teens' lives are more likely than teens whose parents say they have a positive influence to attend religious services only rarely or never.

☙ *Close friends*: Teens with fewer close friends involved in a religious youth group or any other religious group they themselves are involved in are more likely than teens with more friends in religious groups to attend religious services only rarely or never.

❧ *Importance of faith*: Teens for whom faith is less important in their daily lives than other teens are more likely to attend religious services only rarely or never.

❧ *Lower desired attendance*: Teens who would like to attend religious services less often than they do are more likely than those who would like to attend more often to attend religious services only rarely or never.

❧ *Race*: White teens are more likely than black teens to attend religious services only rarely or never.

❧ *Regional location*: Teens who live in the Northeast are more likely than those living in the South and Midwest to attend religious services only rarely or never.

Parental influences again appear to be important in differentiating low-attending from more frequently attending American teens. Low-attending teenagers are more likely to have parents who themselves reflect low levels of religiosity, who are relatively less educated, and who their teens say do not give them enough attention, love, and understanding. Stated differently, teenagers with parents who are more religious, who are better educated, and who are perceived as expressing more love for, attention to, and understanding of their adolescents are more likely to attend religious services more regularly. As with nonreligious teens, youth who are low religious service attenders also tend to be older and so tend to enjoy greater personal freedom from their parents. Their parents are also more apt to say that their friends are a bad influence in their teens' lives—again, often a sign of strained relationships between parents and teens. Low-attending teens are also, as we would expect, less likely to have friends involved in religious groups, to say that faith is important in their lives, and to want to attend religious services. Like nonreligious teens, they also tend to be generally less involved not only in religious congregations, but in all types of organized activities, groups, and programs. Low-attending teens tend to be disproportionately white compared to black and living in the Northeast compared to the South and Midwest. An attempt to draw any picture of low-attending American teenagers, then, would likely depict them as older, raised in low religion and lower education households, experiencing greater strain in their parental relationships, relationally disconnected from religious and other kinds of youth organizations and programs, and having friends who may be more likely to be in trouble. Although there are certainly many well-adjusted American adolescents who do not attend religious services regularly, as a whole, low-attending American teens, like the nonreligious teens, appear to reflect at least some likely signs of family strain and general civic and organizational disconnection.

RELIGIOUSLY DEVOTED TEENAGERS

At the other end of the spectrum from the religiously disengaged teenagers are the highly religiously active. What factors associate with American adolescents attending religious services more often, reporting faith as more important in their lives, and participating in religious youth groups?[8] Table 32 reports the results of regression analyses of these three key measures of adolescent religiosity. Only the associations that are statistically significant after controlling for the possible effects of all other variables examined are noted as positive or negative. Here we see a number of factors that correlate with higher teenage religiosity. While controlling for all other variables in the columns, we see that evangelical and black Protestant and Mormon youth are higher than mainline Protestant youth in religious service attendance and importance of faith. Catholic and black Protestant teens and those from other minority religions are less likely than mainline Protestant teens to participate in a religious youth group. And nonreligious youth are, as expected, lower than mainline Protestants on all three measures of youth religiosity. Table 32 also shows that more frequent religious service attendance, greater importance of faith, teens' personal desire to attend religious services, and youth group participation are all significantly associated with each other. They generally all hang together as religious practices that increase and decrease with each other among more and less religious youth. Parental religious service attendance and importance of faith also exhibits a consistent effect on teenage religiosity: the more religious parents are, the more religious their teens tend to be.

Table 32 also suggests that certain other social variables associate with teen religiosity. Teens who are involved in more organized activities, programs, and groups are also more likely to attend religious services more often and to participate in religious youth groups. All three measures of religiosity are positively associated with teens having higher proportions of their closest friends in their religious groups, which may, of course, be both a cause and an effect of their own higher religiosity. Teens who say that their parents love, accept, and understand them are also more likely to have faith be important in their daily lives and to be part of a religious youth group. And teens whose parents monitor their lives more closely are also more likely to score higher on service attendance and importance of faith. On the other hand, it is less likely that faith is important in the daily lives of teens who say their parents do not give them enough freedom to develop and express their own views on important issues.

Finally, some demographic variables associate with teen religiosity even after controlling for the examined religious and social factors. Girls are more likely than boys and younger teens are more likely than older teens to say faith is important in their daily lives. Black youth are more likely than white to score higher on all three measures of religiosity, even after controlling for black Protestant religious tradition.[9] Teens whose residential parent lives with an unmarried partner are less likely than teens with married parents to participate in a religious youth group, just as teens with divorced or widowed

Table 32. Factors Associated with Increased Adolescent Religiosity, U.S. Adolescents, Ages 13–17

Tested Variables	More Frequent Religious Service Attendance	Greater Importance of Faith	Youth Group Participation
Religious Variables			
Religious Tradition			
Evangelical Protestant	Positive	Positive	
Mainline Protestant*			
Black Protestant	Positive	Positive	Negative
Catholic			Negative
Jewish			
Mormon	Positive	Positive	
Other religion			Negative
Not religious	Negative	Negative	Negative
Teen Personal Religiosity			
Religious service attendance	—	Positive	Positive
Importance of faith	Positive	—	Positive
Desired service attendance	Positive	Positive	Positive
Parent Personal Religiosity			
Attendance/Importance	Positive	Positive	Positive
Social Variables			
Time Demand Factors			
Number teen organized activities	Positive		Positive
Hours teen works paid job			
Peer Influences			
Number of friend ties to faith	Positive	Positive	Positive
Friends a positive influence in life			
Parental Relationship Issues			
Parents love, accept, understand teen		Positive	Positive
Parents monitor teen's life	Positive	Positive	
History of marital breakups			
Parents give too much freedom to think and express themselves			
Parents give too little freedom to think and express themselves		Negative	
Parents give the right amount of expressive freedom*			
Demographic Variables			
Teen is female		Positive	
Teen age older		Negative	
Teen Race			
White*			
Black	Positive	Positive	Positive
Hispanic			
Asian			
Other race			
Family Structure			
Married*			
Never married			
Unmarried partner			Negative
Divorced		Negative	
Widowed		Negative	
Separated			

(*continued*)

Table 32. Factors Associated with Increased Religiosity (*continued*)

Tested Variables	More Frequent Religious Service Attendance	Greater Importance of Faith	Youth Group Participation
Parents' education	Positive		
Higher family income		Negative	
Number of teens in household			
Region of Residence			
Northeast*			
South		Positive	Positive
Midwest			Positive
West/Pacific			Positive
Residential Context			
Rural*			
Suburban			
Urban			
Parental political conservativism			

Source: National Survey of Youth and Religion, 2002–3.

Note: * =Reference group.

parents are less likely to say faith is important in their lives. Teens with more highly educated parents tend to attend religious services more often, although teens in higher-income families tend to say faith is less important in their lives. Finally, youth from all other areas of the country are more likely than those in the Northeast to be in a religious youth group, and those who live in the South also score higher on importance of faith.

In sum, we see that the religiosity of American youth is conditioned by a variety of religious, cultural, and relational factors. Although American teenagers may not be able to see, understand, or articulate such influences on their lives, it is nonetheless clear that certain faith traditions, social relationships, and cultural identities and locations shape their religious lives significantly.

The Most Highly Devoted

Another way to examine factors shaping religiously committed teens is by focusing on the most highly devoted among them: the 8 percent who believe in God, attend religious services weekly or more often, for whom faith is extremely important in their lives, who regularly participate in religious youth groups, and who pray and read the Bible regularly. Kristen in chapter 1 is an example of this kind of teen. But who are these highly religiously devoted teens more generally? What social and personal factors distinguish them from other American youth? As with the analyses above, we used regression techniques to examine the influences of a variety of religious and social variables while controlling for the effects of all of the others to identify which factors are statistically significantly associated with being a religiously devoted teenager, as defined just above. The results reveal these factors as significantly associated, which generally reinforces the findings of the previous analysis:

🪶 *Parent religiosity*: Teens with parents who attend religious services more often and for whom faith is more important are more likely than teens whose parents attend less often and for whom faith is less important to be religiously devoted.

🪶 *Relationship with parents*: Teens who say their parents tend to understand, love, or pay attention to them more, compared to teens who say their parents tend not to understand, love, and pay attention to them, are more likely to be religiously devoted.

🪶 *Parental marital status*: Teens with married parents are more likely than teens with divorced parents to be religiously devoted.

🪶 *Parent education*: Teens with more highly educated parents are more likely than teens with less educated parents to be religiously devoted.

🪶 *Organized activities*: Teens involved in more programs, clubs, hobby groups, sports, or other organized activities are more likely than teens in fewer organized activities to be religiously devoted.

🪶 *Religious tradition*: Evangelical and Mormon teens are more likely than are mainline Protestants to be religiously devoted, and Catholic teens are less likely than mainline Protestants to be devoted.

🪶 *Higher desired attendance*: Teens who themselves would like to attend religious services more often are more likely than those who would like to attend less often to be religiously devoted.

🪶 *Close friends*: Teens with more close friends involved in a religious youth group or any other religious group they themselves may be involved in are more likely than teens with fewer friends in religious groups to be religiously devoted, although this is likely as much a result as a cause of being religiously devoted.

🪶 *Peer influences*: Teens whose parents say their friends have a positive influence on their teens' lives are more likely than teens whose parents say they have a negative influence to be religiously devoted, although this may be as much a consequence as a cause of being religiously devoted.

🪶 *Teen gender*: Girls are more likely than boys to be religiously devoted.

🪶 *Race*: White teens are more likely than black and Hispanic teens to be religiously devoted.[10]

Here we see once again that parents have an important influence on the shape of their teenagers' religious lives. Teens are more likely to be religiously devoted—as measured by this conglomeration of variables—who have more highly religious parents, who have positive and loving relationships with their parents, and whose parents are married.[11] Better-educated parents are also more likely to have religiously devoted teens. Religiously devoted youth also tend to be more broadly involved in a variety of organized groups, programs, and activities; thus religious devotion and involvement in many other kinds of organizations seems to go together in a larger life package of participation and engagement. Teens from religious traditions that are relatively demanding—conservative Protestantism and Mormonism—which also are most likely to offer organized religious youth groups (see table 14 in chapter 2), tend to be more religiously devoted, and Catholic teens tend to be less devoted. Religiously devoted teens want to attend religious services frequently and have a strong personal attraction to life in religious congregation. They also have more close friends in the religious groups in which they are involved and their parents believe their friends are a good influence on their teens' lives, although, as noted above, these are likely as much consequences as causes of teen religious devotion. Finally, girls, who in general are more religious than boys, and white teens, compared to black and Hispanic teens, are more likely to be religiously devoted. Thus, teenage religious devotion is not randomly distributed, but tends to be identifiably socially located in specific types of families, religious traditions, friendship networks, orientations to participation, and gender and racial identities.

Religious on Their Own

There are many other potential ways to examine religious devotion among American adolescents, most of which are beyond the scope of this chapter to explore. Here, however, we do examine one other group of religiously devoted youth: those who attend religious services without their parents. We know that parental attendance is a powerful predictor of teen attendance, but what about teens who do not appear to be encouraged by their parents' attendance? Which teens, that is, among those not accompanied by one or both of their parents—either because their parents do not attend at all or attend services of a different religion or congregation—attend more services on their own? What factors among this group differentiate those who attend religious services more and less? Of all teens not attending religious services with one or two parents, after controlling for many standard demographic variables, the following factors stand out as significantly associated with more frequent attendance:

◆ *Popularity at school*: Teens who say they are part of the popular group at school are more likely than those not part of the popular group to attend religious services without parents more often.

◆ *Organized activities*: Teens in more programs, clubs, hobby groups, sports, or other organized activities are more likely than teens in fewer organized activities to attend religious services without parents more often.

👄 *Regional location*: Teens living in the South and Midwest are more likely than those living in the Northeast to attend religious services without parents more often.

👄 *Religious tradition*: Teens in the conservative and black Protestant traditions are more likely than teens in mainline Protestantism to attend religious services without parents more often; self-identified nonreligious teens are less likely.

👄 *Youth group participation*: Teens who are involved in a religious youth group are more likely than those who are not to attend religious services without parents more often.

👄 *Religious youth activities*: Teens who have participated in more religious youth activities—such as religious missions teams, summer camps, social service projects, and retreats—are more likely than those who have participated less to attend religious services without parents more often, although it is unclear whether this is a cause or a result of greater attendance.

When teenagers do not have parents with whom to attend religious services, other social factors can nonetheless encourage and discourage their frequency of attendance. One appears to be the sociability and confidence of teens as reflected in their greater popularity at school and involvement in a larger number of organized activities. More popular and active teens appear more ready, willing, and able to attend religious services on their own. Another factor is simply living in the South or Midwest, both regions that supply relatively more religious congregations per capita and reflect greater normative acceptability of religious service attendance. Conservative and black Protestant churches also appear to do a relatively better job of drawing teens to church who are not accompanied by their parents. Finally, more frequent religious service attendance without parents is also significantly associated with greater involvement by teens in religious youth groups and other religious youth activities, although we cannot be sure if these are the causes or effects of more frequent service attendance. Among these variables, the most robust are teens' youth group involvement, experience with religious camps and retreats, and conservative Protestant affiliation.

We pressed this analysis of independently attending teens one step further, narrowing down to only those teens who do attend religious services at least more than once or twice a year and thus have a tie to a specific religious congregation, some characteristics of which they are able to report. Which variables significantly predicted greater religious service attendance for this population of teens who attend without their parents? Involvement in more organized activities, in religious youth groups, and with religious camps and missions trips remain significantly associated with their more frequent service attendance. The presence of any designated youth minister in the teen's congregation is also statistically associated with increased teen attendance without parents. However, a closer analysis shows that only the presence of a *full-time* youth minister in the congregation, compared to no designated youth minister at all, significantly increases these teens' attendance. Congregations with only volunteer and part-time youth ministers are not significantly different from those with no designated youth minister in increasing the attendance of teens who do not attend with their parents, when other variables are controlled for. Thus, we see that religious service attendance of independent youth is significantly increased by key institutional factors, particularly by religious youth groups led by full-time youth ministers who can create the kind of relationships and programs that draw youth who do not otherwise have parental support to attend into greater attendance at religious congregations.

Alyssa's Spiritual Mother and Father

The importance of dedicated youth ministers in the lives of teens lacking parental support in faith as evident in the survey analysis above is illustrated in the story of Alyssa, a 15-year-old white girl we interviewed in Milwaukee, Wisconsin, the only member of her family who regularly attends church. Alyssa's mother died of cancer when she was 6, and she and her three siblings have been raised by their father in an urban, blue-collar neighborhood. When Alyssa's mother died, her father stopped attending church: "I think it was a big push when my mom was with it too and it was easier to go along because he had a companion, but I guess now he feels like it's a waste of time. But I still go and I love it." Alyssa says that at her church she enjoys what she calls her "spiritual mother and father":

> It's like real parents, except in a different way. My real dad supports me with money and stuff like that, but these are parents that you can actually talk to like friends. They are very helpful, like when I can't go to my dad on certain things 'cause he won't understand it, I go to them. They're very understanding, but at the same time, if you know better and still do something, they'll tell you what's wrong with that and rebuke you. It's very helpful just to have someone like that around. My spiritual mother, she's very motivated and determined for everything, she'll just go after what she wants, and it's always good things she wants so it's not like a bad motivation. She's just a woman of God, she's really cool. Ever since [we met] she's just been counseling me.

Alyssa says her sister brought her to this church's youth group when she was getting "into drugs and stuff." She says her life without the youth group would be very different because she would probably still be doing drugs. What does she enjoy about her youth group? "Friendships, a lot of friendships, a lot of people who care about you, not because of who you are but they just care about you automatically. It's like so cool." Alyssa also has other support beyond her family for her life and faith. About the teachers at her Christian school, for example, she says, "I love them all. A lot of them have been through a lot in their life and now they're Christians so they tell us testimonies and it's helpful just to hear that they went through something [hard], too, you know? One teacher, she's been really like a mother-figure, too." In addition, Alyssa says that many of her good friends also attend her church and that they talk about faith matters a lot, because she explains, "we have this thing at my church called 'accountability partners.' "

We would expect Alyssa's father's lack of interest in religion and the untimely death of her mother, which Alyssa says caused much grief and trouble in her own life—anger, rebellion, drug abuse, and early sexual activity with many partners—to work against Alyssa's religious faith. Yet it appears that a set of important and densely connected social ties, at the center of which stand her youth group leaders, has come in her middle teenage years to provide her with emotional support and relational connections to a serious, committed life of faith.

CONCLUSION

Spiritual seekers, the religiously disengaged, and the religiously devoted— three interesting and religiously important types of American teenagers. What have we learned about who these various types of teens are and what factors associate with their religious identities and choices? There is much that might be said, but at the very least the following observations seem to stand out:

• The majority of American teenagers appear to espouse rather inclusive, pluralistic, and individualistic views about religious truth, identity boundaries, and need for religious congregation. A significant minority of U.S. teens do hold fairly particularistic attitudes on these matters, but most tend in their attitudes to be fairly liberal, relativistic, and open to differences among religious types. When it comes to their thinking about what is legitimate for other people, most affirm pluralism, religious inclusivity, and individual authority. This is true for notable percentages of teens even in America's more conservative and strict religious traditions.

• Very few American teenagers, however, appear *themselves* to be active spiritual seekers who think of themselves as spiritual but not religious and actually incorporate spiritual practices of other faiths into their own lives. We estimate their number to be about 2 to 3 percent of all U.S. 13- to 17-year-olds. Thus, while most U.S. teens hold the attitude that *other* people should be free to mix and match religious traditions and spiritual practices, almost none of them are actually interested in doing that themselves. Most appear content, rather, to identify with and practice only one religious faith.

• Parents of teenagers appear to play an important role in the character of their children's religious lives. In the immediacy of parenting teenagers, parents may feel a loss of control and influence over their teens, but nationally representative statistics show that the religious practices and commitments of parents remain an important influence on the religious practices and commitments of their teenage children. Family socialization generally seems to work when it comes to teenagers' religious faith and practice. Furthermore, the quality of relationships that parents build with their teenagers and their own choices about marriage relationships, education, and occupations—insofar as they have choices in these areas—also create family contexts that again form the outcome of their teenagers' religious and spiritual lives.

☙ Teenagers' friendships seem related to their religious lives in important, if not always unexpected, ways. Greater and lesser adolescent religiosity appears to be reflected in the composition of friendship groups: the more religiously serious and involved a teen is, unsurprisingly, the more their good friends also seem to be. Moreover, parents of less religious U.S. teenagers are more likely to say that their teens' friends are a negative influence on them, while parents of religiously devoted teens think their teens' friends are a positive influence. We do not know how much of this is the cause or effect of more and less teen religiosity or even a reflection of problematic parent-teen relationships. But we can say that the character of American teenage religion and spirituality has a definite social component or correlation that varies with levels of teen religiosity.

☙ American adolescent religion and spirituality appear to be significantly related to a larger propensity to get involved in a broader range of other organized social activities. U.S. teens who are more religiously serious and active are also more likely to be involved in a larger number of other programs, clubs, hobby groups, sports, or other organized activities; less religiously active teens tend to be involved in fewer. This may reflect differences in personality types, general family orientations toward social involvements, the encouragement and facilitation of religious organizations to get involved in other groups, or some other factor; our data are not able to determine this. But U.S. adolescent religiousness clearly does seem related to a positive propensity toward broader social involvements.

☙ Certain religious traditions in the United States appear more or less capable of eliciting serious, multifaceted religious devotion in their teenagers. Conservative Protestantism and Mormonism seem especially likely and Catholicism appears particularly unlikely to produce highly religiously devoted teenagers (all compared to mainline Protestantism).

☙ Very many religiously disengaged American teenagers appear to be religiously disconnected for what seem to be rather vague or unremarkable reasons. Many cannot explain their disengagement from religion; many seem simply to have drifted. Only a minority of them report definite skepticism, disbelief, or dislike of religion as explanations for their personal religious disengagement. In other words, many religiously disengaged U.S. teens may in fact have fairly low levels of commitment to and investment in their religious disengagement, and so may be more susceptible to religious engagement by proactive religious agents than may be commonly supposed.

☙ In the absence of parental encouragement by example to attend religious services, religious congregations that offer teenagers organized youth groups—particularly those with full-time, paid, adult youth group leaders— seem to make a significant difference in attracting teens to attend congregational religious services. Well-developed, congregational-based youth groups with established youth leaders likely provide teens who lack active parental support appealing doorways into and relational ties encouraging greater religious participation in the life of religious congregations.

As was true of the conclusions of the previous chapter, these observations do not exhaust the details of what we have learned in this chapter's analysis. Nor do they come close to describing all there is to know about American teenage spiritual seekers, nonreligious teens, nonattending teens, and highly religiously devoted teens. There is much room for further research on these types of U.S. adolescents. But this chapter's analysis is a start, we believe, that can begin to fill out our picture of key aspects of the religious and spiritual lives of American teens. What is clear, among other things, is that adolescent religiosity is socially patterned. How religiously serious and involved American teenagers are is not merely randomly or individually determined, but reflects the influence of particular social locations and especially key social relationships and organizations. Parents, friends, youth organizations, religious congregations, and youth group leaders all appear to have significant influence on the shape and extent of American teenagers' religious and spiritual lives.

Beneath our survey measures of factors such as religious service attendance, religious devotion, spiritual seeking, and the like, lay multiple layers of complicated religious and spiritual meanings, perceptions, experiences, assumptions, and feelings that require different research methods to adequately access and interpret. To make better sense of our NSYR survey statistics and findings, therefore, we followed up a subsample of our survey respondents with in-depth, personal interviews conducted in the cities and towns around the country where they actually live. Returning somewhat to and greatly expanding on the method and tone of chapter 1—where we pondered the stories of the two Baptist girls, Joy and Kristen—the next chapter explores in much greater detail what religious faith and spiritual life looks, sounds, and feels like from the perspective and in the words of these teenagers themselves. The systematic, interpretive analysis of hundreds of teen interviews in the following chapter should add greater depth to, more complex meaning around, and clearer understanding of the significance of the survey findings examined in this and the previous chapter. In what follows, the overall picture painted so far becomes more complicated and, from the perspective of many religious traditions, probably more troubling, as the voices of teens explain just what they mean by God, faith, and religion.

4

God, Religion, Whatever

On Moralistic Therapeutic Deism

THERE IS NO SUBSTITUTE for talking with someone for a long time if you hope to understand him or her. Surveys are very useful for providing big-picture descriptions of and sorting out associations between different variables in human life and society. But surveys alone rarely provide enough insight to really understand people's lives. To get beyond the surface descriptions that surveys provide, to get to the important experiences, feelings, contradictions, processes, and complex layers of meaning in most people's lives requires using other methods, such as directly observing and talking with people at length. To better understand the lives of U.S. teenagers, therefore, we traveled around the country to the rural areas, towns, and cities where many of the teens we surveyed live—to 267 teens in 45 states, to be exact, as shown by the map in figure 1—and sat down and talked with these teens at length about many subjects. We also took notes on observations we made about many of the teens we interviewed: about their neighborhoods, interactions with parents, clothing, attitudes, whatever seemed worth noting.

In this chapter we report on what we found, exploring a variety of key themes around adolescent religion and spirituality that emerged from our in-depth interviews. Here we provide an important clarifying follow-up to the survey data presented in the two previous chapters, broadening, deepening, and sharpening our understanding. Much of what follows significantly qualifies the survey numbers we examined earlier; some of it helps us better interpret or put into context the numbers above; and some of it pushes well past what the survey questions addressed. In all cases, the survey findings should be interpreted in light of this chapter's interview findings, as the interview findings must be framed by the survey findings. We need to combine every methodological means at our disposal to portray as complete a sociological picture as possible of the religious and spiritual lives of American teenagers.

The analysis that follows is organized around a number of major themes emerging from our 267 teen interviews. Each of the themes highlights a dominant tendency among U.S. teenagers on various concerns. Each thematic central tendency is also typically flanked on two sides by minority voices representing alternative experiences and views. We thus represent both the typical teen voice that surfaced in our interview discussions, as well as a range of divergent perspectives.

NOT A BIG DEAL

Perhaps the most widespread and persistent stereotype about teenagers in American culture is that they are intractably rebellious. In U.S. culture, the very ideas of "teenagers" and "rebellion" are virtually synonymous. Decades of psychological theorizing about adolescents in the twentieth century, based primarily on observation of adolescent psychological patients, not coincidentally, portrayed the teenage years as inevitably rocked by "storm and stress." For decades, experts taught that adolescence is a time of radical identity change, emotional upheaval, and relational conflict. Thus, in the late 1950s, Sigmund Freud's psychologist daughter, Anna Freud, wrote about teenagers, "To be normal during the adolescent period is by itself abnormal."[1] By the late 1960s and early 1970s, the youth and adults of an entire era came to understand themselves as caught in the crisis of a "generation gap."[2] In more recent decades, adolescents have been habitually framed as "alien creatures" from another planet, who inhabit a "teenage wasteland" and whose rebellion and craziness parents and other adults can only attempt to "survive."[3] Teens today are also framed as "monsters among us," psychopathic freaks driven by "raging hormones" and teetering on the knife edge of frenzied, violent destruction.[4] Although academic adolescent researchers have more recently come significantly to revise this picture of normal adolescence,[5] many books about teenagers and religion continue to employ the "storm and stress" master frame in ways that set teenagers' religious values and interests in opposition to those of adults. They depict youth as "alone," "disillusioned," "irreverent," uniquely "postmodern," belonging to something that is "next" and "new," and "in search of an authentic faith" different from that of existing adult religion, which simply "isn't cutting it."[6] Such stereotypical cultural frames lead to the clear impression that, when it comes to faith and religion, contemporary teenagers are deeply restless, alienated, rebellious, and determined to find something that is radically different from the faith in which they were raised.

But that impression is fundamentally wrong. What we learned by interviewing hundreds of different kinds of teenagers all around the country is that the vast majority of American teenagers are *exceedingly conventional* in their religious identity and practices. Very few are restless, alienated, or rebellious; rather, the majority of U.S. teenagers seem basically content to follow the faith of their families with little questioning. When it comes to religion, they are quite happy to go along and get along. The popular images of storm and stress, generation gap, and teen rebellion may describe the religious orientations and experiences of most teenagers of prior generations, but they do not accurately portray the religious realities of most teenagers in the United States today.

"Just How I Was Raised"

Teenage religious conventionality is most evident in the way contemporary U.S. teens talk about their own religious identity, interests, and beliefs and where these come from. The vast majority of the teenagers we interviewed, of whatever religion, said very plainly that they simply believe what they were raised to believe; they are merely following in their family's footsteps and that is perfectly fine with them. This typical mentality is evident in the following exchange with a 16-year-old white mainline Protestant boy from Oregon (I stands for interviewer, T for teen):

I: Okay, where do you think you get your ideas of what God's like?
T: From my parents.
I: From your parents.
T: What they've told me.
I: And have your parents told you very much about that, or . . . ?
T: No, just kind of what I've figured from them.
I: Okay. And what religion, if any, do you consider yourself to be now?
T: Christian.

For most of the teens we interviewed, many of their answers to our religion questions were just as cut-and-dried as that. To the vast majority of teenagers, it was obvious that a teenager would naturally follow and believe what his or her parents believe. When asked how his beliefs compare to his parents', for instance, this 13-year-old black Protestant boy from Ohio answered, "Not different. I don't know what I'm gonna believe in [the future]. I'm guessing they're just going to be what my parents do, but that's about it." Similarly, when asked about religious influences in his life, this 15-year-old white conservative Protestant boy from Texas responded, "Like I said, I grew up with it, in a Christian home and it's always been that." And this 14-year-old East Indian Hindu girl from California said the most important influences in her life are "My parents, mostly, because I look at them and want to be like them."

Some teens, such as this 14-year-old black Protestant girl from Pennsylvania, were more conscious and appreciative of their parental religious socialization: "I was raised Christian. My mom is a sucker about God, oh my goodness, everything you say, she says, 'Take it to God, take it to Jesus,' and I do it and it works. I'm a Christian, she is a Christian. She has raised me right. She says, 'That's what God wants you to do,' then you do it. She wants me to be the best I can be, but also to know that the way you live has to be a Christian way." When we asked if her religious beliefs were any different from her mother's, she replied: "I don't think we have any different beliefs. I don't want to say I'm not in the mind-set to think on my own, yet when it comes to that I think that she paves the way for what I think. Because she'll say something to me that doesn't make sense, but as I get older it starts making sense, and then I start to listen to what she says more often than I'll listen to others. I just think everything that has to do with Christians, she's right, in my opinion. Even if someone else is right, I'll think she's right, because I'm just biased when it comes to her, so I just, I stick with her." Most teens, however, are more likely simply to take for granted their parents' influence on their own religious identity and beliefs. Their answer to many questions about the main religious influences in their lives most often are "Just my parents," "Parents and church," "My parents, actually," and "I guess my family." We observed no variance in such teens' answers by teen age, sex, race, or other factor.

Religious conventionality was also evident in teen reports of actual and ideal religious service attendance, as illustrated by our exchange with this 14-year-old white Catholic girl from Florida:

I: How often do you go to church?
T: Every Sunday.
I: And do you like that?
T: Yeah.
I: If you could go as much or as little as you wanted, how often would you go?
T: Every Sunday.

There are, of course, some disgruntled teenagers who would much prefer to sleep through their religious services. But the majority, as we also saw in table 6 of chapter 2, seem to be just fine with attending religious services at the same congregation and with the same frequency as their parents.

On the ultraconventional side of this dominant group of family-following teenagers were a small minority who seemed to think that teenagers should *not even yet have* their own, independent religious identity and beliefs. They conveyed the vague idea that sometime in the future they would probably develop their own views, but that for now it is normal to simply mimic their parents' religious beliefs and practices without much thought. One 17-year-old white mainline Protestant boy from Michigan, for instance, reported, "Like when they tell us to give a silent prayer or something, I'll just try to pop something into my head, just to act like I'm doing something, even though nobody can tell. I guess just trying to fit in until I'm ready." "Ready" meaning ready to get the religion thing figured out for himself sometime in the future.

On the other side of the family-following majority of conventional teenagers are a minority who no longer believe in the religion in which they were
raised. Few of these unbelieving teens, however, as we are about to see, appear to make an issue of their divergent view with their parents. Some, such
as Joy in chapter 1, do not even disclose their different views to their parents.
Besides these, a very few other teens claim their own mind, not how they
were raised, as the only source of their religious beliefs. One 17-year-old
Hispanic Catholic girl from California, for instance, replied in answer to our
question about where she gets her ideas about God, "Just my thoughts." She
denied that her ideas came from anywhere other than her own reflection. The
same kind of approach is evident in our exchange with this 18-year-old white
conservative Protestant boy from Wisconsin:

> I: Where do you think you got these ideas about God?
> T: Uh, personal beliefs.
> I: Okay.
> T: Whatever I've come to conclude.
> I: Do your parents have any influence on that or . . . ?
> T: Not really, no they haven't.
> I: Have you ever talked to them about it?
> T: Not really.
> I: So, would you consider yourself to be any particular religion?
> T: I don't really know. I know I'm one but I don't know what.

But such voices were a small minority. The vast majority of U.S. teenagers
are simply not only not hostile to or rebellious against religion generally or
the faith tradition of their parents specifically. They are also quite content to
believe what their parents believe, what they've been taught to believe. In this
way, for most teens, religion is taken as part of the furniture of their lives,
not a big deal, just taken for granted as fine the way it is.

"Not Worth Fighting About"

As a result of this high degree of teenage religious conventionality, our interviews uncovered very little religious conflict between teens and their parents,
other adults, or friends. The vast majority of youth reported that they largely
share their parents' beliefs and have very little conflict with family members
over religious matters. Again, the dominant mentality seemed to be to go
along and get along, especially in families where all members embrace the
same faith. But even in the minority of families where teens and parents
overtly disagree religiously, religious differences rarely seemed to be a point
of conflict. Consider, for instance, the account of this 15-year-old white Catholic boy from Georgia:

> T: Well, I don't know about my brother 'cause I haven't talked to him
> about it, but the rest of my whole family is big on religion. And I'm
> just an "out there" atheist.
> I: So you've become an atheist, but are your parents atheist?

T: No. I'm different from them in that way.

I: Is that a source of conflict at all?

T: Oh no. Not at all, no.

I: Okay. So does religion ever come up in conversation with your parents?

T: No.

This 13-year-old white Jewish boy from Washington, D.C., told a similar story:

T: Oh, everyone's is completely different when it comes to religion.

I: Completely different.

T: I'm probably closest to my sisters. But my parents, I'm completely direct opposite of my dad, closer to my mom, ah, but not really.

I: Would you say religion is a source of conflict or solidarity between people in your family?

T: Um, neither.

I: Neither.

T: It doesn't really come up that much. Religion's just not a big part of my family at all.

Finally, one 16-year-old white boy from New Mexico who thinks of himself as not religious explained that he, his father, and stepmother are all agnostics but that his mother is a Christian. When asked if that difference is a source of conflict with his mother, he answered, "No, it never is. No."

In only a small handful of interviews did teenagers say religion was a source of conflict in their relationships. Usually the conflict in these cases sprang from doubtful teens questioning the beliefs or practices of parents whom they view as too religious. One 18-year-old white Mormon boy from Idaho, for example, said demands of their church create conflicts in his household: "It's a source of major conflict. My mother always puts church before family, like she would miss my graduation if there was a church activity scheduled at the same time. And my mom, dad, and I argue a lot over different religious rules that our church teaches." A 13-year-old Hispanic Catholic girl told how her hyperreligious stepfather, an immigrant from Central America, forced her to learn and recite prayers from a book each night and how he yells at her and pulls on her ears when she stumbles over words in the prayer book. "He's too religious, he wants me to be exactly like him and is always talking about how they used to treat him when he was a boy. That's why he treats me this way now, too." One 17-year-old black Protestant girl from Louisiana also talked about recurrent struggles with her mother about getting ready for church:

On Sunday mornings when we're trying to wake up, it is really hard for us to get out of the house, 'cause nobody's motivated to get up except for her. And we're like, "Just leave us here," and she's like, "No, you have to go to church, you have to do this and that." So we get up and go because she wants us to. If we had a choice I don't think we'd get up. And we do have disputes on certain topics. 'Cause she's one of those people who says, "No, that's not right because God says da da da," and I'll be like, who cares what God says? [laughs] I mean, this is real life, you know what I'm saying? So, yeah, we just had a fight like that.

One 15-year-old Jewish boy from New Jersey also described conflicts with his mother over religion: "We have conflict over the God part and observances just because God wants you to. I tried for many years, but I just couldn't believe in it, even when I said I did, I didn't. And so I finally just admitted that to myself, and then when I told my Mom, that I don't need to be going to synagogue, I don't care, it's not something I want to do, she's like, 'Well when you move out you don't have to. I know you'll want to, I regret now that I didn't when I was a child.' It is a source of conflict, a lot. My dad doesn't get involved, just my mom, she does everything." But, again, these stories nearly exhaust the very small number of cases we heard of religion-provoked family conflicts. And what teens said about lack of family conflict over religion also applies to their relationships with friends. Few U.S. teenagers today talk about religious matters with their friends, and far fewer get into arguments when they do. As one 17-year-old white Catholic boy from Connecticut, whose religious experience with friends is representative of very many teens (and whose story we tell in greater depth in chapter 6) put it, "Some of my friends are religious, but it really doesn't come into play with any of us, not at all in terms of our interactions. Religion may influence them. I have no idea, that sector of their lives is a lot different from interaction with me, they are different chapters." Likewise, a 15-year-old Buddhist girl from Alabama told us about the religious life of her friends, "Um, we don't talk about religion so much."

Thus, to rightly understand the religious and spiritual lives of the vast majority of U.S. teenagers, we need to see that religion is *not a particularly contested or conflictive* aspect of their lives. Rather, it is generally viewed by most teenagers, religious and nonreligious alike, as something that simply *is*, that is just not the kind of thing worth getting worked up about one way or the other.

"It's Good for Lots of People"

Another major dimension of widespread teenage religious conventionality is the benignly positive light in view of which nearly all U.S. teenagers see religion. Practically all teens at every level of personal religious involvement feel quite positive about religion generally and, when they are affiliated with one, about their own religious congregations specifically. Very few U.S. teenagers are rocking the boat when it comes to religion. Rather, most volunteer benevolent and amiable comments, such as that they "don't have anything against religion" and that "it is really good for a lot of people." Most U.S. teenagers thus tend to view religion as a Very Nice Thing.

The substantial majority of U.S. teenagers expressed in interviews that religion is a positive force in individuals' lives, in society, or both. Most commonly, teenagers of all sorts contend that religion helps provide people with strong moral foundations. According to one 18-year-old Hispanic Catholic girl from California, "The moral system of religion is valuable. I think the whole support system is valuable." Likewise, a 17-year-old white conservative Protestant boy from North Carolina maintained, "The morals that you learn, like don't kill people, that's a good thing in religion." A 14-year-old white Jewish girl from Massachusetts said, "I think it's just important to have a belief system because I think it helps you, what you believe is how you live." And this 13-year-old white mainline Protestant boy from Minnesota observed, "More people would do a lot more sin and stuff [without religion]. It helps people behave the better way."

Next most frequently, U.S. teens think positively of religion simply because it "provides something to believe in"—for many, something of value regardless of the content of the belief itself. One 15-year-old mixed-race Catholic boy from Texas observed, "I guess it gives people motivation, it gives them something to believe in." And this 15-year-old nonreligious white girl from Washington said, "Religion gives people something to believe in, something to hold on to. Not everybody needs it, but for people who do, it gives them something to believe in." Other teens made a similar point by saying religion is good simply because it "gives people faith." Yet other teenagers emphasized religion's value in providing people a connection or relationship with the divine, as one 16-year-old black Protestant boy from California remarked: "What's valuable in religion is the relationship between you and God, I guess." Likewise, an 18-year-old white conservative Protestant boy from Arizona commended religion because "It's important to know who God is and who Jesus is, but also important to know who you are as a person and how you related to God and Christ."

Other teenagers, such as this 18-year-old white nonreligious boy from Colorado, stressed religion's positive merit in "helping people": "Just to help people, I think that's really important. A religion should really try to help people, I feel like, anyway." Similarly, this 16-year-old white Catholic boy from Florida stated, "The important thing in a religion is connecting yourself to the spiritual side of yourself and fulfilling that. That's the reason for religion, to make it possible for people to fill the gaps that nature can't explain. As long as you do that, that's the only purpose of religion." A few teens, as with this 15-year-old white conservative Protestant boy from Alabama, claimed that religion is good because it helps people specifically to go to heaven and not go to hell: "People should always have religion, 'cause when you die you can either go to heaven or hell, and if you don't believe that there's a God then you're gonna have a really bad life and there's no way to change that." A few other teens stressed the good of religion as the community relationships provided by churches, prayer, the Bible, and other miscellaneous religious practices or benefits. For the majority of teenagers, however, religion is a positive good simply because it "gives people morals" and provides "something to believe in." Most of the teenagers we talked with seemed to truly value and appreciate religion for helping accomplish those things.

Even most nonreligious teens we interviewed seem very open to religion, not belligerent about it. Typically, nonreligious teens are quite appreciative and interested in religion, even if they say it is "not for them." Consider, for example, the following quotes of boys and girls representing every age, race, social class, and region of the country, all of whom, bear in mind, identify themselves personally as not religious:

> Religion gives people a good foundation, it's a great moral foundation for people who don't have any, a spiritual foundation, it helps a lot of people.

> It's important that people take religion as their own and interpret it as it helps them. It definitely gives people some ground, like my aunt for one. She was heavily into drugs, then found God and has calmed down. So it gives a lot of people hope. I don't believe in pushing anything on people, but if they choose it, then great. It's all up to them.

> I think it's good to have something to hold on to and religion is a very personal thing, so I would never say that religion is not good or that it's stupid. It just depends on the person.

> I think religion is important for people to have. All religions are meant for people to better themselves. That's one way that someone can try to be a better person, through organized religion, so I think that's important and really good for a lot of people. It's not for some people, but I can't think of it as a bad thing.

> Religion is something that should happen in people's lives, it's a good thing—any religion, as long as you believe in God. Because it's just having faith and believing in God, makes you feel like a different person.

> What's good is that it emphasizes how you treat other people. Just ethics in general could be good. The main message of most religions is to love each other. Though in some religions, women are treated with less respect than men and that's not cool.

> I don't think you necessarily have to believe in God and go to church, but I do think you have to believe that there's something more powerful than you and some things you can't control. If you don't have something to believe in, there's just no point in waking up and going to work. If people without religion are happy, that's okay for them. But if they start feeling like there's something missing, then I think they should believe in something.

> Religion teaches treating other people with respect, to show kindness. Religion should be a really strong thing, 'cause a lot of people are in gangs and stuff and if they had a religious influence that would be good.

Religion brings people together, it's a big support. The people in the church and stuff are really supportive. If you need anything, they're always there. It doesn't matter which religious faith, as long as they believe in God. My idea has always been as long as you believe in God, you're doing the right thing.

Religion's another thing that helps instill morals in people when they're young and I think it's important to see God in life. It always shows there's hope, it gives people hope and that kind of thing.

To be clear, not all nonreligious teenagers talked like this. Some did say that they think there is no particular value in religion. Some, for instance, said, "It's all made up" and "Not really, I mean most people think religion's good but I don't, I mean, to go to heaven you don't have to go to church." But these were the minority of nonreligious teens. Most expressed rather open and positive views of religion, like those quoted above. In any case, whether they saw any value in religion or not, no nonreligious teen we interviewed launched any outright attacks on religion as ignorant, destructive, regressive, or needing to be repressed. If nonreligious teens had nothing good to say about religion, they typically just did not say much at all.

Thus, in their general outlooks, the vast majority of U.S. teenagers representing all religious commitments and persuasions express little if any rebellion against, aggravation with, or hostility toward religion, including organized religion. Rather, in keeping with their general religious conventionalism, the vast majority of U.S. teens view religion in a benignly positive light.

"What Do You Mean, 'Spiritual Seeking'?"

Part of the conventionality of contemporary teenage religion in the United States is evident in what we found regarding the lack of spiritual seeking among teens. As we already noted in chapter 3, any teenage interest in practicing the spiritualities of other faiths or being "spiritual but not religious" is present among only a very small minority of teens. Most, in fact, have not even heard of the spiritual but not religious mantra, and many of those who have do not really know what it means. Very few teenagers today have ever considered practicing other faiths. "Why would I ever want to do that?" seems to be the general attitude of the vast majority, even if they typically grant anyone else the right to practice other religions if they wish. But few teens themselves generally have any such interest. When we asked teenagers if they ever experimented with other religious practices, explored alternative spiritualities, or considered adopting or converting to a new religion, they simply replied, "What?," "Nah," "No, never," and "Not really." For many, the idea seemed never to have occurred to them before. Some teens were even unable to comprehend our simple questions about spiritual seeking and experimenting, the very ideas seemingly so inconceivable to them that we had to repeat and rephrase our questions multiple times before they understood what we were asking. Because spiritual but not religious seeking is so far off

the radar screen of so many teenagers, it was difficult to generate much discussion of the topic in interviews, and so we do not have a lot of quotes on
the matter to report here. The vast majority of U.S. teens are simply too
conventional to consider, much less actively pursue, the idea of an eclectic
spiritual quest. Again, however they were raised seems to be good enough
for most.

The few teenagers we interviewed who had explored or were exploring
the spiritualities of religions other than those in which they were raised are
instructive. Many were doing so not because they were seriously considering
changing faiths but wanted "just to learn more." Most were also not seekers
on internally driven quests for enlightenment, but were merely introduced to
some religious practice by a friend or relation who recommended it to them.
Few seemed particularly serious about the possibility that their seeking ex-
periments might significantly change their life or identity. One 16-year-old
black Protestant boy from South Carolina, for example, told us he was interested in looking into Islam for these reasons: "I'm looking for Muslims as
far as the way they treat their body and treat women, I feel that's what God
would want. But on the other hand, I like Christianity, you know that's how
I was brought up and that's the only thing I know, so I wouldn't want to
drop that completely. There's just a lot of things I don't understand right now
and am trying to figure out, like, um, Islamic maybe. I mean, I'm not saying
I want to become a Muslim, I would just like to learn a little bit more about
it. But my own religious beliefs haven't changed." Meanwhile, he continues
to attend his Baptist church weekly, prays alone many times a day, and reports that his Christian faith is extremely important in his daily life. Or consider the case of this 14-year-old white nonreligious boy from Oregon, who
reports:

> T: I've thought about being a Buddhist because my brother influenced
> me. He was a Buddhist for a little bit and told me about a lot of things
> he'd done, that he really felt like he connected with the higher power.
> So I meditate sometimes. You kind of think about one thing over and
> over and almost get a feeling of, like, I'm one with everything. Some-
> times I do that just to go to sleep and sometimes I'm bored so I'll
> meditate, like once or twice a month.
> I: Do you find that helpful?
> T: Somewhat.
> I: Do you think that you would ever become Buddhist?
> T: I've thought about studying it more, I really would like to study
> religions because I do feel that there's a higher power and I kind of
> want to test some of the religions and see what they do, for a con-
> nection with the higher power that I believe is out there. So I might
> keep looking in the future.

This boy, at only 14, definitely sounds like a spiritual seeker. And yet, notice
that he is seeking from a nonreligious, not traditional religious, circumstance;
his interest in Buddhism was introduced to him by his brother; he only med-

itates on occasion when he is bored or wants to fall asleep; he only finds that somewhat useful; and he is unsure if he will study Buddhism more in the future. He clearly is an exception to the vast religious conventionalism of most U.S. teenagers. But, even so, he does not seem to be on much of a quest that will dramatically change his life.

SOMEWHERE IN THE BACKGROUND

The majority of U.S. teenagers are not rebellious toward religion but are generally rather positive about and conventional in living out religion. This fact should not, however, be presumed to mean that religion is among the most important concerns in the majority of U.S. teenagers' everyday lives. Conventionality, after all, very easily lends itself to routine and inertia. We believe, and the findings in chapter 7 help to confirm, that religious faith and practices are quite sociologically important in shaping many of the assumptions, values, lifestyles, and outcomes of the majority of adolescents in the United States. Religion really does matter in the lives of teenagers, we believe, however indistinct and inconsiderable it may sometimes seem on the face of it—especially as teenagers themselves describe it. But, however important or not religion objectively is in the lives of U.S. teenagers, and however generally positive teens may feel about religion, when it comes to getting specific about religion in their lives, most teens seem simply to accept religion as a taken-for-granted aspect or presence that mostly *operates in the background* of their lives. Most exhibit real but definitely limited recognition of religion's influence, importance, or distinction in their experiences.

When we asked teenagers directly how important religion was in their lives, some said frankly that religion is not important or that it is only somewhat important. But many teens did profess that religion is very important to them. They said things like, "Oh, really important, yeah," "It's the center of how I live my life," and "Faith influences many of my decisions." Among these, a substantial minority did express specific claims that religious faith and practices significantly affect their lives. Some teens, for instance, said religious faith has rescued them from severe depression. Some say they quit smoking, doing drugs, and drinking heavily because of their religious convictions. Other teens explained how religion is helping them stay in school when previously they were being expelled or had flunked out. One teen told about how religious faith is all that sustains his hope that his ailing father will not succumb to a life-threatening disease. Others told how, because of their religious beliefs, they operate completely differently from their friends when it comes to sexual relationships; specifically, they are abstinent when their friends are sexually very active. Certain teens describe how religious commitments prevent them from giving in to temptations to steal and get into fights which they otherwise feel powerfully drawn to. The vast majority, however, do not give such specific examples but instead simply claim that religion is very important in their lives and the basis for their fundamental knowledge of moral right and wrong. We have no reason to disbelieve or discount these declarations of religion's importance. Our claim is not that religion makes no difference in any teenager's life.

The following pages, however, do question the relative position that religion occupies in teenagers' lives and examines how poorly many teens, in spite of their claims to the contrary, are able to see and articulate religion's role in their life. Our analysis provides a tempered view of the importance and operation of religion in teenagers' lives that the survey data showed. We suggest that there seems to be among many or even most teenagers a lot more unfocused, "invisible" religiosity than focused, "intentional" religiosity at work in their actual lives. As such, teenagers' responses and reactions to many of our questions and issues regarding religion often seemed quite tepid, not particularly energized or animated or engaged. Again, our interviews did turn up some exceptions to this invisible, background-style of religion. Kristen, whose story we recounted in chapter 1, is an example of a teen practicing a more intentional, foreground approach to religion. Such exceptions tended to come from conservative Protestant and Mormon traditions, but not exclusively so, and certainly not all conservative Protestant or Mormon teens practiced religion intentionally in the foreground of their lives. But viewed as a whole, for most U.S. teenagers, their claims to religion's importance notwithstanding, *religion actually appears to operate much more as a taken-for-granted aspect of life, mostly situated in the background of everyday living, which becomes salient only under very specific conditions.*

"What I'm Really Into"

The first tip-off to the largely invisible and backgrounded nature of religion in the lives of most U.S. teenagers is what they talk about in general, wide-open discussions as being most important, central, and interesting in their lives. We talked with the teens we interviewed about what they get enthusiastic or excited about, what pressing issues they are dealing with, and what forces and experiences and routines seem to them most important and central in their lives. Most teenagers talk about friends, school, sports, television, music, movies, romantic interests, family relationships, dealing with issues of drugs and alcohol, various organized activities with which they're involved, and specific fun or formative events they have experienced. What rarely arises in such conversations are teens' religious identities, beliefs, experiences, or practices. Religion just does not naturally seem to appear much on most teenagers' open-ended lists of what really matters in their lives. This is not surprising. It simply reflects the fact that there is very little built-in religious content or connection in the structure of most U.S. adolescents' daily schedules and routines. Most U.S. teenagers' lives are dominated by school and homework; many are involved in sports and other clubs besides. Most teens also spend lots of time with their friends just hanging out or doing things like going to the mall or bowling. In addition, most teens devote a great deal of life to watching television and movies, e-mailing or instant messaging friends, listening to music, and consuming other electronic media. Boyfriends and girlfriends sometimes consume a lot of teenage time and attention as well. In all of this, religion simply is not an integral aspect of teens' structured lives, does not often come up as a relevant subject of discussion, and is not often involved in many teens' most significant social relationships. As a consequence, religion seems to become rather compartmentalized and backgrounded in the lived experiences of most U.S. teenagers.

"Not Sure How to Explain It"

In our in-depth interviews with U.S. teenagers, we also found the vast majority of them to be *incredibly inarticulate* about their faith, their religious beliefs and practices, and its meaning or place in their lives. We found very few teens from any religious background who are able to articulate well their religious beliefs and explain how those beliefs connect to the rest of their lives, although Mormon and conservative Protestant teens were sometimes an exception. This pervasive teen inarticulacy contributes to our larger impression that religion is either de facto not that important for most teens or that teens are getting very little help from their religious communities in knowing how to express the faith that may be important to them.

A substantial minority of religiously affiliated U.S. teenagers, when asked if they held any specific religious beliefs, simply answered, "No" or "Not really" or "Not that I can think of." We expect such answers from nonreligious teens, but we also heard many religious teens say flatly that they hold no particular religious beliefs. Another large minority did claim to hold religious beliefs but were unable to describe them. Thus, the transcripts of our interviews with U.S. teenagers are littered with the following kinds of answers to our questions about the religious belief, practices, and influences in their lives:

> Uh, I haven't really thought about that [pause]. I don't know.

> Just like, um, what they taught me, what I grew up knowing, I don't know.

> I believe in the [pause], I, ohhh [pause], I don't think I'd really like to talk about that.

> I don't remember.

> I don't think so right now.

> Hm, I don't know, I'd have to like ask somebody or something, I don't know.

> Um, I guess I believe . . . [laughs], um, I don't know. I don't really know how to answer it.

These are a small sample of actual quotes of all kinds of Protestant, Catholic, Jewish, and other types of religious teens of all ages and both sexes.

Mainline Protestants were among the least religiously articulate of all teens. Consider, for example, this 17-year-old white mainline Lutheran boy from Colorado: "Uh, well, I don't know, um, well, I don't really know. Being a Lutheran, confirmation was a big thing but I didn't really know what it

was and I still don't. I really don't know what being a Lutheran means."
This 17-year-old white mainline Presbyterian boy from Kentucky managed
an only slightly stronger answer: "Um [pause], I don't know, I just, uh, just
like anybody else I guess. There's nothing really to say, I don't know, just the
Presbyterian beliefs. Just like I believe in all the sin and stuff and going to
heaven and stuff, life after life." Similarly, here is what one 15-year-old white
mainline Methodist girl from Michigan—who, note, attends two church services every Sunday, Sunday School, church youth group, and Wednesday-night
Bible study—offered regarding her own personal religious beliefs:

> T: [Pause] I don't really know how to answer that.
> I: Are there any beliefs at all that are important to you? Really gen-
> erally.
> T: [Pause] I don't know.
> I: Take your time if you want.
> T: I think that you should just, if you're gonna do something wrong
> then you should always ask for forgiveness and he's gonna forgive you
> no matter what, 'cause he gave up his only son to take all the sins for
> you, so.

That was it. Catholic teenagers also tended to be particularly inarticulate
about their faith. One 18-year-old white Catholic girl from Massachusetts,
for instance, said that what made Catholics distinctive was, "Like, you, you
live better, like you, um, you have like a standard for yourself that's higher
than like other people. Uh, I don't know." Similarly, this 17-year-old white
Catholic boy from Indiana explained about his basic religious beliefs, "Um,
I think if you're a good person and like, you know you don't break any huge,
if, if you live your life around the basic structure, you know. I mean nobody's
perfect so you're gonna do bad things. But like, the whole Ten Commandments and stuff, pretty much a good person, then when you get judged you
get to have another life. If you ask forgiveness and pray a lot you have a
pretty good chance, just 'cause, you know, the whole forgiving God thing."

At the next higher level of articulation, some teens were able to make a
bit more of a stab at explaining their faith. One 18-year-old black Protestant
boy from Georgia, for example, said, "What do you mean, like by living by
the Ten Commandments and stuff like that? Um, I just believe that you
should live your life according to the Bible, and that's it." This 16-year-old
Hispanic Catholic girl from Arizona explained her beliefs as, "Uh, God is
everywhere, you know, helping, he's there when you need him, things happen
for a reason, um [giggles]." In most cases, as with these quotes, even when
teenagers did offer specific accounts of their beliefs, they usually turned out
to be mere snippets or fragments of what is in fact the larger belief system
of their own religious traditions. One 13-year-old black Protestant boy from
Illinois, for instance, recounted his religious beliefs as simply "God is coming
back." One 16-year-old Asian Muslim boy from Michigan described his religion as, "Nothing really, like, just hard work, my parents really believe in
hard work, so it's one thing. Like, concern for other people, things like that,

like just don't be an asshole, you know." A 17-year-old white Seventh Day Adventist girl from New Jersey summarized her religious beliefs as, "Well, we are, hmm, we keep the Sabbath that not everyone does . . . yes, all religions and . . . we don't paint ourselves, like with makeup." And this 16-year-old white Catholic boy from Washington said his "key religious belief" is that "God is forgiving, he's the only one who can judge you, the only one who can be right 100 percent of the time. And basically that's about it."

There were, of course, some teenagers who were impressive in explaining what they believe, what they doubt, why they think what they think, what it means to them, and how it influences their lives. Religiously devoted teenagers were more articulate than nominally religious teens, for obvious reasons. And older teens tended to be slightly more articulate than younger, but not by much. However, impressively articulate teens were few and far between. The vast majority simply could not express themselves on matters of God, faith, religion, or spiritual life.

We do not believe that teenage inarticulacy about religious matters reflects any general teen incapacity to think and speak well. Many of the youth we interviewed were quite conversant when it came to their views on salient issues in their lives about which they had been educated and had practice discussing, such as the dangers of drug abuse and STDs. Rather, our impression as interviewers was that many teenagers could not articulate matters of faith because they have not been effectively educated in and provided opportunities to practice talking about their faith. Indeed, it was our distinct sense that for many of the teens we interviewed, *our interview was the first time that any adult had ever asked them what they believed and how it mattered in their life.* Very many seemed caught off-balance by our simple questions, uncertain about what we were asking, at a loss to know how to respond. It was clear that, for many teens, very little in their lives had prepared them to be able to explain, even in basic terms, what they believe and how that fits into their lives. Some teens came right out and said so. One 14-year-old Hispanic conservative Protestant boy, for instance, replied to our questions about his religious beliefs, "Um, hmm, not really that I can think of, not really. 'Cause no one has ever really asked me." Likewise, this 15-year-old white Jewish boy from Pennsylvania answered our questions about religious belief by saying, "I guess I don't really know, basically I haven't been taught about it." Religious language is like any other language: to learn how to speak it, one needs first to listen to native speakers using it a lot, and then one needs plenty of practice at speaking it oneself. Many U.S. teenagers, it appears, are not getting a significant amount of such exposure and practice and so are simply not learning the religious language of their faith traditions.

"I Believe There Is a God and Stuff"

A closely related observation is, for many, their accompanying meager, nebulous, and often fallacious knowledge of the belief content of their own religious traditions which they claim to embrace. To the extent that the teens we interviewed did manage to articulate what they understood and believed religiously, it became clear that most religious teenagers either do not really comprehend what their own religious traditions say they are supposed to believe, or they do understand it and simply do not care to believe it. Either way, it is apparent that most religiously affiliated U.S. teens are not particularly invested in espousing and upholding the beliefs of their faith traditions, or that their communities of faith are failing in attempts to educate their youth, or both. The net result, in any case, is that most religious teenagers' opinions and views—one can hardly call them worldviews—are vague, limited, and often quite at variance with the actual teachings of their own religion. In the end, many teenagers know abundant details about the lives of favorite musicians and television stars or about what it takes to get into a good college, but most are not very clear on who Moses and Jesus were. This suggests that a strong, visible, salient, or intentional faith is not operating in the foreground of most teenagers' lives.

Some U.S. teenagers' articulated religious beliefs are simply quite paltry. One 15-year-old black Protestant girl from Florida, for instance, stated her personal religious beliefs this way: "[Long pause] Be kind." A 15-year-old white Catholic boy from Michigan said, "God's watching over us, that's it." This 15-year-old white conservative Protestant girl from Oregon reported, "I really don't have any beliefs, but basically just do whatever. I just pay my dues of going to church every Sunday and vacation Bible school things, just that." And one 17-year-old white mainline Protestant girl from Maryland told us, "I'm not one of those people who, you know, believes in these specific things. But I celebrate Christmas and, you know, that kind of thing." Other U.S. teens related to us their core religious beliefs that were not so much paltry as just trivial. A 13-year-old white mainline Protestant boy from California, for example, explained his religious beliefs in this way: "I don't believe in ghosts, they really aren't real. I think God's real and, um, he can see us but we can't see him." One 14-year-old white Catholic boy from New York told us, "I believe there's life after death, but that's about it."

Some teens summarized their central personal religious beliefs in terms representing what are actually at best secondary beliefs in their own religious traditions. One 17-year-old white Catholic boy from Wisconsin, for example, recounted his essential religious beliefs this way: "My religious beliefs, what's good and bad, like you know, if you kill or rape someone, I think you're screwed, give up on life 'cause it's over." Then he added, "I'll never stop being Catholic, even if I stop believing in God, I'll still be Catholic." This 15-year-old white mainline Protestant boy from Virginia stated his beliefs as, "You know, if somebody's in the wrong, you let them know, if you don't, that's a sin. That's pretty much what's been handed down to me." This 13-year-old white mainline Protestant girl from Montana explained, "I just, like, believe that no sins are any different from any other ones, they should all be like, the same rate. And, uh, I don't know, when I die I'm going to heaven." And one 16-year-old white conservative Protestant girl from Washington explained her beliefs in this way: "We go to church, and that God is coming back again and he'll take us to heaven. And what was the other one? I forgot, but we did go over this in Bible class [laughs], I remember." Our exchange with this 14-year-old white conservative Protestant girl from Idaho also conveys some of the lack of focus and enthusiasm about religious faith that many teens manifested in their interviews:

I: When you think of God, what image do you have of God?
T: [yawning]
I: What is God like?
T: Um, good. Powerful.
I: Okay, anything else?
T: Tall.
I: Tall?
T: Big.
I: Do you think God is active in people's lives or not?
T: Ah, I don't know.
I: You're not sure?
T: Different people have different views of him.
I: What about your view?
T: What do you mean?
I: Do you think God is active in your life?
T: In my life? Yeah.
I: Yeah, hmm. Would you say you feel close to God or not really?
T: Yeah, I feel close. [yawns]
I: Where do you get your ideas about God?
T: The Bible, my mom, church. Experience.
I: What kind of experience?
T: He's just done a lot of good in my life, so.
I: Like, what are examples of that?
T: I don't know.
I: Well, I'd love to hear. What good has God done in your life?
T: I, well, I have a house, parents, I have the Internet, I have a phone, I have cable.

A number of Christian teenagers we interviewed conveyed an "Oh-yeah-and-Jesus-too-I-guess" kind of attitude in trying to express their core religious beliefs. For example, a 13-year-old white Catholic girl from South Dakota said, "I'm not sure, not sure, I can't remember what I believe. Oh, mm-mm, yeah, like Jesus and God and them guys. That he is alive and watching over us." This 15-year-old conservative Protestant Hispanic boy from Texas took some reminding eventually to tentatively include Jesus in his beliefs: "I'm sure God exists and like, helps people and answers their prayers, that's pretty much it. [Do you believe in Jesus?] Ah, yes . . . I think [little laugh]. I don't know, I don't know." And this 14-year-old white Catholic girl from Montana summarized her religious beliefs in this way: "I really don't know, um, pretty much I believe in God and Jesus and all those people." Recall, these were not throwaway comments of teens, these were their main answers to our key questions about their basic personal religious beliefs.

A number of religious teenagers propounded theological views that are, according to the standards of their own religious traditions, simply not orthodox. One 13-year-old white mainline Protestant girl from Colorado, for instance, told us, "I think [laughing] I kind of picture God like this man, this woman, all types of animals and I mean no real total definition, can't even see the shape or anything, this great amazing being who, one snap of his or her fingers and a human is born, it's just amazing and really nice." A 14-year-old Hispanic Catholic boy from California said, "I kinda believe in reincarnation and I kinda don't, 'cause like my little brother totally believes in it, that he can become a hawk as soon as he's dead. Sometimes I think it's cool and then my cousin says no, so I'm all lost. So I just kinda believe in it." A 17-year-old Hispanic conservative Protestant girl from California confessed, "I believe that there's heaven and hell and spirits and angels, I even believe that there's still vampires living today." A 15-year-old Arabic Muslim boy from California summarized religious faith as, "I don't know, just like, pretty much try to live life without regrets, try to take responsibility for what you do, 'cause I don't know, just don't be a bitch about things. Try to make things fair, that's another thing, as fair as possible." One 18-year-old black mainline Protestant boy from New York described God this way: "I feel like God is everybody, all the dead spirits together, I feel like that's God combined into one, he's just looking down and watching us. He's in everyone's eyes, know what I'm saying? Like everyone's spirit, like my voice that you're hearing right now, I feel like that's God right now." Similarly, this 15-year-old Native American Catholic boy from Illinois reported, "When I think of God, I think of everything, like everything around us. [Like this desk?] Yeah, like the trees, everything. I don't think you can picture God as a being or a person, he's everything, everywhere, like grass growing, everything."

Viewed in terms of the absolute historical centrality of the Protestant conviction about salvation by God's grace alone, through faith alone and not by any human good works, many belief professions by Protestant teens, including numerous conservative Protestant teens, in effect discard that essential Protestant gospel. One 15-year-old white conservative Protestant boy from Mississippi, for instance, explained, "If you do the right thing and don't do anything bad, I mean nothing really bad, you know you'll go to heaven. If you don't, then you're screwed [laughs], that's about it." Similarly, this 16-year-old black conservative Protestant girl from Pennsylvania told us, "Being a Christian means, um, don't do many sins, read the Bible, go to church, living godly, that's about it. It's basically not committing sin, basically." Likewise, historically orthodox Christian doctrines about the personal nature of God and the authority of revelation are abrogated by more than a few teens' religious views, such as that expressed by this 13-year-old white conservative Protestant boy from Ohio: "God is just this big thing that's been there forever and controls everything, probably not personal, I don't know. [How did you come to that idea?] Ah, like, I was just raised that way I guess, and I guess I believe it till I hear another theory that's more reasonable or something, like from science."

And then there are the teenagers, such as this 18-year-old Hispanic Catholic girl from Maryland, who simply admit that they are confused: "My beliefs are so wishy-washy, like I'll think something one minute, something else the next. I don't know what is most important, 'cause I don't really live by the Bible." Similarly, this 17-year-old black Protestant girl from Illinois confessed, "I guess I'm a Christian, but I'm one of those still trying to figure everything out. I believe there's a higher power, but that's about all I know for sure."

Again, nobody expects adolescents to be sophisticated theologians. But very few of the descriptions of personal beliefs offered by the teenagers we interviewed, especially the Christian teenagers, come close to representing marginally coherent accounts of the basic, important religious beliefs of their own faith traditions. The majority of U.S. teens would badly fail a hypothetical short-answer or essay test of the basic beliefs of their religion. Higher proportions of conservative Protestant teenagers than other Christian teens proved able to summarize the elementary beliefs of their tradition, though often in highly formulaic terms. And teenagers affiliated with minority religious traditions—Mormon, Buddhist, Jewish, and other—who do not have the luxury of taking their religion for granted, also seem somewhat better able to explain the basic outlook and beliefs of their traditions. Otherwise, most teenagers held religious beliefs that, judged by their own religion's standards, were often trivial, misguided, distorted, and sometimes outright doctrinally erroneous. The point here is not that U.S. teenagers are dumb or deplorable. They are not. The point is simply that understanding and embracing the right religious faith and belief according to their religions does not appear to be a priority in the lives of most U.S. adolescents—and perhaps many of their parents. Faith is usually just there, around somewhere, and most teens do believe something religious or other. But religion simply doesn't seem consequential enough to most teenagers to pay close attention to and get right. Rather, most teens seem content to live with a low-visibility religion that operates somewhere in the mental background of their lives.

"Religion's Really Important to Me, I Guess"

Teens may struggle with articulating their cognitive religious beliefs, but perhaps they can better explain what their faith means to them and how their religion forms their identity and actions. We asked them outright how important their faith is to them, why, and in what ways. Here, in fact, the picture is somewhat more complicated than the view on religious beliefs painted above. About 25–30 percent of teens we interviewed said simply that religious faith was not important to them, religious beliefs did not influence their lives, religious practices made no particular difference in who they were and how they behaved. This substantial minority of U.S. teens included many nonreligious teens, as we might expect, but it also included a fair number of religiously affiliated teenagers from a variety of faith backgrounds. That, however, still leaves a substantial majority of U.S. teenagers who, when directly asked, claim that religious faith is indeed between somewhat and extremely significant in shaping and giving meaning to their lives. Within this larger group, there is a range of positions on the matter.

Some teenagers are absolutely exuberant and adamant about how important faith is in their lives. These teens report, "I base everything I do on faith, it affects every action I make," "It's the only thing that gets me through, 'cause if I didn't have faith, I wouldn't even be here," and "It's the center of everything, a top priority of my life." One 18-year-old white conservative Protestant boy from California, for instance, told us, "Absolutely central, it's the basis for everything, who I am, what I think. Like what life is all about, what I'm looking for, what satisfies me." Such teens often elaborate their strong statements by describing how God changed their lives in a religious conversion, how religion structures all of their values and commitments, or how different they feel from "the world" or "secular people" because of their faith. Such intense religious accounts are very striking and seemingly genuine. However, they represent a fairly small minority of teenagers, mostly, but not entirely, conservative Protestant and Mormon teens.

The majority of U.S. teenagers, by contrast, typically speak in more tempered tones about how religious faith and practice influence their lives in various ways. Many teens report that their religion helps them in knowing right from wrong, making good decisions, providing a sense of hope and purpose in life, motivating them to be moral and altruistic, and helping them get through hard circumstances. For example, one 15-year-old black Protestant girl from California said religion is important because "when I'm about to do something wrong, like steal or anything, I'm like, no, I'm trying to be on God's side, trying to go to heaven." A 15-year-old white mainline Protestant boy from Virginia said, "If I wasn't religious, I would be doing a whole lot more stuff, like drugs and smoking, but I think it's leading me to a good, straight path." And this 17-year-old white Mormon girl from Utah explained, "It helps me make decisions. I just pray every night and I keep my religion in mind throughout my day while making my choices." We have no a priori reason to question the sincerity or veracity of these statements. At the same time, we do notice certain clues in some of the interview discussions that raise questions worth considering about the depth or specificity of the professed meanings and influences of religious faith and practice in some teenagers' lives.

For example, what a number of teens, perhaps especially black teens, apparently mean in reporting that religion is very important in their lives is that religion is very important in the strictly *religious* sector of their lives. Religion influences them religiously—that is, when it comes to church attendance, basic beliefs, prayer, and so on—but not necessarily in other ways. One 14-year-old black Protestant girl from Maryland, for instance, elaborated on how religion influences her life: "It affects my life every day in one way or another. I say my prayers every night and we always bless the table before we eat." A 14-year-old black Protestant boy from South Carolina said that faith influences him "because I can call on the name of Jesus and all, he can wash all my sins away." A 15-year-old Hispanic conservative Protestant girl from New Jersey explained that religious practices are important in life because they "strengthen my faith." Avoiding hell was another key theme some teens articulated. One 17-year-old black Protestant girl from Alabama stated, "Very important, because I want to go to heaven, I don't want to go to hell." Likewise, this 13-year-old black Protestant boy from Illinois explained, "It's very important, 'cause when you do bad stuff, even if the cops don't see you, God saw you, and that really puts a hurt-down on you after you die, for your afterlife." And even this 17-year-old white nonreligious boy from Wisconsin says religious practices are important in his life because they "give a sense of security, like, 'Oh, phew, I'm not going to hell now 'cause I repent of my sins.' " Thus, sometimes religion is important to teens for specifically religious purposes but not for reasons beyond that, as this 14-year-old white conservative Protestant boy from North Dakota made clear: "Church makes me learn more about God and Jesus, but that's about it. It doesn't have any effect on my life."

Other teens claimed that religion is important in their lives, but ended up explaining the reason for religion's importance in terms that were so distant and far-fetched as to seem nearly irrelevant. One 18-year-old nonreligious girl from Arizona, for instance, suggested that, despite not being religious, religion "influences me a lot with the people I choose not to be around. I would not hang with people that are, you know, devil worshipers because that's just not my thing, I could not deal with that negativity." Perhaps socializing with Satanists is a real issue in this girl's life; more likely she is simply reaching very far for some explanation of why or how religion influences her at all. Similarly, one 17-year-old Catholic boy from Texas explained that religion influences him in "the things I choose not to do, um, like bad things, like murder or something." Again, perhaps this boy does struggle with murderous tendencies, but more probably, this explanation merely establishes religious influences in a way that is not too demanding or threatening to his routine life. Another version of citing largely irrelevant factors in teen explanations of religion's importance is commending what for most would be fairly negligible or unrelated accomplishments of religion. One 16-year-old Seventh Day Adventist girl, for instance, explained the difference her faith makes in this way: "Well, without my faith, my life would be different, um, I'd go shopping on Saturday 'cause they always have sales on Saturdays. That's the only thing I can really think of." A 13-year-old white Jewish girl from Georgia suggested, "I think it influences me to not do things that aren't acceptable in my religion, like getting tattoos." One 17-year-old white mainline Protestant boy from Tennessee said his faith is "kind of" influential in that "I don't cuss because it's a sin." A 13-year-old Hispanic Catholic girl from Connecticut told us that "faith helps me understand things better, like why the sky is blue and where trees come from, those questions." And one 15-year-old white conservative Protestant girl from California stated that her faith influences her this way: "Um, I'm conservative, a card-carrying Republican! Conservative, like the way I dress, the music I listen to—I'm one of the few teenagers that considers 'Rhapsody in Blue' and Rachmaninoff's Concerto some of my favorites." Again, it may be that for certain teenagers Saturday clothing sales, tattoos, curse words, explanations for why skies are blue, and "conservative" music tastes really are momentous life issues. But our impression is that, in most such cases, the teens are simply groping for something, anything that might confirm their claim that religion is indeed important in their lives. And sometimes they seem to have to grope hard because it actually is not very important.

Yet other teens we interviewed exhibited some slippage between the idea of religion's actual importance in their lives and its ideal importance. One 18-year-old white Catholic girl from Ohio, for instance, explained that religion is important to her in these terms: "I think it *should* be the, for me, I think it should be the central thing, um, yeah." Here she seems caught between the socially desirable answer that religion is in fact important and the apparent actual reality that it really is not that important. Similarly, this 16-year-old white Catholic boy from New York switched from discussing how religion does influence him to how it *would* if he were a serious believer: "I know it influences my personality, 'cause everything does, but I don't know how. *If* I was a devout Catholic, I'd probably have some more conservative and strict beliefs, like premarital sex and stuff." Another form of slippage that a few teens exhibited concerns differences in the objects in which one's faith is placed. One 17-year-old black conservative Protestant boy from New York, for instance, readily slid from discussing how religious faith influences him into how having faith *in himself* has been helpful: "How is religious faith important? Well, like school. If I didn't have faith in myself, I wouldn't be going to school right now, wouldn't have the motivation."

A final reason why, even though many teens said religion is important in their lives, it still seemed to us to be mostly part of the furniture in the background of their lives is the repeated lack of specific examples of religion's importance many of them offered in other sections of our interviews. In addition to our general discussions with teens about religion's value and significance in their lives, throughout the interviews, in sections on other topics— such as family relationships, dating, school, sexual activities—we also asked questions about whether and how religious faith influenced their thinking or living in these specific areas. Quite often, teens said they did not think their religious faith affected their family relationships, they did not believe religion was relevant to the conduct of a dating relationship, they did not see that religion affected their life at school, and so on. This was often even true for teens who in the religion discussion explicitly said that faith was important and influential in their lives. One 16-year-old white mainline Protestant girl from Michigan, for example, who explicitly stated, "Religion is very important to me," denied in every other section of the interview that religion had anything to do with her relationships, dating, school work, or any other aspect of her ordinary life. This is not to say that she or any others are frauds or hypocrites, simply that it is easier to say generally that religion is important than to specify exactly how and why it is important in particular areas of one's everyday life.

Related to this observation, we also asked teenagers whether they observe that religion makes any difference in the lives of their peers and friends. Do they notice that religious teenagers around them live any differently than nonreligious teens because of their faith? About half of the teens we interviewed said they did observe a difference, such as this 14-year-old East Indian Hindu girl from Oregon: "My peers who are religious are very disciplined and know what is right and wrong, but those who aren't religious, it's kind of hard for them." But half of the teens also said they did not notice that the religious teens were any different from the nonreligious teens around them. Matching teens' observations about religion's importance and influence in their *own* lives (often said to be quite important) compared to the lives of their *peers and friends* (often observed to be not that important) reveals a discrepancy that is difficult to explain. Either the teens we interviewed underestimate or fail to notice religion's real influence on their friends and peers, or they overestimate and give undue credit to religion's influence in their own lives. The reality is probably some of both. The bottom line, however, is that, for whatever reason, most U.S. teenagers seem to view strong religiosity as a socially desirable trait, such that at least some seem inclined to give themselves the benefit of the doubt in reporting how important and influential religious faith is in their own lives. We have no doubt that for many teenagers, religion indeed is meaningful and influential, even in ways about which many teens are only vaguely aware. But for the majority of U.S. teenagers, we think it consistent with teens' frequent professions of the importance of faith in their lives that, for the most part, religion actually operates largely as an invisible factor situated in the backgrounds of their lives.

"I'm Not Too Religious"

As we talked with U.S. teenagers about what it means to be religious and spiritual, we also noticed a particular category helping to structure the larger cultural framework of religious understanding assumed by many teens, namely, the category of being "too religious." Many U.S. teens across all religious traditions seem to hold in their minds a negative image of people who are too religious, which they definitely seek to avoid by muting their own religiosity. Consider, for instance, the following quotes drawn from our discussions with teens about what it means for them to be religious:

I'm not a big religious person where I go around preaching all the time, like this kid in my school who carried his Bible all the time and said really scary things, like whoa. I'm not that religious. (16-year-old white conservative Protestant girl from Virginia)

I'm not religious as in, you know, holier than thou or sanctimonious, praying all the time and whatnot. (17-year-old black Protestant boy from New York)

I think it's important to keep tradition, but I don't think it's too important to do, to like dive too much into it. (16-year-old Asian Hindu boy from Michigan)

I mean, I go to church but I'm not like, "Oh my God, I have to do what God tells me," I'm not, no I'm not like that. (17-year-old Hispanic Catholic girl from California)

I mean, I believe in God and Jesus but I'm not like, holy rolling Christian type person. (16-year-old white mainline Protestant boy from South Carolina)

I'm pretty religious I guess, but I'm not like Ned Flanders [evangelical neighbor on *The Simpsons* television show] or anything, you know? (16-year-old white conservative Protestant boy from Indiana)

There are some really, really religious Jews I know, they even go to my synagogue, who like, won't associate with anyone who is not Jewish, like they're protecting themselves and their religion. (15-year-old white Jewish girl from Maryland)

I do have a lot of knowledge of my religion, but I don't go around and preach. (13-year-old Catholic girl from Connecticut)

I'm not, like, very highly religious but I mean, I have faith and everything, but I'm not a really religious person, not the kind of person, you know, who carries around a Bible and stuff like that. I follow my religion, but I don't try to tell other people about it. (17-year-old while conservative Protestant boy from West Virginia)

I go to church but it's not like I'm deep into church, I'm not like, really, really religious. (16-year-old conservative Protestant Hispanic girl from New York)

I think of myself as a person who knows and is into her religion, but not like, a religious person, because people who go to my church have to wear really long skirts and I don't like to dress that way, or like reading the Bible every day. I know my Bible and I pray but, you know, not really strong, like religious, religious people do. (13-year-old black Protestant girl from Illinois)

I go by what I'm feeling. If I were religious I would be like my mom and I would be really, really literalist. People are like that, religious gets really weird, really weird, church-y candles with the crosses. (15-year-old conservative Protestant Hispanic girl from New York)

I don't really follow anything, like too much, not like I'm following everything to a T, but like, I do have basic principles and morals and stuff. (16-year-old white pagan girl from Wisconsin)

I am religious but you know, not too, I wouldn't consider myself a strict Methodist, I don't base my life around it, but you know, when it comes to church and all, I'm into it and stuff. (15-year-old white mainline Protestant girl from Virginia)

I'm not a fanatic, I don't, you know, go up and down the street waving a Bible. (14-year-old white conservative Protestant boy from Texas)

I'm not religious, like holy roller, constantly talking about God and stuff like that. That would very much bother me, would get very annoying after a while. I'd probably want to slap the person and say, "Get a life." (16-year-old white mainline Protestant girl from New Mexico)

Well, religious kids tend to be less accepting of people that aren't religious, sometimes kind of stick together. That's the reason why religion may suffer, it's made into something that, like, people shouldn't limit themselves to certain people just because of religion. (16-year-old white Jewish girl from New York)

I'm not a big Jesus freak or something. I mean, some people live their life by the Bible! (17-year-old white conservative Protestant from Kentucky)

I do, but not, like, to the extent where there's these fanatics going to people's doors. Sometimes people just go overboard. (17-year-old white mainline Protestant boy from Pennsylvania)

Sometimes people that are more religious take it to an extreme, like sure, but after a point, when are you going to finally live your life? (16-year-old white Catholic boy from Washington)

Thus, many teenagers, including many evangelical teens, have negative images of people who are "too religious." And in the larger cultural field of religiosity in which they see themselves operating, very few teens want to be too religious. So they position themselves in relation to that negative image as more modulated and irresolute in the practice and expression of their own religious faith. This structured contrast of too religious versus modestly religious is yet another factor helping to place religion in the background, not the foreground, of U.S. teenagers' lives.

EVERYONE DECIDES FOR THEMSELVES

American youth, like American adults, are nearly without exception profoundly individualistic, instinctively presuming autonomous, individual self-direction to be a universal human norm and life goal. Thoroughgoing individualism is not a contested orthodoxy for teenagers. It is an invisible and pervasive doxa,[7] that is, an unrecognized, unquestioned, invisible premise or presupposition. U.S. teenagers' profound individualism informs a number of issues related to religion.

"Who Am I to Judge?"

For most teens, nobody *has to* do anything in life, including anything to do with religion. "Whatever" is just fine, if that's what a person wants. Consequently, certain traditional religious languages and vocabularies of commitment, duty, faithfulness, obedience, calling, obligation, accountability, and ties to the past are nearly completely absent from the discourse of U.S. teenagers. Instead, religion is presumed to be something that individuals choose and must reaffirm for themselves based on their present and ongoing personal felt needs and preferences.

Second, most U.S. teens are at least somewhat allergic to anything they view as *trying* to influence them.[8] They generally view themselves as autonomous mediators or arbitrators of all outside influences; it is they themselves who finally influence their own lives. Other people and institutions provide information that youth see themselves as filtering, processing, and assimilating. Based on this information, they then make their own decisions for themselves. Or so the story goes. This autonomous individualism, not incidentally, helps to explain why teens have such difficulty articulating how religion influences them. They have difficulty imagining how religion influences their lives because they tend to imagine that *nothing* influences them, at least without their final choice that it does so. The idea that one's life is being formed and transformed by the power of a historical religious tradition can be nearly incomprehensible to people who have allergies to outside influences. Such a perspective lends itself instead to thinking of religion as something one chooses to *use*, as we will see below, not something to which one devotes oneself or gives away one's life.

A third consequence of American individualism for teenagers' relating to religion is that most teens embrace a very strong ethos that forswears judging any ideas or people that may be different. When each individual has his or her own unique and self-authenticating experiences and felt needs and desires, it is impossible for any other (alien) individual to properly evaluate or judge those chosen beliefs, commitments, desires, or lifestyle. The typical bywords, rather, are "Who am I to judge?" "If that's what they choose, whatever," "Each person decides for himself," and "If it works for them, fine." As one 16-year-old black Jehovah's Witness girl from California said of a friend who has switched between four different religions, "Whatever floats her boat." In this context, as it is often pointed out, the very idea of religious truth is attenuated, shifted from older realist and universalist notions of convictions about objective Truth to more personalized and relative versions of "truth for me" and "truth for you." In fact, despite the rhetoric, few teenagers actually consistently sustain such radical relativism. In certain ways and areas of life, teens do actually draw clear lines, often quite moralistic lines. Like many of the adults who are socializing them, they also often readily proffer decisive judgements as obvious facts that they take as self-evident to any reasonable person, such as, "Well, obviously you shouldn't hurt someone else" or "It's totally wrong to have sex with someone you don't really care about." What almost all U.S. teenagers—and adults—lack, however, are any tools or concepts or rationales by which to connect and integrate their radical relativistic individualist selves, on the one hand, with their commonsensical, evaluative, moralist selves, on the other. So teens continually seesaw, with little self-awareness that they are doing so, between their individualist Jekyll and moralistic Hyde selves, incapable of reconciling their judgments with their anti-judgmentalism, and so merely banging back and forth between them. In matters of religion, however, it is the latter, the nonjudgmental demeanor, that normally wins out. For some, this position seems couched in the civic notion that, in the United States, by virtue of the First Amendment, all citizens enjoy freedom of religion as a sacred right of conscience. But for many more teens, that limited civic and legal notion appears to have morphed into a more comprehensive epistemological and metaphysical sensibility that truth either does not exist or cannot be known, such that individuals can do no better than to choose whatever version of truth happens to work for them.

"There Is No Right Answer"

When we asked the 15-year-old Native American Catholic boy from Illinois—who maintained that God was present in the desk, trees, and grass—what he says to people who have a different view of God, he replied:

> T: I couldn't say anything. It's their opinion. I have my own opinion.
> I: Are you right?
> T: Ah, I don't know. I have no idea, but.
> I: Is there a right or wrong answer when it comes to God?
> T: There is no right answer.
> I: Why not?
> T: There isn't a wrong answer. 'Cause it's God, you can't prove, it's just what you believe.

Some teenagers champion this skeptic's view of individual, relativistic truth with great relish. Others concede it only very reluctantly, often intuitively believing in one truth, but not knowing how or being too cautious to try to express or defend it. In either case, whether through active embrace or compliant acquiescence, some version of this individualistic subjectivism and relativism is the dominant, assumed viewpoint about religion among most contemporary U.S. adolescents.

A very small minority state uncompromisingly not only that other people should practice some religion but that there is one right and true religion that people should practice. Most of these are conservative Protestants, with a few Catholic and Mormon teens mixed in; these are the U.S. religious traditions that still appear capable of socializing at least a few of their youth into a definite sense of religiously exclusive truth. This small minority of religiously particularistic teens, of various ages and sexes, boldly expressed the following views:

> Other religions do not worship the one true God. They're not teaching what's right about the one and only God. That's not right.

> The Bible says that everyone should praise the Lord and everyone *will* praise the Lord. I'm not going to knock anyone's religion, but that's the way I was raised. They should become the same as mine, Christianity.

> Jesus died for you on the cross, I mean, that's a matter of life and death. If you're practicing another religion, it's pretty pointless, it

doesn't matter what religion you're believing if you don't believe in Jesus and the cross.

If I said people could practice whatever, I'd be two-faced, 'cause I believe I found something great and I want other people to also, so yeah. Not Buddhism or anything, nothing that worships an idol. If you believe in God and Jesus then that should be enough. If you know the truth, he is the truth, then I think you're set.

I would influence others to pick my religion and my God over some-body else's. Everyone else thinks theirs is right, and I think mine is right. When it comes down to it, when Jesus comes back, they're gonna wish that they had believed in my God as opposed to their statues that they worship.

There can be only one truth, so you can only really be religious with one belief. If they're not gonna practice the right one then don't bother. If they practice something else, it's not only wrong, it's also not the truth.

I know this is completely against PC, but you know people like Mus-lims and stuff, they're not all about peace and love. Completely ridic-ulous. Their scripture tells them to kill Jews! If you want people to believe in a faith, you would want them to believe in a particular faith, not any old faith. The best would be to be a Christian.

If you're not believing in the truth, what does it amount to when you die, if it's not the truth? The Bible is the truth and Holy Spirit lives in me and I know it in my heart, it's evident. I'd say I know it's the truth.

I think a lot of other people live better lives than Christians do, more respectful. But being a Christian, I think everyone should be a Chris-tian, yes, I think that there's only one true God.

These are the more steadfast teen voices of religious particularism, though not necessarily behavioral intolerance, as most of these teens still appear to take civil, accommodating approaches to their interpersonal relationships.[9] But among U.S. teenagers, at least as far as our personal interviews with teens are able to tell, these teens represent only a minor fringe of dissenters skirting a vast majority of religiously individualistic, relativistic, subjectivistic teen-agers. The dominant position on the matter among contemporary adolescents in the United States is more evident in the following voices, representing Jewish, Catholic, conservative, black, and mainline Protestant, and nonreli-gious teens of all ages and both sexes:

When it comes to religion, people should do what they want. I shouldn't be the one to say what they do.

Everybody has their own stuff, people are all different, so our religions are very different. People have a right to choose to be religious or not.

I think everyone is capable, if they choose to believe in a higher power, I think they are capable of dealing with it themselves. Some people prefer a group method, but there's other ways to go about it.

They can just do whatever they want. If people want to believe in something they should, but it wouldn't matter at all, they're all pretty much the same.

I basically believe in guardian angels. I believe if you're really bad you will get punished sooner or later, but I don't believe in hell, that's just too, it's not right for me.

People who aren't religious? It's up to them, I don't know. It's their belief and stuff like that, it doesn't really matter. It's their own choice, their own choice.

Religious practices can make my life hard because they say to do something and I don't want to 'cause nobody else is doing it. Sometimes I do, sometimes I don't.

It's up to everybody to choose their own religious path, and mine are made up of various beliefs, a weird mixture of sorts.

My religious beliefs? I believe everybody should be treated with respect and everybody should have peace and just [be] treated fairly and have all kinds of opportunities to do things and stuff.

Religion is very important to me. I don't do everything by the book. I'll do stuff that I'm told not to do.

I can't speak for everybody, it's up to them. I know what's best for me, and I can't, I don't preach to nobody.

In these voices we hear the core underlying ideas constituting American religious individualism: that each individual is uniquely distinct from all others and deserves a faith that fits his or her singular self; that individuals must freely choose their own religion; that the individual is the authority over religion and not vice versa; that religion need not be practiced in and by a community; that no person may exercise judgments about or attempt to change the faith of other people; and that religious beliefs are ultimately interchangeable insofar as what matters is not the integrity of a belief system but the comfortability of the individual holding specific religious beliefs. From the wells of radical American religious individualism, contemporary U.S. teenagers have drunk deeply, no doubt following the example of their parents and other adults. For most, religious individualism appears to be all U.S. teens can actually conceive of.

HELPS YOU DO WHAT YOU WANT

Most U.S. youth tend to assume an instrumental view of religion. Most instinctively suppose that religion exists to help individuals be and do what they want, and not as an external tradition or authority or divinity that makes compelling claims and demands on their lives, especially to change or grow in ways they may not immediately want to. For most U.S. teenagers, religion is something to personally believe in that makes one feel good and resolves one's problems. For most, it is not an entire way of life or a disciplined practice that makes hard demands of or changes people. Stated differently, for many U.S. teenagers, God is treated as something like a cosmic therapist or counselor, a ready and competent helper who responds in times of trouble but who does not particularly ask for devotion or obedience. The latter might make a person feel awkward or uncomfortable. Thus, one 14-year-old white Catholic boy from Ohio told us, "Faith is very important, I pray to God to help me with sports and school and stuff and he hasn't let me down yet, so I think it helps you."

"Helps Me Feel Happy"

This instrumental image of religion is not the invention of teenagers. It seems to be a dominating image of religion embraced by many adults in the United States. Numerous other scholars have already observed that American parents use religion instrumentally to achieve prosocial outcomes for their children, to help their kids be more healthy, safe, and successful in life. The family sociologist Nicholas Townsend, for example, makes this incisive observation:

> Many men [hold an] . . . instrumental view of religion. Particularly when talking about the role of religion in their children's lives, the men I talked to emphasized its practical or behavioral aspects and never mentioned transcendence or fulfillment. For many people in the United States, religious observance is imposed on them as children, dropped when they are young adults, and resumed once they become parents. Parents of young children enlist religion as a source of values to inoculate their children against danger. Their motivation is in line with their view of children as malleable . . . Given this image of children as sponges, and a sense of the world as full of bad influences, it is hardly surprising that many parents turn to the churches as allies in their struggle to protect their children . . . The men I talked to . . . equated "high morals" with not using drugs and with wearing a seatbelt, rather than with a thirsting after righteousness, sacrificing for the common good, or speaking truth to power.[10]

Our interviews with hundreds of teenagers around the United States reveal that such an instrumentalist view of religion has also been deeply and widely embraced by the vast majority of American adolescents. We discussed in depth with teens what religion was all about, whether religion has any value, why anyone would want to practice a religious faith, what religion does and does not do in their own lives. What we heard from most teens is essentially that religion makes them feel good, that it helps them make good choices, that it helps resolve problems and troubles, that it serves their felt needs. What we hardly ever heard from teens was that religion is about significantly transforming people into, not what they feel like being, but what they are supposed to be, what God or their ethical tradition wants them to be. What U.S. teenagers very infrequently said, for instance, is that God is the one who calls and people are the ones who respond. What our interviews almost never uncovered among teens was a view that religion summons people to embrace an obedience to truth regardless of the personal consequences or rewards. Hardly any teens spoke directly about more difficult religious subjects like repentance, love of neighbor, social justice, unmerited grace, self-discipline, humility, the costs of discipleship, dying to self, the sovereignty of God, personal holiness, the struggles of sanctification, glorifying God in suffering, hungering for righteousness, or any other of a number of historically key ideas in America's main religious tradition, Christianity. What very few U.S. teens seem to believe, to put it one way, is that religion is about orienting people to the authoritative will and purposes of God or about serious, life-changing participation in the practices of the community of people who inherit the religiocultural and ethical tradition. As far as we could discern, what most teens appear to believe instead is that religion is about God responding to the authoritative desires and feelings of people. In simple terms, religion is essentially a tool for people to use to get what they want, as determined not by their religion but by their individual feelings and desires. Of course, very few teenagers, or adults, come out and say it in these crude terms. But such a view emerges rather clearly from a systematic analysis of our interviews.

Before exploring this dominant view of religion among U.S. youth, however, we first consider the minority alternative voices flanking the majority on either side. On the one end, there is a minority of youth, fewer than 10 percent, who are either so disconnected from anything religious that they simply have no opinion, or who merely suspect that religion could not accomplish much of value for anyone. Religion is not something one can use to accomplish anything important; religion is just an incomprehensible thing that some people do for reasons unknown. Such teens express sentiments like, "I have no idea what religious people think they are doing" and "I don't see religion has any point, it's just whatever."

On the other end, there is a very small minority of teenagers, mostly conservative Protestants and Mormons, who are devoted to following their religious faiths and who can speak in at least fragments of terms other than that of individual instrumental benefits. One 15-year-old white conservative Protestant girl from Indiana, for instance, explained that religion shapes everything she does and pushes her "to want to be who I can be just for the kingdom of God." This was one of only two Christian teens we interviewed who referred to "the kingdom of God." One 16-year-old white Mormon girl from Utah told us, "I want to be like Christ and try to live that way, and I think that changes the goal." A 14-year-old white conservative Protestant boy from Delaware explained that praying and reading the Bible are important to him because he needs them "to live for God." One 17-year-old white conservative Protestant girl from California explained that when she does good things "I've glorified God in some way." A 15-year-old white conservative Protestant girl from Georgia spoke of God as in charge of "everything that goes on in my life and his will in my life is for my own good and for his own glory. He is a compassionate, loving God, but can be wrathful against his enemies, both judging and loving at the same time. Even God's enemies bring him glory. That he defeats them and protects his own brings him glory." One 13-year-old white conservative Protestant boy from Kentucky talked about the need to "have Christ in your heart and live every day for him." A 16-year-old black Protestant boy from North Carolina said, "I try to do everything the Bible says to do, that's what I try to govern myself by, the Bible." One 13-year-old white conservative Protestant boy from California said, "My religious practices strengthen my spiritual walk and make me more of the person God would want me to be." And a 13-year-old white mainline Protestant girl from Colorado described how, before she came to faith, she took part in any poor behavior she wanted to, but that when she "got saved" that "changed the type of person I am, it changed my mind, so now it's just like I don't want to do that stuff." Whatever anyone thinks of the theologies and spiritualities represented in these statements, they nonetheless illustrate something of a departure from the individualistic instrumentalism that dominates U.S. teen religion by making God and not individuals the center of religious faith. But such statements and the religious outlooks they convey are rare among U.S. teenagers.

The overwhelming number of U.S. teens engage and value religion, not for the sake of God, or the common good of a just society, or for composing through identity and observance a distinctive community of people, but for the instrumental good it does them. So many are the interview quotes illustrating this observation that we simply enumerate them thematically in groups, without giving specific religion and demographic information for each statement. What follows, however, represents the broad view of most teenagers from all religious traditions.

First, one of the most important things that teens say religion provides them is guidance in being a "good person." Most teens say they want to be good and most understand that good people generally do well in life and bad people often fare poorly. Religion is good because it supplies useful guidance and training in being the good person they think it is important to be. Hence, they answer questions about religion's value, importance, and role in their lives in the following kinds of terms:

It's important 'cause you have to have some kind of guidance in life, so I look to God.

Pretty important, without it it'd be harder to judge what's right and wrong.

Religion helps me make like a lot of decisions, gives just a guidance.

Training myself to be a moral person.

It's sort of guidelines for my life.

It's my blueprint for life, my guideline, it helps me through life.

It teaches me how to be like a good Jew, you know, go out and be a good person, moral.

Makes me a better person.

Just makes me a nicer person, 'cause before I hated adults but now it's a lot easier just to be, like, lovable and caring to people.

Closely related to the practical moral guidance and training that religion provides teenagers are the boundaries it sets to help teens stay out of trouble:

It helps me not to do a lot of bad things.

It's important to me to keep my life in order and stuff, to keep me straight.

Without religion, I'd be a troublemaker, I'd get out of hand.

I guess it keeps me on the right track.

It's probably good for me, helps keep me out of trouble.

Protects me from a lot of things, like a bunch of sex and AIDS.

I'm not in trouble no more, so it fixed my life and I don't get into trouble.

Makes me a better person, you don't just go out and do immoral things.

Most U.S. teens also value religion greatly for its ability to help them get through their problems and troubles:

It helps me get through trying times, helps me face problems.

Faith is important when I need God to comfort me and like that.

It's important, not like major important, but religion can help you get through a bad day.

If I ever have a problem I go pray, so.

You can do all things possible with Christ, it's true, you believe and he'll make a way for you to make a bad day turn into a good thing.

It's very central, whenever I need support with bigger problems I go to my parents, but with little problems, you know the little pushes, I ask God with that.

It affects day-by-day life, you can turn a bad day into a good day.

Yes, sir, they help me like in my problems or when I'm down, they help me see my way through.

It helps me deal with problems, 'cause I have a temper, so it calms me down for the most part.

It's influenced how I face problems, like there's this security and no matter what I'll be fine, I'll get over it and God's always there.

Whenever I have a problem, I can just go bear it and he'll always be supportive.

If I'm having a hard time, it makes me feel better.

Teenagers also report that religion gives them feelings of mental and psychological security, which they appreciate:

Praying just makes me feel more secure, like there's something there helping me out.

I know that doing religious practices will eventually bless me, that's why I do it.

Praying is a way to get something out, if you want to say something you go ahead and say it, like if you feel sorry, you ask forgiveness and that.

I'll pray to do the right thing and it kind of reassures me.

It's always there, helping you mentally, supporting you, you think things are okay.

Religion also helps teens keep a positive attitude about life:

If you don't live a godly life you will always think negative things.

Positive beliefs are important and valuable in religion.

Without my religious beliefs, I wouldn't accept the world or people for who they are, I wouldn't be able to tolerate or accept them.

We have a better day when we have family prayer, we just come home in a better attitude and atmosphere.

Many teens also often report that one of religion's mental and emotional benefits is in helping them keep a good perspective on life:

They help me to relax and remember all the little things that are important, to not worry about what isn't important. I forget that when I don't go to church.

It makes me see life clearly.

Gives me something to balance my outlook with and to check things against.

Gives me time. You need to think about and consider things that go on in your life.

They change my perspective on life, my perspective on problems, how I look at stuff.

They change what I focus on in life, focus on what's important instead of all these little things.

Just gives direction and puts a new focus on something.

A number of U.S. teenagers say that their religious faith has given them a personal confidence and direction which has proven helpful in living their lives:

> Faith lets me move forward, like I have a shield in front of me that nobody can come past.

> It gives more motivation to get up in the morning and do the same thing again, go to school and all that again.

> Religious practices just provide me with something, like some support I'll always hold onto, faith that what I'm doing is all right and everything will work out the way it should.

> It reinforces that I can do stuff, like helping friends, it's like, wow, I actually did something, I can do something about things.

> Encouragement and enlightenment to go forward.

Teenagers also report that religion is good because it contributes to their growing maturity as they pass from childhood to adulthood:

> It helps me understand more about what I can expect when I grow up.

> I'm bettering myself by doing it, I become a better person, more mature and responsible in my life.

> Makes me more prepared for the challenges that will come.

> Helps me gain a sense of respect, that I'm supposed to do things, helps me understand and be more respectful of things.

Some U.S. teens even suggest that religion has served to help them be successful, socially involved, and healthier:

> I would say prayer is an essential part of my success.

> If I need something I can just pray.

> Affects my life a lot 'cause I wouldn't be part of the youth movement, one of the biggest events of my life, and the experience of summer camp.

> Ever since I've been praying, we've been eating healthier and I haven't been getting hurt as much.

But one of U.S. adolescents' highest compliments to religion and faith is simply that they help teenagers to feel good and to be happy:

> It's pretty central, it helps me feel better.

> If something's wrong, just a way to escape it and make things better, just feel better, whatever, positive.

> I would probably feel lost, feel that emptiness, there would be that space nobody but God can fill.

> It makes you feel better.

Our religious observances, some of them are a lot of fun and can really make you happy to do them.

Going to church makes me feel better, like if I go in angry, when I come out I am really happy.

It makes me feel better, kind of confident about my beliefs.

I guess it just makes me feel at ease knowing that I did something good.

Probably just more happy, 'cause it keeps reminding you of all the stuff.

Like the practices help me be a happier person with less problems going on.

It makes me a happier person, that I'm doing everything I'm supposed to do.

Broad swaths of U.S. teenagers—girls and boys, young and old, wealthy and poor, rural and urban, Southern and Northeastern, white and black and Hispanic and Asian—tell us that religion is very valuable, important, and influential in their lives. This is no doubt true in many cases. But observers should know that the religion to which most of them appear to be referring seems significantly different in character from versions of the same faith in centuries past. The religion that many U.S. teens acclaim today is not commendable for youth because, for example, it is revealed in truth by holy and almighty God who calls all to a turning from self and a serving of God in gratitude, humility, and righteousness. Nor is it commendable, alternatively, because it inducts them into a community of people embodying a historically rooted tradition of identity, practices, and ethics that define their selfhood, loyalties, and commitments. Rather, the religion that many U.S. teenagers acclaim today is for them commendable because it helps people make good life choices and helps them feel happy.[11] What legitimates the religion of most youth today is not that it is the life-transformative, transcendent truth, but that it instrumentally provides mental, psychological, emotional, and social benefits that teens find useful and valuable. This is not an unambiguously bad (or good) fact. Most people would hope and expect that religious faith would indeed help youth to behave well, avoid trouble, solve problems, feel supported, and be happy. No American religious tradition actively promotes poor behavior, negative attitudes, and unhappiness. But all major American religious traditions have historically been about more than helping individuals make advantageous choices and maintain good feelings. However one evaluates the character and texture of contemporary American religion as reflected by most U.S. youth, it must be acknowledged that it seems qualitatively quite different from the faith of the same traditions in previous eras. And a key aspect of that difference is the primarily instrumental use value that it offers and is praised for by individual believers.

"You Don't Have to Be Religious to Be Good"

For all of religion's functional value in the eyes of most U.S. teenagers, particularly in providing moral guidelines, religion actually bears a complicated relationship in teenagers' minds with what goes into moral living. Most U.S. teens think that one of religion's primary functions is to help people be good. But they do not view religion as *necessary* for anyone being good, because they see many means to being good and many good nonreligious people. Hence, most U.S. teenagers conclude that religion is a nonnecessary condition for achieving one of its primary functions. In other words, the thing religion specializes in does not actually require religion to achieve. Consequently, many U.S. teenagers construct religion in nonessential terms, as an optional individual lifestyle choice that does indeed help many people but is certainly not itself ultimately necessary.

One of the key teenage assumptions in this religion-morality equation is that right and wrong are simply common sense, something everyone just knows. For most teens, morality is not something that requires much thought or discernment. Everyone just knows it; whether they choose to live morally or not is simply their individual choice. Nobody therefore finally needs religion to specify what is right and wrong. The good, the right, and the true are not per se defined as the will or word of God, for instance. They are just things that any reasonable person knows. For many youth, the Bible, for example, nicely specifies what is right and wrong, but in any case pretty much everyone knows what is right and wrong, Bible or no Bible. In achieving the effect of living a good life, religion is therefore not a necessary condition. For some, it may be a sufficient condition. But for others, it may be entirely optional.

Despite the widespread teenage belief that moral right and wrong are obvious matters of common sense, U.S. teenagers actually disagree significantly among themselves about what actually is moral and immoral and why a person should be motivated to act morally. Some teens cite religious referents like the Ten Commandments and afterlife consequences to define moral boundaries and motives. They may believe that such a morality is universally known and applicable and not ultimately grounded in a particular religious tradition, but they nonetheless locate its clearest expression—at least "for them"—in teachings found in places like the Bible. On the other hand, for many U.S. teens, morality's core or covering law seems to be essentially "Thou shalt not hurt oneself or others." For these teens, morality has little substance or content other than the general rule, needing application in various situations, that it is wrong to hurt other people or oneself. What these teens learn in school about the dangers of drug and alcohol abuse and unprotected sex plays a significant role in defining key moral issues. There also seems to be some connection here to the new American "bourgeois bohemian" morality described by David Brooks.[12] A more explicitly utilitarian version of the "Thou shalt not hurt" rule that more than a few teenagers seem to have adopted is that what is "immoral" is defined as that which significantly puts at risk being successful in life, that which would screw up one's life chances as defined by school, science, and cultural common sense. In this approach, it seems that behaviors such as cheating, lying, stealing, getting into fights, and abusing drugs are wrong simply because they might cause an automobile accident, get one expelled from school, reduce one's chances of getting into a good college, and so on. In this consequentialist morality, not succeeding per se seems to be that which constitutes the wrong and immoral. Last, there are a small minority of U.S. teenagers who claim to be consistent moral relativists. For them, moral goodness is simply whatever people want it to be, whatever they happen to want to think and do. Although some give in on this hard line when pressed, others continue to insist on no existing objective moral standard or even general rule of thumb. They profess to be pure moral social constructionists who are unflinching about the larger Machiavellian implications.

A Brief Excursus: On Living in Morally Significant and Insignificant Universes

We have just said that some U.S. teenagers openly profess to be Machiavellian moral relativists who regard right and wrong as little more than contingent and relative cultural constructions that people, being more or less aware of what they are doing, use to feel good about themselves and to manipulate others. This observation relates closely to another that we made in our interviews, which we think is worth taking a brief detour here to discuss. Namely, we observed in our interviews that at least some contemporary teenagers seem to live in what we might call a "morally insignificant universe." In such a universe, moral commitments, decisions, obligations, and actions have little if any larger meaning, purpose, significance, or consequence; that universe is, in short, a morally empty reality. The next two paragraphs contrast this kind of universe with what we might by comparison think of as a morally significant universe.

Contrasted with living in the morally *in*significant universe, to live in a morally *significant* universe means living one's life within a larger, morally meaningful order that provides significant direction and purpose to one's thoughts, feelings, and actions. Such a universe provides weight and gravity to living. It impregnates life's choices, commitments, and moral actions with purpose. To exist in a morally significant universe means that one's single, modest life is at another level also inescapably bound up to a larger framework of consequence. In a morally significant universe, one's decisions and practices and deeds bear the burden and reflect the significance of a much bigger story or system of import. In such a reality, moral temptations are serious business, as choices for right and wrong reverberate far beyond our own lives and affirm or violate a larger cosmic order. That order may be an inexorable and self-evident natural law woven into the fabric of reality against or with which our lives run in ways that over the long haul reveal that we inevitably reap what we sow. It may be the work of a perfect and loving God in history and in the lives of men and women whose daily choices and habits either resist or respond to God's redemptive purposes. It may be a long and hard historical human struggle for freedom, equality, justice, or sisterhood and brotherhood in which one expends one's life to play a small but perhaps notable role in moving history forward. Whatever the exact universe may be, it is a morally significant one and in a big way. Its significance is not derived from one's own life. Significance rather emanates to selves from the very order of things, the creation, the cosmos, the human story, or the light and force of history. One's own single life finds its significance not in relation to itself, but by becoming connected to this larger moral order, by living a life in tune with and reflecting that order. In which case, so many desires, struggles, disciplines, and deeds signify not only themselves but also much larger purposes and consequences. One at once bears in one's living the burden of history and the cosmos, and yet is simultaneously relieved of that burden by knowing that their momentum and outcome are somehow formed by forces much larger than one's own life. A morally significant universe has a telos, an end, goal, and standard, by which one knows where one is and to where one is headed. It thus provides individuals the big script of a very real drama, in the sense both that the story is intensely dramatic and that the drama is reality, within which the living out of one's life really means something significant because of the role it somehow plays in helping to perform the larger dramatic narrative. In a morally significant universe, actions really do embody and reflect bigger challenges, struggles, failures, and victories—and all things really are finally going somewhere important. Many teenagers in the United States today live with more or less self-awareness in such a universe. But not all do.

When a person lives in a morally *in*significant universe, by contrast, as some teenagers we interviewed appear to, all of what is described in the previous paragraph evaporates. Instead, there are only the specific people, pains, pleasures, and opportunities concretely before a person at any given time. There are no demons tempting or angels watching over anyone. There is no natural law or world-historic struggles and achievements. When one looks up into the stars, one sees not the gods, nor the handiwork of God, nor the portentous alignment of planets; one simply sees empty space in which nobody else is at home. People living in such a universe find themselves in a small corner of that empty space of which their short lives have come by chance and for reasons nonexistent into being on this minor and insignificant bit of carbon floating in a galaxy destined for extinction. There is no Creator who set humanity here and guides our lives and history with Providence. There is no larger law-like order in nature that structures the moral living of the human race. There is little worth spending life to fight for that does not seem arbitrarily chosen. There is no judgment, no final retribution or punishment, not even a remembrance of one's life or anything human after time and physics have run their course. There is no telos, but simply the given self and world and experience. Nothing more. In such a morally *in*significant universe, the four dimensions of the morally significant universe collapse into two dimensions. What matters is simply what is in front and back and sideways. What is above and below doesn't particularly matter. And what some other people may believe is mysteriously hidden or present within the material world we occupy is either simply not on the radar screen of conceivable possibilities or is just not plausible—mere fairy tales left over from more credulous ages. In such a universe, one's decisions and actions may indeed have certain pleasurable or painful consequences, but they have no particular meaning, purpose, or significance beyond that.[13]

We cannot here elaborate the sources, social locations, and social consequences of U.S. teenagers living in morally significant versus insignificant universes. Such a task would require its own dedicated chapter at least, which present space limitations will not allow. Suffice it to say here, however, in anticipation of a future elaboration elsewhere, that the living of U.S. teenagers in morally significant and insignificant universes strikes us as strongly correlated with teen religious commitment and lack thereof. For reasons not hard to grasp, those Christian, Jewish, and other religion teens we interviewed who are strong believers in and followers of their faith traditions tend to have lives that are quite firmly embedded in morally significant universes. By contrast, many of those teens who were quite serious about their nonreligious identities were also the ones who struck us as definitely living in morally insignificant universes. Such big-picture contrasts and associations are difficult to measure or quantify. But the association between levels of religious commitment and types of moral universes occupied seems to us, at least, to be very strong. Further research will have to determine if these observations are accurate and worth pursuing. Meanwhile, the remainder of this chapter returns to the more immediate task of describing the complex character of contemporary adolescent religion in the United States.

WHAT YOU'RE "SUPPOSED" TO DO

We have said that teenagers in the United States typically consider themselves to be self-directing, autonomous individuals, the key mediators or arbiters of all outside influences, fully in charge of their own interests, choices, and actions. The irony is that most teenagers are, of course, subject to all kinds of cultural directives and pressures which powerfully govern their assumptions, decisions, and behaviors. For example, although most teens went to great pains in our interviews to deny the operation of peer pressure in their lives, such peer pressures were patently obvious to us in many of the stories they recounted. Most teenagers simply could or would not see them.

"It'll Be More Important When I'm Older"

The religious and spiritual lives of most U.S. teenagers are significantly shaped by what are to them largely invisible cultural scripts about how people of various ages are supposed to engage religion. Most American youth, in other words, bring strong life course assumptions and expectations to their experiences of religion, often tacitly viewing faith's relevance and importance in terms of "age-appropriate" stages.[14] This is a very natural and necessary social ordering process. In any given society, individual human lives are always structured and guided by particular cultural expectations about what is normal and expected at different stages of the life course. What is normative for a preteen is different from that for a middle-aged adult, for instance. As part of this invisible cultural life course script, most U.S. teens view numerous other behaviors as also life stage–driven. Many consider drinking and partying, for example, to be things that teenagers are *supposed* to be doing, but that they will give up when they get older and settle down. Such culturally scripted stereotypes of the "typical" teenage lifestyle often greatly influence the thinking and behaviors of many youth.

One related background assumption of at least some U.S. teenagers, perhaps especially Catholic, Jewish, and mainline Protestant teenagers, is that religion should play quite a different role in the life of teenagers than that of adults. Some youth, for instance, seem to assume that while religion is mostly good for teens, as we saw above, it is not necessarily a naturally important part of teenage life. And it is sometimes presumed that it will be even less important for older, more independent teens and young adults, when it is often assumed that its role will diminish. More than a few teens also seem to assume that religion is something they will likely return to when they are older, especially when they have children—either because it is something they themselves will be more interested in learning about, or because their children will need it, or both. Some teens also expect that their future spouse will significantly shape their religious involvements, especially in encouraging religious service attendance. It would be misleading to overstate this point. Religiosity as culturally demarcated by presupposed life course–scripted social roles is not the most common or obvious theme in adolescents' discussions about religion. But the theme is definitely there for some. For example, this 14-year-old Asian Jewish girl from California expressed it clearly: "At the moment religion's not that important. I guess when I get older it might become more so, but right now being with my friends and having fun and being a teenager is more important to me." This 15-year-old white mainline Protestant girl from Alabama made the same point a bit more subtly: "Praying and reading devotionals and going to church is just something I do. I don't think I've gotten to the how-it-affects-me yet. But I'm pretty sure that it will, I'll get to that point." One 17-year-old black mainline Protestant girl from Louisiana elaborated the point about age-appropriate religious differences in this way: "A lot of people I know get caught up to think that it's more acceptable when you're a teenager to not understand everything with religion. You do know what's right and wrong. But you take chances and do things that feel good at the moment. But when I'm older, I think, like a lot of people, you think you've done everything that is possible for you to do, so you just try to settle down, be mature. Grow more and help others to grow." Approaching religion with such a presumed life course script in hand means that at least some U.S. teenagers feel free not to pay much attention for the moment to what religious faith means and how it ought to shape their lives. One 14-year-old Hispanic Catholic boy from Texas, for instance, told us, "It hasn't influenced me yet, but I'm hoping when I become more active that it will have influenced me." Likewise, this 15-year-old white Jewish girl from California answered our question frankly: "Does my religious faith influence me? Um, not right now." One 17-year-old white Catholic boy from Connecticut (whose story we describe in greater depth in chapter

6) went so far as to postpone the time he said he would take religion seriously to just prior to his death: "I'm sure when I get older I'll have to do more [with religion], but it's something that becomes a lot more important later on, you know, like when you're about to die." Again, not every teenager we interviewed said such things. Not even the majority of teens did. But enough teenagers did speak in such terms that we did notice the theme, suggesting that expectations of life course–scripted, low-level teen religiosity serves as a background cultural structure that shapes the religious assumptions, interests, and actions of at least some U.S. youth.

"I Don't Want to Be Offensive or Anything"

A second major cultural influence on U.S. adolescent practices of religion that emerged from our interviews concerned the expression of their personal religious beliefs in public. Nearly all U.S. teens seem to have adopted a posture of civility and a careful and ambiguous inclusiveness when discussing religion with possible "others," especially in public. It is possible that some teens especially comported themselves in this way with us, seeing us as strangers, professional interviewers from a secular research university. But this was clearly not the entire explanation for their civility. By so much of what so many of them said, it was clear that American teenagers have been very well trained to avoid religious particularity and possible discomfort in discussions. Their natural tendency is to studiously avoid personal expressions of religious specificity, seemingly in deference to normative rules governing the public-private divide in our culture. We assured and reminded our interviewees that our questions had no right or wrong answers, that everything they said was confidential, and that we really wanted to know whatever they actually thought, felt, and believed, not what they think we might want to hear. Despite that fact, many of the teens we interviewed seemed to take great care not to offend us, not to say things that would be politically incorrect. We believe that over the course of our interviews we did manage to put our teens at ease and help them be comfortable speaking frankly and honestly. But their natural first instincts were to be civil, inclusive, and nonoffensive when it comes to discussing the subjects of religion and spirituality.

Part of this careful civility seems rooted in the high premium that most teenagers place on being open to a vast variety of ideas, people, and experiences. It is normative in contemporary U.S. youth culture both to be open to if not accepting of nearly everything that comes along, and not to be "too" committed to or earnest about anything absolute or contentious. This itself is another expression of anti-judgmentalism derived from the American individualism that adolescents have thoroughly assimilated, as described above. Individuals can decide only for themselves and so cannot strongly evaluate or judge anyone or anything other. Part of obeying that general rule is being careful not to speak any potentially upsetting or exclusive things, particularly about religion. It is also obvious that, in all of this, public schools have served as an effective training ground for teaching teenagers to be civil, inclusive, and nonoffensive when it comes to faith and spiritual matters. In addition to the general official promulgation of tolerance and acceptance of all cultural difference that normally begins in kindergarten, most teenagers report that their school teachers avoid discussing religion like the plague and that their school friends largely act as if religion is not part of anybody's life. Thus, we found many of the teenagers we interviewed to be—at first, at least—polite, judicious, and ambiguous. We sometimes had to work to create a comfort level for teens to admit, for example, that they love contemporary Christian music, that they believe their religion is the one true religion, or that they think some people will go to hell. We are confident that in the end most teens we interviewed were open and honest with us in discussing religion. But, again, that did not seem to be their first, natural, or most comfortable response.

SOMEWHERE ON THE PRIORITY LIST

One final general observation from our interviews: in the ecology of American adolescents' lives, religion clearly operates in a social-structurally weak position, competing for time, energy, and attention and often losing against other, more dominant demands and commitments, particularly school, sports, television, and other electronic media. If we conceive of adolescents' lives as bundles of finite interest, energy, and investment, then we can think of the various social institutions that touch adolescents' lives as seeking to lay claim to shares of those resources. Different institutions enjoy different capacities to extract and consume teenagers' attention, energy, and investments. School, for example, enjoys a tremendous amount of legitimacy and authority in demanding significant portions of teenagers' waking lives and disposable resources. Few teenagers seem to form their most significant social relationships in their religious congregations; instead, school appears to be the center of their most important social ties. Sports, peer groups, shopping and consuming, television, paid work, computers, and romance also compete to capture teenagers' attention and energy.

So what place is religion able to secure among these vying institutions and activities? For most U.S. teenagers, quite a small place at the end of the table for a short period of time each week (if that). Indeed, given religion's limited structured access to typical U.S. teenagers' lives, it is remarkable that as many teens insist on religion's high importance and great influence in their lives as do. Religion simply occupies a largely losing structural position when it comes to most adolescents' obligations, schedules, routines, and habits. When it comes to institutions possessing opportunities to form the lives of youth, religion is not among the more advantaged players. This general situation is evident in the way many teenagers talk about, for instance, their religious practices. Despite frequent declarations about religion being a "top priority" or "extremely important" in their lives, more than a few teenagers we interviewed seemed to consider religious service attendance, for example, a nice thing to do if and when it is feasible. "I go to church whenever I can, when there isn't homework pressing or a game scheduled" was a common statement on the matter. For many teenagers, then, religion is often the thing that gives; school, sports, television, friends, and the like are the things that demand the giving. As one 16-year-old black Jehovah's Witness girl from California related:

> I'm supposed to read the Bible by myself every day, but I don't because of that little magic box called TV and this other little magic box called computer. So my Bible reading kind of goes bye-bye [laughs]. Like I said, if I'm not pushed and it looks like work, I'm not gonna do it. I mean I appreciate the Bible and everything but some parts are kind of [hard to] wade through. I also like attending religious services, then I don't like going, 'cause that means I have to stop what I'm doing, get ready, and leave my house, and it's just [hard], you know, when you're sitting at home on the couch in front of one of your magic boxes.

Especially when religion is structurally isolated from the primary schedules and networks that comprise teenagers' daily lives are teens' religious and spiritual lives most weak. It is, by contrast, when teens' family, school, friends, and sports lives and religious congregations somehow connect, intersect, and overlap that teens exhibit the most committed and integral religious and spiritual lives. It does not take a Ph.D. to understand why. But such effects are nonetheless substantial. That parents are typically the primary agents in making such connections and overlapping happen or not is yet another way that parents are crucial influences in forming the religious and spiritual lives of their teenage children, for better or for worse.

A SUMMARY INTERPRETATION: MORALISTIC THERAPEUTIC DEISM

The themes and analyses explored in this chapter have followed varied topical trains of thought and sometimes pursued diversions and digressions. But what does the whole look like when one puts it all together? When we get past adolescent inarticulacy about religion, systematically sort through the myriad stories and statements about religious faith and practice, and pull apart and piece together what seem to be the key ideas and relevant issues, what might one conclude? Here we attempt to summarize our observations by venturing a general thesis about teenage religion and spirituality in the United States. We advance our thesis somewhat tentatively as less than a conclusive fact but more than mere conjecture: we suggest that the de facto dominant religion among contemporary U.S. teenagers is what we might well call "Moralistic Therapeutic Deism." The creed of this religion, as codified from what emerged from our interviews, sounds something like this:

1. A God exists who created and orders the world and watches over human life on earth.
2. God wants people to be good, nice, and fair to each other, as taught in the Bible and by most world religions.

3. The central goal of life is to be happy and to feel good about oneself.
4. God does not need to be particularly involved in one's life except when God is needed to resolve a problem.
5. Good people go to heaven when they die.

Such a de facto creed is particularly evident among mainline Protestant and Catholic youth, but is also visible among black and conservative Protestants, Jewish teens, other religious types of teenagers, and even many nonreligious teenagers in the United States. Note that no teenager would actually use the terminology "Moralistic Therapeutic Deist" to describe himself or herself. That is *our* summarizing term. And very few teenagers would lay out the five points of its creed as clearly and concisely as we have just done. But when one sifts through and digests hundreds of discussions with U.S teenagers about religion, God, faith, prayer, and other spiritual practices, what seems to emerge as the dominant, de facto religious viewpoint turns out to be some version of this faith. We could literally fill another chapter of this book with more quotes from teen interviews illustrating Moralistic Therapeutic Deism and exploring its nuances and variants. Given space limitations, however, suffice it here to examine merely a few more representative quotes depicting this religion's core components.

First, Moralistic Therapeutic Deism is about inculcating a moralistic approach to life. It teaches that central to living a good and happy life is being a good, moral person. That means being nice, kind, pleasant, respectful, responsible, at work on self-improvement, taking care of one's health, and doing one's best to be successful. One 17-year-old white Mormon boy from Utah said this very clearly: "I believe in, well, my whole religion is where you try to be good and, ah, if you're not good then you should just try to get better, that's all." Being moral in this faith means being the kind of person that other people will like, fulfilling one's personal potential, and not being socially disruptive or interpersonally obnoxious. As more than one teenager summarized morality for us, including the Hindu boy quoted above, "Just don't be an asshole, that's all." Such a moral vision is inclusive of most religions, which are presumed ultimately to stand for equivalent moral views. Thus, a nonreligious white girl from Maryland said, "Morals play a large part in religion. Morals are good if they're healthy for society. Like Christianity, which is all I know, the values you get from, like, the Ten Commandments. I think every religion is important in its own respect. You know, if you're Muslim, then Islam is the way for you. If you're Jewish, well, that's great too. If you're Christian, well good for you. It's just whatever makes you feel good about you." Feeling good about oneself is thus also an essential aspect of living a moral life, according to this dominant de facto teenage religious faith.[15] Which leads to our next point.

Moralistic Therapeutic Deism is, second, about providing therapeutic benefits to its adherents.[16] This is not a religion of repentance from sin, of keeping the Sabbath, of living as a servant of a sovereign divine, of steadfastly saying one's prayers, of faithfully observing high holy days, of building character through suffering, of basking in God's love and grace, of spending oneself in gratitude and love for the cause of social justice, etcetera. Rather, what appears to be the actual dominant religion among U.S. teenagers is centrally about feeling good, happy, secure, at peace. It is about attaining subjective well-being, being able to resolve problems, and getting along amiably with other people. We have already examined numerous quotes to this effect in the pages above. A few more will help to complete the picture. One 15-year-old Hispanic conservative Protestant girl from Florida expressed the therapeutic benefits of her faith in these terms: "God is like someone who is always there for you, I don't know, it's like God is God. He's just like somebody that'll always help you go through whatever you're going through. When I became a Christian I was just praying and it always made me feel better." Making a similar point, though drawing it out from a different religious tradition, this 14-year-old white Jewish girl from Washington State describes what her faith is all about in this way: "I guess for me Judaism is more about how you live your life. Part of the guidelines are like how to live and I guess be happy with who you are, 'cause if you're out there helping someone, you're gonna feel good about yourself, you know?" Thus, service to others can be one means to feeling good about oneself. Other personal religious practices can also serve that therapeutic end, as this 15-year-old Asian Buddhist girl from Alabama observed: "When I pray, it makes me feel good afterwards." Similarly, one 15-year-old white conservative Protestant girl from Illinois explained: "Religion is very important, because when you have no one else to talk to about stuff, you can just get it off your chest, you just talk [to God]. It's good." And this 14-year-old East Indian Hindu girl from California said of her religious practices, "I don't know, they just really help me feel good." It is thus no wonder that so many religious and nonreligious teenagers are so positive about religion, for the faith many of them have in mind effectively helps to achieve a primary life goal: to feel good and happy about oneself and one's life. It is also no wonder that most teens are so religiously inarticulate. As long as one is happy, why bother with being able to talk about the belief content of one's faith?

Finally, Moralistic Therapeutic Deism is about belief in a particular kind of God: one who exists, created the world, and defines our general moral order, but not one who is particularly personally involved in one's affairs—especially affairs in which one would prefer not to have God involved. Most of the time, the God of this faith keeps a safe distance. He is often described by teens as "watching over everything from above" and "the creator of everything and . . . just up there now controlling everything." As one 15-year-old Arabic Muslim boy from California put it: "God is like an entity that decides when, if he wants to intervene with a lot of things. To me God is pretty much like intervention, like extreme luck. Say you're $50 away from something and you find $50 on the floor, then that's probably God's intervention or something like that. But other than that it just seems like he's monitoring. He just kind of stays back and watches, like he's watching a play, like he's a producer. He makes the play all possible and then he watches it, and if there's something he doesn't like he changes it." For many teens, as with adults, God sometimes does get involved in people's lives, but usually only when they call on him, mostly when they have some trouble or problem or bad feeling that they want resolved. In this sense, the Deism here is revised from its classical eighteenth-century version by the therapeutic qualifier, making the distant God selectively available for taking care of needs. As this 14-year-old white mainline Protestant boy from Colorado said, "I believe there's a God, so sometimes when I'm in trouble or in danger, then I'll start thinking about that." Like the deistic God of the eighteenth-century philosophers, the God of contemporary teenage Moralistic Therapeutic Deism is primarily a divine Creator and Lawgiver. He designed the universe and establishes moral law and order. But this God is not trinitarian, he did not speak through the Torah or the prophets of Israel, was never resurrected from the dead, and does not fill and transform people through his Spirit. This God is not demanding. He actually can't be, because his job is to solve our problems and make people feel good. In short, God is something like a combination Divine Butler and Cosmic Therapist: he is always on call, takes care of any problems that arise, professionally helps his people to feel better about themselves, and does not become too personally involved in the process. As one 14-year-old white Catholic boy from Pennsylvania, in response to our inquiry about why religion matters, said, " 'Cause God made us and if you ask him for something I believe he gives it to you. Yeah, he hasn't let me down yet. [So what is God like?] God is a spirit that grants you anything you want, but not anything bad." Similarly, this 17-year-old conservative Protestant girl from Florida told us, "God's all around you, all the time. He believes in forgiving people and whatnot and he's there to guide us, for somebody to talk to and help us through our problems. Of course, he doesn't talk back." This last statement is perhaps doubly telling: God, being distant, does not directly verbally answer prayers, according to this girl, but he also does not offer any challenging comebacks to or arguments about our requests. Perhaps the worst the God of Moralistic Therapeutic Deism can do is simply fail to provide his promised therapeutic blessings, in which case those who believe in him are entitled to be grumpy. Thus, one 16-year-old white mainline Protestant boy from Texas complained with some sarcasm in his interview, "Well, God is almighty, I guess [yawns]. But I think he's on vacation right now because of all the crap that's happening in the world, 'cause it wasn't like this back when he was famous." Likewise, this 14-year-old white conservative Protestant boy from Ohio told us, "God is an overall ruler who controls everything, so like, if I'm depressed or something and things aren't going my way I blame it on him, I don't know why." But few teens we talked to end up blaming God for failing them, because Moralistic Therapeutic Deism usually seems to be effective in delivering its promised benefits to its many American teenage believers.

We want to be very clear here about our thesis. We are not saying that all U.S. teens are adherents of Moralistic Therapeutic Deism. Some are simply disengaged from anything religious or spiritual, and others embrace substantive religious beliefs and practices that effectively repudiate those of this revisionist faith. Some teens do appear to be truly very serious about their religious faith in ways that seem faithful to the orthodox claims of the faith traditions they profess. We are also not saying than anyone has founded an official religion by the name of Moralistic Therapeutic Deism, nor that most U.S. teenagers have abandoned their religious denominations and congregations to practice it elsewhere or under another name. Rather, it seems that the latter is simply colonizing many established religious traditions and congregations in the United States, that it is becoming the new spirit living in the old body. Its typical embrace and practice is de facto, functional, practical, and tacit, not formal or acknowledged as a distinctive religion. Furthermore, we are not suggesting that Moralistic Therapeutic Deism is a religious faith limited to teenage adherents in the United States. To the contrary, it seems that it is also a widespread, popular faith among very many U.S. adults. Our religiously conventional adolescents seem to be merely absorbing and reflecting religiously what the adult world is routinely modeling for and inculcating in its youth.

Moreover, we are not suggesting that Moralistic Therapeutic Deism is a religion that teenagers (and adults) either adopt and practice wholesale or not at all. Instead, the elements of its creed are normally assimilated by degrees, in parts, admixed with elements of more traditional religious faiths. Indeed, this religious creed appears to operate as a parasitic faith. It cannot sustain its own integral, independent life; rather it must attach itself like an incubus to established historical religious traditions, feeding on their doctrines and sensibilities, and expanding by mutating their theological substance to resemble its own distinctive image. This helps to explain why millions of U.S. teenagers and adults are not self-declared, card-carrying, organizationally gathered Moralistic Therapeutic Deists. This religion generally does not and cannot stand on its own, so its adherents must be Christian Moralistic Therapeutic Deists, Jewish Moralistic Therapeutic Deists, Mormon Moralistic Therapeutic Deists, and even nonreligious Moralistic Therapeutic Deists. These may be either devout followers or mere nominal believers of their respective traditional faiths, but they often have some connection to an established historical faith tradition that this alternative faith feeds on and gradually co-opts if not devours. Believers in each larger tradition practice their own versions of this otherwise common parasitic religion. The Jewish version, for instance, may emphasize the ethical living aspect of the creed, while the Methodist version stresses the getting-to-heaven part. Each of the believers then can think of themselves as belonging to the specific religious tradition they name as their own—Catholic, Baptist, Jewish, Mormon, whatever— while simultaneously sharing the cross-cutting, core beliefs of their de facto common Moralistic Therapeutic Deist faith. In effect, these believers get to enjoy whatever particulars of their own faith heritages that appeal to them, while also reaping the benefits of this shared, harmonizing, interfaith religion. This helps to explain the noticeable lack of religious conflict between teenagers of apparently different faiths. For, in fact, we suggest, very many of them actually share the same deeper religious faith: Moralistic Therapeutic Deism. What is there to have conflict about?

One way to gauge people's interest in different matters is to track their language use. What do people talk about? How often do they use different kinds of key words and phrases? The idea behind this approach is that people's discourse roughly reflects their concerns and interests. We used this method as one means of assessing U.S. teenagers' relative orientations to religious and therapeutic concerns. We systematically counted in our interview transcripts the number of teenagers who made reference to specific subjects or phrases of interest. We found, first, that relatively few U.S. teenagers made reference to a variety of historically central religious and theological ideas. The following list shows the number of teenagers who explicitly mentioned these concepts in their interviews:

47	personally sinning or being a sinner
13	obeying God or the church
12	religious repentance or repenting from wrongdoing
9	expressing love for God
8	righteousness, divine or human
7	resurrection or rising again of Jesus
6	giving glory to or glorifying God
6	salvation
5	resurrection of the dead on the Last Day
5	the kingdom of God (2 Christian, 3 Mormon)
5	keeping Sabbath (of 18 Jewish interviews)[17]
4	discipleship or being a religious disciple
4	God as Trinity
4	keeping Kosher (of 18 Jewish interviews)
3	the grace of God
3	the Bible as holy
3	honoring God in life
3	loving one's neighbor
3	observing high holy days (of 18 Jewish interviews)
2	God as holy or reflecting holiness
2	the justice of God
0	self-discipline
0	working for social justice
0	justification or being justified
0	sanctification or being sanctified

When teenagers talked in their interviews about grace, they were usually talking about the television show *Will and Grace*, not about God's grace. When teenagers discussed honor, they were almost always talking about taking honors courses or making the honor role at school, very rarely about honoring God with their lives. When teens mentioned being justified, they almost always meant having a reason for doing something behaviorally questionable, not having their relationship with God made right.

For comparison with these tallies on religious terms, we also counted the number of teens who made reference to the key therapeutic ideas of feeling happy, good, better, and fulfilled. What we found, as shown in the following list, is that U.S. teenagers were much more likely to talk in terms broadly related to therapeutic concerns than in the religious terms examined above:

112 personally feeling, being, getting, or being made happy
99   feeling good about oneself or life
92   feeling better about oneself or life
26   being or feeling personally satisfied or enjoying life satisfaction
21   being or feeling personally fulfilled

Note that these are not total number of times that teenagers used a word or phrase, but simply the number of teens who used them. In fact, our teenagers used the single, specific phrase to "feel happy" *well more than 2,000 times.* In short, our teen interview transcripts reveal clearly that the language that dominates U.S. adolescent interests and thinking about life, including religious and spiritual life, is primarily about personally feeling good and being happy. That is what defines the dominant epistemological framework and evaluative standard for most contemporary U.S. teenagers—and probably for most of their baby boomer parents. This, we think, has major implications for religious faiths seriously attempting to pass on the established beliefs and practices of their historical traditions.

What we are theorizing here, in other words, is the very real existence of a shared American religion that is analogous to the American civil religion that Robert Bellah astutely described in 1967,[18] yet that operates at an entirely different level than civil religion. It is not uncommon for people to think of the United States as containing a variety of diverse religions that coexist more or less harmoniously: Protestant, Catholic, Jew; Freewill Baptist, Irish Catholic, Conservative Judaism, Reformed Presbyterian, Latter Day Saint, and so on. But the reality is actually more complicated than that. "Religion" in the United States in fact separates itself out and operates at multiple levels in different ways. American religion is most obvious at the level of formal organizations, the plane on which denominations, seminaries, religious congregations, publishing houses, and other religious organizations operate. But religion also often operates distinctively at a level below the organizational plane, at the level of individual belief and practice. Here religious faith is often eclectic, idiosyncratic, and syncretistic, inconsistently—from the perspective of most organized religious traditions, at least—mixing together elements as diverse as belief in infant baptism, interest in horoscope predictions, and the collection of religious kitsch. This is the dimension that some scholars have called "lived religion" or "popular religion."[19] Beyond these two levels, Bellah's major contribution in 1967 was to reveal civil religion operating at yet another level, above the plane of formal religious organizations. Bellah very insightfully showed how religious symbols and discourse, appropriated and abstracted from the Judeo-Christian tradition, are mobilized at a national civic level for purposes of national order, unity, and purpose.

What we are suggesting in our observations about Moralistic Therapeutic Deism is that, to understand the fullness of religion in the United States, we need to see yet another level or plane of religious life or practice operating in this social order, as shown in figure 2. At the bottom are the eclectic, idiosyncratic, and discretely syncretistic faiths operating at the level of individual religion. Higher up abide the more coherent, systematized faiths operating on the plane of organizational religion. Even higher exists the nationally unifying political faith of American civil religion. But situated between the individual level at the bottom and the organized religions and civil religion on planes above that, there operates yet another distinct level of religion in the United States: the widely shared, interfaith religion of Moralistic Therapeutic Deism. Like American civil religion, Moralistic Therapeutic Deism appropriates, abstracts, and revises doctrinal elements from mostly Christianity and Judaism for its own purpose. But it does so in a downward, apolitical direction. Its social function is not to unify and give purpose to the nation at the level of civic affairs. Rather, it functions to foster subjective well-being in its believers and to lubricate interpersonal relationships in the local public sphere. Moralistic Therapeutic Deism exists, with God's aid, to help people succeed in life, to make them feel good, and to help them get along with others—who otherwise are different—in school, at work, on the team, and in other routine areas of life.

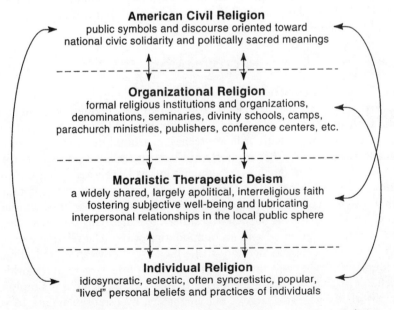

American Civil Religion
public symbols and discourse oriented toward
national civic solidarity and politically sacred meanings

Organizational Religion
formal religious institutions and organizations,
denominations, seminaries, divinity schools, camps,
parachurch ministries, publishers, conference centers, etc.

Moralistic Therapeutic Deism
a widely shared, largely apolitical, interreligious faith
fostering subjective well-being and lubricating
interpersonal relationships in the local public sphere

Individual Religion
idiosyncratic, eclectic, often syncretistic, popular,
"lived" personal beliefs and practices of individuals

Figure 2. A Model of the Distinct Levels of Operative American Religion.
Arrows indicate permeability and limited mutual influence.

Finally, to suggest that religion in the United States operates complexly and distinctly on different levels does not mean that those levels never interact or influence each other. They do, as indicated by the arrows in figure 2. Purely individual beliefs, for instance, are shaped in part by the teachings of organized religion as well as by horoscopes, advice columns, talk show hosts, and so on. And American civil religion is affected both by liberal religious activism and by the Religious Right operating at the level of formal religious organization. The same observation about interlevel interaction and influence is also true of Moralistic Therapeutic Deism. It helps to organize and harmonize individual religious beliefs below it. It also both feeds on and shapes, one might say infects, the religious doctrines and practices at the organizational and institutional level above it. It also mirrors and may very well interface with American civil religion at the highest level by providing the nation's inhabitants a parallel and complementary common, unifying, functional faith that operates at a more apolitical, private, and interpersonal level of human life. The cultural influence of Moralistic Therapeutic Deism may also be nudging American civil religion in a "softer," more inclusive, ecumenical, and multireligious direction. What in American civil religion that is conservative becomes more compassionate, what is liberal becomes more inclusive, and aspects that are particularistic are increasingly universalized. All can then together hold hands and declare in unison, "Everyone decides for themselves!" And those who believe that only the born again go to heaven who are justified by the spilled blood of Jesus Christ, or that the Angel Moroni really did appear to Joseph Smith with a new and commanding revelation, or that God's chosen people really must faithfully observe his laws are suspect. The flock of sheep is diversified and expanded, but certain goats remain part of the picture nonetheless.[20]

CONCLUSION

Adults in the United States over the past many decades have recurrently emphasized what separates teenagers from grown-ups, highlighting things that make each of them different and seemingly unable to relate to each other. But our conversations with ordinary teenagers around the country made clear to us, to the contrary, that in most cases teenage religion and spirituality in the United States are much better understood as largely reflecting the world of adult religion, especially parental religion, and are in strong continuity with it. Few teenagers today are rejecting or reacting against the adult religion into which they are being socialized. Rather, most are living out their religious lives in very conventional and accommodating ways. The religion and spirituality of most teenagers actually strike us as very powerfully reflecting the contours, priorities, expectations, and structures of the larger adult world into which adolescents are being socialized. In many ways, religion is simply happily absorbed by youth, largely, one might say, by osmosis, as one 16-year-old white Catholic boy from Pennsylvania stated so well: "Yeah, religion affects my life a lot, but you just really don't think about it as much. It just comes natural I guess after a while."

However, it appears that only a minority of U.S. teenagers are naturally absorbing by osmosis the traditional substantive content and character of the religious traditions to which they claim to belong. For, it appears to us, another popular religious faith, Moralistic Therapeutic Deism, is colonizing many historical religious traditions and, almost without anyone noticing, converting believers in the old faiths to its alternative religious vision of divinely underwritten personal happiness and interpersonal niceness. Exactly how this process is affecting American Judaism and Mormonism we refrain here from further commenting on, as these faiths and cultures are not our primary fields of expertise. Other, more accomplished scholars in those areas will have to examine and evaluate these possibilities in greater depth. But we can say here that we have come with some confidence to believe that a significant part of Christianity in the United States is actually only tenuously Christian in any sense that is seriously connected to the actual historical Christian tradition,[21] but has rather substantially morphed into Christianity's misbegotten stepcousin, Christian Moralistic Therapeutic Deism. This has happened in the minds and hearts of many individual believers and, it also appears, within the structures of at least some Christian organizations and institutions. The language, and therefore experience, of Trinity, holiness, sin, grace, justification, sanctification, church, Eucharist, and heaven and hell appear, among most Christian teenagers in the United States at the very least, to be supplanted by the language of happiness, niceness, and an earned heavenly reward. It is not so much that U.S. Christianity is being secularized. Rather more subtly, Christianity is either degenerating into a pathetic version of itself or, more significantly, Christianity is actively being colonized and displaced by a quite different religious faith.

5

American Adolescent Religion
in Social Context

EVERY HUMAN PERSON is a distinct individual with a unique story. But, as we have already suggested, all people also live within larger cultural and institutional contexts that profoundly shape their lives and stories. If we want to understand the experiences of individuals, it is necessary to understand these larger social contexts in which people's lives unfold and by which they are shaped. Only by appreciating the power of these social forces that define and influence people's lives can we adequately make sense of their individual hopes, problems, commitments, actions, and experiences. This chapter continues our analysis of the religious and spiritual lives of American teenagers by stepping back and observing some important cultural and institutional features of the world in which they live that we believe influence the character of their religious and spiritual lives. The previous chapter described the *what* of teens' religious and spiritual lives. This chapter attempts to help explain *why*.

THERAPEUTIC INDIVIDUALISM

The cultural ocean in which American adolescents swim saturates them in the ethos of therapeutic individualism.[1] Therapeutic individualism is not so much a consciously and intentionally held ideology, but rather a taken-for-granted set of assumptions and commitments about the human self, society, and life's purpose that powerfully defines everyday moral and relational codes and boundaries in the contemporary United States. The evidence of previous

chapters suggests that therapeutic individualism is having a significant influence in shaping American youth's religious and spiritual practices and experiences.

Therapeutic individualism defines the individual self as the source and
standard of authentic moral knowledge and authority, and individual self-
fulfillment as the preoccupying purpose of life. Subjective, personal experience is the touchstone of all that is authentic, right, and true. By contrast,
this ethos views the "external" traditions, obligations, and institutions of
society as inauthentic and often illegitimate constraints on morality and behavior from which individuals must be emancipated. James Nolan observes,
"Where once the self was to be brought into conformity with the standards
of externally derived authorities and social institutions, it now is compelled
to look within. . . . No longer is society something a self must adjust to; it is
now something the self must be liberated from. . . . Where once the self was
to be surrendered, denied, sacrificed, and died to, now the self is to be es-
teemed, actualized, affirmed, and unfettered."[2] In a society governed by therapeutic individualism, the traditional authority and functions of priests, pastors, parents, and lawmakers are largely displaced by a new authoritative
class of professional and popular psychologists, psychiatrists, social workers,
and other therapeutic counselors, authors, talk show hosts, and advice givers.
In the process, many activities and behaviors once defined as moral failures—
alcoholism, drug abuse, financial debt, domestic violence, gambling, family
neglect, obesity, sexual promiscuity—are redefined as either perfectly legitimate "lifestyles" or as psychological and medical dysfunctions, diseases, syn-
dromes, codependencies, or pathologies. The latter are then, for better or for
worse, treated with therapy, medications, self-help seminars, support groups,
and rehabilitation programs. Meanwhile, the self increasingly comes to be
viewed as the victim of abusive or oppressive personal pasts and current social
experiences that violate the self's right to personal health and fulfillment.
Members of therapeutic individualist cultures are encouraged in various ways
to "get in touch with their honest feelings" and to "find" their "true selves"—
presuming that they have essential, self-originating emotions and selves that
are distinct from any social formation and lost or hidden from everyday
awareness. Moreover, moral duties, pain, and suffering are not seen, as they
traditionally often were, as an inevitable part of life to be endured or perhaps
through which one should grow in personal character and spiritual depth.
Rather, these are largely avoidable displeasures to be escaped in order to
realize a pleasurable life of happiness and positive self-esteem.

Moral decision making in therapeutic individualism is always profoundly
individually self-referencing. Right and wrong are determined not by external
moralities derived from religious teachings, natural law, cultural tradition, or
the requisites of collective social functioning. Rather, clearly unaware that
feeling itself is profoundly socially formed, individual subjective feeling establishes for individuals what is good and bad, right and wrong, just and
unjust. In general, therapeutic individualism significantly displaces substantive reason and rational analysis with personal sentiments and emotions as

the grounds of knowledge and morality. In a therapeutically individualistic culture, the reasoned arguments, assertions, and professions implicit in the phrases "I think that . . ." and "I believe that . . ." are increasingly supplanted by the personal expression "I feel that . . ." Therapeutic individualists come to *feel*, for example, that murder is wrong, that the Bible teaches the deity of Jesus Christ, that a particular tax policy will stimulate the economy. Moreover, people shaped by this ethos are loath to claim that their own beliefs and morals necessarily apply to anyone else, for other people may have different feelings about matters, and no one person has the right to violate any other person's subjective sentiments, which are, after all, what determine what is truly authentic and real for each individual. In the end, the most assertive of moral arguments are expressed as "Poverty sucks," "*For me*, it is wrong when . . . ," and "I'm not trying to impose this on anyone, but that's how I personally feel about it."

Therapeutic individualism did not drop out of the sky, nor is it the spontaneous creation of its individual advocates and adherents. Ironically, given its emphasis on individual autonomy, subjectivity, and self-creation, therapeutic individualism is the collective cultural product of a historical complex of social and institutional forces that generated and sustain its ethos. At one level, therapeutic individualism is a reaction against the impersonal, bureaucratic, rationalized, instrumentally utilitarian institutions of modern public life. Its ethos provides a way for moderns to rescue some sense of individual uniqueness, spontaneity, and meaningful emotion in the face of a massive, proceduralistic, mechanistic, and alienating public sphere. At another level, therapeutic individualism's ethos perfectly serves the needs and interests of U.S. mass-consumer capitalist economy by constituting people as self-fulfillment–oriented consumers subject to advertising's influence on their subjective feelings, a point elaborated in the following section. In yet another way, the rise of therapeutic individualism corresponds to the secularization of the U.S. public sphere as the decline of the authority of religious traditions over the institutions of public life.[3] Publicly irrelevant pastors and priests are, for good or ill, displaced by their functional equivalents, therapists and psychologists, who are taken to be very relevant and authoritative. Then again, therapeutic individualism is also a by-product of modernity's cultural pluralism, in which increased frequency of routine interaction with "the other," who may be quite different from oneself, may problematize objectively maintained shared epistemological and moral orders.[4] What then becomes collectively shared is a much thinner ethos of personal subjectivity, feeling, and self-fulfillment.

Whatever its social and institutional sources, therapeutic individualism is, for better or worse, now pervasive in American culture and society, both in many people's personal lives and increasingly in public institutions themselves. Its assumptions and commitments infuse every level of the educational system; practices of courtship, marriage, family life, and divorce; some public social programs; key cultural elements of the economy, such as the advertising industry and mass media, entertainment, and recreation; the health care sector and public health system; very many elements of religion; and, increasingly, the justice system and the government itself.[5] Most every youth growing up in the United States today, perhaps Amish youth excepted, will receive some significant exposure to therapeutic individualism. Many will receive very heavy and consistent doses of socialization into its assumptions, precepts, and ethos, even as its social pervasiveness renders it natural, intuitive, and invisible to most people being inducted into its worldview. Therapeutic individualism thus seems to be the obvious way things are.

All of this appears to have had important influences on the character of the religious and spiritual lives of American adolescents. As therapeutic individualism has institutionalized itself as a natural dominant framework not only for much of social life around religion, but in American religion itself, we expect youth's assumptions about religious teachings, faith, church, and spiritual development and experiences to be transformed. Religion as an external authority or tradition that people encounter and that makes authoritative claims to form their believing, thinking, feeling, desires, and living becomes increasingly inconceivable. Therapeutic individualists instead seek out religious and spiritual practices, feelings, and experiences that satisfy their own subjectively defined needs and wants. Faith and spirituality become centered less around a God believed in and God's claims on lives, and more around the believing (or perhaps even unbelieving) self and its personal realization and happiness. The very idea and language of "spirituality," originally grounded in the self-disciplining faith practices of religious believers, including ascetics and monks, then becomes detached from its moorings in historical religious traditions and is redefined in terms of subjective self-fulfillment. For example, during the writing of this chapter, our secular state university's Training and Development Department posted on its Web page an offering for an employees' education class on "Spirituality at Work," taught by a university "Health Education Specialist," described as follows: "Work, home, family, friends—so many different hats in life! And each one requires different pieces of our self to shine through: employee, family member, confidant. Learning to integrate who we are both at home and work can lead to a greater sense of self and feelings of purpose and well-being. Come explore practical tips for integrating various facets of life in a healthy and holistic way as we strive to balance who we are both on and off the job." Spirituality is thus renarrated for all comers as personal integration, subjective feeling, and self-improvement toward individual health and personal well-being—and no longer has anything to do with, for example, religious faith and self-discipline toward holiness or obedience.

Sociologists of religion and other scholars have already observed the influence of therapeutic individualism on American religion, although their studies have usually focused on religious young adults or the middle-aged or on religious subcultures or organizations.[6] This book helps to reveal the extent to which the therapeutic individualist ethos appears to be forming the religion and spirituality of contemporary American youth and with what possible effects.

MASS-CONSUMER CAPITALISM

People normally think of the economy and religion as two separate spheres of life that affect each other very little. In fact, however, American religion and spirituality, including teenagers' involvement in them, may be profoundly shaped by American mass-consumer capitalism. Capitalism is not merely a system for the efficient production and distribution of goods and services; it also incarnates and promotes a particular *moral order*, an institutionalized normative worldview comprising and fostering particular assumptions, narratives, commitments, beliefs, values, and goals.[7] Capitalism not only puts food on the table, it also powerfully defines for those who live in it in elemental terms both what is and what should be, however taken for granted those definitions ordinarily may be.

Consider, for example, how mass-consumer capitalism fundamentally constitutes the human self. There are many ways to conceive of what the human person is and should be: a fundamentally morally responsible agent, an illusion of individuality destined to dissolve into cosmic unity, a sinner being divinely redeemed and sanctified, and more. As an institution with a specific historical and social location, mass-consumer capitalism constitutes the human self in a very particular way: as an *individual, autonomous, rational, self-seeking, cost-benefit-calculating consumer.* This, of course, is not what human selves have always been, nor what they inevitably must be. This is also not the definition of the human self that most American religious historical traditions have sought to constitute in their adherents. But it *is* the human self that the moral order of mass-consumer capitalism constitutes, that its institutions and practices very powerfully bring into being, promote, and reinforce. Note that we are not simply talking here about particular ethical problems that the capitalist market may pose for religious teenagers, such as whether or not to buy and smoke cigarettes, but fundamental, taken-for-granted presuppositions about what is real about the world and ourselves, which, once established, are difficult to recognize, much less resist.

One of the possible consequences of this capitalist constitution of the human self is the way it can reshape the character of religion itself over time. The more American people and institutions are redefined by mass-consumer capitalism's moral order, the more American religion is also remade in its image. Religion becomes one product among many others existing to satisfy people's subjectively defined needs, tastes, and wants. Religious adherents thus become spiritual consumers uniquely authorized as autonomous individuals to pick and choose in the religious market whatever products they may find satisfying or fulfilling at the moment. And the larger purpose of life comes to be defined as optimally satiating one's self-defined felt needs and desires, as opposed to, say, attaining salvation, learning obedience to God, following the Ten Commandments, achieving enlightenment, dying to oneself and serving others, or any other traditional religious purpose. Where does this profound shift, this novel approach to religion originate? Not from the individuals who end up espousing it, for they are themselves profoundly formed by larger historical transformations and social structures. It comes instead in good measure from the life-defining power of the pervasive and deeply rooted moral order and institutions of mass-consumer capitalism.

One way to describe this process is as a shift, which happened concurrently with the historical expansion of mass-consumer capitalism, from tradition-centered to individual-centered religion. The central question here is: In what does religious *authority* reside? Who or what has authority to define religious truth, to adjudicate religious differences and conflicts? In a mass-consumer capitalist-shaped society, authority increasingly resides not in the church nor in millennia of tradition, the prayer book, theological experts, or the scriptures. Rather, authority resides in the individual human self. Religious knowledge and authority thus become increasingly privatized, subjectivized, customized, and therapeutically psychologized around the controlling authority of individual selves, and not religious communities, traditions, and institutions.[8] The historical, dynamic tension in living religions between the received traditions and interpretations and the ongoing human collective experience living and interpreting those traditions in new times and contexts increasingly collapses into mere one-dimensional subjective individualism. People then less frequently say, "I do not fully understand it or naturally agree with it, but because my religious tradition teaches thus-and-such, I embrace it and try to better understand it." Rather, people shaped in the image of capitalism's moral order and into the human self it constitutes personally decide on and define for themselves what they are willing and able (and not willing or able) to believe and practice religiously—based on what feels comfortable to them, what resonates with their personal subjective experience, what meets their personally felt needs. Although this is a relatively new situation historically, for some readers this version of religion may be so pervasive that it is hard even to recognize as other than entirely obvious and natural. (The irony in all of this apparently nonconformist, strong individualistic, selective acceptance of religious traditions' teachings and practices in order to suit one's own preferences, tastes, comforts, and subjective moral judgments is that it in fact is a major act of *conformity* to the larger moral authority of mass-consumer capitalism—whether any of its subjects realize that as such or not.) In this way, the religious assumptions and options available to American adolescents are shaped by the larger context of the reigning economic order.

Another way of understanding mass-consumer capitalism's influence on American adolescents and the religious and spiritual terrain they inhabit is by examining the morally charged appeals that its most obvious promotional arm, the advertising industry, persistently and pervasively advances. Many Americans complain about "the culture," "the media," "television," and "Hollywood" for the evident roles they play in generating teenage problems. But if we think *systemically*, we see that these are for the most part euphemisms for mass-consumer capitalism. For what drives television, the media, and Hollywood? What are they really about? They are often both commodities for sale themselves and the means of gathering and organizing buying

audiences of consumers to whom to sell other products. Commercial television, for instance, is not ultimately about entertainment, but about delivering
segmented purchasing audiences to advertisers who want to sell products.
There was once a time in earlier days of market capitalism—up until the
early twentieth century—when increasing production was more important
than increasing consumption. But eventually, increased production required
increased mass consumption to move the new masses of more efficiently produced goods. The inherent, internal logic of mass-consumer capitalism is the
drive of an impersonal profit motive and perpetual capital accumulation.
Capitalism as a system must ever grow or it will die. The intrinsic problem
in capitalism's logic, however, is that *actual* human needs are somewhat limited and modest: it takes only so many goods and services to sustain a healthy,
potentially satisfying human life. For mass-consumer capitalism to forever
grow, therefore, it must constitute masses of people as consumer selves who
misrecognize new wants as essential needs, whose basic sense of necessity
always expands. Consumer demand thus must always escalate if capitalism
is to succeed. And because this does not necessarily happen naturally or automatically, it must be actively and intentionally promoted. This is the job of
the $240 billion-a-year American advertising industry.[9]

What is evident about the advertising industry's efforts when it targets
youth is that to accomplish its goals it often appeals to what has always and
pervasively been understood to be some of the *worst* of human potentials:
insecurity, envy, vanity, impulsiveness, pride, surface images and appearances,
the sexual objectification of others, emotional impulses habitually trumping
rational thought, short-term gratification, and so on. How many successful
youth ad campaigns appeal to, say, contentment, self-control, humility, rationality, inner character, selflessness, or any other traditional virtue? Playing
to the darker side of human nature seems to be, for whatever reason, often
easier and more successful in selling products than appealing to humanity's
brighter side.[10]

All of this becomes tremendously important for our purposes when understood in light of American adolescents' immense purchasing power, which
makes them a prime advertising target. Industry experts estimate that American teenagers spend about $170 billion of their own dollars annually and
influence upwards of $500 billion of their parents' spending.[11] American teen-
agers thus have an immense amount of money to spend in the market. In
addition, they are both highly brand-sensitive and brand-flexible. This means
that, while they will spend extra money to purchase a particular product
brand that is in fashion, their brand preferences are often not firmly established. Brand loyalties become firm later in life.[12] In an effort to line up potential lifetime consumers behind allegiances to particular product brands
while they are still open to switching, therefore, advertisers especially target
youth with massive promotions campaigns. Thus, a massive and powerful
advertising industry expends immense amounts of resources on very sophisticated efforts that shape the basic assumptions, feelings, desires, and commitments of American youth.[13] This is not because they care a hoot about

the well-being of teenagers, but because they want the dollars that are burning holes in teenagers' pockets. In short, the consciousness of American adolescents is being powerfully formed by expert agents with enormous resources motivated not to achieve youth's good but rather to acquire youth's money. And what it often takes for them to acquire that money turns out to be not very good for youth, at least from most historical religious perspectives.

For all of the good things that modern capitalism has clearly achieved, which cannot be ignored, we would also be remiss not to see, again, mass-consumer capitalism's relevance for understanding the religious and spiritual lives of American youth. If we conceive of the culture as distinct moral orders competing for the attention and allegiance of its members, and if the elemental assumptions and moral commitments of traditional religions and mass-consumer capitalism are often at odds, as described above, then American religious communities are in fact up against overwhelming competitors in their efforts to shape the lives of youth. The average American teenager watches 21 hours of television per week and views 360,000 television advertisements before graduating from high school; furthermore, 65 percent of 8- to 18-year-olds have television sets in their bedrooms.[14] That kind of exposure dwarfs the exposure to religious influences that even the most religiously active American teenager might encounter. Aside from this simple volume of exposure, the elementary assumptions and expectations shaped by mass-consumer capitalism that youth bring to religion, as described above, also affect their interests in and responses to religion. And in America's religious economy, these consumer "preferences" over time shape the available religious "products" on the market, for American religions tend to some degree to accommodate the transformed definitions of self, faith, and purpose to avoid becoming culturally outmoded. Exactly how different religious traditions, denominations, and congregations negotiate this process inevitably shapes both the larger character of American religion and ways that different kinds of youth engage religious beliefs and practices. Some of the outcomes we have already seen in the previous chapter.

THE DIGITAL COMMUNICATION REVOLUTION

Critical in working out the dynamics described above (and some below) and in shaping the religion and spirituality of American teenagers are recent, profound transformations in technologies of communication. Radio revolutionized mass communication in the 1930s, and television in the 1950s and 1960s. But the emergence of digital communication technologies—computers, the Internet, e-mail, digital video recording, cellular telephones, and so on—have dramatically transformed the character of human communication in recent years. Predigital communication technologies tended toward centralization, the authority of gatekeepers, and fixity of location. Television programming was provided by a handful of networks, well-capitalized record labels controlled most music distribution, and telephones were attached to kitchen walls. The digital revolution, by contrast, has not only vastly expanded the amount of available information and imagery, but also diffused access to media production and consumption, promoted the mobility of individual communicators, replaced centralized channels with dispersed networks of communication, and integrated technological links between different media forms.[15] Many American youth now talk on their own cell phones day and night, e-mail and instant-message any number of friends and strangers at any time, download hundreds of music CDs onto portable hard-disk jukeboxes, and access a world of unregulated information and images with a few keystrokes.[16]

Many theorists of these new technologies suggest that they bring with them important social psychological and cultural consequences.[17] For one thing, the digital communication revolution, especially its visual side, accelerates the trend begun with the advent of television away from typographic-based, linear, rational thought and discourse and toward noncognitive, image-based, entertainment-centered public discourse.[18] The new communication technologies also seem to produce a world of information and images that is more disjointed and fragmented, that does not hang together as an organized whole. Anyone can, for instance, post for global consumption almost whatever content on the Internet, unregulated by traditional standards gatekeepers, without having to account for its relation to everything else on the Internet. Stated differently, the new technologies open up greater opportunities for unfettered authorship, for more reciprocal flows of information, and for multiple horizontal connections through hyperlink structures instead of the more linear and hierarchical structures of traditional texts and producers. Authority over standards of knowledge thus becomes radically democratized and decentralized, filling the open market with a congestion of ideas and information that have not been reviewed, judged, and sorted by evaluating authorities. Thus, Internet searches on any subject—on the nature of God, for example—produce many thousands of hits with no built-in means to sort through which information among those hits is more valid, reliable, or authorized by the institutions that once controlled that knowledge. Discernment is left up to the individual. All of this not only increases the amount of information publicly available, but more important, embodies for and promotes among its users a new epistemology—a novel definition of human knowledge and interaction per se—that represents an alternative model of what the very world itself is and how the world itself works. The new world of knowledge, and perhaps the human consciousness that flows from it, is, for better or worse, increasingly visual, decentralized, unclassified, disjointed, unregulated, fragmented, and unevaluated. Alien to it, therefore, are many of the continuities and organizing principles of historical tradition, canon, authority, rules of order, systematic doctrine, and many other features that have historically defined American religions. Youth socialized into the new digital order may therefore find the substance of historical religious traditions difficult to assimilate—as, indeed, prior chapters suggest they do.

On the other hand, American youth now have easy access to masses of information about an endless array of religious systems and spiritual practices that might broaden their religious horizons and kindle new spiritual interests. Furthermore, many traditional American religious communities are capitalizing on the novel communication technologies to reach new audiences, increase communication efficiency within and between congregations, raise funds, experiment with new worship styles and visuals, enhance religious education programs, train ministers from a distance, and much more. Not all American religious groups are behind the curve on social and cultural change, for good or ill. There are many conceivable ways that the communication revolution can and does serve the purposes of American religious communities. Finally, historically rooted religious traditions may provide a grounded counterbalance to what may feel lacking or unsettling in the new digital age, making religion more attractive to youth. What matters for our purposes in all of this are the multiple consequences of the digital revolution at various levels on the youth who do and do not engage religion and spirituality, and on the texture and character of the religious ideas and organizations they may engage.

RESIDUAL POSITIVISM AND EMPIRICISM

Ironically, at the same time that American teenagers are confronting the consequences of major contemporary technological revolutions in communication technologies, many of them also continue to assume popular but antiquated cultural mentalities about science and knowledge rooted in nineteenth- and early twentieth-century thought: logical positivism and naïve empiricism. These schools of thought claimed, in short, that there are only two sources of real knowledge, logical reasoning and empirical experience, and that statements are meaningful only if they can be positively proven true by logic or experience—making traditional, metaphysically oriented philosophy and theology simply meaningless and useless. Although logical positivism and naïve empiricism have been discredited in the academy for decades as philosophically untenable—their claims cannot be supported, after all, by their *own* criteria of knowledge and meaning[19]—residual, taken-for-granted forms of them remain fast in popular culture, including among American youth. The popular, residual version of these old doctrines automatically assumes that no idea should be embraced or commitment made for which there is no irrefutable material or logical evidence providing positive verification. The naïve assumption, which hardly anyone ever actually thinks about, is that everything we legitimately hold to has beneath it an indubitable and universally accessible foundation of knowledge that provides a means to identify positive knowledge of the truth. Normally, this means of identifying truth is thought to involve sensory observation of the material world. Because most religions and spiritualities reference superempirical realities, this taken-for-granted residual positivism and empiricism often have a corrosive effect on religious faith and practice. Thus, while writing this chapter, we received the following e-mail from a worried father who had accessed our project's Web site in search of help with his teenage son: "I would appreciate your help to refer me to resources to talk to my soon-to-be 15-year-old son on religion. He has recently expressed his non-belief in God. We are a regular church attending (Catholic) family. His point of view is there is no proof for the existence of God. Thank you for any help you can offer." It is unreasonable to expect most teenagers, who are merely operating with widespread cultural assumptions, to be current on contemporary views in epistemology and the philosophy of science. But clearly, what most informed intellectuals now think about the character and limits of all human knowledge has not trickled down to American youth at the grassroots nor, apparently, to their high school teachers and parents. Many contemporary American youth thus approach religion and spirituality unconsciously assuming certainty and proof in knowledge and belief that are more than a century old and now largely philosophically discredited. But taken-for-granted cultural beliefs, however intellectually lacking, are still powerful, and so many American adolescents engage religion with the old framework in the back of their minds that pitches faith against fact, positive knowledge against personal belief, verified truth against subjective opinion. For some youth, this framework poses few problems for their religious and spiritual faith and practice. "That's just the way I was raised," we have seen, is good enough for them. For others, while it does not destroy their religious faith, it diminishes religion's reliability and importance in their minds. For yet other youth (such as Steve in chapter 3), this assumed framework helps to undermine the very possibility of religious belief and commitment. Thus, American 14-year-olds with cell phones, instant messaging, and Internet access can lose their religious faith in part under the influence of lingering cultural residues of intellectual doctrines that exhilarated science and philosophy in the 1880s and 1930s but that are now untenable. Whatever the exact effect on specific youth, residual positivism and empiricism continue in American popular culture as influential, taken-for-granted presuppositions. They envelop people's intellectual imaginations and often have real consequences for their religious and spiritual lives, even though few people are even aware of the real philosophical issues involved.

STRUCTURAL DISCONNECT FROM THE ADULT WORLD

Throughout most of human history in most societies, the lives of youth were closely integrated into the world of adults.[20] One need not hold a romanticized view of "traditional society" to see that, in premodern social settings lacking modernity's radical splits between public and private, production and consumption, and education and work, at relatively early ages youth typically were important contributors to the tasks of survival and economic production. They participated in herding, gathering foods, planting, irrigating, and harvesting, hunting, fishing, fending off predators, running errands, transporting and selling goods, assisting in crafts, caring for animals, and much more. Children and youth were also tightly integrated into the workings of the domestic life of families, clans, tribes, villages. Early on in life they took on such responsibilities as tending fires, food preparation and cooking, spinning and weaving, child care, the construction of shelter, and the disposal of wastes. As recently as 175 years ago, for better or worse, many American boys at the age of 12 were sent away from their families to become apprentices working long days under the eyes of craft masters in whose homes they lived out their teenage years. The days of most American girls at that age, if not younger, consisted of helping older women accomplish household chores and perhaps, in certain times and places, taking in some home-based book learning. Young people in many cultures have often carved out for themselves some minimal degree of distance from the adult world and sometimes developed in those spaces something somewhat like what we think of as youth culture. But the much more striking reality is that the lives of most youth in all but the most recent generations have generally been closely involved in the productive activities of and supervised by the watchful eyes of adults.

All of that was profoundly changed by the industrial revolution and the rapid technological and social transformations that followed in its wake. America's nineteenth-century industrial revolution separated work from home, production from consumption, and public from private life. In larger, related processes, domestic nurture was differentiated from national economic advance, and the education of youth was increasingly formalized and detached from household life. In the early industrial revolution, many children and teenage boys and girls worked long hours in the factory under the foreman's discipline. In due time, however, economic production by youth increasingly came to be viewed, often rightly, as pernicious and exploitative child labor, which was gradually suppressed by social reforms. Throughout, childhood and adolescence were being culturally redefined as particular developmental phases of life profoundly different from adulthood.

Further social changes in the twentieth century accelerated the structural disconnection of youth's lives from the adult world. The invention of the automobile provided teenagers with a mobility and privacy they had never before known. Commercial movie theaters, dance halls, and other centers of entertainment had similar effects. Most important of all, however, was the near complete institutionalization of universal public education. In fact, it was not until the 1930s that the majority of American youth of high school age became school students. Comprehensive national child labor laws were finally put into effect in 1934, and state and local governments made major efforts to get youth into schools. This new state crackdown on truancy was fueled in part by the need prompted by the Great Depression to remove youth from the labor force so they would not compete with adult men for scarce jobs. With little work to be done, mandatory schooling for teenagers became a means to keep youth off the streets and from being drawn into "hobo jungles" and other worrisome places and activities.

A mere 70 years ago, then, the majority of teenagers were for the first time in history gathered up together for most of the day, for most days of the week, in single buildings with masses of other boys and girls of their same age, with relatively few adults around to supervise and intervene into the details of their lives. Mass schooling was the perfect incubator for a new, distinctive youth culture, which blossomed in the following decades. The word "teen-ager" (its first spelling) was coined during World War II, and by 1945 "teenager" had become a widely used label naming a cultural reality newly come into being. Postwar prosperity, a widespread perceived "return" to the traditional nuclear family, and the desire of Depression- and war-weary parents to provide their children all the good things they had never enjoyed provided the resources and attitudes further enhancing adolescents' free time, mobility, and privacy—in short, autonomy from adults. Peer groups now became significant new and powerful sources of knowledge and influence in the lives of youth, competing with parents and other adults in teenagers' socialization. The postwar GI Bill also helped rapidly to expand American higher education, further postponing entry into the adult world for millions of young college students and further fostering the evolution of a distinct American youth subculture. By the 1960s, the civil rights, student, free speech, and anti–Vietnam War movements—in all of which youth played major roles—signified new levels of youth independence from the control of the adult world. The trend continued. Macroeconomic changes after 1970 accelerated the entry of women, including mothers of adolescents, into the paid labor force. The no-fault divorce revolution of the 1970s and other social forces significantly increased the number of single-parent households in which teenagers lived and live.[21] These and other related factors left youth increasingly on their own, both alone and with other youth, for growing numbers of hours of the day and night. This high degree of youth autonomy has become the normalized reality for very many adolescents among working poor, middle-class, and upper-middle-class families alike.

Interacting with this structural disconnect is our society's cultural construction of adolescence as an Incredibly Long Wait for full participation in genuine adulthood.[22] In American culture adolescence can begin at age 10, 11, or 12; at the latest, official teenage status begins at age 13. On the other end, many youth do not pass the symbolic cultural markers of full adulthood—school graduation, full-time work, financial independence, marriage—until the age of 18, 22, 25, or, for some, even their late 20s and early 30s. Thus, American youth live for between five and 20 years in a kind of socially constructed developmental limbo, ever waiting, delaying, anticipating, preparing for the day when they will take on and enjoy the freedoms and responsibilities of being real grown-ups. The cultural message to youth is that they are not mature or prepared enough to enter the adult world and so must continue for years to wait, even as other powerful, contradictory messages implore them to act fully responsibly, be self-directed, and make very good choices as independent decision makers. Furthermore, even as improved nutrition (and perhaps the increased use of hormones in some farm products) lowered the age of the onset of puberty by about three years during the twentieth century, extended educational expectations, career startup requirements, and increasing lifestyle consumption expectations postponed the average age of marriage for young men and women from the years 1950 and 2000 by an extra four to five years.[23] Part of adolescents' Incredibly Long

Wait, then, involves the tension of being physiologically able and hormonally very interested in activities that make babies, while normally lacking the emotional, relational, and financial capacity to parent babies. Adult American culture, working through the media, schools, and other institutions, thus sends its youth the conflicting messages that sex is one of the greatest and most important experiences in life, that youth should abstain from sex until marriage, that boys will be boys (and, increasingly, girls will be girls) and cannot be expected as teens not to party wildly, that youth should practice "safe" and "responsible sex," and so on.[24] The wait is therefore not only incredibly long but often very confusing.[25] The larger situation this can create for many youth is a widespread gnawing restlessness and frustration, underlying tension with parents over continually renegotiating boundaries of freedom and responsibility, and sometimes a feeling of uselessness and inertia. Teenagers are forever waiting, continually preparing, perpetually coming of age, and are meanwhile for the most part socially superfluous. Thus, they experience a disconnect from the adult world not only in the structures of their routine activities and schedules, but also through the many years of limbo through which they must hang in suspension before passing into full-fledged adulthood.

The degree to which specific, individual adolescents today are connected to or disconnected from the adult world is of course highly variable. Some American teens do have close ties to many adults. But viewed in broad historical perspective, contemporary teenage autonomy from adults is unprecedented and astounding. Significant numbers of teens today live their lives with little but the most distant adult direction and oversight. They spend the greater part of most weekdays in schools surrounded almost exclusively by their peers. Their parents are working and otherwise busy. Members of their extended family live in distant cities. Their teachers are largely preoccupied with discipline, classroom instruction, and grading. Their neighbors tend to stay out of each others' business. These teens may have their own cars, cell phones, spending money, and televisions in their bedrooms. Or they may simply spend all their free time hanging out with friends and associates at the mall, on the streets, at friends' houses, or other places away from home. In any case, when school lets out, it may be hours before a parent gets home from work. If the teen works, his or her coworkers are mostly other teenagers who are also flipping burgers or working cash registers; their supervisors may be adults, but few teens have significant relationships with them beyond taking orders and collecting paychecks.

This structural disconnection of many contemporary American adolescents from the world of adults has potential important ramifications for the character of their religious and spiritual lives. If a teenager defines serious religion as mostly an adult affair, as many do, then religion comes automatically to feel distant to them, as something that they may "get into" someday when they are older, but not now; this feeds into the age-appropriate life course scripts mentioned in the previous chapter. Furthermore, when teenagers have little daily experience socializing with adults generally, they likely find it more difficult to form meaningful relational ties with members of their congregations who are not their peers. Some youth may demand religious expressions and experiences that resonate with the symbols, images, language, and practices of popular youth culture. This may, in turn, shape the religious programming that religious institutions offer to youth, potentially altering the texture of the religious tradition itself. In addition, our culture's structural disconnect between youth and adults has fostered among some religious adults an insecurity about their ability to "relate to" youth, a lack of confidence in their capacity to teach and train youth well in matters of faith, a reluctance to speak to teenagers about spiritual or theological issues with direction and authority for fear of coming across as square, boring, or irrelevant to teenagers' real lives, in which many adults are not very involved. In such cases, religious adults may back away from adolescents and so fail to provide them with the kind of nurture, instruction, and direction in the faith that they might actually need or want.

At the same time, the structural disconnect of youth from adults may generate in at least some youth a hunger for meaningful relationships with mature adults, for many youth do in fact desire the boundaries, teaching, direction, wisdom, and caring that adults can offer. In some cases, this can create opportunities for religious adults effectively to reach out to youth, to satisfy this need, and to use such relationships to foster religious conversions and deeper commitments to faith among youth. For good or ill, many religious institutions have also mirrored society's separate and parallel worlds of youth and adults by creating youth-only religious groups, worship services, and service projects that may, given the culture, recruit teenagers into religious organizations more effectively than mixed-age religious meetings and activities. For these and other possible reasons, the significant contemporary structural disconnection between youth and adults and its possible consequences is a fact we must bear in mind as we seek generally to understand the religious and spiritual lives of American teenagers and specifically to make sense of the survey and interview findings in the previous and following chapters.

ADULTS WITH PROBLEMS

Despite their daily routines being structurally disconnected from the adult world, most American adolescents still also have to negotiate their lives dealing with specific adults—parents, teachers, coaches, family members, friends—who may have their own personal problems. Many adults truly love and care for the teenagers in their lives. Yet adults are also often far from perfect. They sometimes have their own haunting emotional and psychological problems and unmet needs. Adults can be selfish, neglectful, abusive, manipulative, distant, or smothering in subtle or obvious ways. Adults have bad conflicts. They get divorced. They have midlife crises. They lose their jobs. They spiral into depressions. They can be too busy with their own concerns and so substitute "guilt money" for time with and attention to their teens. Adults can burden youth with the emotional pressure to meet their own needs or make them happy through achievement, success, and goodness. Adults can lack parenting skills and appropriate judgment. Sometimes adults, even some parents, simply do not care much about the teenagers in their lives. Adults can be too poor, too rich, mentally ill, in and out of prison, or consumed by their careers in ways that hurt teens. However loving and self-less adults may profess themselves to be and may in fact be, there is also often a shadow side in humanity that can be self-centered, lazy, dishonest to self, or oblivious to the needs of others. It is not that many adults are particularly wicked. Adults are simply human. And adults, like teens, live in larger social and cultural contexts that both enable and constrain, in which they make choices, sometimes bad choices. But for whatever complex of reasons, adult humans have problems, both large and small, which can often make trouble for the teenagers in their lives.

Nevertheless, it is common for adult talk about teenagers in the United States to focus on *teenagers'* problems, on their possible or actual bad attitudes, rebellion, offensive music, materialism, drinking, smoking, drugs, gangs, delinquency, obesity, pornography, sex, pregnancy, STDs, abortions, violence, school shootings, suicide, and more. Parents are often concerned about these issues in their kids' lives, and often rightly so. The media always headline crimes committed by teens. Bookstore shelves are lined with myriad advice books telling parents not how to enjoy, but how to *survive* the teenage years. One can readily get the impression from all of this not only that adolescents sometimes have problems, but that teenagers *are* a problem, that adolescence itself *is* a social problem.

But this viewpoint is ultimately deceiving and self-deceived. The truth is, first, that American adults have as many or more of most of the problems with which youth struggle. Compared to teenagers, American adults consume more alcohol, cigarettes, and drugs, commit more crimes and violence, contract more STDs, have more abortions, and more often become obese, drive drunk, commit suicide, and engage in a host of other problems that worry adults about youth.[26]

Second, every teenage problem is finally rooted in and perpetuated by the adult world problems. In their often very real troubles, American youth are normally only acting out problems ingrained in the grown-up world into which they are being socialized. It is precisely adults, at least some adults, and not teens who are the primary inventors, suppliers, promoters, and beneficiaries of most "teenage problems." Where do adolescents get the Marlboros they smoke and Budweisers they drink, and the very idea that smoking and drinking are cool? Who or what supplies and promotes the expensive sneakers, jeans, and myriad other commodities that adults then complain represent shallow teen materialism? Who develops and makes the money from pornographic videos and Web sites? Where do teens, especially girls, get the idea that body weight and outward physical appearance are paramount in defining and projecting one's self-identity? From where do teens learn that sex is an individual right of self-expression and the pinnacle of all human experiences? From where have youth learned that they should be autonomous individuals wary of authority? Who transports the drugs from South America to New Jersey? Who develops, records, sells, and promotes offensive and degrading music? Who has taught teens that making a lot of money is a paramount goal of life? From whom have youth learned that problems are rightly solved with force and guns? Where does all this come from? Not primarily from 13- and 16-year-olds, assuredly, but from 33- and 55-year-olds. From business entrepreneurs, multinational corporations, shopping malls, Hollywood, Madison Avenue, Wall Street, American history textbooks, U.S. political parties and interest groups, the Pentagon, sometimes the White House, and sometimes even teenagers' baby boomer parents themselves—which is to say: from *the institutions of mainstream adult American society*. Few teen problems in fact are invented or promoted by teenagers. Most are prevalent in and developed, modeled, and handed down to teens by the adult world. Adolescents are often less sophisticated than adults in how they act out their problems and less able to cover up their negative consequences. But in the end, teens are simply learning through socialization how to live in the problematic world they are inheriting from adults.

At the very least, then, adults' obsessions with adolescents' problems represents a double standard. It may also be worse, however, in representing a collective adult process of what psychologists call "transference": the projection of one's own problems onto other people or situations in order through denial and blaming of others to avoid having to confront one's own responsibilities, problems, and failures. When teenagers become the cultural lightning rod for deep concerns about what are actually adult personal and social problems, it helps relieve adults of the discomfort of the fact that teenage troubles merely reflect back to adults problems of their own adult world. Adults may not consciously intend to engage in such transference, denial, self-deception, or scapegoating, but we also know that these kinds of psychological and cultural processes are rarely conscious and intentional. At the very least, these are possibilities meriting consideration.

If all of this sounds judgmental, all we can say is that through our research interviews around the country, we came across more parents and other adults with problems than one might ever want to know, just some of whom we have seen in this book—parents and other adults oblivious to their children's multiple suicide attempts, who buy drugs and hard liquor for their teenagers and their friends, who communicate with their kids only by yelling, who ignore obvious evidence of their kids' breaking major family rules and even the law, and much more. The more truth telling we can do about adults' problems, we think, the better position we may be in to understand adolescents' lives.

All of this is relevant for understanding teenagers' religious and spiritual lives. First, adolescents often associate faith and religion with adults. When adults in teenagers' lives have problems that injure them, religion can become negatively associated with those problems. Youth can view religion as a source of hypocrisy when adults fail to live up to the standards professed by religion. In this and other ways, religion can become for some youth a symbolic field of resistance or rebellion on which to work out their anger or hurt over the adult problems that bother or injure them. Thus, adult problems imposing on the lives of teens may create subjective dissonances with religion, causing some youth to drift from their congregations and discard their beliefs. Recall the lives of Raymond and Joy, for example. On the other hand, religion can provide youth with resources to help them deal with problems adults may pose in their lives. Faith can become a sanctuary from pain and struggle, a spring of strength and hope. Fellow believers, both adults and peers, can be to youth sources of support, encouragement, counsel, and direction. Consider, for instance, the lives of Kristen and Alyssa. Thus, adult problems can cut both ways in the religious and spiritual lives of youth, helping to explain both defection from and commitment to the institutions and practices of American religion.

OTHER RELEVANT CULTURAL CONTRADICTIONS

In no culture do all expectations, ideals, and lived practices add up. All cultures contain some contradictions, loose ends, and discrepancies between what is said and what is done. This is true of American culture in many ways that we might expect to create tensions and confusion in the lives of American adolescents, even if teens are not always consciously aware of and articulate about them. We have already alluded to some of these contradictions. Adults fear and condemn teen violence, for instance, yet we are a nation birthed by a violent revolution we celebrate annually; our right to own and bear guns is constitutionally protected; graphic violence in the media is defined by an "R" rating that defines violence as appropriate to enjoy when one is grown up enough; and the ready use of violence to achieve goals is integral to U.S. foreign policy. The point here is not whether any of these things are good or bad per se, but rather that our culture is actually ambivalent and multivocal about violence, sending mixed messages to those being socialized into the culture.

We might observe many other American cultural contradictions that may affect teenagers. Adults often impress on adolescents that what really counts is the personal character of one's inner self. And yet, in many other ways, American culture sends the clear message that what really counts is outward appearance and good looks. Which are teens supposed to believe? Adults often tell teenagers that they must learn to respect authority, yet most sacred of all American values is the inviolability of the individual conscience, derived from liberal individualism,[27] embedded in widespread American distrust of the government and other institutions of authority, and incessantly depicted in television and movies, particularly those aimed at youth. Is it any wonder that American teens sometimes disrespect or rebel against parents, teachers, school principals, and other authorities? Adults say they want kids to learn to be financially responsible, but, except among the poorest Americans, teenagers with jobs are freed from the responsibility of helping to support their household, so nearly all of their income is used for discretionary consumer spending on themselves. Moreover, the U.S. economy itself has become dependent on high levels of consumer debt.[28] Adults often complain about how stupid television is and how much of it teenagers watch, but American adults actually watch just as much (stupid) television as teenagers do.[29] Adults constantly preach to adolescents about sexual responsibility, yet many adults engage in extramarital sex and have unwanted pregnancies; the world portrayed by adult-produced media is one of relatively free sex without negative consequences; and all manner of pornographic sex (much of which can hardly be called "responsible") our society labels "adult," implying that, though kids should not view pornography, it is a perfectly appropriate pastime for grownups to enjoy. Should we be surprised that teens, who are itching to enjoy the freedoms of grown-up life, act out their sexuality in ways not always responsible? Much American public discourse is spent agonizing about improving the health of youth yet we structure the lives of youth in ways that obviously undermine their health: we schedule early school hours and overbearing homework requirements, for example, so as to virtually guarantee that teenagers routinely get less sleep than their bodies need—and then wonder why teens are surly, lazy, and complain about being hassled. Our culture wakes up adolescents at 5:30 and 6:00 in the morning, not because it is healthy for their bodies and spirits to do so—we know scientifically that it is not—but so their parents can get to work for the corporation on time.

Thus, although many Americans talk about what a pro-family, youth-loving society ours is, it is not entirely clear that many of our actual practices and institutions support those claims. Most of the structures and routines of American life actually pull families apart regularly and effectively. American work and education practices separate family members for most daytime hours of every weekday. Day care centers and preschools remove children from their parents at a very young age. After school, many parents, middle-class parents particularly, schedule their children's lives with so many programmed activities that they find themselves with very little unstructured time simply to spend together as families. A minority of American families with teenagers eat most of their dinner meals together.[30] And our legal systems and cultural practices around divorce make clear that keeping families together is not a particularly high societal priority. Contrary to our culture's pro-family rhetoric, an alien anthropologist might have good reason to conclude that members of American families actually have little interest in spending time together. To be clear, the point here is not that individual parents and other adults are rotten people who do not love their children. These, rather, are largely matters of routine cultural practices and institutional structures from which it is very difficult to deviate. But they do send messages to and have consequences for the youth of our society.

In these and other ways, many of the messages and practices of American culture do not add up. We often say one thing but do something else. Whether or not American teenagers have the perspective to be able to recognize and articulate such cultural contradictions, they may intuitively feel them in their lives and react to them in various ways. As with the other big-picture factors described above, these cultural contradictions can thus have significant effects on the religious and spiritual perspectives and experiences of American teenagers. They may provide the occasion for youth to feel frustrated, angry, guilty, overburdened, or confused, which, in certain cases, may be projected onto religious experiences and organizations in ways that influence their religious beliefs and commitments. Religion, as one high-profile institutional representative of mainstream adult society, may become the focusing point of more generalized frustrations with double standards and unfairness. Then again, in other cases, religious people, programs, organizations, and experiences may become for youth sources of integration in or resolution to an otherwise disjointed life experience. Religious faith and religious communities may provide a shelter from what some youth may perceive to be a crazy, mixed-up world.

CONCLUSION

It is difficult to understand adequately the religious and spiritual lives of American adolescents without considering their lives within the framework of the larger cultural and institutional influences described above. Exploring the faith of youth with this big-picture context in mind can thus yield valuable insights about the condition of contemporary American teenage religion and spirituality. One of the benefits that attention to the larger social context of teenage life makes possible is helping us to realize both how thoroughly shaped by and reflective of their social and cultural order American youth are and how much they actually have in common with adults. Teenagers are often spoken of in popular culture as alien creatures, strange beings from another planet, unpredictable animals driven by mysterious forces and motives, to whom parents and other adults have little chance of relating or understanding. In fact, however—their lack of maturity and emotional volatility notwithstanding—American youth actually share much more in common with adults than they do not share, and most American youth faithfully mirror the aspirations, lifestyles, practices, and problems of the adult world into which they are being socialized. In these ways, adolescents may actually serve as a very accurate barometer of the condition of the culture and institutions of our larger society. Far from being alien creatures from another planet, American teenagers actually well reflect back to us the best and worst of our own adult condition and culture. This approach, we believe, proves to be a much more helpful perspective for making sense of adolescent life today than the more typical alien-creatures framing of American teenagers.

We seek to understand the religion and spirituality of contemporary American adolescents. To adequately do so, we must frame that understanding in the larger social and institutional contexts of therapeutic individualism, mass-consumer capitalism, the digital communication revolution, residual positivism and empiricism, the structural disconnect of teenagers from the world of adults, the problems of adults, and other relevant cultural contradictions that may affect the religious and spiritual lives of contemporary youth. This is not because youth are normally consciously aware of or articulate about these big-picture social influences, but because these larger contexts are objective, structural, institutional, and cultural realities that powerfully form youth's lives. Making these kinds of connections between larger social contexts and the unique stories of particular individuals by examining the "intersection of history and biography" is one of the important contributions to social understanding that the sociological imagination has to offer.[31]

In the next chapter, we shift our focus back to religious teenagers more specifically by zeroing in on youth in the major religious tradition of U.S. Catholicism. Chapter 6 is a kind of case study seeking to help better explain the apparent relative religious laxity of Catholic teens. There we shift from examining statistics across religious traditions and interpreting teen interviews to trying to make sense of a pattern of findings specifically in terms of Catholic religious history, socioeconomic mobility, and other organizational factors. Had space allowed, we might have written similar chapters on, for instance, U.S. teens in mainline Protestantism and Judaism. However, space constraints focus our attention on Catholic teenagers. It is to try to explain their relative religious laxity that we now turn.

6

On Catholic Teens

IT WAS AN AMAZING scene. There I sat among 23,000 exuberant Catholic teenagers mobbing the entire field floor and first seating level of the Houston Texans' Reliant Stadium.[1] This mass of rollicking Catholic teens, gathered from all over the United States in November 2003 for the biannual National Federation of Catholic Youth Ministry's National Catholic Youth Conference, was for four days alternately bouncing to the throb of Christian hip-hop bands, fervently praying the Hail Mary and Our Father, wildly cheering the testimonies and messages of young and old Catholic speakers, and reverently celebrating the Eucharist en masse. These kids, by all appearances, were splendidly proud to be Catholic. They wore T-shirts emblazoned with in-your-face Catholic slogans, creeds, and Bible verses. They thunderously applauded the attending bishops and priests and screamed adoration for the Pope whenever his name was mentioned. Groups from parishes and dioceses roved about the stadium and convention grounds in packs, waving parish banners and bellowing Catholic cheers and chants. The throng's palpable energy was generated by this congregation of many thousands shouting, hugging, swaying, singing, and sharing together in unity—a real religious collective effervescence at work, a massive sacred experience, a distinctively Catholic spectacle that was jubilant, intense, exhausting, inspiring.

Many of the teens attending told me they had come mostly to have fun at this major event about which they had heard so much. But it was also clear that most came from lives and families much involved in their parishes

193

and well grounded in Catholic identity. More obvious to me was how powerfully drawn many of them were to the conference's vision of practicing faith
more seriously and consistently, living Catholic lives of distinctive integrity,
being active members of a Church that is a force for love and justice in the
world. These teens listened intently to speakers challenging them to devote
their lives to Christian peacemaking and the work of justice, for instance,
visibly moved by the idea that they could actually make a difference in the
world. In one breakout session offering three workshop options, 14,000 teens
packed to standing-room-only a workshop on "Romance without Regret"
led by two dynamic Catholic youth speakers teaching the sacredness of bodily
intimacy, sexual abstinence before marriage, and full commitment to Catholic
moral teachings. The workshop message was veritably countercultural, yet
the youth in attendance were captivated. They received the message, it
seemed to me, not as oppressive traditional moralizing but as a breath of
fresh air, a radical challenge. Many of the girls seemed exhilarated by the
idea that they might actually take charge of their romantic relationships and
may not have to barter their bodies simply to get boys' attention. Many of
the boys in attendance seemed compelled by the evidently novel idea of living
lives of romantic and sexual purity, integrity, and self-discipline. Afterward,
I wandered to an adjacent, sprawling convention hall jammed with teens
gallivanting among hundreds of booths featuring the goods of Catholic colleges, Catholic musicians, Catholic religious orders, Catholic service ministries, Catholic clothing manufacturers, Catholic seminaries, Catholic publishers, Catholic radio and television programs, Catholic religious devotional
objects, Catholic videos and cassette series, and other vendors of Catholic
jewelry, stuffed animals, home decor, lawn ornaments, fashion accessories,
novelties, church supplies, gifts, and other Catholic kitsch that I had no idea
even existed. The sheer massiveness of the Catholic products and opportunities displayed in that convention hall was extraordinary.

What I observed at this conference might suggest that Catholic teenagers
in the United States are doing quite well religiously, that Catholic youth are
generally committed, enthusiastic, and serious about their faith and Church.
But such a conclusion would be mistaken. There are, of course, U.S. Catholic
teenagers who are very religiously engaged, but they are not typical. In our
study, Catholic teenagers, who represent nearly one-quarter of all U.S. teens,
stand out among the U.S. Christian teenagers as consistently scoring lower
on most measures of religiosity. Scanning many of the tables in chapter 2,
for example, reveals Catholic youth scoring 5 to 25 percentage points lower
than their conservative, mainline, and black Protestant peers on many of a
variety of religious beliefs, practices, experiences, commitments, and evaluations. Perhaps more important for Catholics, our findings regarding Catholic
teenagers show many of them to be living far outside of official Church norms
defining true Catholic faithfulness.[2]

The question is Why? Why do U.S. Catholic teenagers as a whole seem
so less religiously engaged than their teenage counterparts in other U.S. Christian traditions? What might help explain the apparent overall higher levels

of religious laxity among Catholic teenagers compared both to other U.S. Christian teenagers and authoritative Catholic norms of faithfulness? This chapter explores possible answers to these questions. We begin by regarding the stories of three Catholic teens whom we interviewed to see some of the specific instances of teenage cases behind our statistical findings. We then examine alternative explanations for this observed relative religious laxity, considering empirical evidence that helps adjudicate among alternative explanations.

THREE CATHOLIC TEENS ON TWO COASTS

A share of U.S. Catholic teenagers are religiously and spiritually very serious, informed, and committed. In the course of conducting our 267 NSYR personal interviews with various kinds of teens living in 45 states, we did come across some white, black, and Hispanic Catholic teens who loved God and the Church, who understood and could talk about what Catholics are supposed to believe, who were involved in the ongoing life of their parishes, and who sincerely sought to live their lives as faithful Catholic believers. But they were the definite minority among the Catholic teenagers we interviewed. The majority instead tended to be rather religiously and spiritually indifferent, uninformed, and disengaged. To help convey a concrete sense of what this looks like in specific teenagers, we recount here the stories of three Catholic teenagers we interviewed from Connecticut and California: a 15-year-old white girl named Heather from Connecticut; a 17-year-old white boy, John, also from Connecticut; and a 16-year-old Hispanic boy, Alano, from Southern California. We do not present them as representative of all Catholic teens[3] but as specific cases of what the lives of religiously indifferent and permissive Catholic teens can look, feel, and sound like.

Heather

I met Heather and her mother at a funky coffee shop on the main commercial street of an old town neighborhood at a time scheduled between Heather's school and a babysitting job. There seemed to be some tension between Heather and her mother when they arrived, but both were friendly enough to me. Mom hung around the coffee shop for a while, to keep an eye on me, it seemed, so Heather and I set up at a wobbly table far off in a corner, laughing over trying not to spill our drinks. Thin, blonde, with blue eyes and a smile full of braces, Heather is the oldest of four siblings in what seems to be a reasonably happy family. She is a typical kid: a B student in school, does gymnastics, plays softball, and likes hanging out with her friends at the mall, by the pool, or at the movies. She's been going out with a boy for two weeks. She likes watching reality TV shows. She gets stressed out a lot, but not often depressed. "I'm a good kid," she reports about herself.

Heather had recently gotten into trouble with her parents. Freaked-out friends had called her to come over to the house of a girlfriend who had drunk too much alcohol and had started passing out. It was a day off from school and the girl's parents were not home. Heather rushed over and helped keep her friend conscious by slapping her on the face repeatedly. They all got caught. Heather's parents feel she broke their trust. Since then, Heather reports, her mother has been keeping a much closer eye on her. She thinks her parents are too strict, mostly because she's the oldest and so setting all of the child behavioral precedents. Heather says she feels somewhat close to her father but definitely closer to her mother and more able to talk with her, " 'cause she's a girl." Even so, Heather says that, as a very private person, she maintains some distance from her mother. She does wish they could be closer, but says that "it's kind of like I don't really know how to."

Heather's mother is a practicing Catholic and her father is a not very religiously observant Jew. Grandparents and aunts and uncles on both sides are very religious; they do not live nearby. Heather has been raised Catholic, goes to church every week, and takes CCD classes. Her mother, in fact, is a CCD teacher. The family also observes some Jewish holidays. Heather's mother has encouraged but not forced her in the Catholic faith: "She's always been like, 'You can go, I'm not going to force you to be this religion.' She was like, 'We're gonna expose you to Catholic first and if after that you want to decide to be Jewish, fine, that's your decision.' " Heather appreciates that approach: "Nobody should be forced into a religion. I think it's a matter of faith and what you believe." When she was younger, she thought she might become Jewish, but has changed her mind: "I do think there was, like, Jesus or whatever, so I don't think I would ever turn back to Judaism." I asked if she thinks religion has any influence on how people get along in her family. "I don't think it has anything to do with it," she replied, "other than when we get in fights at church Mom says, 'Come on, knock it off, this is God's house.' " Heather can think of only one nonfamily adult, an ex-nanny she is close to, whom she can turn to in times of real trouble. She has no significant adult relationships at her church. "Not really, like I don't, no, I don't really hang out at church," she says.

Asked whether she thinks of herself as a religious or spiritual person, Heather replies, "I go through the actions but I think the faith is kind of missing. I think I believe it, but a lot of people are like, 'God talked to me,' and I don't think I really ever felt any connection like that or anything." Why not? "Maybe 'cause I'm not really waiting, not really looking for it, 'cause I just don't pay attention or whatever." But none of that bothers or worries her, she says. Who, I ask, is God? What is God like? "Just a big guy up there who just kind of like watches, looks out for you, I guess." Heather tends to view God as more loving and forgiving than demanding and judging, but says God is not particularly involved in her own life. Sometimes she doubts Catholic beliefs, thinking "this is a bunch of crap that someone just made up, 'cause I haven't really experienced anything [myself], so I'm like, someone probably just made this up." She says she ultimately doesn't really think that is true, however. But "a lot of times when things don't go how I want them to, sometimes I'll be like, 'Yeah, whatever, like thanks a lot, like wow, this wouldn't have happened if God was, like, paying attention or whatever.' " I ask Heather to summarize her most basic religious beliefs. She responded: "I admit there is a God and there is a heaven and a hell and, like, if you're a horrible person you're going to hell. But I don't think I'm being judged or whatever, I don't think I'm totally conscious of that. Like, I'm gonna do what I'm gonna do and if God doesn't like it then I really don't think about that. I think God is, like, what I think of him and I'll be, like, 'Oh, help me with this,' but I'm not, like, 'God is watching so I better not do this.' Like, that doesn't really enter my head."

What about Jesus, I ask? Anything about Jesus? "Jesus. I believe in Jesus," she answers. "I don't really get the whole thing about how, well, with the Catholics, how God is Jesus and Jesus is God, I don't understand that." Anything about the crucifixion or resurrection, I probe? "Like, I believe that and, like, okay, he died and rose, rise or whatever. But that's not something I really think about unless it's like Easter, that Jesus like rose." Overall, Heather seems unclear on exactly what people in her religion are supposed to believe. "I don't think I've ever really, like, gotten it, like figured it out." She doesn't refer to her own religious ideas and views as beliefs but as opinions.

Heather says she doesn't like church that much and sometimes falls asleep during services. "I don't think it really does anything," she says. "It's just more one of those actions, like I agree with what they're saying in church but other times I'm like, 'What time is it?' 'cause I wanna go home." She says the homilies and sermons usually do not engage her. "It doesn't really feel [interesting]. I think maybe when I get older it will be different." She is not involved in any church activities besides Sunday Mass and CCD. Her parish does have an active youth group, but she has never been involved, despite her mother's encouragement. "I just don't want to go," she says. Heather does not read the Bible. As to praying, her mother used to remind her to say her prayers when she was younger but no longer does. "I wouldn't say that I pray regularly, I don't think about it that much, I guess. But if something's bothering me maybe I'll pray. If I'm not sure about something, I'll ask, 'Help me out on this one.' And sometimes my opinion is, yeah, I kind of got a little help with that." Heather once attended a Christian camp with a Protestant friend; she enjoyed it and says it had a lasting impact on her because her mom said she was nicer when she came home. Heather says she never expresses her religious faith at school. When asked whether the Catholic Church teaches anything about dating relationships, Heather says no. What about sex, I ask, does Catholicism teach anything about sex? "They kind of teach the whole no-sex-before-marriage thing, but I don't know," she answered, "even though that's one of the main things they stress, I don't think the Church has that much of an impact on what I think about that. I know it teaches that—and I'm Catholic and know I probably shouldn't—but I just don't think I pay much attention to it. I more just ignore it than anything else." So what does Heather, who has not yet been physically involved with anyone, believe about when or under what conditions it is appropriate to have sex?

I don't know. If you're comfortable and you really want to do it, I don't think there are, like, any lines. I don't think I'm ready for anything like that. I still hear in my head "Don't do that," like maybe that's from my parents or from the Church, I don't really know. But I think a lot has to do with how comfortable you are with the person, how much you trust them and stuff, I guess. And be careful, with like STDs and pregnancy. I don't think it necessarily has to be no sex until marriage. I think that's good and nice, but maybe other times, if you want to and really feel like that for a person, you want to take it to the next level, then go ahead and do it.

Heather says that teens are under a lot of pressure to experiment with sex, to drink, and to cheat in school. She has consumed alcohol some but not to the point of getting drunk. She tried marijuana once but didn't like it. Heather cheats in school some, feeling bad about it but feeling even more pressure to get good grades to get into college. She says she also lies to her parents on occasion about things she is doing when she thinks they are being overprotective. "They need to just, like, trust me and know that I'm not going to kill myself," she insists. She says she does believe in moral rights and wrongs, she is no relativist. But her views of morality mostly seem oriented around not getting caught for doing wrong things. About drinking alcohol, for example, she recalls, "The first time I did it, I was a wreck, like paranoid [about getting caught], but other times when I think I won't get caught it's taken a lot of pressure off, so a lot depends on if I think I'm gonna get caught." Like very many U.S. teenagers, Heather cannot explain what it is that makes things right and wrong beyond immediate consequences. "I'm trying to think!" she laughs. "I don't really think about this stuff too much! I don't know, I don't really know where morality comes from." She reports that more bad behaviors go on among teenagers, such as keg parties among eighth-graders, she says, than many parents and other adults probably want to know about. Adults, she says, "realize it, but I think a lot of times they just look the other way, they don't acknowledge it. A lot of times they just turn their heads and they kind of like put up a wall, like they don't want to get involved, don't want to have to deal with it." To illustrate, she cites an example of a male friend of hers who has been smoking pot regularly, was grounded by his mother when she first found out, but who recently got caught again and is not being punished at all. "And his dad doesn't even know yet," she reports. "His mom doesn't tell his dad, 'cause they don't like each other, like, they sleep in separate bedrooms. I really don't know why they're not divorced."

It's time for Heather to get to her babysitting job. I close by asking what she thinks she will be like religiously when she is 25 or 30 years old. She replies, "I think like, maybe I'll want to go to church by myself. Maybe, yeah. Kind of depending on what happens in that, I think I probably will, 'cause that's how I grew up, that's just like kinda routine. But," she adds to close, "maybe by then it won't be routine anymore." Whatever happens in

Heather's future, I think, it's clear that, despite regularly attending Mass and CCD, the Catholic Church seems to have made only a rather small dent in her believing and thinking. There are small signs here that she is hungering, exploring, and may grasp a rudimentary sense of Catholic faith. But she is hardly what the Catholic Church hopes for and expects of its faithful.

John

I interviewed John on a cold afternoon in the public library study room of an older, affluent suburban neighborhood. John had been hard to get in touch with to set up the interview, but, with his mother's help, I finally managed to arrange to meet him after school at the library. I arrived early and staked out the small, upstairs study room in which to conduct the interview, spreading my jacket, bag, and papers around the table and chairs to make clear the room was occupied. Anxious that my digital recording equipment might get lifted, I returned to the downstairs lobby to meet my interviewee. John finally arrived, late. He drove a car and, because his parents work, came to the interview by himself. We climbed the broadly winding stairs to the study room. John, a tall and chubby guy with short brown hair and green eyes, seemed a little nervous and fidgety as he signed his consent forms and we began.

John's parents divorced when he was very young. His mother is remarried to a policeman, whom she lived with for six years before marrying and who now seems to have a lot of free time that he spends hanging around the house. John's mother, by contrast, spends most of her waking hours at her job. John says that he often argues with his mother, but that they are somewhat close and get along okay. About his stepfather, John says, "We're not close at all, he's the type you can't be close to, he puts up a big barricade. I've tried talking to him but he didn't respond very well, was kind of a dick. I don't think he likes me." John says his mother and stepfather do not communicate with each other very much. The parent John feels closest to is his biological father, a nominal Protestant whom he characterizes as irresponsible and lazy, and whom he visits every other weekend. Other than that, John has no significant adult relationships with relatives, teachers, or people at church. Regarding the latter, he says, "Ah, no, our church, it's not, we're not involved anymore, really we just go [to Mass]." John says he does not particularly admire anyone that he can think of.

John calls himself "a pretty boring person, just sitting at home after school all day." He has no job or girlfriend, feels in limbo as a senior in high school, and spends lots of time playing video games, hanging out with friends, and sleeping. "Now is not, you know, a peak time in life," he says. "Hopefully it'll improve. I haven't really been too successful with, you know, girls this year. I do need to muscle up a bit in the gym, with summer coming up and the beach, to be able to take off my shirt and still be able to pick up the chicks." He says he has no idea what the purpose of life is, what humans are doing on earth. No clue. "There's not really much substance to my life right now and if I think about it too much I'm gonna be miserable. I don't do anything, you know. I want my life to go somewhere but I'm also not the type of kid to beat himself up about it. You don't think about it, you just sit in front of the TV and chill and do your own thing instead of being miserable. I just don't really let myself feel sad and depressed. When I have problems, I just think about something else."

In general, John observes, "teenagers today are a lot more emotionally fragile, too much pressure is put on them to succeed nowadays. Everyone has these feelings, everyone's depressed. Teenagers right now, like, no matter what, sometimes you're always gonna be bummin' about something. You know, you have to wake up at 6:30 and get to school, all these kids walking around like zombies, asleep, everyone's sleep-deprived." What most excites John is skiing, because of how fast he can fly down the mountain. He also likes bowling and driving to Boston to watch Red Sox games, but without a job he does not have the money now to afford those. So he spends time at home trying to ignore his stepfather and arguing with his mother when she comes home from work. "They give me a hard time about stuff, make doing everything a pain in the ass." I ask for an example. He says that recently he and friends were caught smoking pot in a parking lot and arrested. "Not a big deal, you know," he assures me. "I'm not a get-into-trouble kid, I mean I do stuff which normal public school kids do, but it's not a big deal, I don't make a big deal out of it." How did his parents react to his arrest? "They're assholes. Yeah, they suck," he replies laughing. "When I got arrested my mom took my car for a month and it's just like, 'Come on, I didn't do anything that bad. I got caught, I won't do it again.' But they give me a hard time." Normally, however, "I can get by doing what I want to do. It's rare that I have to suffer a couple of consequences severe enough that it's any big deal." John is looking forward to going away to college. "When I get into college it's just gonna stop, I can kick back, Mom's not gonna give me a hard time about grades. Things here just suck, my senior class sucks. Last year's was good, next year's will be better. Whatever, it's no big deal, I'm not really sweating it." That's what he says. In fact, throughout the interview he continued to act nervous and fidgety, not at ease.

John's mother and stepfather are Catholics. John also identifies himself as Catholic but says he does not think of himself as a religious or spiritual person. "It's just something that hasn't come into play with me yet. I think probably it will sometime but not now, but after I have a better understanding of the way things work, I'll get more religious and spiritual. I don't question why about most stuff, but when I get older I'll do that a lot more than I do now." He attends church about every two to three weeks. "We don't go to Mass every week, but I mean, we're pretty every-week people. Except the weekends that I'm with my dad." John says he believes in God. "I do, but that's a whole 'nuther part of me which really doesn't get visited much, I don't really like to think about it that much, like I told you." What does John envision God to be like? "I think there's something else out there and at some point in my life I'll think about that a lot more but, as it is, you know, I'm Catholic and I don't really necessarily have to think about it, don't have to question it, 'cause you know it works, I mean Jesus and it all makes sense to me, it works just fine for me." I ask John what he means by the phrase "I'm Catholic" in this context. "Just, you know, everything which has been told to me. Jesus came down, did all these things, you know, he's the one, you can look up on that picture up there on the wall of him and follow, you know, it makes sense to me, I don't question it. I accept it and I don't feel the need to ask why. I just believe everything which they say at church, I don't disagree with any of it. And I hope that there's something after [death]. That's pretty much all. I mean, I don't intentionally wrong anybody, I try to be nice and think about them and hopefully that's good enough." I press John on his view of God. "I don't think he's demanding at all," he elaborates. "I think most people are good and forgiving and I think, he's okay, I like God." I ask if God has any expectations of him. "All I know is," he answers, "I'm not angry at God, everything's okay, I'm not pissed off at anyone. Hopefully that's good enough for me right now." John says he has never had any kind of religious experience. When I ask what he thinks about angels, demons, and life after death, he simply says, "Nothing. I just hope it's okay, that I don't have to go to hell. I hope it doesn't just end, I hope I'm reincarnated as someone else." So then, I ask, does he believe there is a punishment after death for bad people? "No, I don't think bad people are really that bad," he replies. What about people like Hitler, I ask? "I knew you'd bring up Hitler," he exclaims, laughing, "I knew it. I mean, I'm not a big fan of Hitler, in any way, shape, or form. But probably [he] thought he was being a good guy, you know."

John engages in no religious practices other than attending Mass. He doesn't pray, read the Bible, rest on Sundays, or anything else. "But," he notes, "I do like the Bible, I like the stories in it." He also says religion plays no role in his family's relationships and it is a taboo topic at school. "No, it can't [play a role] at school, teachers wouldn't touch it with a ten-foot stick. Religion? Our school? Half of my school is Jewish so you gotta be sensitive to it, it's just such a sensitive topic. A teacher's not gonna say 'Merry Christmas,' you can't even say that. You gotta be neutral." John is not involved in his parish's youth group and has never been involved in any religious retreat, missions trip, or summer camp. "I'd never go on one of those, no matter how religious I might be. It's all just people trying to feel secure about their religious beliefs. That's one thing I'd never do." He says if it were up to him he would be an "E and C Christian"—one that attends only on Easter and Christmas. How good a job has John's church been at teaching him about his religious faith? "It's been okay, I mean, CCD was just a chance to clown around on Sundays after church. I didn't like it, you couldn't like it, it sucked." But when I ask specifically about his feelings about the Catholic Church, he grows a bit defensive on its behalf:

I think it's gotten kind of a bum rap. On an everyday basis, you're not going to run into a bad priest. Most priests are good guys, well-intentioned. [The priest abuse scandal] is too bad, really too bad that they're getting such a hard time about this. I mean, I'm not a big fan of the people sitting around in Rome, that's just people milking it in the Vatican. But the priests in church, they get shipped around. My priest is kind of new, but I've talked to him a few times. He seems like a good guy. All priests are pretty good guys. They just do what they believe and give up a lot for it. There's nothing wrong with priests, I don't have anything against them.

And what does he think of other religions, like Buddhism and Hinduism? "I think they're all right, you know, all well intentioned. I kind of like Christianity, it seems the most, not reasonable, but practical. I think Voodoo is fake. I don't like Judaism and I don't like Muslim. Nothing against the people, just as religions. Like if you were given a list of all the beliefs and asked to point to the one you want, I'd point to Christianity every time."

I ask John if he is involved in any volunteering or community service. "Oh, speaking of community service," he replies, "I should be talking to a woman downstairs about, I have to do 20 hours a week for probation [since getting arrested], sorting books." I express curiosity. He laughs, "Well, no, I'll scheme the hours, I'll sneak out, I know the back door here, my buddy did it. I'll do one hour for them and then take off." I try to engage John in a discussion about morality, but with some difficulty. "It's not a big deal," he repeats, "most stuff's not that big a deal. I'm not really a big fan of pondering the meaning of life, I don't see the point." It comes out, however, that he believes that morality is relative and that people only act morally in order to feel good. About himself, he reports, "I think I'm a pretty honest person. I don't cheat people, don't lie, don't deceive people, don't trick people, I'm up-front." He says he does not feel guilty about anything.

I notice that John's agitated fidgeting is getting worse. He is acting slightly odd—jittery, distracted, perturbed, a bit frenetic, not about the interview meeting per se, it seems to me, but rather about the subjects we are talking about. The thought enters my mind that maybe John is on the edge of some kind of minor emotional crackup, and I find myself hoping he does not have a breakdown during our interview.

We get into some moral specifics. John says he does not think it is wrong to cheat on tests or assignments at school. "No! When you cheat from someone, you're not taking away from them. It's high school, it's not that important, that's why. That's not a big deal at all, if it's some stupid math test, senior year, when you're not gonna take math ever again, not gonna use the stuff, who cares about if you look over and write down their answer?" He also does not think it wrong to lie to parents. "Everyone does it," he says. "If you lie too much then that's a problem, because what are you having to lie so much about? But if you don't lie at all and follow them in every wish, I think the people who don't lie to their parents, you know, I think there's also a problem. People have to be balanced, you gotta do a little bit of everything." He says he drinks alcohol and does drugs. "Yeah, sure, why not? Yeah. All of them. Everything in moderation." He started in his sophomore year. He explains that because he is big, he can drink two six-packs and not get sick. "It takes a lot to get me puking." Still, he comments, he does not drink and drive: "I don't want that on my record." In fact, getting caught seems to be John's key moral concern here. "I just like to have a good time with friends, have a few beers, some laughs, nothing wrong with that, smoke a nice big fattie every now and then. I'm careful, but not like from a safety point of view, it's for not-getting-caught point of view. Yeah, I mean, which might be wrong." John says that about 75 or 80 percent of students in his school drink alcohol and smoke pot. He says there is no peer pressure to drink and smoke, mostly because everyone already does it. "I mean, I don't really find any people who don't do it. Most people smoke all the time, you know, it's always there." He says he probably would do more of other, harder drugs, but doesn't have the money to afford them. He also reports that it is common for teens in his and nearby towns to hold parties when parents are away traveling, where there is a lot of alcohol, music, and some sex upstairs; eventually the neighbors call the police and the parties get broken up. John says he's looking forward to parties at college.

In the meantime, he is bummed out because, in his words, "I haven't gotten any girls recently. I'd be lying to you if I said I don't want, you know, some pussy." John thinks it is fine for teenagers to have sex—"I like sex, it's good, nothing against it"—as long as it does not create stress or guilt. He confesses, "I don't like feeling guilty. I take every possible, I'll go to any ends not to feel guilty." Teens have got to be able to handle sex mentally, he then explains, need to use birth control, and need to not hurt each other's feelings. "Sex is no different from other things: just don't be an asshole and don't make people feel bad." He says boys are motivated to have sex partly for the feeling of "achievement," but he also expresses that he thinks it is wrong for boys to take sexual advantage of drunk girls. He says he has no idea what motivates girls to have sex. John himself had a lot of sex with different girlfriends and some girls he met at parties in eleventh grade, but he has not scored with any girls in his senior year. He figures not much more will happen till he gets to college, because he's not feeling in a very outgoing mood lately. Do his parents know he was having sex? "Well, if you went up to my dad," John ventures, "and asked him if he thought I was having sex, he'd probably be like, 'Yeah, I hope so.' " Does he think his Catholic religion teaches any sexual morality? "I think it's so old," he responds, "any sort of rules about sex in Christianity made up 200 years ago were pretty much so that people didn't pop out like 20 babies. They were to keep 14-year-olds from having babies 'cause they didn't have condoms back then, not some sort of moral thing. Meaning, if I have sex with a condom when I'm 17, I'm not going to hell." What does he think about pornography? "It's not bad, nothing wrong with it. I don't go looking up porn on the Internet or anything, that's cheap. I've just gone to a couple shops and bought some DVDs, bought a couple online too, so I have a nice little selection of DVDs." He says his mom suspects he watches porn but he plays dumb and nothing has come of it. "It just relaxes me," he explains, "it's a nice relaxing way to spend the afternoon.

I just get out of school, go home, close the bedroom door, pop on a porno, fall asleep, wake up, it's still on. Nothing wrong with that. When I get some more money I'll get some more, you know, keep up the variety."

After college, John looks forward to being successful, having money and a nice life. He thinks he will want to have a string of girlfriends, then get married. "Just a nice, good-looking wife, you know, a few kids, that type of thing. Just a normal American dream type of thing." Before getting married, however, he suspects he'll live with some romantic partners. "Yeah, nothing wrong with waking up to a nice honey next to me." He expects to raise his kids in the Catholic Church and looks forward to his children getting married in the Church. What will he himself be like religiously when he is 25 or 30 years old? "I don't know. No clue. Hopefully when I'm like 50 or 60 I'll be a little bit better than I am now. Then I'll be going to church a little bit more actively, one of the guys who teaches CCD or, you know, that type of thing." Meanwhile, he says, he doesn't know if he'll get more involved in church or not. "Maybe, we'll see, we'll see."

Alano

Alano pulled up to the public library for his interview in his 1967 Ford Mustang, wearing black shorts, white T-shirt, baseball shoes, and a black Air Jordan baseball hat. Alano lives with his mother, father, and two younger sisters in a basic Southern California bungalow located in a primarily Hispanic working-class suburb near Los Angeles. In the parking slot, Alano's car engine sputters and dies. It won't restart. We agree to work on a jump-start after the interview.

Alano is a really nice guy who loves his family, works hard in school, plays and coaches city league baseball, and is infatuated with his girlfriend, whom he has been dating for four months. He is earning A's and B's in school, is hoping to attend a good college and become a successful civil engineer. He tries to only hang out with friends who are also serious about school. Besides baseball, he enjoys bowling and roller skating. Having earlier suffered watching his grandfather mistreat his grandmother when he got drunk, Alano studiously avoids alcohol and drugs. He believes they are immoral. He seems to get along well with his parents, although, if he could change anything, he wishes his father would open up more. "I want him to talk about what he feels to me, to have a close relationship with my dad and when I have a question I want an answer."

For Alano, family is much more central to life than for most of the white teenagers we interviewed. When asked who he most admires, for instance, he says, "My dad, in a sense my family, probably my dad." Why? "Because he'll go out and work the whole day for the family, just give up his whole life for us. He takes care of us and never has, never, never has any regrets or complaints, just does it." When asked how he decides between right and wrong in different situations, Alano replies, "I think about what my parents would think, what choice they would want me to make." He knows right and wrong, he says, from "just my parents and my conscience." Besides being a successful engineer, Alano's purpose in life, he says, is to "raise a family and teach them right so they can go on and do the same." Later in the interview, he says he prays to God no more than a few times a month, but when he does pray, it is "to be happy, for my family to be happy, just to continue the way things are. It would be like, 'Thank you for my family and, dear God, please keep my family safe.' " This is very much in keeping with sociological research on the centrality of family in Hispanic American culture. Very few white teenagers we interviewed talked this warmly about their families.

When it comes to religion, Alano is very positive about Catholic faith, though not practicing it much. His family is "Catholic, but," he says, "we don't go to church. I could definitely improve on that. I know the following behind it and the stories but I don't go to church enough to learn. I want to but I just don't." Alano did attend church regularly until his First Communion at age 10, but his family stopped attending a month after that. He says that his religious beliefs do mean a lot to him. "That's why I would like to go more, I would like to learn more." He does not know any adults in his church. "No, I haven't been there enough to develop relationships." He says he knows that he could become closer to God, whom he describes as "a spirit looking over everything, he can look over everything but you can have a direct relationship with him also." He contends that God is more loving and forgiving than judging, is both personal and impersonal, but more removed from life than active in it. "I don't think he's active, I just think he's looking over everything." Alano summarizes his own religious beliefs this way: "That God does exist and that he's looking on all of us. All of us." Alano also believes in heaven and hell, the latter in which bad people are punished after they die. All of this, he says, he learned from his family.

As to religious practices, Alano says that "prayer is hoping for good in your life and making the good decisions so that those things will come true, so God will help you out." He reports that he has read the Bible in his life but does not now. "Nu-uh, I don't know enough about it to read it. I would want to read it, I just don't." Although he does not attend church, he says that Sunday is a holy day on which he tries to rest and reflect. "I know I should be in church but I just sit back and think. It makes me grateful for the things I have, like that my family is safe. And I think about what actions I could do for God to help me still." A stronger faith is, for Alano, "something that I want to do, that I strive for, I just, for some reason I just haven't. It's something that I'm going to do, it's just that other things take up my time."

Despite not actively practicing his Catholic faith, Alano does think it influences his own moral decision making, such as refusing to drink or do drugs. When asked if he approaches social problems or world events differently because of his faith, he answers, "No. Um, well, religion comes into that a little. If a problem comes up, religion's going to come up sooner or later." He cites abortion as something he opposes because of his faith. His general view is that many religious people do the same bad things that nonreligious people do, like drinking, but at least feel sorry for it and try not to drink so much later. Curiously, he says he does not think that religion affects his relationships in his family at all. He also says being Catholic does not affect his life at school, that most of his classmates are Catholic and that religion as a topic of conversation simply does not come up much. But he does report that he has friends who he knows choose not to have sex before marriage because of their religious beliefs.

Alano thinks religion is generally a good thing that everyone should practice, "but it's by choice, I'm not going to force a person." Religion is valuable, he explains, because of "faith and I guess purity not to sin, to make the right decisions, not to lie about it. Just to know what's really out there and what life is about." It does not matter, however, *which* religion a person practices; it could be one of many religions. "You could make a case for all of them to be true, it just depends on the individual, the truth in probably every religion." However, he also believes people should accept all of the teachings of whatever religion they choose and not be selective. "I don't agree with that. If you're going to be Catholic you should take in the whole, because if you just take in parts you're just looking for ways to go against it. You have to believe in the whole." Alano also opposes the idea of practicing more than one faith. "You should learn about other religions but not practice both. You should learn to see what you want to follow and then follow that, find one that pertains to you and follow it. You can't pick two and go follow both."

Alano spends a lot of time with his girlfriend—much to his mother's chagrin, one learns in talking with her on the phone while trying to arrange an interview. He is attracted to her because "she's a caring person, her inner beauty I guess, how she treats others." He says she is good to talk to and that she pushes him to do well in school. He thinks a lot of teens date simply to have sex, and observes that lots of his friends have sex for purposes of social status and acceptance. He is against that. "It's wrong if that's all you're looking for in a relationship. But, yeah, if you really get to know a person and it's not just about sex but about having a real relationship, then there's nothing wrong in that, when it's not pressured but something that both want to do because they care about each other." Does he think people should wait to have sex until they are married? "Yeah. But if you find the right person, I think it could be different." Why does he think that? "It's just, I don't know [pause], just how I feel." He and his girlfriend are having sex. He has not told his friends and his parents do not know; he does not know how they would react if they found out. Does he think his religion teaches anything in particular about sexual morality? "To wait before you get married." Does he agree with that? "I agree with it," he says, "but I've gone against it." What does he think about that? "It's not that big of an issue," he simply says. Alano wants someday to get married, but is open to living with a romantic partner before that. "I guess it would depend on the situation. Maybe."

What does he think he will be like religiously when he is 25 or 30 years old? "More involved than I am now. I will attend church." How religiously similar or different will he be then? "The same but just more aware of religion. Because I want to learn more, and I think I will start attending."

Our time is up. We gather our things and head outside to jump-start his car. It doesn't work; we keep trying, but to no avail. Alano's girlfriend, who had cell-phoned him partway through the interview, then shows up in her own car. He assures me that they can get his Mustang started, so I take off.

The same caveat that we have given about interview subjects before applies here. Neither Heather nor John nor Alano are representative of all U.S. Catholic teenagers, either white or Hispanic. They may not even be representative of religiously apathetic Catholic teens. They simply help to illustrate what the lives of some religiously indifferent and permissive U.S. Catholic teens look like. Sociological methods, such as multivariate statistical analyses, often pull apart different factors and variables that they assume compose aspects of people's lives. Recounting the stories of people like Heather, John, and Alano helps us to also see how such factors and variables can fit together into larger, connected wholes.

TOWARD EXPLAINING TEENAGE CATHOLIC RELIGIOUS LAXITY

The relatively lower levels of religiosity among U.S. Catholic teens compared to teenagers in other U.S. Christian traditions asks for explaining. What social factors might help account for these observed differences? The following pages propose and evaluate some possible explanations.

Demographic Differences

One possible explanation for relatively lower Catholic teenage religiosity is the existence of simple demographic differences associated with lower religiosity. Catholic teenagers' overall relative religious laxity, in other words, may not reflect their being Catholic per se, but rather other demographic factors known to associate with lower religiosity. Examining differences in table A.12 in Appendix A, we see, for example, that Catholic teenagers tend to be more likely to reside in the Northeast, a generally less-religious region of the country. Perhaps it is something about their greater Northeastern regional location and not Catholicism per se that pulls down Catholic teen religiosity. Catholic teenagers are also much more likely to be Hispanic than other Christian teens, and U.S. Hispanic teens generally are, according to NSYR data, slightly less likely to attend church, for example, than white and black teens. Table A.12 also shows minor differences between Catholic teens and their Protestant counterparts around parental marital status, age, and sex, all of which normally correlate with levels of teen religiosity—although admittedly not in any direction that would consistently explain differences in religiosity. But might these demographic differences together, rather than something about being Catholic per se, help explain Catholic teenagers' relative religious laxity?

To test this hypothesis, we ran multivariate regression analyses statistically removing the effects of these demographic differences from the negative association of Catholic teens with church attendance, importance of faith, and religious youth group participation, using mainline Protestant teens as the reference group. These regression analyses examined whether the significant negative effect of teens being Catholic on these three religiosity outcomes was diminished or made statistically insignificant when controlling for the effects of possibly related demographic factors. The statistical results show, however, that none of these demographic factors explain away the Catholic factor. That is, the statistically significant negative correlations between U.S. teens being Catholic and levels of church attendance, importance of faith, and youth group participation compared to mainline Protestant teens are hardly reduced when the possible effects of Northeast regional location, Hispanic race, parental marital status, teen age, and teen sex are removed. The statistical coefficients with demographic controls entered remain nearly the same as without the controls. In other words, even if there were no demographic differences in regional location, race, teen age, and so on, U.S. Catholic teens would still score significantly lower on these religiosity measures. The evidence therefore fails to support a differential demographics hypothesis of lower Catholic teen religiosity. Some other factors must be at work.

Parental Religiosity

One of the major themes of this book has been the profound influence, both positive and negative, that parents and other significant adults often exert in the lives of U.S. teenagers. The religion of U.S. teenagers often follows and looks a lot like the religion of their parents.[4] Perhaps the relatively lower levels of Catholic teen religiosity simply reflect relatively low levels of Catholic parent religiosity. Perhaps the issue is not U.S. Catholic *teen* religious practice at all, but overall U.S. Catholic religious practice generally, as engaged and modeled by adults. That Alano's family stopped attending church immediately after his First Communion when he was 10 years old is an example of that. Is there broader evidence for or against this possibility?

As recently as the mid-twentieth century, U.S. Catholic adults attended church at far higher rates than U.S. Protestant adults. But the second half of the twentieth century saw a major decline in Catholic church attendance, particularly among its younger adult members.[5] By the late twentieth century, U.S. Catholic adults showed similar if not lower levels of reported church attendance and importance of faith in life than U.S. Protestant adults.[6] But any such differences between Catholic and Protestant adults in general are not large. What about for the specific population in question, Catholic parents of teenagers? Table 33 shows that, compared to their Protestant peers, U.S. Catholic parents of teenagers are somewhat less likely than conservative and black (but not mainline) Protestant parents of teens to attend church regularly and are more likely than the same to attend infrequently or never. U.S. Catholic parents of teenagers are also much less likely than all of their Protestant counterparts to participate in organized activities at church other than regular worship services, such as Bible studies, potluck meals, music practices, and small groups. Catholic parents of teens are less than half as likely as all U.S. parents, including nonreligious parents, to do so weekly or more often, and nearly 10 percent more likely never to do so at all. The U.S. Catholic parents of teenagers, in other words, are less involved in the community lives of their parishes outside of regular services than are U.S. Protestant parents of teens. Furthermore, table 33 shows that Catholic parents of teenagers are somewhat less likely than their conservative and black (but not mainline) Protestant counterparts to say that their religious faith is very or extremely important in their lives and to be married to a spouse who shares the same religious faith. Altogether, such relatively lower levels of religiosity and parental religious solidarity among U.S. Catholic parents of teenagers could help explain relative lower levels of religiosity among U.S. Catholic teens. But do they?

To answer this question, we again ran multivariate regression analyses removing the possible effects of parental religiosity from the negative correlation of Catholic teens with church attendance, importance of faith, and religious youth group participation, again using mainline Protestant teens as the reference group. These analyses thus examined whether the significant negative effect of teens being Catholic on our three religiosity outcomes was diminished or made statistically insignificant when controlling for the possible effects of lower parental religiosity. The statistical results show that they indeed are. The originally statistically significant differences between Catholic and mainline Protestant teen religious service attendance, for example, are reduced when controlling for parental church attendance, importance of faith, and shared parental religious faith separately in addition to demographics. And that difference is made statistically insignificant when the effects of parental involvement in church beyond regular worship services is removed.

Table 33. Religious Practices of Christian Parents of U.S. Adolescents, Ages 13–17 (Percentages)

	U.S.	U.S. Christian Traditions of Parents			
		CP	MP	BP	RC
Parental religious service attendance					
2–3 times a month or more often	56	67	49	68	58
Many times a year or less often	37	27	43	27	34
Participates in activities of church other than regular worship services					
Once a week or more often	23	30	23	41	11
Never	18	15	19	16	28
Importance of faith shaping major life decisions					
Very or extremely important	73	84	67	90	72
Not very important or not important at all	6	4	6	1	4
Both parents share same faith (2-parent families)	77	83	69	80	77

Source: National Survey of Youth and Religion, 2002–3.

When all four parental religiosity variables are entered into the same regression model, three of the four parental religiosity variables (all except parental importance of faith) remain statistically significantly associated with frequency of teen church attendance, while the coefficient for the Catholic teen variable is reduced by nearly one-third and becomes statistically insignificant. In plain English, the lower levels of church attendance by U.S. Catholic teens compared to their mainline Protestant peers can be significantly explained by the lower levels of religiosity of their *parents*. The differences among teens, in other words, disappear when we account for the differences among the parents.[7]

A similar but less clear-cut pattern emerges for our regression analysis of teen importance of faith. Controlling for the four parental religiosity variables reduces the coefficients for the negative Catholic teen association with importance of faith. And that association is made statistically insignificant when one of the four parent variables tested individually (church activities beyond attendance) is controlled for. In ordinary language, the lower levels of importance of faith reported by U.S. Catholic teens compared to mainline Protestant teens can be explained partly by the lower levels of religiosity of their parents. The religious (Catholic versus mainline Protestant) differences in importance of faith among teens again are reduced and, for one parent religiosity control, disappear when we account for the religious differences among the parents.

The same findings do *not* emerge, however, from our analysis of teen religious youth group participation. Even when we control for four different parental religiosity variables, U.S. Catholic teenagers remain statistically significantly less likely to participate in a church youth group than mainline Protestant teens. This is partly because mainline Protestant teens participate in church youth groups at relatively very high rates (see table 14), such that the gap between Catholic and mainline Protestant teenagers is larger for youth group attendance than for church attendance and importance of faith. This remaining significant Catholic teen difference thus suggests that differences in parental religiosity, though very important in explaining aspects or degrees of relatively lower Catholic teenage religiosity, do not explain all of the differences. There are probably other factors worth considering to answer our larger question.

Parish and Diocesan Institutional Commitment and Infrastructure

Another likely explanation for the comparatively lower levels of Catholic teen religiosity is an apparent lower level of institutional commitment and investment of the U.S. Catholic Church to and in youth ministry at the parish and diocesan levels. Simply put, the U.S. Catholic Church appears in its institutional infrastructure to invest fewer resources into youth ministry and education than do many other Christian traditions and denominations in the United States. Take parish-level youth groups, for example. We have already seen in table 14 that while between 81 and 86 percent of Protestant teens belong to church congregations that offer youth group programs, only 67 percent of Catholic youth do.[8] Table 14 likewise shows that about half the

percentage of Catholic youth compared to Protestant youth belong to
churches with full-time, paid youth ministers (21 percent Catholic compared
to 37–44 percent other Christian).[9] This may help to explain why only 12
percent of Catholic teens attend youth group once a week or more often,
compared to 23–43 percent of other Christian teens (see table 14).

The impression given by these numbers is reinforced by the church evaluations of Catholic parents of teens. According to reports presented in table
22, Catholic parents are much less likely than other types of Christian parents
to say that ministry to teenagers is a very important priority in their church
congregation (47 percent compared to 56–80 percent, depending on the Protestant tradition). Catholic parents are more likely than other types of
Christian parents to say that ministry to teenagers is only a somewhat important priority in their congregations (23 percent compared to 9–14 percent). Similarly, U.S. Catholic parents of teenagers are noticeably less likely
than other Christian parents to say that their church has been very or extremely supportive and helpful to them as parents in trying to raise their
teens, and are more likely to say that their church has been somewhat or a
little supportive of them as parents of teens (see table 22). At the parish and
perhaps diocesan level, therefore, the Catholic Church seems to be relatively
weak when it comes to devoting attention and resources to its youth and
their parents.[10]

Effective youth ministry and the engagement of teenagers in vibrant lives
of faith cannot be manufactured through simple organizational programs. At
the same time, churches are social organizations. It is difficult for them to
mobilize for successful youth ministry and the Christian education of teens
when those are not institutional priorities of dioceses and parishes providing
the kind of attention, budgets, training, personnel, publications, and other
infrastructural supports needed.[11]

Transformed Catholic Schools and CCD

Another piece of this larger puzzle involves understanding the historical transformation of Catholic schools and CCD in the United States. One of the
reasons the U.S. Catholic Church may somewhat neglect youth ministry, considered broadly, at least in comparison to other Christian traditions and denominations, may be because Catholic schools and CCD no longer function
as well as they had for decades as means by which the Church evangelized,
ministered to, and educated its youth. Youth groups as they are popularly
known today do not have a strong legacy in the U.S. Catholic Church. Rather,
Catholic schools and CCD have historically been the primary vehicle for
Catholic youth ministry and education. Beginning in the nineteenth century,
the U.S. Catholic Church mobilized its own schools to maintain control over
the formation and training of its young people, as a structural bulwark
against the cultural pressures of U.S. public schools, which often sought to
acculturate and Protestantize Catholic youth. For many decades, Catholic
schools provided a reasonably strong Catholic grounding and education for
the Church's youth. Catholic parents, priests, and bishops thus rested assured
that their youth were being well socialized and educated as Catholics, taught

the doctrines of the Church, and nurtured in their faith. After 1935, thanks to the promotional work of the Vatican's Sacred Congregation of the Council[12] and the organizational initiatives of Bishop Edwin O'Hara of Great Falls, Montana, any Catholic students lacking an adequate Catholic school education could otherwise be taught through a parish-based catechetical CCD program.[13]

But much of that has changed. Many of today's Catholic schools and CCD programs are very different from those of, say, the 1960s. Various historical forces, beyond the scope of this chapter to elaborate, have profoundly transformed Catholic schools in recent decades. Catholic schools of a previous era, for instance, were normally guided and staffed primarily by priests and nuns educated and dedicated by life calling to distinctively Catholic instruction and pedagogy. But only 5 percent of the staff of today's nearly 8,000 Catholic schools consist of priests, nuns, and religious brothers. And the Catholic theological knowledge and commitments of the 95 percent of today's lay Catholic school teachers—not all of whom are necessarily Catholic themselves—is sometimes quite thin, however solid are their mainstream academic credentials and aptitudes. According to J. Fraser Field, executive officer of the Catholic Educator's Resource Center:

> Having received their training in secular universities, most Catholic teachers are poorly equipped to appreciate the positive historical and cultural impact of Catholicism and are therefore generally lacking in the background necessary to share these riches with their students. As a consequence, most Catholic schools . . . depend on the same textbooks and other resources as those used in the public schools, and, staffed, for the most part, by graduates of the same universities as the public schools, are, outside of the subject of religious education, teaching almost exactly the same content as the public schools, content that is decidedly impoverished in the rich heritage and meaning of Christian faith and culture.[14]

Changing family demographics have also helped to transform U.S. Catholic schools. Originally founded to serve primarily an immigrant Catholic working class, Catholic schools have increasingly become institutions for affluent Americans. The proportion of well-to-do students in Catholic schools doubled between the early 1970s and the late 1990s, by which time nearly half of all Catholic secondary school students came from the wealthiest quarter of U.S. households.[15] There are cases of inner-city Catholic schools for which simply attending to the basic educational, nutritional, and social needs of poor students consumes most of the schools' resources, such that educating students in distinctive Catholic theology, ethics, and identity is an unaffordable luxury. In more typical cases, however, Catholic schools have grown into college prep academies with competitive admissions standards and hefty tuition rates, serving the more privileged of their communities, whether Catholic or not, and more dedicated, by demand of parents, to getting their students admitted to prestigious colleges than to teaching them about the Trinity, sin, the Virgin Mary, the atonement, and faithful Christian living. In related situations, some Catholic schools have developed into regional sports powerhouses, dedicated in recruitment and programming to maintaining their football or basketball prowess, perhaps to the detriment of distinctively Catholic socialization and education. Thus, Pennsylvania State University education sociologist David Baker rightly observes:

> Higher social class students and their families are more demanding customers, they are very adept at having schools provide what they want . . . rigorous academic preparation. As Catholic schools continue to attract and adapt to this kind of a student, priorities at schools change radically. . . . Catholic school leadership is compromising an older basic religious mission in favor of intensive academics. . . . In short, the old common Catholic school is fast becoming an elite private school in which indoctrination into the faith may be taking a back seat to academic preparation.[16]

Furthermore, although in 1970 only 2.7 percent of students enrolled in Catholic schools were non-Catholic, by 2003 that number had quadrupled to 13.5 percent—a size reaching a critical mass with the potential to reshape school cultures and faculty and administration perceptions of pluralism, inclusivity, and mission.[17] So, according to David Baker, fewer than half of Catholic high school principals today identify "religious development of the student" as their school's primary mission, a drop to nearly the same percentage of principals who state "academic excellence" as their school's chief objective.

What happened to CCD? Reorganizations of the United States Conference of Catholic Bishops (USCCB) in 1975 and 1980 abolished what had been the well-staffed organizational hub of CCD, the National Center of Religious Education, and reduced and disbursed its education specialist personnel in other departments and programs. Since then, the work of developing and promoting CCD in the Church has been much more fragmented and piecemeal in approach. According to Berard Marthaler, since the reorganizations,

> there has been no single agency that keeps abreast of developments in the field, no coordinating effort either in identifying the issues or of plotting a strategy for the catechetical mission of the Church in the U.S. . . . By 1989, mention of the Confraternity and CCD has all but disappeared from the Catholic Directory. . . . CCD has come to be a label for generic programs, makeshift substitutes for parochial schools concerned entirely with the instruction of children. Many diocesan offices no longer use the term CCD because of its negative connotations, and individuals have invented new meanings for the acronym, e.g., "Christian Character Development."[18]

None of this is to deny that there are very many highly competent, extremely dedicated, distinctively Catholic educators working in the U.S. Catholic Church today. There most definitely are. But they themselves will often be the first to say that today's Catholic school system and CCD are not at all what they used to be, that something profound about the "Catholicness" of the education has been lost in recent decades. In any case, even if Catholic schools were doing a superb job at distinctively Catholic youth formation and ministry, their influence would still be limited, for fewer than 15 percent of secondary-school–age Catholic teens in the United States now attend a Catholic school.[19] Furthermore, as the stories of Heather and John illustrate, the CCD program has declined in its ability effectively to reach, educate, and form contemporary Catholic youth who do not attend Catholic schools.

The institutional systems that the U.S. Catholic Church has long relied on—for good reason or not—to accomplish its youth ministry and education have thus become structurally and culturally weakened in recent decades. And not enough has been done in response to shore up the system. It appears, in other words, that too many U.S. Catholics have through inertia continued to rest assured that old organizational structures were taking care of their children when in fact they increasingly have not been. And so many or most Catholic teenagers now pass through a Church system that has not fully come to terms with its own institutional deficit and structural vacuum with regard to providing substantial and distinctive Catholic socialization, education, and pastoral ministry for its teenagers. As a result, the Catholic Church today comprises large proportions of teenagers like Heather, John, and Alano.

Upward Mobility and Acculturation

Until recent decades, Catholics in the United States were commonly regarded by many other Americans as dangerous outsiders. Their faith was seen as threatening the dominant Protestant evangelical religious order and their hierarchical Church polity and allegiance to Rome as threatening the American democratic political order. Moreover, most Catholics came to the United States as poor immigrants from European countries other than England, and so were often viewed by established Anglo-Americans as racial minorities, ethnic aliens, dirty riffraff. For these reasons, U.S. Catholics were recurrently maligned, persecuted, and socially excluded.[20] During the twentieth century, however, U.S. Catholics made remarkable gains in socioeconomic status, which helped to facilitate their eventual growing social acceptance in U.S. culture and institutions, the election of the Roman Catholic John Kennedy as president in 1960 being the key symbolic turning point in this process. By the 1970s and 1980s, U.S. Catholics had become among the best-educated, occupationally privileged, and most affluent Americans.[21] That rapid upward mobility was paralleled by a major decline, though not elimination, of anti-Catholic sentiment in U.S. culture.[22] This major transformation in the social position of U.S. Catholics has, in turn, had profound consequences on U.S. Catholicism itself. Sociologist James Davidson, for example, observes that "U.S. Catholics have gone from being a relatively small, working class, and highly segregated population of largely white Europeans who trusted social institutions, especially their pre–Vatican II Church, and stressed the importance of obeying church teachings, to being a larger, more privileged . . . population that is more highly integrated into American society and culture, more skeptical of all social institutions, including the post–Vatican II Church, and more inclined to stress the importance of thinking for themselves."[23]

Everything that sociologists of religion know about how socioeconomic status and cultural difference shape religiosity—whether Troeltsch's "church-sect" theory, Stark and Finke's "religious tension" theory, or Smith's "sub-cultural identity theory"—predicts that this upward mobility and social and mainstream cultural integration would have had the consequence of weakening American Catholics' religious identity and commitment.[24] By most accounts, this is precisely what has happened, although, not to oversimplify, the effects of Vatican II also seem to have played a role in this process. In the second half of the twentieth century, U.S. Catholicism saw a significant decline in regular church attendance, in the strength of religious orders, in the number of new priestly vocations, and in ordinary American Catholics' readiness to learn, embrace, and live out Church doctrines and teachings. American Catholics generally became more acculturated, more individualistic, and more selective in appropriating elements of the Catholic worldview as they personally saw fit. What is more, such new approaches to faith and Church tended to be expressed generationally; that is, they were especially concentrated among younger Catholics.[25] These trends clearly show up in the stories of Heather, John, and Alano.

To understand the greater religious laxity of contemporary U.S. Catholic teens compared to the other Christian teens we observed in this study, we need to set their experience within this larger historical experience of upward mobility, mainstream acculturation, and declining religious strength in twentieth-century U.S. Catholicism. Today's Catholic teenagers are, often without even knowing it, living out their lives on the cutting edge of a profound religious transformation that pushes forward with a half-century of momentum and that has in recent decades weakened the religious identities and commitments of multimillions of U.S. Catholics. As a whole, today's Catholic teens come from relatively prosperous families and enjoy great chances for success in mainstream society. There is little about their religious identity that, in their cultural context, automatically reminds them of their distinctiveness or tension with the larger culture. Thus, the Catholicness in their larger personal identities and lives is increasingly able to slip into the background of their overall concerns, activities, practices, and commitments. Whether contemporary U.S. Catholic teenagers attend Mass regularly, understand what Catholics believe, and live up to Catholic morality is simply not a pressing issue for many of them. This is exactly what we heard from the majority—though not all—of Catholic teens we interviewed around the country.

CONCLUSION

We do not intend this chapter to convey the impression that U.S. Catholic teenagers are uniquely religiously or spiritually in trouble. Most of the aspects of religious laxity that we focus on and illustrated in this chapter are also readily evident in the lives of teens in other Christian traditions in the United States. The differences are not categorical, but mostly a matter of degree. Furthermore, this chapter in no way claims to have comprehensively analyzed the religious and spiritual lives of U.S. Catholic teenagers. That would take an entirely separate, in-depth book dedicated to that task. The U.S. Catholic Church and its adherents are simply much too complex racially, ethnically, regionally, theologically, generationally, and social-class-wise to cover in a single chapter. Simply addressing differences between Hispanic and white Catholic youth would require much more analysis and discussion beyond the scope of this book to engage. Our more modest purpose has been simply to ask a question that seems to us to emerge from many of this book's findings and to offer some preliminary possible answers to focus attention, generate discussion, and stimulate further research.

To summarize, then, both our quantitative survey data and qualitative personal interview evidence point to the same conclusion: compared both to official Catholic norms of faithfulness and to other types of Christian teens in the United States, contemporary U.S. Catholic teens are faring rather badly. On most measures of religious faith, belief, experience, and practice, Catholic teens as a whole show up as fairly weak. We think this can be attributed to a number of causes. In general, the U.S. Catholic Church seems to have become at least somewhat devitalized as a result of Catholic upward mobility and mainstream acculturation in the later part of the twentieth century; Catholic teenagers today merely reflect the leading edge of that larger trend. In addition and as part of that broader process, the organizational means that the Catholic Church historically employed to more or less successfully accomplish its work with youth, Catholic school and CCD, have in recent decades had the world around them change and have themselves changed in ways that, for whatever good they do accomplish for Catholic and other youth, render them inadequate to serve as the primary vehicles for contemporary youth socialization, education, formation, and ministry. The old wineskins cannot hold the new wine, and so it is often spilled and lost. Complicating these factors is the apparent relatively low institutional priority that youth evangelization, formation, and ministry appear to garner at the parish and diocesan levels, at least, of the U.S. Catholic Church. Evidence suggests that more than a few of today's Catholic youth may be falling through the organizational cracks without much notice.

Finally, many of these processes appear to get played out at the family level by Catholic parents of teenagers. As we wrote in chapter 2, the best general rule of thumb for religious adults considering the possible faith outcomes of their youth is "We'll get what we are." Most American teens turn out religiously to look a lot like their parents—not always, but very often— for understandable reasons. It does not appear to be the case that most U.S. Catholic parents of teenagers are struggling mightily to live out vibrant lives of Catholic faith and yet find their teenagers to be religiously apathetic and resistant. Rather, it appears that the relative religious laxity of most U.S.

Catholic teenagers significantly reflects the relative religious laxity of their parents. Once again, teens effectively embody and reproduce the larger adult world of which they are a part. Thus, we think the evident "problem" of Catholic teens is rightly seen in part as a larger challenge of Catholic adults generally and parents specifically.

During one plenary session of the Houston National Catholic Youth Conference described in this chapter's opening, I sat next to a very friendly, middle-age chaperone for an attending group of teens from the Midwest. Chatting with him, I asked exactly how many teens were attending the conference from his diocese. He answered with an amused smirk, "Oh, I think our bus brought twenty-three of the little shits . . . er, I mean kids, including one of my own little sh—, uh, kids." He was clearly tired of boisterous teenagers, understandably, and needed a good night's sleep. Later, I mentioned his comment to a life-long Catholic youth minister, one of the Conference organizers. "Well," he replied wearily, "sometimes it seems we have as much work to do educating and training our adults as we do our teens."

The jubilant, intense, exhausting, and inspiring Houston Conference reveals the great potential that the U.S. Catholic Church has for seriously engaging and forming its teenagers. But our research findings show that the Church has a long way to go to reach that immense potential. Getting from where the majority of U.S. Catholic teens currently are with regard to their religious faith and lives to achieving the huge religious potential that appears to exist for them would seem to require that the Church invest a great deal more attention, creativity, and institutional resources into its young members—and therefore into its own life. Undeniably, the future shape of the U.S. Catholic Church vitally depends on it.

7

Adolescent Religion and
Life Outcomes

A S WE SAW in chapter 4, the majority of teenagers we interviewed said
that religion is a good thing. But they had difficulty explaining how faith
is particularly consequential or influential in their own lives. Instead, religious
faith seems to operate largely invisibly, taken for granted and in the background of their lived experiences. Faith seems to help teens to feel good and
maybe to behave better. But then again, many said that their nonreligious
peers can be just as good and happy as believers. Many of the religious
teenagers we interviewed actually had a difficult time imagining how their
own lives would be much different if they were not religious, did not attend
church, were not in a youth group.

The question is: Do teenagers know the truth about their own lives? This
chapter examines the relationship between different levels of American adolescent religious involvement and a broad variety of outcomes in adolescents'
lives. Such an examination allows us to assess whether religion is associated
with any difference in teenagers' experiences. Are religious youth any different from nonreligious youth? Is faith actually consequential in the lives of
American teenagers or not? Ironically, although many teens cannot see it or
are not able to articulate it, according to the findings presented in this chapter,
the differences between more religious and less religious teenagers in the
United States are actually significant and consistent across every outcome
measure examined: risk behaviors, quality of family and adult relationships,
moral reasoning and behavior, community participation, media consumption,

sexual activity, and emotional well-being. Religiously active teenagers are in fact quite different from religiously disengaged teens in a host of ways, illustrated anecdotally by the contrast between Joy and Kristen in chapter 1, which suggests that there is definitely something about religious belief and practice that shapes adolescents' lives in positive directions. Perhaps it is the work of what remains of America's historical religious traditions. Perhaps Moralistic Therapeutic Deism is actually accomplishing some of the goals for which its adherents commend it. Perhaps it is both.

After first explaining the method used to compare different types of religious and nonreligious U.S. teenagers, we examine a variety of findings showing clear associations between religiosity and youth outcomes. We then take up the tricky question of causality and selection effects, seeking to clarify whether and to what extent we can with confidence attribute causal influence to the effects of teens' religion per se in the observed positive associations between religiosity and life outcomes. We conclude that we indeed can.

RELIGIOUS IDEAL TYPES

The first goal of this chapter is to assess whether different groups of religious and nonreligious American teenagers vary on different measures of adolescent outcomes. The initial question to answer toward this end is how best to categorize teens along different religious lines to reveal any differences in outcome measures that may exist. Different levels of religiosity in American religious culture are determined not by one but by a variety of dimensions of religion: beliefs, practices, experiences, affiliations, group participation, and so on. One option, therefore, is to run multiple analyses of all outcomes by each religion measure separately, presenting one set of tables focused on outcomes by religious service attendance, another on all of the same outcomes by importance of faith, a third on all of the same outcomes by frequency of prayer, and so on. That, however, would have the undesirable effect not only of multiplying the number of tables of findings beyond what is reasonable, but would also pull apart aspects of religion that in real people's existence conglomerate into lived, organic wholes. Ideally, we would instead devise a measure of religious difference that pulls the various dimensions of religiosity together into meaningful categories. Therefore, to be as clear and crisp as possible in our presentation of findings and in a way that reflects common understandings of religious types of people, we have chosen to create four ideal types of religious and nonreligious teenagers to compare to look for possible differences in their life outcomes. By ideal types we do not mean that no real people actually fit into those categories; most American teens do fit into one or another of the four categories. Rather, we simply mean, first, that the categories have been created around common cultural understandings of specific religious types of people and, second, that to fit into any of the categories the teen survey respondents have to reflect a number of specific characteristics that qualify them to be categorized that way. All of those who do fit those characteristics then belong together in that ideal religious type, and those who don't do not. Specifically, we have created and defined for analysis these four categories:

The Devoted (8% of American youth)
Attends religious services weekly or more.
Faith is very or extremely important in everyday life.
Feels very or extremely close to God.
Currently involved in a religious youth group.
Prays a few times a week or more.
Reads scripture once or twice a month or more.

The Regulars (27% of American youth)
Attends religious services two to three times a month or weekly.
Faith ranges from very to not very important in everyday life.
Closeness to God, youth group involvement, prayer, and scripture reading are variable but less religious than for the Devoted.

The Sporadic (17% of American youth)
Attends religious services a few times a year to monthly.
Faith ranges from somewhat to not very important in everyday life.
Closeness to God, youth group involvement, prayer, and scripture reading are variable.

The Disengaged (12% of American youth)
Never attends religious services; or attends many times a year and identifies as not religious.
Faith is somewhat, not very, or not important in everyday life.
Feels only somewhat close to God or less close.
Is not involved in a religious youth group.
Prays one to two times a month or less.
Reads scripture one to two times a month or less.

Sixty-three percent of U.S. teens fit one of these four categories. Thirty-seven percent do not fit cleanly into one of these four ideal-type categories and so are categorized as "other/mixed." Some of them might, for example, satisfy five of the features defining a Devoted teen but not the sixth; these closely approximate the type categorized but do not perfectly fit the ideal type, so are not included. All of those who do fit are ideal types of the category. The following analyses do not focus on those who do not fit cleanly into one of the ideal type categories. This means that not all American teens are included in the analyses represented in tables 34–42. There are nevertheless three important advantages of using this ideal-type approach. First, the ideal types we use to compare teens reflect the concrete way many ordinary Americans normally think about categories of religious people—extradevoted believers, regular churchgoers, sporadic participants, and so on—much more than any abstract, numerical "scale of religiosity" we might construct from multiple survey variables. Second, we can more clearly identify any differences that exist between the 63 percent of American teens who do fit these quintessentially distinct kinds of religious and nonreligious categories without having the comparisons and differences clouded by more ambiguous cases. Third, by combining the multiple dimensions of religiosity into a single set of concrete type comparisons, instead of examining each dimension separately, we can keep the number of tables of findings in this chapter to a reasonable and focused limit.[1]

Many of the outcomes we examine are also known to sometimes be affected by teen gender, age, race, family structure, parents' education, and so on. The religious ideal types used in this chapter's analyses also reflect significant, though not major, differences among them on many of those demographic variables (see table B.4 in Appendix B). To remove the possible effects of those related variables influencing the outcomes indirectly through the religious ideal types, we use multivariate regression analyses to control for seven key demographic variables—teen gender, age, race, region of residence, parental marital status, parental education, and family income—when testing for statistically significant differences between the religious types on outcome measures, the results of which are reported in the notes of each table. Thus, some of the observed percentage differences between Devoted and Disengaged teens, for instance, may be due to the fact that the former comprises more girls than the latter. But by using appropriate regression techniques to control for teen gender and the six other related variables, we can be confident that differences across the religious types are statistically significant even when the effects of these demographic variables are removed. This can reduce our worries that the observed differences across the religious types are really being produced by nonreligious factors and so making the religion association spurious. The religious associations remain statistically significant in every table, as explained in the table's notes, even after controlling for other key variables. What appear to be religious associations can thus confidently be understood as religious associations in fact.

ADOLESCENT RELIGIOUS TYPES AND LIFE OUTCOMES

What difference does religion make in the life outcomes of American teens? According to the following tables, actually quite a significant difference. Table 34, for example, compares differences in risk behaviors and getting into trouble across our four ideal religious types. We see there that the more religiously involved teens are much less likely to smoke cigarettes regularly, drink alcohol weekly or more often, and get drunk every few weeks or more often. More religiously involved teens are also more likely to not drink alcohol and not smoke marijuana. By comparison, it is the least religiously active teens who smoke marijuana the most. Among those attending school, the more religiously active teens are much less likely to cut classes in school, to cut a lot of classes when they do cut, and to be expelled from school. They also tend not to earn poor grades in school. Finally, the more religiously involved teens are much less likely to be said by their parents to be rebellious or to have a bad temper. Note that, as explained above, all of the observed differences

Table 34. Risk Behaviors of and Getting into Trouble by Religious Ideal-type U.S. Adolescents, Ages 13–17 (Percentages)

	U.S.	Religious Ideal Types			
		Devoted	Regulars	Sporadics	Disengaged
Smokes cigarettes at least once a day	7	1	6	9	14
Drinks alcohol					
Weekly or more	5	~	4	7	11
Never	63	88	62	50	49
Has gotten drunk every few weeks or more in the prior year	5	1	4	9	10
Smokes marijuana					
Regularly	4	~	2	6	8
Occasionally	7	1	6	9	13
Tried once or twice	14	6	13	19	16
Never	75	93	78	66	63
Cut class in school last year (school attenders)					
Six or more times	7	2	5	10	12
Never	64	76	67	61	48
School grades are usually Cs, Ds, and Fs	10	3	8	13	14
Suspended or expelled from school four or more times last two years (school attenders)	5	1	3	6	9
Parent reports teen is fairly or very rebellious	13	3	13	13	17
Parent reports teen has a somewhat or very bad temper	43	32	36	46	49

Source: National Survey of Youth and Religion, 2002–3.

Note: Percentages may not add to 100 due to rounding and unreported don't know and refused answers, and omission of some middle-range answers. Cells of <1 are reported as ~. All differences between Devoted and Regulars compared to the Disengaged are statistically significant at the 0.05 level after controlling for teens' age, sex, race, region of residence, parental marital status, parental education, and family income using linear, ordered logit, or logistic regression techniques; differences between the Sporadics and the Disengaged are statistically significant at the 0.05 level with those controls only for the "cuts class" variable.

between the Disengaged teens and the Devoted and Regular teens are statistically significant after controlling for seven other demographic variables that we might expect to effect these outcomes. The Disengaged and Sporadic teen differences are, with the one "cuts class" exception, not statistically significant. In sum, American teens who are Regulars and Devoted, as defined above, are doing noticeably better than their religiously Disengaged peers on a variety of risk and trouble behaviors and attitudes. Furthermore, there appears to be a genuine religious difference at work here, net of the effects of seven other potentially related variables.

Turning to table 35, we see a similar pattern played out around issues of media consumption. The most religiously involved American teens appear to watch less television during the week and on the weekends and are much less likely to watch R-rated movies. They are also less likely to use the Internet

Table 35. Media Consumption of Religious Ideal-type U.S. Adolescents,
Ages 13–17 (Percentages)

	U.S.	Religious Ideal Types			
		Devoted	Regulars	Sporadics	Disengaged
Average weekday hours spent watching TV	2.6	1.8	2.6	2.5	2.5
Average weekend hours spent watching TV	5.9	4.4	6.1	5.8	5.4
All or most movies and videos teen watches are rated R	29	14	25	32	42
Used the Internet last year to view X-rated, pornographic Web sites (Internet users only)					
Once a week or more	3	0	2	3	8
Never	83	96	84	74	74
Average number of X-rated, pornographic movies, videos, and cable programs viewed last year	2.7	0.5	1.6	2.6	2.5
Average hours spent playing action video games per week	2.9	1.2	2.9	3.1	4.1

Source: National Survey of Youth and Religion, 2002–3.

Note: All differences between the Devoted and the Disengaged are statistically significant at the 0.05 level after controlling for teens' age, sex, race, region of residence, parental marital status, parental education, and family income using linear, ordered logit, or logistic regression techniques; differences between the Regulars and the Disengaged are statistically significant at the 0.05 level with those controls only for the "R-rated movies," "pornographic Web sites," and "pornographic movies" variables; differences between the Sporadics and the Disengaged are statistically significant at the 0.05 level with those controls only for the "R-rated movies" variable.

to view pornographic Web sites and watch, on average, fewer pornographic movies, videos, and cable programs per year. Finally, they spend considerably less time playing action video games. Again, all of these differences between the Devoted and the Disengaged are statistically significant after controlling for seven potentially related demographic variables, and some of the difference between the Regulars, the Sporadics, and the Disengaged are significant as well. We may conclude, in other words, that real differences exist along religious lines between religiously Disengaged and Devoted teens when it comes to the extent and kind of media teens consume, including kinds that concern many parents and other adults.

Table 36 examines the sexual beliefs and activities of American teenagers across the religious ideal types. Here we see major differences in beliefs about appropriate sexual conduct. Nearly all Devoted teens believe in waiting for marriage to have sex, compared to less than one-quarter of the Disengaged who believe the same. Likewise, only 3 percent of the Devoted believe it is okay for teenagers to have sex if they are "emotionally ready for it," compared to 56 percent of the Disengaged. As to actual physical and sexual behavior, differences in the teens' beliefs are at least somewhat reflected in

Table 36. Sexual Belief and Activity of Religious Ideal-type U.S. Adolescents, Ages 13–17 (Percentages)

	U.S.	Religious Ideal Types			
		Devoted	Regulars	Sporadics	Disengaged
Believe in waiting for marriage to have sex	56	95	57	37	24
Believe it is okay for teens to have sex if they are emotionally ready for sex	30	3	27	42	56
Have been physically involved with another person, more than holding hands and light kissing, since turning 13	42	29	41	50	53
Have ever willingly touched or been touched by another person in private areas under clothes	34	18	34	43	43
Have had oral sex	21	11	20	27	30
Have had sexual intercourse	20	9	19	23	26
Average number of sexual intercourse partners (among sexually active teens per group)	3.8	2.7	2.6	3.8	4.1

Source: National Survey of Youth and Religion, 2002–3.

Note: All differences between the Devoted and the Disengaged are statistically significant at the 0.05 level after controlling for teens' age, sex, race, region of residence, parental marital status, parental education, and family income using linear, ordered logit, or logistic regression techniques; differences between the Regulars and the Disengaged are statistically significant at the 0.05 level with those controls for all but the "willingly touched" variable; differences between the Sporadics and the Disengaged are statistically significant at the 0.05 level with those controls only for the "sex before marriage" and "teen sex okay" variables.

differences in their actions. Twenty-four percent more of religiously Disengaged teens than Devoted teens have been physically involved with another person more than merely holding hands or light kissing. Whereas only 18 percent of the Devoted teens have willingly touched or been touched by another person in private areas under their clothes, 43 percent of the religiously Disengaged have done the same. About three times the proportion of Disengaged teens have had oral sex and sexual intercourse than Devoted teens. And, of the sexually active teens in each ideal type group, the less religious teens on average have had intercourse with significantly more partners than the more religious teens. Again, we see across a variety of sexual outcome measures noticeable correlations between the degree of teen religious seriousness and cautious teen sexual attitudes and behaviors. Moreover, statistical significance tests again show the differences between all of the Devoted and the Disengaged outcomes, many of the Regulars and the Disengaged outcomes, and two of the Sporadics and the Disengaged outcomes to be statistically significant after controlling for seven possibly related other variables. As with the risk and problem behavior and media consumption findings, religious variations seem to make significant differences in the life outcomes of American teens.[2]

Continuing this exploration of religion and adolescent life outcomes, we turn to table 37 to examine measures of teenage emotional well-being and

Table 37. Emotional Well-being and Attitudes about Life and the Future of Religious Ideal-type U.S. Adolescents, Ages 13–17 (Percentages)

	U.S.	Devoted	Regulars	Sporadics	Disengaged
		Religious Ideal Types			
Feelings about own body and physical appearance					
Very happy	42	54	43	36	29
Very unhappy	3	1	2	3	7
How often feels sad or depressed					
Usually or always	7	2	5	7	8
Never	19	23	21	17	14
Feels alone and misunderstood					
A lot	9	6	7	9	13
Never	39	52	40	37	32
Feels invisible					
A lot	4	3	3	3	6
Never	59	69	60	56	54
Feels cared for by people responsible for teen					
A lot	80	92	81	78	73
Never	1	~	1	1	3
Feels guilty about things in life fairly or very often	14	7	12	12	12
Thinks about and plans for the future					
Very or fairly often	75	87	74	71	60
Rarely or never	6	~	6	6	13
Thinks about the meaning of life					
Very or fairly often	40	47	35	33	26
Rarely or never	29	20	32	34	43
How often life feels meaningless to teen					
Always or usually	7	3	6	9	8
Never	40	56	40	37	30

Source: National Survey of Youth and Religion, 2002–3.

Note: Percentages may not add to 100 due to rounding, unreported don't know and refused answers, and omission of some middle-range answers. Cells of <1 are reported as ~. All differences between the Devoted and the Disengaged are statistically significant at the 0.05 level after controlling for teens' age, sex, race, region of residence, parental marital status, parental education, and family income using linear, ordered logit, or logistic regression techniques, except the "feel guilty" variable, which is significant at the 0.10 level; differences between the Regulars and the Disengaged are statistically significant at the 0.05 level with those controls for all but the "feel guilty" and "invisible" variables; differences between the Sporadics and the Disengaged are statistically significant at the 0.05 level with those controls for the "feel sad," "plan for future," and "think about meaning" variables.

life and future attitudes. Here again we find significant differences between the more religious teens and religiously Disengaged teens, contrasted in this table with opposite answer categories. The more religiously serious teens are more likely than the Disengaged to feel very happy and less likely to feel very unhappy about their body and physical appearance. The Devoted and the Regulars are likewise significantly less likely to feel sad and depressed, alone and misunderstood, and invisible as a result of nobody paying attention to them. Furthermore, the less religious the teens are, the less they feel cared for by people responsible for them. Moreover, very religious teens are no more likely than other teens to feel guilty, popular stereotypes notwithstanding. The more religious teens are also more likely to think about and make plans for the future, as well as to think about the meaning of life. And life tends much less often to feel meaningless to more religious teens than to less religious teens. Again, on every measure examined, teen religious seriousness and involvement is positively associated with greater well-being and more positive perceptions of and attitudes about life and the future, net of the possible effects of all seven control variables.

Much existing research has suggested the crucial importance in adolescents' lives of meaningful relational ties to parents and nonparent adults—grown-up friends, teachers, mentors, coaches, other parents—who can help watch over, care for, and provide resources to teens. Are there differences across our religious ideal types in such ties to nonparent adults? Table 38 shows there are indeed significant differences. The more religiously involved teens, first, tend to be more comfortable talking with adults other than parents or relatives. The Devoted in particular have a larger number of nonparental adults in their lives whom they can turn to for support, advice, and help. Moreover, the parents of the more religiously serious teens are more likely to know more of the supportive adults in their teen children's lives well enough to talk to them, expanding the reach of what sociologists call "net-

Table 38. Adult Ties of Religious Ideal-type U.S. Adolescents, Ages 13–17 (Mean averages unless otherwise noted)

	U.S.	Religious Ideal Types			
		Devoted	Regulars	Sporadics	Disengaged
Fairly or very comfortable talking to adults other than parents or relatives (percentages)	52	67	53	49	49
Number of adults teen can turn to for support, advice, help, not including parents	5.7	8.4	5.5	4.9	5.0
Number of supportive adults teen's parents know well enough to talk to	4.6	7.3	4.6	3.8	3.4
Average afternoons per week spent without adult supervision	2.6	2.1	2.7	2.8	2.9
Average evenings per week spent without adult supervision	1.9	1.5	2.1	2.1	2.1

Source: National Survey of Youth and Religion, 2002–3.

Note: All differences between the Devoted and the Disengaged are statistically significant at the 0.05 level after controlling for teens' age, sex, race, region of residence, parental marital status, parental education, and family income using linear and ordered logit regression techniques; differences between the Regulars and the Disengaged are statistically significant at the 0.05 level with those controls for only the "comfortable talking with adults" and "parents know supportive adults" variable.

work closure" around religious teens more than nonreligious teens.[3] The religiously Devoted teens are also less likely than their less religious peers to spend their afternoons and evenings without adult supervision. In sum, the lives of more religious teens are, compared to less religious teens, statistically more likely, net of all seven control variables, to be linked to and surrounded by adults, particularly nonparent adults who know and care about them and who themselves have social ties to the teens' parents. All of which tends to contribute to more positive, successful outcomes in youth's lives.

What about teenagers' relationships with their parents and siblings? Does religion appear to make a significant difference? Table 39 shows that Devoted and Regular teens are significantly more likely than Disengaged teens to feel close to, get along with, and hang out and have fun with both their mother and their father. Both are also more likely than the Disengaged to feel that their parents understand them, love and accept them for who they are, and pay enough attention to them. The more religious teens are least likely to think their parents give them either too much or not enough freedom to develop and express their own views about important issues, and thus are most likely to say their parents give them the right amount of freedom. Moreover, the Devoted and Regulars tend to eat more dinners per week with one or both of their parents than do the Disengaged. Finally, the more religious teens tend to get along better with their siblings than the less religious teens. Again, as the table note explains and as with the many differences examined above, these religious differences remain statistically significant even when the possible effects of other control variables are removed. There seems to be something about religion per se that positively associates with better family relationships.

Table 40 explores the comparative moral reasoning and honesty behaviors of American teens as categorized into our four religious ideal types. Once again we observe some remarkable differences. As measured by one survey question, 22 percent of Devoted teens and 61 percent of the Disengaged are moral relativists. When asked how they would decide what to do if they were unsure of what was right or wrong in a particular situation, only 1 percent of the Devoted said they would choose to "do what would help them get ahead," and 6 percent said they would "do whatever would make them feel happy."[4] By comparison, 16 percent of the Disengaged said they would choose what would help them get ahead and 40 percent chose what would make them feel happy. Furthermore, four times the number of Disengaged than Devoted teens often lie to their parents, while more than twice the proportion of Devoted than Disengaged say they never lie to their parents. Finally, the most religious teens are significantly less likely to cheat on schoolwork and to do things they hope their parents never find out about. All told, when it comes to moral reasoning and honesty, the differences between the most and least religious American teens are conspicuous and significant.

What about compassion for less fortunate, more vulnerable people? Do American teens differ in moral compassion and commitment to justice by religious type? Table 41 shows that the more religious teens, indeed, profess

Table 39. Quality of Family Relationships of Religious Ideal-type U.S. Adolescents with Mothers and/or Fathers, Ages 13–17 (Percentages) (Teen reports)

	U.S.	Religious Ideal Types			
		Devoted	Regulars	Sporadics	Disengaged
Feels extremely or very close to mother	78	88	77	74	66
Gets along with mother extremely or very well	68	80	70	66	51
Has fun hanging out and doing things with mother very or fairly often	50	67	46	44	38
Feels extremely or very close to father	59	70	63	55	46
Gets along with father extremely or very well	61	70	65	56	49
Has fun hanging out and doing things with father very or fairly often	48	57	48	46	40
Teens feel parents understand them a lot	41	53	38	39	28
Teens feel parents love and accept them a lot for who they are	83	93	85	79	74
Teens feel parents pay a lot of attention to them	70	78	70	67	63
Amount of freedom parents give teen to develop and openly express own views on important issues					
Too little freedom	13	8	12	15	19
The right amount of freedom	81	89	83	77	75
Too much freedom	6	4	4	7	6
Average nights per week teen eats dinner with parent or adult guardian	5.1	5.7	5.3	5.0	4.6
Gets along with siblings in household (teens with siblings only)					
Very or extremely well	44	54	43	38	36
Not so well, pretty poorly, or very badly	11	5	10	10	18

Source: National Survey of Youth and Religion, 2002–3.

Note: Some percentages may not add to 100 due to rounding, unreported don't know and refused answers, and omission of some middle-range answers. All differences between the Devoted and the Disengaged are statistically significant at the 0.05 level after controlling for teens' age, sex, race, region of residence, parental marital status, parental education, and family income using linear, ordered logit, or logistic regression techniques; differences between the Regulars and the Disengaged are statistically significant at the 0.05 level with those controls for all but the "get along with siblings" variable; differences between the Sporadics and the Disengaged are statistically significant at the 0.05 level with those controls only for the "close to mother," "get along with mother," "have fun with father," and "parents understand" variables.

on our survey to be much more compassionate than the less religious teens. The Devoted are more than twice as likely than the Disengaged to say they care very much about the needs of poor and elderly people in the United States. The Regulars and even the Sporadics are also significantly different from the Disengaged on these questions. The Devoted are likewise significantly more likely to say they care about racial equality. Once again, as stated

Table 40. Moral Reasoning and Honesty Behaviors of Religious Ideal-type U.S. Adolescents, Ages 13–17 (Percentages)

	U.S.	Religious Ideal Types			
		Devoted	Regulars	Sporadics	Disengaged
Believes that morals are relative, that there are no definite rights and wrongs for everybody	45	22	46	57	61
If were unsure about what was right or wrong in a particular situation, would choose to do whatever would help them to get ahead	11	1	12	13	16
If were unsure about what was right or wrong in a particular situation, would choose to do whatever would make them feel happy	27	6	27	36	40
Lied to parents in the prior year					
Fairly or very often	10	4	9	11	16
Never	16	26	12	10	11
Cheated in a test, assignment, or homework in school in the prior year					
Fairly or very often	7	6	8	7	8
Never	38	45	33	33	33
Did things they hoped their parents would never find out about in the prior year					
Fairly or very often	16	7	15	17	22
Never	17	24	13	12	13

Source: National Survey of Youth and Religion, 2002–3.

Note: Percentages may not add to 100 due to rounding, unreported don't know and refused answers, and omission of some middle-range answers. All differences between Devoted and Regulars compared to the Disengaged are statistically significant at the 0.05 level after controlling for teens' age, sex, race, region of residence, parental marital status, parental education, and family income using linear, ordered logit, or logistic regression techniques, except for the "cheated" and "did things hoped parents would not find out about" variables, which were not significant for the Regulars only; differences between the Sporadics and the Disengaged are not statistically significant for any variables.

in the table notes, these differences are statistically significant even when controlling for other demographic variables that may also affect the outcomes. Thus, more religious teens appear to possess greater moral compassion and concern for justice than their nonreligious peers—and apparently for religiously related reasons and not simply because of differences in their demographic compositions.

Finally, do professed feelings and attitudes of concern for others appear actually to get worked out in actions differently among more and less religious American teenagers? Table 42 examines differences in levels of community participation, volunteering, and giving between different types of American teens. First, we see that religious seriousness is associated with involvement in all types of organized activities. The Devoted and Regulars are involved in more than the average number of organized activities of all

Table 41. Moral Compassion of Religious Ideal-type U.S. Adolescents, Ages 13–17 (Percentages)

	U.S.	Religious Ideal Types			
		Devoted	Regulars	Sporadics	Disengaged
Personally cares about the needs of poor people in the United States					
Cares very much	51	69	43	44	33
Does not really care	3	2	4	3	6
Personally cares about the needs of elderly people in the United States					
Cares very much	49	64	45	41	31
Does not really care	3	2	3	5	5
Personally cares about equality between different racial groups					
Cares very much	47	62	45	43	39
Does not really care	19	11	18	23	23

Source: National Survey of Youth and Religion, 2002–3.

Note: All differences between the Devoted and the Regulars compared to the Disengaged are statistically significant at the 0.05 level after controlling for teens' age, sex, race, region of residence, parental marital status, parental education, and family income using linear, ordered logit, or logistic regression techniques, expect for the "care about racial equality" variable for the Regulars; differences between the Sporadics and the Disengaged are statistically significant at the 0.05 level with those controls for all but the "care about racial equality" variable.

U.S. teens, while the Sporadics and Disengaged are involved in fewer. We also see large differences by religious type in teens' giving of their own money to organizations or causes. The Devoted are more than three times as likely as the Disengaged to have given more than $20 of their own money. More religious teens are also significantly more likely to do noncompulsory volunteer work or community service, with the Devoted twice as likely as the Disengaged in doing so (50 compared to 25 percent). Furthermore, the most religious tend to volunteer or do community service more *often* than the less religious. They are also significantly more likely to engage in the kinds of volunteer and service activities that bring them into contact with racial, economic, and religious differences, which helps generate what social theorists call "bridging" social capital that fosters social cohesion and trust.[5] Moreover, religiously Devoted teens have helped homeless people, needy neighbors, family friends, or other needy people a lot directly, not through an organization, at twice the rate of the national teen average (20 compared to 10 percent), while the Disengaged have done so at less than half of the rate of the national average (4 compared to 10 percent). The Disengaged are also more than twice as likely as the Devoted never to have helped other needy people directly (37 compared to 17 percent). Last, in their community participation, religiosity also correlates with organizational involvements that provide teens with experiences that cultivate their leadership skills. Whether or not those organizations include religious organizations, the more religious teens are much more likely to have been part of planning an event, leading

Table 42. Community Participation of Religious Ideal-type U.S. Adolescents, Ages 13–17 (Percentages)

	U.S.	Religious Ideal Types			
		Devoted	Regulars	Sporadics	Disengaged
Average number of regular, organized activities, clubs, classes, or organizations involved in	2.1	3.1	2.4	2.0	1.5
Has given more than $20 of own money to any organization or cause	38	65	41	33	21
Regularly or occasionally did volunteer work or community service in the prior year (not counting required service, e.g., by school, juvenile justice program)	32	50	34	29	25
Average total number of times per month teens did volunteer work or community service in the prior year (not counting required service, e.g., by school, juvenile justice program)	.65	1.07	.52	.61	.53
Did volunteer or service work that brought teen into a lot of direct contact with people of a different race, religion, or economic class	24	31	25	22	19
Helped homeless people, needy neighbors, family friends, or other needy people, not through an organization					
A lot	10	20	9	9	4
None	26	17	26	27	37
Involved in an organization last year in which teen planned an event, led a meeting, or gave a presentation or speech	31	56	33	30	20
Involving organizations not exclusively religious	27	44	30	30	20

Source: National Survey of Youth and Religion, 2002–3.

Note: All differences between the Devoted and the Regulars compared to the Disengaged are statistically significant at the 0.05 level after controlling for teens' age, sex, race, region of residence, parental marital status, parental education, and family income using linear, ordered logit, or logistic regression techniques; differences between the Sporadics and the Disengaged are statistically significant at the 0.05 level with those controls for all but the "times per month volunteered" and "planned an event" variables.

a meeting, and giving presentations or speeches. Thus, far from being "too heavenly minded to be of any earthly good," it is the more religious teens who are the most involved in their communities. And, as with the findings in the tables above, these observed differences in community participation, volunteering, and giving between more and less religious teenagers are statistically significant even when using statistical techniques that neutralize any effects of demographic composition differences between the religious ideal types. In other words, even if there were no differences between the examined religious types in race, sex, region of residence, parental marital status, parental education, and family income, religious differences in outcomes would remain significant.[6]

Religious communities may be tempted simply to feel good about these findings—and they clearly do have some reason for taking heart that their work with teens may not be inconsequential. But viewed from a different, more self-critical perspective, as judged by the norms and expectations of their own teachings and traditions, some religious communities have some cause for concern. A glass half full is also half empty. These tables do show that religiously involved teenagers are doing relatively better than religiously inactive teens. But they also show that significantly large minorities of teens who regularly attend religious services, for example, do not have particularly good relationships with their parents, appear to be moral relativists, act dishonestly in various ways, are sexually active, do not particularly care about racial equality in the United States, do not feel comfortable talking with adults, are not in any habit of giving money to other organizations or causes, and are not particularly involved in the civic life of their communities. Nobody is perfect. And different people and communities have different standards on many of these issues. Still, very many American religious communities have commitments, teachings, and expectations to which some of these results suggest more than a few quite religious American teens are not living up. The point is not that sociology stands in a position to chastise religious communities or people. The point is simply that the findings above can be interpreted from more than one perspective and that fair-minded observers of American religion, including American religious believers themselves, do well to consider the insights and implications of multiple points of view—including those that may provide unhappy news or difficult challenges.

That said, standing back from all of these tables and viewing them as a whole, we can draw some larger summarizing conclusions. First, ironically, contrary to many youth's own inability to see or articulate the influence or importance of religion in their lives, religion does in fact appear to be a significant factor that does make a considerable difference in a host of life outcomes. And these observable differences are not scattered and uneven but emerge regularly across a wide variety of adolescent attitudes, experiences, relationships, behaviors, and beliefs. The consistency across outcomes is truly striking. Moreover, as we have repeatedly noted, the religious differences across the outcomes are consistently statistically significant, at least when comparing the most and least religious, even after controlling through multivariate statistical techniques for the effects of seven other key demographic factors that might affect the outcomes through the religious types. The religion-outcome association remains, net of these controls, suggesting that there is something about different levels of teen religiosity per se that correlates with differences in teen life outcomes. Religion itself indeed does appear to matter in some way in the formation of teens' lives.[7] Furthermore, we can observe in the tables a certain threshold of teen religiosity below which the religious association appears not often to operate. Mere sporadic investments

and involvements by teens in religion usually prove indistinguishable in outcomes from those of teens who are completely disengaged from religion. Religious associations with more positive life outcomes generally appear to require teens reaching the level of religiosity of at least the Regulars to be
statistically significantly different from the Disengaged. A modest amount of
religion, in other words, does not appear to make a consistent difference in
the lives of U.S. teenagers. It is only the more serious religious teens, the
Regulars and Devoteds, whose outcomes are more consistently and significantly more positive than those of their entirely religiously Disengaged peers.

   If all of this is so, then why do teens have such trouble seeing and articulating this religious difference in their own lives and that of their friends?
We believe there are two answers to that question. First, most American
teenagers lack perspective on their own lives. Because they are young and
their personal experiences are so immediate, they simply have a difficult time
understanding and describing their lives from any larger, more objective, comparative viewpoint. And because for so many teens religion is such a taken-
for-granted aspect of their lives, they have a nearly impossible time thinking
about how their lives would be different if they were more or less religious.
Second, and we think most important, nearly all American teenagers believe
that they are not influenced directly by *anything* at all, religious or otherwise.
Like most of the adults who have socialized them, teenagers take for granted
an image of themselves as autonomous and self-defining individuals fully responsible for and capable of the formation of their own lives. Many teenagers
actually bristle at the suggestion that they are directly influenced by people
and institutions outside of themselves. Their conventional view, rather, is that
others—peers, friends, parents, the media—merely provide them with information and options, but that they as autonomous individuals fully in control
of and responsible for themselves make their own choices and actions independent of any external influence. This unselfconscious embrace of American
individualism thus makes it very difficult for teens to perceive and explain
how religion may directly influence their lives. Religion cannot, because *nothing* does. They are influenced by themselves. We know, however, that Americans' faith in autonomous individualism is naïve. People's lives are normally
in fact profoundly defined and shaped by many of the social relations, cultures, and institutions in which their lives are embedded.[8] All of sociology
teaches this basic insight. This chapter's tables also suggest the real religious
difference in teen's lives.

   But is it religion itself that is causing the difference? That is the next
question.

EXCURSUS: THE COMPLEXITIES OF CAUSAL INFLUENCE

Religion is significantly associated with positive outcomes across a variety of
important youth attitudes and behaviors.[9] But can we make the inference that
religious faith and practice themselves play a causal influence role in explaining these associations? Social processes of causal influence are complicated

and worth thinking through carefully. The cross-sectional data on which many analyses of youth religion and outcomes are based, including the analyses in this chapter—which are gathered at one point in time rather than with the same subjects over multiple points in time—make it difficult to determine the time-ordering of key factors and the direction of cause and effect between religion and youth outcomes. Normally, all we can say with confidence is that a certain *correlation* exists between certain religious factors and other outcome variables. We can legitimately speak of *differences* in levels of youth outcomes between religious groups or types, and of statistical *associations* between religious variables and outcome measures. With cross-sectional data, however, we typically cannot clearly establish the time-order of potentially important factors or claim that religious factors actually *causally influence* outcomes in the lives of youth. This is because the observed associations may be the result of different (or combinations of different) possible processes involving dissimilar relationships and directions of causal influences.

In the following pages we draw on current social research about religion as a possible causal influence in the lives of U.S. teenagers to help properly interpret the findings of tables 34–42. In short, below we suggest that the observed positive association between greater teen religiosity and positive life outcomes cannot be explained by one simple causal mechanism. Rather, the observed association is most likely the result of a *combination* of complex causal social processes, some of which recognize the operation of what scholars call the "endogeneity problem" in specifying sociological causal relations. This combination, we believe, likely does involve the possibility that higher teen religiosity may select on certain personality types, such as "risk-averse," "conventional," or "joiner" personalities, which themselves may be more likely to be correlated with more positive life outcomes. Such selection processes complicate the commonsense inference that greater religion causes more positive outcomes in adolescents' lives. We further suggest that some self-selection or reverse causation processes also likely *partially* explain the observed religion-outcomes association above.

Nevertheless, although we do believe that these other complicating processes likely help to explain *some* proportion of the religion-outcomes associations observed in tables 34–42, we also believe that established, solid empirical research and theorizing justify the inference that various features of religious faith and practice themselves influence more positive outcomes in U.S. teenagers' lives. We thus conclude that it is not mistaken to interpret the greater positive outcomes in the lives of more highly religious U.S. teenagers as likely caused in significant part by direct influences of features of committed religious faith and practice. Religion, we suggest, is part of what helps produce the more positive observed outcomes in teenagers' lives.[10] Before going there, however, we must consider other likely causal mechanisms in the larger, complicated combination of causal processes that help to interpret the findings in tables 34–42.

Personality Selection

One potential causal process that may help partially explain why more religious U.S. teenagers appear to enjoy better life outcomes is the possibility that certain hard-wired personalities tend both to be attracted to religion and to have better life outcomes. Some scholars have suggested that certain genetically grounded personality types—variously described as risk-averse, conventionalist, conformist, clean-living, and joiners—affect both religiosity and outcomes. Some studies seem to support this hypothesis. Steven Reiss has found that young people valuing order, honor, and family is correlated with higher religiosity, while their valuing vengeance and independence is correlated with lower religiosity. In another study, Reiss and S. M. Havercamp found that devoutly religious people display lower levels of an independence trait. Other scholars have suggested an empirical relationship between religion and risk aversion. Mark Regnerus reports finding among teenagers an association between certain personality factors—having a hot temper, liking to take risks, and a lack of planning—and religiosity. More highly religious teens are less likely to possess those personality traits, and the more teens possess those personality traits, the more likely they are, according to Regnerus, to have trouble with outcomes like family relationships, health, and stealing.[11] Hard-wired personality selection on religion and better outcomes, therefore, may help to account for some of the observed positive association between greater religiosity and more positive life outcomes.

Available evidence, however, suggests that personality selection does not itself entirely explain away the religion-outcomes association. Regnerus's most systematic effort to test the personality selection hypothesis with national adolescent data, for example, finds that, although personality, religiosity, and outcomes are indeed all related, the strength of the direct associations between religion and positive life outcomes are barely diminished when multiple personality factors are introduced into multivariate regression models. In other words, both personality and religion variables predict life outcomes, but personality type does not attenuate religion's statistically significant direct effects on life outcomes.[12] It also deserves mentioning that hard-wired personalities do not necessarily mean absolutely immutable personalities. It could well be that, for some youth, religion can act back on personality types, softening, redirecting, or stretching them in new ways. For example, religion could channel a risk-seeking teenager away from the allure of drug abuse, unprotected sex, or skipping school and toward the challenges of a third world missions project or teaching rock climbing at a religious summer camp. In any case, evidence suggests that personality selection may play some role in the religion-outcomes association observed among U.S. teenagers. Still, if that is so, it is nevertheless likely only one causal process among others operating in a larger, more complex combination of influences.

Reverse Causation

A second causal possibility that we suspect is at work in the religious lives of some U.S. teens is a reverse causation process. The idea here is that some youth likely self-select out of religion when they get into trouble or experience some other negative outcome in life. In other words, some religious youth who, for whatever reasons, develop negative or self-destructive attitudes and behaviors subsequently reduce their religious involvement and so count on surveys as less religious, thus creating observed associations between religiosity and positive outcomes for those who did not drop out of religion because of their lack of negative outcomes. In which case, religion is *not* influencing positive or negative outcomes in the lives of youth. Instead, other, nonreligious factors explain different levels of family problems, delinquency, substance abuse, civic involvement, and positive attitudes about life among youth. Yet, if teenagers do for these other reasons become depressed, begin taking drugs, get in trouble at school, or develop poor relationships with their parents, they also may tend to reduce or drop out of whatever religious involvements they previously had. As a result, these negative-outcome youth sort themselves out of the pool of youth who are religiously involved. So, when researchers find positive correlations between religiosity and constructive youth outcomes, it is not because youth religiosity influenced those outcomes; rather, it is because the youth with the negative outcomes moved themselves out of the higher religious categories, leaving behind other youth with (not religiously influenced) better average outcomes.

For example, in a hypothetical church youth group of 20 teenagers, four youth from bad neighborhoods, broken families, and poor schools may start to get into trouble for selling drugs, shoplifting, and fighting. Feeling uncomfortable for various reasons with the program and other kids in the church youth group, to reduce their cognitive and emotional dissonance these four now delinquent teens stop attending church and youth group altogether. A subsequent survey of these 20 youth would then observe a strong correlation between higher youth group involvement and avoidance of delinquency. But the church and youth group themselves could hardly take credit for producing that association, because it was actually the troubled neighborhoods, families, and schools that helped produce the negative outcome of their delinquency, which religion was not able to prevent. To the extent that this process is operative, religion itself is not influencing youth toward good outcomes, but is only being avoided by youth with worse outcomes by making them feel uncomfortable and driving them away.

The best available evidence suggests that this kind of reverse-causation process *may* help to explain *some* but not all of the positive association between adolescent religion-outcomes observed in tables 34–42. Good empirical studies on the question using longitudinal data have produced mixed results. Brent Benda and Robert Corwyn, for example, have found not only that religion predicts lower levels of delinquency on certain outcomes, but also the reciprocal effect: that delinquent behaviors predict a subsequent decline in youth religiosity. Similarly, Arland Thornton and colleagues have found that while marriage without previous cohabitation tends to increase the religious involvement of young adults, cohabitation also tends to reduce religious service attendance. Using longitudinal data, Mark Regnerus has likewise found that adolescent involvement in theft decreases subsequent religious service attendance and self-reported importance of religious faith. On the other hand, Ann Meier's two-wave panel study of 15- to 18-year-olds shows that first sexual intercourse between the survey waves did not significantly reduce or increase religiosity for boys or girls, contradicting her "religiosity adaptation" hypothesis that having sex will result in lower levels of religiosity among adolescents. And Steven Burkett's three-wave panel study of high-schoolers likewise shows that eleventh-grade girls and eleventh- and twelfth-grade boys who had been drinking alcohol more heavily in the previous year were not more likely to reduce their religiosity as a result; heavier consumption of alcohol the previous year exhibited only a weak significant association with reduced religiosity for twelfth-grade girls.[13]

Recall, too, that our own study specifically asked teens who had reduced their levels of religiosity why they had done so. Of the nonreligious teens in the NSYR who had been raised in a religion and were asked why they had become not religious, few said something like they were beginning to get into trouble in life and started to feel uncomfortable in religious settings (table 28). The majority of them mentioned intellectual skepticism about faith or other quite vague reasons for losing their religion. Likewise, few of the NSYR teens who had stopped attending religious services that they had previously attended more often, when asked why they reduced their attendance, suggested anything like selecting themselves out of religious participation because delinquency, sexual activity, deteriorating relationships with parents, trouble at school, or other signs of poor outcomes made them feel disinterested in or uneasy with religion (table 31). Again, the vast majority had no clear reason for stopping attending, were simply disinterested, moved locations of residence, or stopped believing what religions taught. It could be that getting into trouble and consequently feeling uncomfortable in religious settings really were the reasons many of these teens became not religious and stopped attending religious services, and that they simply did not want to say so. But, if so, we found scant evidence for it.

In sum, it appears plausible if not likely that, at least with some outcomes, some teens who engage in religiously nonnormative behaviors may subsequently tend to reduce their levels of religious involvement. And this may help to account for *some* of the religion-outcomes associations observed in tables 34–42. We do not believe, however, that the available quantitative and qualitative evidence support the conclusion that reverse causation explains most or all of the variance in outcomes among different religious types. Most likely, reverse causation is one among a combination of relevant causal processes.

Direct and Indirect Religious Effects

A third causal process that we believe helps to explain the findings of tables 34–42 is what to many people will be the commonsense interpretation: that religion actually does causally influence positive outcomes, that *religious practices themselves influence youth in ways that produce positive outcomes in their lives.* The idea behind this possibility is straightforward: there are certain features in religious practices per se, some of which we elaborate in the next section, that have the capacity directly and indirectly to produce positive outcomes in the lives of youth. Something about religion itself causes the good outcomes for youth. By general implication, teens who increase their religious involvement should, net of other factors, reduce their chances of experiencing negative and harmful outcomes; and teens who reduce their religious practices should, net of other factors, increase their risk of negative and destructive outcomes. There are, of course, a number of specifying sub-variants of these processes worth noting, accounting for conditions, exceptions, and limits possibly affecting religion's influence. One subvariant could be that religion particularly influences teenagers who are more at risk for negative outcomes, but exerts less influence among more typical adolescents. Alternatively, religion may effectively promote and maintain positive outcomes among those already doing well in life, but may not possess the ability positively to influence youth who are already heading or deep into trouble. It could be that religion exerts a protective influence on early and middle adolescents but becomes less of an influence among late adolescents, or vice versa. It might be that the dominant religion in the United States, Christianity, exerts significant causal influences over its adolescent adherents, but that minority religions for different reasons exert less influence. A number of other subvariant hypotheses are conceivable and potentially empirically testable. In any case, each of them essentially represents a specification of the basic idea that something about religious practice itself causally affects outcomes in youth's lives.

Another possible complication of this religious influence process is that religion may exert causal influence on the outcomes in youth's lives not directly, but indirectly, through nonreligious mechanisms of influence. The idea is that religion need not *directly* influence some outcome in order to have a significant influence on that outcome. Religion can exert influences indirectly, through other factors. For example, religion may reduce delinquency in the lives of teenagers, not in some direct way, but indirectly by strengthening families, which in turn reduces delinquency; thus, greater religiosity produces stronger families, which then reduces delinquency. Religion still exerts causal influence, but strengthening families is the mechanism by which religion reduces delinquency. If this process were modeled incorrectly, a researcher might wrongly conclude that it is strong families and not religion that reduces delinquency, when in fact religion *would* reduce delinquency by its influence on and through the quality of family life.

Still another model of this religious influence process might suggest that youth and families who, for perhaps nonreligious reasons, are already predisposed toward the outcomes of positive attitudes and practices choose to become more religiously involved as one strategy to achieve that end. This hypothesis suggests that observed positive outcomes in youth's lives are not only the result of the influences of religious practices per se, they may be driven by larger, preceding, perhaps nonreligious life orientations of youth or their families to be good and do well in life, to avoid trouble, to be as happy and involved in life as possible. Such people then choose to implement a variety of strategies at different levels and in different areas of their lives to achieve this kind of generally positive, constructive life. Religion is one such instrumentally chosen strategy, which itself is as much the result of a more fundamental, potentially nonreligious orientation toward positive life outcomes as it is a causal influence on those outcomes. Note that it is extremely difficult here to sort out which factor was causally prior to the other. Perhaps the general life orientation to be good and do well in life, to avoid trouble, and to be as happy and involved in life as possible is as much the result of generationally prior family religious involvement as it is the cause of it. Much here depends on the limits of our assumptions and adequacy of measures. But note that either version of this possible causal process locates significant religious effects on youth attitudes, behaviors, and experiences. This view posits that religion can have an influence on positive youth outcomes. It merely attempts to move back one step in the causal sequence by suggesting some antecedent factor that explains religious involvement and positive outcomes. But clearly religious practices still exert some causal influence on outcomes; that is precisely why in this model basically constructively oriented people become involved in religion: because religion actually helps them achieve their purpose of living positive, constructive lives. Recognizing that positive outcomes are likely also the results of other, nonreligious factors, such as basic positive life orientations, does little to challenge the idea that religion likewise influences outcomes, because nobody claims that religion is the *only* factor influencing youth's outcomes in life. What these other versions of the religious effects process do is point out possible complexities in the ways religion may influence people's life outcomes.

To summarize: sorting through the alternative causal processes potentially involved in explaining the observed association between greater teen religiosity and more positive life outcomes is complicated business, more technically complicated than this chapter can thoroughly address.[14] The bottom line, however, is this: our review of existing scholarship, our analysis of NSYR and other survey data, and our experience interviewing hundreds of teenagers around the United States persuades us that no single causal process or mechanism entirely explains the positive religion-outcomes findings in tables 34–42. Human life is too complicated for that. We believe that some proportion of certain of the religious differences in outcomes observed in the tables are likely explained by such processes as personality selection and reverse causation. We also believe, however, that religious faith and practice can and often do exert causal effects on outcomes, that religion itself can and often does operate as a causal influence in youth's lives.[15] Moreover, we must bear in mind that there are prima facie reasons for supposing that religion possesses the capacity to socialize, motivate, constrain, and direct human, including teenagers', assumptions, values, preferences, moral commitments, choices, and behaviors. It is in fact one of the bread-and-butter tasks of the sociology of religion to show empirically that religious beliefs and practices do causally shape outcomes in people's lives. Decades of research in that field accumulate to suggest the plausibility of the idea that religion can exert a causal influence on human consciousness and action. Again, in any given case, the possibility of spuriousness is real, but until it is demonstrated, it remains only a possibility. Meanwhile, scholars are justified in getting on with the business of providing most plausible interpretations of research findings. And this may well involve interpretations positing that religious influences per se can and may indeed have causal effects in forming the lives of people, including youth. More empirical research is needed to help better sort through the alternative and conjunctural causal possibilities around this question.[16] This chapter is merely one piece of a larger puzzle.

Another key task in interpreting the findings of tables 34–42 is theorizing more specifically the sociological processes by which religion might influence outcomes in adolescent lives. If religion does influence outcomes in youth's lives, as we have suggested, can we explain how exactly that might happen? Possible religious effects on teen outcomes can only be as plausible as the specific causal mechanisms we can theorize by which that may operate. So, why or how might religion influence the lives of American teenagers? It is to answer these questions that we turn next.

THEORIZING RELIGIOUS INFLUENCES IN ADOLESCENTS' LIVES

If we are to believe that religion exerts some causal influence in the lives of youth, we must better specify how or why it may do so. What is it about religion that might produce positive outcomes in the lives of teenagers? We suggest that religion may exert positive sociological influences in the lives of American youth through nine distinct but connected and potentially mutually reinforcing factors. These nine distinct factors cluster as groups of three beneath three larger conceptual dimensions of social influence. These three larger dimensions are moral order, learned competencies, and social and organizational ties. The nine specific factors that exert the religious influences are moral directives, spiritual experiences, role models, community and leadership skills, coping skills, cultural capital, social capital, network closure, and extracommunity links. The following pages elaborate these nine distinct but connected and potentially mutually reinforcing factors that we suggest account sociologically for religion's recurrent positive, constructive influence in the lives of American adolescents.[17]

Moral Order

The first three factors influencing youth we conceptualize as dimensions of the cultural moral orders into which religions induct their adherents. By moral order, we mean to suggest the idea of substantive cultural traditions grounded on and promoting particular normative ideas of what is good and bad, right and wrong, higher and lower, worthy and unworthy, just and unjust, and so on, which orient human consciousness and motivate human action.[18] Importantly, these distinctions of judgment and valuation within moral order are understood as not established by people's own desires, decisions, or preferences, but are believed to exist apart from and above them, providing standards by which human desires, decisions, and preferences can themselves be judged. It is under this larger category of moral order that the first three of the nine factors should be understood, as follows:

1. Moral directives: *American religions promote specific cultural moral directives of self-control and personal virtue grounded in the authority of long historical traditions and narratives into which members are inducted, such that youth may internalize these moral orders and use them to guide their life choices and moral commitments.*

This is to say that, as American adolescents go about forming practices and making choices that compose and shape their lives, religion can provide them with substantive normative bearings, standards, and imperatives to guide those practices and choices. Normally, these substantive normative directives and orders operate to foster forms of self-control toward the learning of virtues and values often expressed in positive, constructive ways. For example, different religious traditions teach their young adherents moral commitments, such as tithing from one's income for the church, synagogue, and the common good; seeking reconciliation instead of vengeance; treating one's body as the temple of the Holy Spirit; honoring one's parents and elders; avoiding self-indulgent gluttony and sexual promiscuity; respecting the dignity of others because they are made in the image of God; faithfully fasting during Ramadan; acting in honesty and fairness even at a cost to oneself; practicing Zakat, the giving of alms to the poor as Allah commands, the Four Noble Truths, the Eightfold Path, the Five Precepts, and so on. Most religious organizations bring to these moral commitments the authority of long historical tradition and compelling narratives. The observable significant associations that religion does have with youth in various outcomes may in part be explained by the cultural moral orders that religion provides that orient consciousness and motivate action.[19]

Of course, religions are not the only source of such moral directives and orders. Indeed, all cultures are constituted by and expressive of moral order.[20] American youth, therefore (as do all modern people), live within and between multiple moral orders among which they have to negotiate, balance, compromise, and choose. Religion represents one of many potential normative orders claiming youth's allegiance and adherence. While other nonreligious moral orders (which may have deep historical roots in religious moral orders, yet have subsequently been secularized) may promote virtues and values similar to those of a religious moral order, clearly not all do. For example, as the previous chapter noted, the moral order of mass-consumer market capitalism and the advertising industry it deploys with great influence on American youth does little to promote self-control, moderation, the common good, sacrifice, honor for others, and other traditional religious virtues. Rather, contemporary American capitalism and advertising tend to promote among youth a moral order whose "virtues" include self-gratification, self-assertion, competition, insecurity, conformity, perpetual experimentation, contempt for traditional authorities, the commodification of all value, and incessant material acquisition. Thus, when various religious speakers say that they struggle against "the culture," they mean that they are up against other moral orders antithetical to their religion's moral order that vie for loyalty and conformity.

2. Spiritual experiences: *American religions provide the organizational contexts and cultural substance fostering in youth spiritual experiences that may help to solidify their moral commitments and constructive life practices.*

The point here is that moral directives are not simply imposed from the outside by traditions and organizations. Individuals do not simply conform their consciousness and actions to moral orders like chameleons changing colors to match their environment. Rather, humans internalize moral directives and orders in their subjective mental worlds of identity, belief, loyalties, convictions, perceptions, interests, emotions, and desires. And these subjective commitments prove often to have a fair amount of stability and continuity (if not consistency and coherence) for individuals over time. They also help to frame the issues and inform the motivations that shape outcomes in the lives of youth. Religious youth are facilitated in this process by personal spiritual experiences that often legitimate and reinforce their religious moral order. Whether it is a conversion experience, an answer to prayer, a sensation of deep spiritual peace, a perceived word of divine guidance, the witnessing of a miracle, or something else, the religious moral orders of youth (and adults) are substantiated and reinforced in ways that bolster the influence of the moral orders on outcomes in their lives. From a sociological perspective, religious experiences tend not to float down from the sky as autonomous or self-generating encounters. Rather, sociologists are attuned to how spiritual experiences often arise from the immediate or distant contexts of religious traditions and organizations. Youth normally have conversion experiences in churches that emphasize conversion, just as youth typically witness miraculous faith healings who belong to religious cultures that emphasize prayers for healing. This does not make the experiences any less real or authentic or perhaps divinely inspired. It simply acknowledges that humans are socially constituted beings. Consequently, religious organizations and traditions possess the contexts and resources to help facilitate such spiritual experiences, which, in turn, often solidify the moral orders that shape various outcomes in youth's lives.

3. Role models: *American religions can provide youth with adult and peer group role models, providing examples of life practices shaped by religious moral orders that constructively influence the lives of youth, and offering positive relationships that youth may be invested in preserving through their own normatively approved living.*

Also solidifying the moral orders that shape various outcomes in adolescents' lives are the embodied normative models provided to youth by adult and peer role models. Religion supplies not only moral order and spiritual experiences that authenticate and fortify moral order. Religion also supplies fellow congregants, companion disciples, wise elders, exemplary representations of life shaped by the religious moral order. In many cases, religion also provides or points out the opposite: explicit cases of examples of people who have violated the moral order, fallen from grace, exemplified vice and foolishness, and so on. These help to make moral order tangible. They provide a teleological direction for growth and development. They show what a good (and perhaps bad) human life looks like, furnishing an instructive example of right (and wrong) living.[21] Moreover, when youth develop relationships with such positive role models, that raises the cost to youth of violating the moral order, because that would likely damage the relationship. The youth come to be personally invested in sustaining the relationships, which normally will involve affirming and enacting the religious moral order. This can often have positive, constructive consequences in various outcomes in the lives of youth. For example, a young person in a religious context may come to know and admire and prize a relationship with his or her youth leader, or devout aunt, or young adult friend who has taken a particular interest in him or her. This relationship communicates to youth that people they hold in positive regard are committed to the religion's moral order and have learned with some success how to live it out in their lives. This provides them with a microplausibility structure for that moral order and a model for possible emulation.[22] Furthermore, the valued relationship with the youth group leader (or aunt or young adult friend) as role model tends to provide an incentive for the youth to continue to enact the religious moral order himself or herself in order to sustain the conditions for maintaining the valued relationship. All of this, we suggest, can work to reinforce the positive attitudinal and behavioral outcomes noted above.

Learned Competencies

Religion shapes the lives of American adolescents in ways beyond the formative influence of moral order. A second major way that religion can influence the life outcomes of youth is by increasing their competence in skills and knowledge that contribute to enhancing their well-being and improving their life chances. Here we explicate three distinct learned competencies that religion may afford American youth.

4. Community and leadership skills: *American religions provide organizational contexts where youth can observe, learn, and practice valuable community life skills and leadership skills, which are transposable for constructive uses beyond religious activities.*

Most American religions take concrete form as congregational voluntary associations. As such, they provide their members, including adolescent members, with multiple and continuous opportunities to observe, learn, and practice the skills of community life and leadership. Religious congregations are ever in need of members to serve on committees, to organize programs, to provide leadership, to coordinate initiatives, and so on. Functional religious congregations also require ongoing member involvement in fundamental organizational processes. In and through this, religious youth may find themselves organizing a car wash, facilitating a Bible study, arranging a trip to Israel, sitting in as a youth delegate on a church committee, serving as altar boy or girl, helping to coordinate a social justice march, assisting in a tutoring program, planning a retreat, sitting in on a congregational meeting, reading scripture in a service, and much more. In so doing, religious youth are exposed to and have the chance to acquire and practice a series of useful capacities and skills. These may include group decision making, raising and budgeting funds, leading discussions, mobilization consensus, public speaking, enacting rituals, building coalitions, conducting meetings and services, and resolving disagreements. Learning such skills clearly enhances the religious capital of youth.[23] But, following the Tocquevillian tradition, we can see that these skills may also be transposed and deployed for use in multiple nonreligious settings.[24] The community and leadership capacities that American youth learn in religious congregations may serve them equally well throughout their lives, in study groups, student government, sports, neighborhood organizing, political activism, professional activities, business ventures, civic involvement, and beyond. Thus, religious communities may inculcate in youth abilities that can increase their confidence and functional capacities, which may enhance their well-being and life outcomes.

5. Coping skills: *American religions promote a variety of beliefs and practices that can help believers cope with the stress of difficult situations social psychologically, to process difficult emotions, and to resolve interpersonal conflicts, and so enhance the well-being and life capacities of youth.*

Life presents most people with various degrees of ongoing problems, obstacles, troubles, crises, and tragedies. Different people possess differing capacities to confront and deal with these difficulties. In general, people who are better able to address, cope with, negotiate, and resolve life's problems prove also to be more healthy and functional. Most American religions comprise and foster many beliefs and practices that can strengthen young people's ability effectively to cope with life's problems.[25] Religions often offer youth a variety of cognitive and behavioral resources to address and process life's mental, emotional, and interpersonal stresses and troubles. These may include practices of prayer, meditation, confession, forgiveness, reconciliation, Sabbath keeping, small group sharing, funeral rites, cleaning rituals, and more.[26] They may also include the beliefs that a loving and omnipotent divinity is in control of one's life, that all things work together for the good of those who love God, that God understands and shares in one's suffering, that ultimately good will be rewarded and evil punished, that a divine Providence is guiding one's steps, that suffering builds character, that God gives the strength to confront and overcome injustice, and much more. Clearly, nonreligious youth are able to draw on coping mechanisms that are not obviously religious, such as "live and let live," "one day at a time," "they'll get theirs," and "try to put things into perspective"—although many of these maxims in fact do ultimately have religious roots. But religion at least can greatly expand the range of possible beliefs and practices that adolescents may draw on to deal with their life problems. Beyond that, it is possible that for some people, the sacred, divine, transcendent, cosmic, and historically traditional nature of many religious coping-enhancing beliefs and practices provides them with greater significance, depth, and power than perhaps their secular counterparts.[27] For many, "nothing can separate you from the love of God" is somehow more profound and compelling than "it'll all work out in the end." Likewise, participating with countless generations of believers in prayer and affirmation by reciting a millennia-old liturgy is somehow more meaningful and comforting than reading the various quips in the most recent edition of *Chicken Soup for the Teenage Soul*. Thus, religion may provide American adolescents with extra or more effective coping mechanisms for negotiating and resolving their mental, emotional, and interpersonal stresses and problems.

6. Cultural capital: *American religions often provide youth with alternative opportunities (beyond family, school, and the media) to acquire elements of cultural capital that may directly enhance the well-being of youth, and may be transposable to other social settings for constructive purposes in youth's lives.*

Scholars have suggested how important possession of cultural capital may be in enhancing one's life chances.[28] Cultural capital in this context consists of unevenly distributed and socially distinctive tastes, skills, knowledge, and practices that are embodied as implicit practical knowledge, skills, and dispositions and objectified in particular cultural objects and credentials.[29] American youth enjoy a variety of contexts in which they might acquire cultural capital, including family, school, voluntary associations, and the media. American religions, however, often provide their youth with increased and alternative opportunities to appropriate more and distinct kinds of cultural capital. For example, in American religions, children and adolescents may grow in biblical literacy, so that they better understand the Western historical context, the prophetic and wisdom traditions, scriptural moral teachings, and more. Furthermore, in religious congregations, youth can also acquire substantial musical education through participation in choirs and choruses, exposure in services to rich traditions of sacred music, learning to sing four-part harmonies for hymns, and opportunities to play piano, guitar, or other musical instruments for worship. In addition, in the course of their religious education and practice, American youth are often exposed to and may learn about world civilizations and empires (the Babylonians, the Egyptians, the Roman Empire, etc.), Western history (the Middle Ages, the Reformation, etc.), major religious traditions (Jewish, Protestant, Catholic, etc.), major holiday traditions (Easter, Ramadan, Rosh Hashanah, etc.), major ethical traditions (ascetic, pietistic, sacramental, natural law, etc.), and important theological categories (holiness, moral law, incarnation, repentance, etc.).[30] All of this, of course, enhances for youth the meaning and value of their religious participation. But, in addition, simply because familiarity with the Jewish and Christian (and Greek and Roman) traditions is a precondition for truly understanding Western history, civilization, and culture, acquiring through religion the knowledge and appreciation of such matters described above can also tremendously advantage youth who accumulate this cultural capital. Adolescents who have soaked up the various kinds of cultural capital available through involvement in their religion may have gained a relative edge over those who have not, in a variety of ways.[31] Other factors being equal, they will likely converse more comfortably with a broader array of social contacts, perform better in their humanities and social science classes, be more impressive in the lunch and dinner conversations of their job interviews, and more. All of this tends to work toward positive, constructive outcomes in youth's lives.

Social and Organizational Ties

The third major hypothesized dimension of religious influences on American adolescents concerns the social and organizational ties religion affords young people. In this we move beyond the cultural orders that shape moral judgment and action, and beyond the advantaging skills and capacities individuals can acquire. Here we are discussing structures of relations that affect the opportunities and constraints that young people face, which significantly affect outcomes in their lives.

7. Social capital: *American religion is one of the few, major American social institutions that is not rigidly age-stratified and emphasizes personal interactions over time, thus providing youth with personal access to other adult members in their religious communities, affording cross-generational network ties with the potential to provide extrafamilial, trusting relationships of care*

and accountability and linking youth to wider sources of helpful information, resources, and opportunities.

It is difficult to overestimate the importance for youth of the transgenerational and age-variable character of most religious organizations in the United States. Most American adolescents live the vast majority of their extrafamilial lives in age-stratified institutions and consuming age-targeted products and services. Perhaps most important, American youth spend about 35 to 40 waking hours per week for between 12 and 17 years in mass-education schools that sort them into classes by single-year age differences. Teens thus spend the greater part of their weekdays with and being socialized by their age-identical peers. In off-school hours, they often spend many hours watching television programs that are also targeted for their specific age groups. Another major use of time by young people is in sports, hobbies, and play, also very often spent with other youth of similar age.[32] Structurally, therefore, the schedules and institutions that organize youth's lives tend to isolate and limit their contacts, exposures, and ideas to those available from others their own age. In such situations, trends in and pressures from peer groups become highly influential and narrow.

American religious congregations, by contrast, represent one of the few remaining major social institutions in which adolescents participate extensively that emphasizes continuity of interaction and yet is not rigidly stratified by age.[33] In these religious organizations, adolescents gather together with fellow believers of all ages and life course stages. While some religious programming may be age-stratified, most central congregational functions (worship services, fellowship gatherings) mix participants of all ages. As a result, youth are exposed to many adult members of their religious communities. This creates the possibility for forming significant relational network ties that cross age boundaries. And those ties generate the potential for relationships with older congregants who may express care for youth. Adolescents' ties to older members of their religious congregations may also afford them access to otherwise less available sources of opportunities, resources, and information. The more (strong and weak) adult ties youth have in their religious congregations, the more likely they are through them to land a good summer job, be recommended for acceptance into a competitive program, know someone who can and will help them fix their broken computer or car, and much more. All of this helps to foster and reinforce positive life choices, behaviors, and outcomes.[34]

8. Network closure: *American religious congregations can provide relatively dense networks of relational ties within which youth are embedded, involving people who pay attention to the lives of youth and who can provide oversight of and information about youth to their parents and other people well positioned to discourage negative and encourage positive life practices among youth.*

The oftentimes unique cross-generational network ties that religious congregations facilitate not only potentially provide youth with important flows of information, resources, and opportunities; they also structure relational networks that facilitate more informed and effective oversight and control of youth by adults who care about them. James Coleman has theorized the importance of network closure, suggesting that higher densities of social relationships among youth, parents, and other interested adults, and among parents whose children are friends, are associated with improved youth outcomes.[35] Others have also suggested that high levels of social network closure benefit youth indirectly by enabling parents more effectively to monitor and supervise their activities, communicate with other parents about their expectations and behavior, and feel supported in their own parenting.[36] As one of the few major American social institutions that emphasizes ongoing social interaction not rigidly stratified by age, religious congregations provide ideal settings for increasing closure in networks involving youth. In religious congregations, adolescents are able to form relationships with youth ministers, Sunday school teachers, choir directors, rabbis, parents of friends, and other adult acquaintances, who can relationally tie back to the adolescents' parents. These ties can operate as extrafamilial sources reinforcing parental influence and oversight. Because of the social setting, parents of adolescents in religious congregations, compared to schools or sports teams, for instance, are better able to build relationships over time with their children's friends and the parents or kin of their children's friends. Moreover, these relationships are very likely to exist among people who share similar cultural moral beliefs, facilitating higher levels of agreement and cooperation in collective oversight and social control. All of this we expect to create conditions of increased support for and supervision of youth, encouraging positive and discouraging negative behaviors among youth.

9. Extracommunity links: *American religions typically comprise links to national and transnational religious organizations, providing youth with connections to positive experiences and events well beyond their local communities, which can expand their horizons and aspirations, foster developmental maturity, and enhance competencies and knowledge.*

Finally, participation in the organizations of American religion very often affords youth structural connections to beneficial programs and organizations at the regional, national, and international levels. The vast majority of American religious organizations are not completely autonomous, but are linked to larger associations, denominations, conventions, and other regional and national organizations. This is as true for Southern Baptists and black Muslims as it is for Reform Jews and Roman Catholics. These regional and national organizations and associations very often involve denominational and parachurch programs, organizations, and other opportunities specifically designed to serve youth. As a consequence, local religious involvement can plug adolescents into an almost endless array of summer camps, youth retreats, missions projects, teen conferences, service programs, Holy Land trips, music festivals, denominational conventions, the hajj to Mecca, and any number of other socioreligious activities. These programs and activities likely strengthen the religious faith and commitment of youth but they probably often do more than that. We may expect that, by moving youth out of local contexts and presenting them with new experiences and challenges, these programs also open up youth's imaginable aspirations and horizons, encourage their developmental maturity, and increase their knowledge, confidence, and competencies. This should, in turn, tend to reduce unhealthy and antisocial attitudes, choices, and behaviors among these youth. Once again, religion is not the only means by which adolescents might link to these kinds of larger programs and organizations. There certainly exist plenty of nonreligious summer camps, service projects, and travel opportunities. Yet, organized religion adds to these a massive superstructure of youth-oriented programs and activities that significantly increases the chances that youth will participate in and benefit from them.

Here, then, are nine sociological factors that we hypothesize as helping to explain significant observed positive associations between higher teen religiosity and more positive life outcomes. To add nuance to our argument, however, it is necessary to offer three qualifications. First, this theoretical account presumes that these nine influences do not typically operate independently, but often together and in combination as mutually reinforcing social processes. For instance, the social capital effects of religious communities could not be operative were it not for the religious moral order factor drawing cross-generational networks together over time in the first place. At the same time, those social capital effects help to reinforce in youth the cultural moral orders that religious communities promote. This reality of interdependence can present the researcher with interpretive difficulties in assessing the source or type of religious influence from a standard measure of religiosity.[37] Nevertheless, we suggest that although these factors are believed to be interrelated and mutually reinforcing and interpretive difficulties abound, it may still be best to conceptualize these factors as analytically distinct influences.

The second qualification of the theory is that obviously not all religious organizations provide their youth with the same quantity or quality of these constructive resources and influences. Some provide most of them in high quality; others provide only few of them or offer them in weak form; and yet others may neutralize whatever good they do provide by including other detrimental practices and influences, such as abusive leaders, adult hypocrisies, and dysfunctional organization. We are not advancing a categorical claim about the effects of American religion on youth, merely theoretically exploring processes and forces that may help explain the religion-outcomes associations seen in the findings above.

Third, as we have already acknowledged, American religion is not the only place where many of these kinds of social influences might affect the lives of youth. Alternative parallel contexts include community programs, purchased lessons and instruction, and other nonreligious voluntary associations. Nevertheless, religious organizations are uniquely pervasive organizations in American society that do strongly encourage youth participation. And religious organizations can provide cultural moral orders characterized by impressive scope, depth, and authority, often typically matching and often surpassing other kinds of voluntary associations or purchasable services. Therefore, we suggest they deserve particular theoretical and empirical attention for their effects in the lives of youth.

At the same time, we must also pay attention to the possibility that religion sometimes does not positively influence adolescent outcomes and may even negatively influence adolescent outcomes. None of the above suggests that religion always or invariably has positive, constructive effects in the lives of youth. First, the larger claim here is probabilistic, not categorical. Second, religious traditions do vary, and certain religions and particular circumstances may produce negative effects in the lives of adolescents, which deserve to be investigated and theorized. We might hypothesize, then, that when religious involvement does not have significant positive effects among American youth it may be for the following reasons:

1. Inadequate supply: Some religious communities in which youth are involved provide few of the influences enumerated above, or only weak versions of them.
2. Failure to appropriate: Some youth in religious communities that do offer constructive influences may, for whatever reasons, choose to remain largely detached, marginal, and uninvolved, and so fail to engage and benefit from positive religious influences.
3. Disruptive events: Some youth who are being constructively influenced by religious involvement may have that influence disrupted and negated by specific detrimental events (such as the divorce of parents, abuse by a religious authority, disorienting tragedy, or unreconciled falling-outs with people in the religious community) that the positive religious influences are for various reasons unable to counter or overcome.
4. Competing influences: Some youth being constructively shaped by religious involvement may have those influences overwhelmed by counterinfluences from interactions in other social associations (neighborhood, work, school, the media, etc.) that promote competing moral orders and practices (risk behaviors, delinquency, family conflict, apathy, school dropout, etc.).

Some research has investigated destructive tendencies among mainstream clergy.[38] Other scholars have noted potentially destructive aspects and outcomes of youth participation in some religious movements.[39] Religion may also hinder the educational attainment of some types of youth.[40] Thus, religion's potential for detrimental and antisocial effects in the lives of American youth is also an issue deserving further consideration and development in future empirical and theoretical work. But those avenues of research should not overshadow the broader, important observation of religion's generally positive associations observed in this chapter.

HOPE AND PRAYER IN THE CITY

What do these processes of religious influence look like in actual teenage lives? They can, of course, look quite different in various cases. We conclude this chapter by recounting the story of one teen whose life illustrates many of the kinds of positive religious influences discussed above. The teen in this case qualifies among the categories analyzed above as religiously Devoted and so quite clearly illustrates the religion-outcomes association observed in this chapter.

Antwan is a 16-year-old African American Southern California boy who, along with a 13-year-old cousin, lives with his grandparents in a rented house in a working- and middle-class neighborhood troubled by racial tensions between blacks and Mexicans. Antwan's mother lives nearby, and his father, a recovered drug addict, lives about an hour's drive away. Antwan is tall and thin. An extremely happy and outgoing kid, he wore shorts, a red T-shirt, and a black Nike headband and wristbands to the interview. His parents divorced when he was a baby. At first, he lived with his mother, then, when he was 8 years old, he moved in with his father, but his father's drug problem forced him to move in with his grandparents three years prior to our interview. Antwan likes, respects, and obeys his grandparents, who are in their 50s, and today gets along very well with both of his parents, who have since settled their differences and are now friends. "I'm real close to all of them, we can talk about anything, we get along real good," he reports. Antwan enjoys music, sports, movies, and video games. He plays the drums, the trumpet, the French horn, and the saxophone. He also plays basketball and football and hopes someday to be a professional sports player. What Antwan says he most enjoys in life, however, is "seeing my parents get along well."

Antwan is highly involved in his church, where many of his extended family relatives are members. He describes people at his church as warm, caring, loving, and accepting. While he was growing up, neither his mother nor his father took him to church much, so it wasn't until moving in with his grandparents that he began attending. "With my grandma I had no option, I just had to go to church [laughs], and I appreciate her for doing that." Antwan greatly enjoys church services: the singing, the dancing, the praying. He is an usher at church and serves on the church security team. He also attends Bible study on Wednesday nights and church youth group on Sunday evenings. He says of his youth group, which calls itself YES for Youth Experience Success: "It's real powerful and encouraging. We have our own dance group and host our own breakfasts. We're having our own back-to-school jam in September with live music and singers. It's important 'cause we're all in unity and it gives youth a place to go that's positive, so you won't have to go to wild parties, you'll always have a positive place to go. If I wasn't in this group, I'd say about 30 percent of my friends would be real bad." Antwan once attended a regional religious youth conference called "Acquire the Fire," which he remembers fondly for its fun activities and the teens he met there.

Antwan is so enthusiastic about his faith community and experience that he has gotten all of his friends involved in church. "My grandmother," he explains, "always tells me I'm a leader and not a follower, 'cause I led a lot of people to church. I told them, and once I started going, they saw me and started going, too. I think they view me as a positive role model. Not all go to the same church, sometimes we visit each others' churches." Antwan also clearly benefits from adult role models at church. In particular, he names his youth group leader, Craig: "He's real tall, like, man, like 6'9", yeah, and he looks exactly like Shaq [Shaquille O'Neal], too. I really get along well with him 'cause he takes us to lots of stuff and shows us that he really cares about us." Antwan described how Craig helped him work through personal struggles and doubts by helping him see that everyone struggles with such issues. More generally, he explains, "When I was younger, I had anger problems, about my dad, and had an attitude and took it out on everybody. But people at church still loved me for that and were really good 'cause they accepted me and encouraged me. Church has done a really good job at helping me to learn. It's a good place to go 'cause they're not gonna lie to you, they're gonna keep it real and tell the truth." Antwan says he has good relationships with all the adults in his life, except one uncle, who he says "tortures" the younger cousins. Besides his grandparents, he really admires his favorite pro basketball player, Tracy McGrady, " 'cause he's a cool basketball player, plus he does wise stuff with his money, he doesn't spend it on drugs or fancy cars, but helps people and helps his family and stuff."

Antwan claims that he did not believe in God when he was younger, "but some things that happened I knew it could only be God in that situation." One of those situations solidifying his faith was his father's religious conversion and turning away from drugs:

> My dad used to be a rapper and had a real drug problem and would leave me at home by myself and stuff. When I moved in with my grandparents, he said he didn't want to have nothin' else to do with me, which hurt me. I was very angry. My grandmother told me, "Just pray about it and God will figure it out for you, he'll help you," and I said okay and I prayed about it. Later, my dad became a Christian and went into rehab and now he goes to church and is a Christian rapper. And I knew it was God that made him change his mind, and now we're really, really, really, really close together now. He comes and picks me up about every other weekend. I can talk to him about anything. Now we're like, me and my dad are like the bestest friends. Oh, yes, faith changed it, really, and I was like, if God can do that, then he can do other things for me, too.

Antwan says he has also witnessed miracles, such as crippled people in wheel-chairs being able to walk after his pastor prayed over them: "They got out of the wheelchair and started walking and I was like, 'Yeah, that's a mira-cle.'"

Antwan says his religious faith is "the top priority" in his life. "I'm very religious and I'm very spiritual," he reports. "I'm always praying for someone 'cause they always ask me to pray for them. The main thing is to lead people to God, that's what makes me spiritual." And what is God like? "I think about, like, this almighty person that made heaven and earth and stuff. He's the highest of the highest, like, doesn't go no higher than him." All this, he says, he learned from reading the Bible. He states that he feels "really close to the Lord, I could talk to him like, about anything." He reads the Bible every day because "it gives me wisdom and shows me how to deal with certain situations, like with anger and lust and lying and stuff like that." He also prays very often, making up his own prayers that rhyme: "It's like talking to God, some of it sounds like a song, like a little rhyme or a poem." On Sundays, Antwan says, he worships, rests, prays, listens to Christian music, and gets together with his friends "to pray for the people who can't pray, like in the hospital and stuff, 'cause they're in pain, so we pray for them." Antwan's aunt also coordinates a continual prayer group at church in which participants are assigned to pray throughout a particular hour during the week, so he spends regular time praying for his friends and family in that way. Does he resent having to spend two nights a week at church? "Um, I feel it's fair [laughs], 'cause God only asks us for, like, two days and I think that's fair. It's fairer than school, school asks for five days and God asks for only two, so, that's fair." Antwan also tithes 10 percent of his allowance and paycheck, " 'cause that's what it says in the Bible, and really 10 percent is not that much, once you think about it." How often would he attend church if it were entirely up to him? "Um, as much as I could. You have to practice faith, you can't live it all by yourself, you need to go to church because church helps you get closer to God." And how do his religious practices affect his life? "They're very important. It makes me a happier person to know that I'm doing everything that I'm supposed to and that my grandparents and them don't have to go behind me and watch what I do. It used to be less, I didn't used to read the Bible every day, but now I'm doing it every day on a consistent basis and I see it affecting my life." Is it okay to pick and choose religious beliefs or to practice more than one faith? "No, 'cause that's like playing with God and making him mad, 'cause there's a God and some people believe in different gods, but I think you should believe in the one and only God because he's the one that made the earth and stuff. I don't think that's okay, that's being disloyal to your own religion."

Antwan says that he disagrees with moral relativism. "There is right and wrong, it's just some people they don't wanna own up to it." Where do his moral views come from? "Um, nothing but my training and my grandpar-ents." He believes it is wrong to smoke, drink, do drugs, cheat in school, get into fights, and lie to parents. "Your parents, they brought you into the world for a purpose, to obey your parents, so you shouldn't have to lie if you're obeying them in everything," he says. Antwan's grandparents are also consistent but forgiving disciplinarians, he reports. There is a lot of opportunity and pressure to get into drinking, drugs, and sex: "People keep coming and say, 'Oh, if you don't do it then you're not cool,' but we basically just say, 'It may not be cool but we ain't gonna be the ones dying from it either.' It's pressure on us but we don't let it pressure us, 'cause we know we're gonna say no." Knowing his father's history with drugs, Antwan also says he takes extra care to avoid situations that might tempt him. "Usually I don't put myself in those kind of positions 'cause I have some of my dad's DNA, so I don't put myself in positions to make me want to use it." Neighborhood teen parties, he says, routinely involve drinking and drugs and "girls flashing their private parts, yeah, they show everything, they're crazy girls." Does he party? "Me and my friends, we sometimes go to those parties but we usually don't stay very long because we know something's gonna end up happening, so usually we just go out and eat somewhere."

Antwan describes his very best friends as trustworthy, very loyal, and "kind of the popular crowd." His grandmother knows all of his friends and their parents. "She makes sure she's close to them," he says, "just in case something happens. She has little get-togethers to have my friends over just so she can get to know them, she does that intentionally to get to know them better." Antwan says religious faith makes a big difference among teens in his neighborhood: "I can see a big difference, like my friends that are Christians, when they have a problem they go and pray about it, but when kids who aren't Christians have problems, they go and fight it out. Yeah, that's different." According to Antwan, a lot of kids try to join his group of friends by "acting gangster and gang-banging and stuff," but that just turns him off. "We really don't like that gangster acting, it really pushes us away from them more." He thinks he and his friends have a positive Christian influence on other teens: "They could be talking about shooting somebody or planning something bad, but when I come around they'll be like, 'You can't talk about that now 'cause here comes Antwan,' like they have to stop talking about bad things when I come around, so that kind of encourages me." Clearly, Antwan is not concerned about being "too religious." Is he ever ridiculed by other teens because of his faith? "I'm pretty sure I am, but I don't really care," he replies matter-of-factly.

Antwan says he tries regularly to help other people: "I pray for them and I say encouraging words and usually it makes them feel good and helps them during the days." He also says he tries to take care of the world around him, " 'cause it's the place that I have to live in and who wants to live in something all messed up, trash all over everywhere?" All of this, he says, is " 'cause of my moral and spiritual beliefs." He says he sometimes feels sad about the pain caused by his grandmother's arthritis and asthma, but he never feels alone, invisible, or neglected. He says he is happy with his body and physical appearance. When he gets upset or has a problem, "usually I talk it through with someone, like my grandmother, and if that doesn't work then I go pray about it."

Antwan reports that his lowest grade at school is a B+. "I care about school a lot," he says, " 'cause I want to go to college and make my grandmother proud. And in the Bible it says to do the best you can in everything, in every aspect of life, and that includes in school and out of school." About his teachers, he reports, "I like all of my teachers, they're fantastic." He also regularly attends the Bible club at school. "I'm always in there," he says. He openly expresses his faith at school in other ways, including "letting people know that I'm a person you can come to and talk to and pray with you and stuff. Plus, you don't do all the drinking and cussing and use the profanity all the other kids use." Antwan is also involved in an Omega Psi Phi fraternity organization, which an elder at church connected him to, through which he has had opportunities to participate in day-long workshops led by famous black athletes about earning, saving, and spending money wisely. He himself works a part-time job at an amusement park, in order, he explains, "to make stuff easier on my grandparents, 'cause instead of them buying for me, spending money on me, I buy my own school clothes and shoes. It kind of gives them freedom to do what they want to do [with their money]."

Antwan is dating a girl whom he found attractive because "she conducted herself like a lady instead of like a wild girl." He says the Bible influences his dating because it teaches that finding a wife is a good thing and that people shouldn't have sex until marriage, which is good because it makes people base their dating relationship on something other than sex. "The teaching in my religion is wait till you're married," Antwan insists. Besides, he notes, sex poses the risks of conceiving a baby when one is not prepared to care for it, having to drop out of school, being emotionally hurt in an uncommitted relationship, and getting STDs. One of Antwan's 17-year-old acquaintances has been infected with HIV from having sex. Antwan reports that despite a lot of pressure from friends and dates to have sex, he has never been physically involved with anyone more than holding hands and light kissing. What does Antwan do with the pressures he feels to have sex? "Usually I pray about them." He also recounts that before he became a Christian, his father used to force him to view pornography, which "made me not want to see it again, like I had a bad experience with it. It's nasty to me."

Antwan says he is thinking and praying a lot about his future, that "I'll make my life all that it's supposed to be." He wants to get good grades in school, go to college, succeed in sports, and get married. When he is 25 or 30 years old, he thinks religiously he will be "stronger, a little bit wiser, more experienced, more spiritual, more of a person to inspire you." So what, when all is said and done, does he think is the ultimate purpose in life? "To worship God, that is what I think. I definitely want to accomplish with my life giving to the kingdom of God, me giving to my parents and family, and giving back to charity and the community."

Antwan's is a life that could easily have ended badly. Growing up amid family breakup, paternal disaffection, pervasive drug abuse, racial conflict, and neighborhood violence, he has faced many factors predicting unhappy outcomes. What mostly seems to have saved him from a bad fate are the belief commitments, moral teachings, faith practices, and social relationships of his religious tradition and faith community and family. Many of the general themes we have seen in previous chapters—the profound positive and negative influences of adults in the lives of teens, the readiness of youth to follow the religion of their family, the importance of youth groups and youth ministers in the formation of teenagers' faith lives—emerge again in Antwan's story. His experience also well illustrates that the nine factors described earlier are at work forming his life in positive directions. His religion clearly provides him with moral directives by which he has learned to negotiate his life in largely helpful ways. Antwan has a clear sense of right and wrong, a strong moral compass by which he lives. His religion has also exposed him to spiritual experiences of worship, healing, and transformation that have solidified his faith, moral commitments, and constructive life practices. Furthermore, he has benefited from many positive role models, particularly his grandmother and his youth leader, Craig, who have helped him to grow in his faith and navigate life's challenges. Involvement in church and youth group is also providing him with basic community and leadership skills that he is putting to use in coordinating security for meetings, influencing peers, negotiating conflicts, helping to organize youth and school activities. Moreover, his faith has equipped him with coping skills that have enabled him constructively to process his hurt, anger, and other troubles and emotions. Rather than turning to outrage and violence, Antwan has learned to turn to prayer and to hope, which in his case, eventually paid off in his reconciliation with his father. The unity and positive atmosphere with which he describes his Youth Experience Success youth group also appear more generally to channel his energy and feelings in positive directions. The acquisition of cultural capital is less obvious in Antwan's story, although it is not unlikely that through the programs, activities, and relationships at church he has picked up certain pieces of cultural knowledge, sensibilities, dispositions, and manners that will serve him well as he moves into life in the adult world. Antwan's ties to church, along with his grandmother's intentional efforts to get to know all of his friends, have also created a situation of network closure. He is thus situated in a system of relational ties in which adults and teens know each other, information about teenagers can flow among adults, and parents and guardians can better exercise oversight of youth. His connection to church has also enhanced his social capital, strengthening his ties to a network of adults and extended family who are positioned to provide him resources and connections to such things as national fraternity organizations. He has also benefited from religious ties to extracommunity links, such as the regional Acquire the Fire youth conference and the Omega Psi Phi organization, where he has learned to handle money wisely.

In sum, whatever one thinks about the specifics of Antwan's beliefs and morals, it is clear that religion has provided him with boundaries, directions, habits, aspirations, structures, expressive outlets, and social relationships that have crucially helped him make good choices and overcome disadvantage. None of this is to suggest that religion is a panacea for all at-risk teenagers. Life is never that simple. Antwan is only one case of a religiously Devoted teen, quite different from the average U.S. teenager as depicted in previous chapters, and so the positive religion-outcomes connection that statistics show pertain to all U.S. teens is particularly clear in his case. For other, less religiously devoted teens, we would expect religion's connection to outcomes to be less strong and obvious. Nor does religion's constructive role in Antwan's life mean that we can, in seeking to understand teenagers' lives, ignore other social structures and forces that also powerfully shape youth's outcomes. Religion or no religion, for example, Antwan still lives in a racialized society, the life chances of the members of which are still significantly shaped by structured social and institutional inequalities.[41] Nevertheless, these caveats notwithstanding, Antwan's story, like many of those in previous chapters, helps concretely to illustrate the ways that religious faith and practice can and, we believe, often does help to form teenagers' lives in positive and constructive ways. Antwan is only one of the 3,290 teenagers we surveyed, only one of the 267 teens we interviewed. But we believe that, in at least some ways, his particular story sheds a helpful light on the larger story of this chapter.

CONCLUSION

The religious difference and, we argue, influence of religion in the lives of contemporary American teenagers observed in this chapter provides a clear illustration of powerful sociological processes at work. Ironically, relatively few American teens, as chapter 4 suggested, reflect a religion that is centrally important in shaping their lives. And yet, we have seen that religion does indeed seem to make a significant difference in forming the lives of youth, that there are consistent and impressive differences in outcomes between highly religious American teens and nonreligious teens. There actually are real differences between the lives of the Joys and the Kristens that we think are not reducible to nonreligious factors. If so, youth's lives are being at least in part significantly shaped by religious and social identities, practices, cultures, relational ties, resources, and institutions *in ways that many teens themselves often cannot even recognize or describe*. Social facts and forces that are not merely the sum of individual properties appear to exert real and powerful influences in human life, whether anyone involved knows it or not. Sociological analysis helps us to see this. In part, American teenagers' taken-for-granted individualism simply fits many of them with blinders so they are not able to see well larger social influences on their lives. The same is often true about adults. But simply because teenagers cannot see it does not make religion's influence any less real or important. To what extent these differences among all U.S. teens result from the influence of their particular historical religious traditions versus that of Moralistic Therapeutic Deism we are not able to determine here. In any case, it appears that religion really does matter, even, ironically, in the lives of religious believers who are not aware that it does. Such believers, it would seem, might be warranted in having, like Antwan, a little more faith in their own faith.

Conclusion

THE TITLE OF THIS BOOK is intended to suggest three meanings. First, in the research project this book reports on, we as sociologists were embarked on a kind of sociological search for the souls of American teenagers. We were not trying to save their souls, simply to do our best to reach and better understand them. Second, what we found when we did so is that many, though certainly not all, U.S. teenagers are themselves engaged in a kind of search for their own souls—trying to sort through their life and faith identity, beliefs, commitments, and practices in their long passages from childhood to adulthood. Teenagers, however, are not a people apart, an alien race about whom adults can only shake their heads and look forward to their growing up. Teenagers are part of us, fully members of our families, religious congregations, neighborhoods, communities, and nation. Teenagers and adults, it turns out, have much more in common with each other than not, and so need to learn better to care for each other. Communities of faith in particular often profess to care about the youth in their midst. Therefore, third, we hope that the findings of this book set various groups and communities of adults on their own processes of soul searching, for when it comes to American adult attitudes and practices regarding adolescents, we think a good deal of soul searching is warranted. To that end, we intend this book to be, among other things, a catalyst for many soul-searching conversations in various communities and organizations about the experience and place of adolescents in our society, in particular the significance of the religious and spiritual lives of teenagers today.

So what have we learned? Having analyzed NSYR survey and interview data, what do we better understand about the religious and spiritual lives of contemporary teenagers living in the United States? A number of recurrent general themes have emerged from our analysis, which we briefly review here. First, religion is a significant presence in the lives of many U.S. teens today. Most have not dropped out of the religious congregations in which they were raised. Many remain regular participants in their families' communities of faith. Many profess that religious faith is important in their lives and that faith exerts a significant influence on their moral views and choices. The fact that they may not have particularly well-articulated beliefs about their own religious traditions does not alter the fact that the vast majority of U.S. teenagers embrace some religious identity, the majority are affiliated with a religious organization, and a sizable minority are regular participants in local communities of faith. In short, U.S. teens as a whole are anything but areligious or irreligious.

Second, contrary to many popular assumptions and stereotypes, the character of teenage religiosity in the United States is extraordinarily conventional. The vast majority of U.S. teens are not alienated or rebellious when it comes to religious involvement. Most are quite content to follow in their parents' footsteps. Most feel quite positive about religion, pointing out many advantages and benefits they see religion offering individuals, society, or both. When it comes to practicing religion, most U.S. teens appear happy to go along and get along.

Third, as part of their general religious conventionality, very few U.S. youth, younger than the age of 18 at least, appear to be exposed to, interested in, or actively pursuing the kind of "spiritual but not religious" personal quests of eclectic spiritual seeking about which we have heard so much lately. Most contemporary teenagers readily grant other people the theoretical right to pursue a religious seeker's quest and to explore and practice multiple religions. But very few teens are interested in doing that themselves. And very few even know of another teen who is a seeker. Rather, the vast majority are happy simply to accept the one religion in which they were raised. And those with dual-religion parents normally either embrace one, try to pay respect to both, or decide they are not interested in any religion. Whether spiritual but not religious seeking is or is not prevalent among older youth, we cannot say, but it is not among contemporary 13- to 17-year-old teens in the United States.

Fourth and somewhat related to the previous point: comparing statistics over time shows that the religiodemographic diversity represented by U.S. adolescents is no more varied today than it has been for a very long time. The vast majority of contemporary teenagers living in the United States identify themselves as Christians, and most of the balance of non-Christian teenagers identify themselves as either nonreligious (many of whom actually turn out to be nominal Christians), Mormon, or Jewish. Recent popular and scholarly claims that the United States has become the most religiously diverse nation in the world are simply false as a matter of empirical religiodemographic proportions, at least when it comes to adolescent religious identity. Whatever ideological or political interests it may serve to promote the alleged dramatic religious pluralism of the contemporary United States, empirically that idea is simply an overblown and erroneous claim.

Fifth, in general comparisons among major U.S. religious traditions using a variety of sociological measures of religious vitality and salience—which, to give a standard sociological disclaimer, may or may not have anything to do with the truth content of religious traditions or their adherents' actual subjective spiritual life and health—it is Mormon teenagers who are sociologically faring the best. Why is a story beyond the scope of this book to tell, but an interesting and important one to consider. After Mormon youth, conservative Protestant and black Protestant teenagers tend to score the next strongest on most of our sociological indicators. Mainline Protestant teens come next in religious strength, followed by Catholic, Jewish, and nonreligious teenagers. Interreligious comparisons of these sorts are notoriously tricky and perilous to make, because not all religious traditions can be lined up against each other on commensurate scales of comparison. Serious and faithful Judaism cannot be directly compared to black Protestantism, for instance, in an apples-to-apples way. Ultimately, such comparisons inevitably involve theological judgments beyond the competence of sociology to engage. At the very least, however, comparisons within the major Christian traditions are somewhat plausible. Such differences should contribute additional empirical fodder to debates in the sociology of religion about what social factors best explain religious vitality and debility.

Sixth, contrary to popular misguided cultural stereotypes and frequent parental misperceptions, we believe that the evidence clearly shows that the single most important social influence on the religious and spiritual lives of adolescents is their parents. Grandparents and other relatives, mentors, and youth workers can be very influential as well, but normally, parents are most important in forming their children's religious and spiritual lives. Teenagers do not seem very reflective about or appreciative of this fact. But that does not change the reality that the best social predictor, although not a guarantee, of what the religious and spiritual lives of youth will look like is what the religious and spiritual lives of their parents *do* look like. Parents and other adults, as we have suggested, most likely "will get what they are." This recognition may be empowering to parents, or alarming, or both. But it is a fact worth taking seriously in any case.

Seventh, our findings suggest a significant supply-side dynamic operative in the religious and spiritual lives of U.S. teenagers. It appears that the greater the supply of religiously grounded relationships, activities, programs, opportunities, and challenges available to teenagers, other things being equal, the more likely teenagers will be religiously engaged and invested. Religious congregations that prioritize ministry to youth and support for their parents, invest in trained and skilled youth group leaders, and make serious efforts to engage and teach adolescents seem much more likely to draw youth into their religious lives and to foster religious and spiritual maturity in their young members. This appears to be true of local congregations, regional organizations such as dioceses and state conventions, and entire religious traditions. Stated negatively, when religious communities do not invest in their youth, unsurprisingly, their youth are less likely to invest in their religious faith. Supplies of resources, personnel, organizations, and programs are not the whole story, but they are a significant part of it. If, as we have said, when it comes to the religious outcomes of youth, parents and adults "will get what they are," we think it is equally true that, when it comes to youth, religious congregations, denominations, and other religious organizations generally "will get back what they invest" and normally not a lot more.

Eighth, at the level of subjective consciousness, adolescent religious and spiritual understanding and concern seem to be generally very weak. Most U.S. teens have a difficult to impossible time explaining what they believe, what it means, and what the implications of their beliefs are for their lives. Many say they simply have no religious beliefs. Others can articulate little more than what seem to be the most paltry, trivial, or tangential beliefs. And others express beliefs that are, from the official perspectives of their own religious traditions at least, positively erroneous. Religion seems very much a part of the lives of many U.S. teenagers, but for most of them it is in ways that seem quite unfocused, implicit, in the background, just part of the furniture. For very many U.S. teens, religion is important but not a priority, valued but not much invested in, praised but not very describable. Our distinct impression is that very many religious congregations and communities of faith in the United States are failing rather badly in religiously engaging and educating their youth.

Ninth, and closely related to the previous point: a particular religious outlook that is distinct from the traditional faith commitments of most historical U.S. religious traditions, what we are calling Moralistic Therapeutic Deism, appears to have established a significant foothold among very many contemporary U.S. teenagers. At the very least, it seems that when the engagement and education of youth by their religious communities is weak, then the faith of teenagers in those traditions tends to degenerate into Moralistic Therapeutic Deism. More significant than that, however, it seems to us that the relatively new and popularly compelling religious faith of Moralistic Therapeutic Deism is, in the context of their own congregations and denominations, actively displacing the substantive traditional faiths of conservative, black, and mainline Protestantism, Catholicism, and Judaism in the United States, which comprise the vast majority of teenagers. Moralistic Therapeutic Deism may not simply be what an ill-informed or nominal faith sounds like in a teen interview. It may be the new mainstream American religious faith for our culturally post-Christian, individualistic, mass-consumer capitalist society. Continued research will have to investigate this possibility.

Tenth, it is impossible adequately to understand the religious and spiritual lives of U.S. teenagers without framing that understanding to include the larger social and institutional contexts that form their lives. It is not sufficient to focus only on teenagers' individual psychological issues or moral character or smart or poor choices and behaviors, for those are often themselves powerfully shaped by the social and cultural forces of therapeutic individualism, mass-consumer capitalism, the digital communication revolution, residual positivism and empiricism, the structural disconnect of teenagers from the world of adults, adults' own problems, and other relevant cultural and social contradictions and tensions. Complicating this fact is the largely marginal social structural position in which religion typically finds itself among the mix of activities and organizations that organize teenagers' schedules and priorities. Teens and parents are not often consciously aware of these big-picture social influences and organizing structures. But these larger contexts nevertheless are objective, structural, institutional, and cultural realities that powerfully form contemporary lives.

Eleventh, and finally, despite the fact that religion seems quite weak at the level of adolescent subjective consciousness, that most teens can hardly coherently articulate their own beliefs, that religion seems to operate mostly as an unfocused, invisible dynamic operating in the background of teenagers' lives, and that many social and cultural forces exert effects that tend to undermine serious religious faith and practice, we nevertheless observe sizable and significant differences in a variety of important life outcomes between more and less religious teenagers in the United States. Highly religious teenagers appear to be doing much better in life than less religious teenagers. We suspect that some of these differences are explained by selection and reverse-causation effects. But we also believe that the empirical evidence suggests that religious faith and practice themselves exert significant, positive, direct, and indirect influences on the lives of teenagers, helping to foster healthier, more engaged adolescents who live more constructive and promising lives. Most teenagers do not insist that religion is "good for people" for no reason at all. They are merely reflecting, however inarticulately, what seems to be an actual empirical association between religion and adolescent outcomes. More research using longitudinal data is needed, however, to better sort through the empirical correlations and causal relations and directions involved in the religion-outcomes associations. At the very least, what appears to be clearly not true is the idea that religious teenagers are essentially no different from nonreligious teenagers, that religion seems to make no difference in adolescent outcomes. Far from that, religion correlates with big differences and arguably exerts significant effects on important outcomes in teenagers' lives.

If the previous finding is correct, then such a conclusion beautifully illustrates sociological forces at work: religious identities, organizations, and practices are significantly shaping people's lives, despite the fact that at the level of subjective consciousness most of them are only dimly aware of how or why that is happening. People, sociology helps us to see, are formed by more than their own personal, individual intentions and choices. Their lives are also profoundly shaped by the patterns and structures of the cultures, organizations, and institutions that undergird and organize their lives, including religious ones. This perspective opens up an important larger horizon for better understanding the lives of adolescents in the United States today.

One of the biggest obstacles to our understanding teenagers' lives is the common apparent inability to see their lives within the larger, very powerful social and cultural context that forms it. We began to address this concern in chapter 5. In all of this, a specific, important impediment to making sense of adolescent life in the United States worth reemphasizing is the routine failure of adults to recognize the responsibility of their own adult world, into which youth are being socialized, for presenting huge challenges for youth. Instead of owning this responsibility, however, adults typically frame adolescence in ways defining teenage life per se as *itself* a social problem and adolescents as alien creatures, strange and menacing beings, perhaps even monsters driven by raging hormones, visiting us from another planet. Teenagers—our own children—this theme suggests, are more dissimilar to us than they are like us, separated from the adult world by light years of distance and difference. Who could possibly hope to understand or relate to teenagers?

In contrast to these and other distancing stereotypical interpretations of American adolescents, our analysis and research experience suggest that adults ought to stop thinking about teenagers as aliens or even others. Any generation gap that exists between teens and adults today is superficial compared with and far outweighed by generational continuities. Contemporary teenagers have almost entirely bought into the mainstream social system, literally anxious above all to succeed on its terms.[1] They are well socialized to want to enjoy the consumerist and experiential benefits of U.S. society as much as they are able. Most problems and issues that adults typically consider teenage problems are in fact inextricably linked to adult-world problems. Furthermore, most teens appreciate the relational ties they have to the adult world, and most of those who lack such ties wish they had more and stronger ties. The traditional "storm and stress" model of adolescence accurately depicts only a minority of teens, about the same number of adults at any given time who are suffering storm and stress, and, in our view, is a counterproductive lens through which adults view youth. That lens unnecessarily and unhelpfully creates distances when what is greatly needed is connection. Adults need alternative mental and discursive models that emphasize grown-ups' similarities to, ties to, and common futures with youth.

Religious congregations and other religious organizations are uniquely positioned in the array of social institutions operating in the United States to embrace youth, to connect with adolescents, to strengthen ties between adults and teenagers. This could only be good for all involved. But it will not happen automatically. It will require intentionality and investment. We hope that by drawing attention to and broadening and deepening our understanding of the religious and spiritual lives of U.S. youth, this book will make some positive contribution in that direction.

Concluding Unscientific Postscript
Observations and Implications of NSYR Findings
for Religious Communities and Youth Workers

We said in the conclusion that we intend this book to be, among other things, a stimulus for soul-searching conversations among adults in various communities and organizations about the place and importance of adolescents in our lives and, in particular, the significance of the religious and spiritual lives of teenagers today. We anticipate that our findings will provoke such discussions in communities of faith and religious organizations in particular. To provide a bit of initial input to those discussions, in this brief, unscientific postscript we step out of our normal sociological roles—with more than a little trepidation—to try to imagine some of the book's possible prescriptive implications for communities of faith. To be perfectly clear about our purpose here: we are academic sociologists, not religious ministry consultants or promoters. Nevertheless, detailed knowledge and understanding of the social world often raises real questions about cultural and institutional practices and commitments that can make real differences in people's lives. We expect that communities of faith will be interested in pondering the implications of our research and so we offer here some preliminary ideas that seem to us to emerge from our findings. Readers who are not involved or interested in religious work with youth can stop reading at this point. For the rest, what follows is not conclusive or exhaustive, nor does it apply to every religious community or institution. It will finally be up to various communities and organizations to, if they wish, digest our findings and consider implications relevant for their own contexts, constituencies, and activities. However, certain possible, initial implications of NSYR findings do seem worth offering for consideration. When we reflect on what we have discovered about youth and religion, the following possible implications for communities of faith come to mind.

To begin, we suggest that religious communities would do well to stop accepting and promulgating what may be simplistic generalizations about American youth—which, in our observation, they sometimes do. We have observed a noticeable tendency when it comes to youth, including among some youth ministry workers, to overgeneralize, overstate issues, frame situations in alarmist terms, and latch onto simplistic answers to alleged problems. But the fact is that the lives, including the religious lives, of American youth are diverse and complicated. Thus, religious communities may do well to learn to be more discerning, more skeptical of alarmist claims, less captivated by trendy books, and more perceptive about the diversity and complexity of the experience and situation of U.S. teenagers. We suspect that they would likely then be more effective in planning programs, prioritizing initiatives, and working with teens in ways more true to their own traditions and identities and more effective over the long run.

Moreover, our findings suggest to us that religious communities should also stop—again, as we not infrequently observe—presuming that U.S. teenagers are actively alienated by religion, are dropping out of their religious congregations in large numbers, cannot relate to adults in their congregations, and so need some radically new "postmodern" type of program or ministry. None of this seems to us to be particularly true. Some middle-aged religious leaders may project their own experience of the 1960s and 1970s onto teenagers today, but that is a mistake. Youth culture today is different from that of that more tumultuous era. Most religious communities' central problem is not teen rebellion but teenagers' benign "whateverism." As long as religious communities presume falsely apocalyptic scenarios, they likely set themselves up for overreactions and pendulum swings in their ministry to youth. In fact, huge numbers of U.S. teenagers are currently *in* congregations, feel okay about them, mostly plan to continue to stay involved at some level, and generally feel fine about the adults in their congregations. But the congregation simply *does not mean that much or make much sense* to many of them. This realization is likely a useful corrective of vision for communities of faith to know and work with as they relate to youth today.

Along those lines, it is important to realize that the allegedly widespread phenomena of spiritual seeking and a spiritual-but-not-religious identity among teenagers is, at this time at least, a bogeyman. Serious spiritual seekers make up only about 2 percent of U.S. teenagers. The majority of U.S. youth appear to believe it is okay for *others* to be eclectic seekers, but they themselves are not particularly interested. They are happy being part of the tradition they were raised in, which to them feels largely satisfactory even if not terribly central or important. Religious leaders should stop worrying that their youth are heading by droves into Wicca, experimenting with Buddhism, or searching for alternative transcendent experiences. Instead, religious leaders might get on with the business of simply better animating and educating the youth in their midst.

It appears to us, in other words, that parents, pastors, ministers, religious educators, and congregational leaders concerned with youth largely need simply to *better engage and challenge* the youth already at their disposal, to work better to help make faith a more active and important part of their lives. The problem is not that youth won't come to church (most will), or that they hate church (few do), or that they don't want to listen to religious ministers or mature mentoring adults (they will and do). But this does not mean that youth are currently being well engaged by their religious congregations. They generally are not. Better engagement could involve multiple approaches, depending on the specific religious group in question, but some possibilities that present themselves in light of the above findings may include the following.

First, the best way to get most youth more involved in and serious about their faith communities is to get their *parents* more involved in and serious about their faith communities. For decades in many religious traditions, the prevailing model of youth ministry has relied on pulling teens away from their parents. In some cases, youth ministers have come to see parents as adversaries. There is no doubt a time and place for unique teen settings and activities; still, our findings suggest that overall youth ministry would probably best be pursued in a larger context of family ministry, that parents should be viewed as indispensable partners in the religious formation of youth. More broadly, one of the most important things that adults who are concerned about how teenagers' religious and spiritual lives are going to turn out can do is to focus attention on strengthening their own and other adults', especially parents', religious and spiritual lives. For in the end, they most likely will get from teens what they as adults themselves are. Like it or not, the message that adults inevitably communicate to youth is "Become as I am, not (only) as I say."

Second, in general, parents and faith communities should not be shy about *teaching* teens. Adults do not hesitate to direct and expect from teens when it comes to school, sports, music, and beyond. But there seems to be a curious reluctance among many adults to teach teens when it comes to faith. Adults often seem to want to do little more than "expose" teens to religion. Many adults seem to us to be almost intimidated by teenagers, afraid to be seen as "uncool." And it seems many religious youth workers are under a lot of pressure to entertain teens. In fact, however, we believe that *most teens are teachable*, even if they themselves do not really know that or let on that they are interested. Parents, ministers, and adult mentors need, it seems to us, to develop more confidence in teaching youth about their faith traditions and expecting meaningful responses from them. Teaching happens, in fact, by somebody or other. Teens learn everything they know from someone, somewhere. Many youth actually consciously do want to be taught; they are open to being influenced by good word and example. Faith communities have no reason to apologize for or be insecure about teaching their youth. Adults should be aware, however, that better adult teaching of youth will require stronger adult relationships with youth. More important in the effective religious teaching of teens than, say, new pedagogical techniques will be the building of sustained, meaningful, personal adult relationships with the teens they teach. This will require investments of time, attention, and readiness to be open and vulnerable with teens.

Third, it seems to us that religious educators need to work much harder on *articulation*. We were astounded by the realization that for very many teens we interviewed, it seemed as if our interview was the first time any adult had ever asked them what they believed. By contrast, the same teens could be remarkably articulate about other subjects about which they had been drilled, such as drinking, drugs, STDs, and safe sex. It was also astonishing how many Christian teens, for example, were comfortable talking generally about God but not specifically about Jesus. Philosophers like Charles Taylor argue that inarticulacy undermines the possibilities of reality.[1] So, for instance, religious faith, practice, and commitment can be no more than vaguely real when people cannot talk much about them. Articulacy fosters reality. A major challenge for religious educators of youth, therefore, seems to us to be fostering articulation, helping teens to *practice talking about* their faith, providing practice at using vocabularies, grammars, stories, and key messages of faith. Especially to the extent that the language of faith in American culture is becoming a foreign language, educators, like real foreign-language teachers, have that much more to work at helping their students learn to practice speaking that other language of faith. Our observation is that religious education in the United States is currently failing with youth when it comes to the articulation of faith.

Fourth, religious youth workers may have an opportunity to tap into teens' strong inclination toward individualism to challenge their often highly conventional styles of doing religion and to bring faith issues out of the background and into the foreground of their lives. How can religious youth workers help to make problematic and interesting issues of religious belief, practice, theology, commitment? We suspect that there are opportunities to show youth how very conventional they are actually acting, how unexciting they are in their approach to faith, to create discomforts to motivate them to more seriously engage what faith is and might be in their lives. One example of this is to challenge the strong life course assumptions that inform youth's thinking about faith, provoking them to question why they should necessarily go along with standard cultural scripts about what religious people do at different life stages. Why should they not be different? The individualism American youth have absorbed will never be displaced, but it may be able to be somewhat leveraged to better ends as defined by the perspectives of their respective faith communities.

Fifth, religious communities might themselves think more carefully and help youth think more carefully about the distinctions among (1) serious, articulate, confident personal and congregational faith, versus (2) respectful, civil discourse in the pluralistic public sphere, versus (3) obnoxious, offensive faith talk that merely turns people off. Most U.S. teens keenly observe the second and avoid the third of these. Because of a common lack of distinction observed among these three, however, it appears that the first often gets lost. It seems to us that youth, and adults too, no doubt, need to learn that committed and articulate personal and congregational faith does not have to be sacrificed for the sake of public civility and respect for others who are different. Pluralism does not have to produce thinness and silence. But for it not to, people need to learn to distinguish among the three distinctions above. Along similar lines, it seems to us that religious communities would do well to better attend to their faith particularities. In efforts to be accessible and civil, it seems that many youth, and no doubt adults, are getting the wrong messages that historical faith traditions do not matter, that all religious beliefs are basically alike, that no faith tradition possesses anything that anybody particularly needs. This seems to produce a bland, oatmeal approach to faith or a lifestyle-preference view of religion, which either ends up holding little challenge or interest for youth or forms them into consummate religious consumers. We suspect that there is plenty of room for faith traditions to claim and emphasize confidently their own particularities and distinctions without risking religious division or conflict. Youth should be able to hear and embrace (or reject) what are the particularities of their own faith traditions and why they matter, without having to be afraid that this inevitably causes fighting and discomfort.

In our view, this last point also connects to the issue of moral foundations and commitments: youth need to be challenged about their often incoherent presumptions that everyone instinctively shares the same morality, that individuals can be free to choose whatever morality they want for themselves, and that the human good is self-evident to all. Religious communities might better engage their youth with the ideas of the actual diversity of moral traditions, the potential not only for human goodness but also for potential human failings and evils, the arguably relative long-term vulnerabilities of broadly humanistic moral and social systems, and the de facto impossibility of never judging other people's moral actions. Having been formed to see these realities, youth may then better appreciate the strengths and weaknesses of the moral grounding and teaching of their own religious traditions and take more seriously in their own lives the particularities of their own faith communities and commitments.

Another important general way religious congregations may better engage youth is through simple, ordinary adult relationships with teenagers. Adults other than family members and youth ministers could be intentionally encouraged to make better efforts to learn teens' names, to strike up conversations with teens, to ask them meaningful questions, to be vulnerable themselves to youth in various ways, to show some interest in them, to help connect them to jobs and internships, to make themselves available in times of trouble and crisis, to work toward becoming models and partners in love and concern and sacrifice. This would no doubt resound positively in broader areas of youth religious belief, commitment, and practice and in youth outcomes more generally. None of this takes a Master of Divinity degree. It is simply a matter of appreciation, attention, effort, and continuity from ordinary mature adults. But fostering this will require intentionality on the part of leaders. It will also, to be sure, require care around the issue of possible interested adults who are not adequately mature or trustworthy. In general, many U.S. teens greatly need more and better relational ties to adults who care about them, and religious congregations are a natural place for that to occur.

Furthermore, regular *religious practices* in the lives of youth beyond those in and of collective weekly congregations seem to be extremely important. There is no question that, empirically, more seriously religious teens intentionally engage in a variety of religious practices, and less religious teens do not. This, of course, is in part the definition of "more and less religious." But beyond that, it is also clear that very basic practices such as regular scripture reading, prayer, and intentional works of service and mercy mark and structure the lives of teens committed to faith, and do not for teens not committed to faith. There is no single, simple causal direction in this. Yet we observe a clear empirical fact that comports with theoretical and theological expectations: strengthening the faith lives of youth does, and so should, involve the formation of religious practices. Youth should be taught to *practice* their faith, not only in the sense of acting it out (as with, "She's a practicing Catholic"). They should also be taught to practice their faith in the sense of consistently working on skills, habits, and virtues in the direction of excellence in faith, analogous to musicians and athletes practicing their skills. Many religious teens in the United States appear to engage in few religious practices. But even basic practices like regular Bible reading and personal prayer seem clearly associated with stronger and deeper faith commitment among youth. We suspect that youth educators and ministers will not get far with youth, in other words, unless regular and intentional religious practices become an important part of their larger faith formation.

Although religious congregations are not particularly losing out to neopaganism and New Age spirituality, our research suggests that religious congregations *are* losing out to school and the media for the time and attention of youth. When it comes to the *formation* of the lives of youth, viewed sociologically, faith communities typically get a very small seat at the end of the table for a very limited period of time. The youth-formation table is dominated structurally by more powerful and vocal actors. Hence, as we wrote earlier, most teens know details about television characters and pop stars, but many are quite vague about Moses and Jesus. Most youth are well versed about the dangers of drunk driving, AIDS, and drugs, but many haven't a clue about their own tradition's core ideas. Many parents also clearly prioritize homework and sports over church or youth group attendance. This is, of course, complicated business and we do not pretend to have answers. It is hard to argue from a faith perspective, for instance, that school per se is bad or that believers should stop all media consumption. One possibility to consider, however, is that religious families could significantly reduce their time spent watching television and pointless movies and be more critical and discriminating about the television programming and movies they do watch. In any case, one way or anther, religious communities that are interested in the faith formation of their youth simply must better address the structural competition of other, not always supportive institutions and activities. This will likely require developing new and creative norms, practices, and institutions appropriate to specific religious situations and traditions.

Another possible implication of our findings that communities of faith might consider is this: just because many teens are not actively involved in a religious congregation does not mean that they would not become active under certain conditions. It is a minority of nonreligious teens who are positively and strongly hostile to religion. Most have rather vague to nonexistent reasons for their lack of religious involvement and commitment. Many actually profess to feel positively about religion. Many religious leaders and clergy may perceive nonreligious youth as a hard-to-reach population. We have come to think, however, that, on the contrary, many seemingly nonreligious teens could be drawn into active religious lives with more initiative and greater expressions of interest by sincere religious believers, good youth programming, increased proactive invitations by friends and adults to attend and participate, and readiness to have friendly and honest discussions around issues on nonreligious youth's minds and hearts.

Communities of faith would also do well, we think, to become more aware that a primarily instrumentalist view of faith is a double-edged sword. For many parents, religious congregations are good and valuable because they produce good outcomes in their children. Many clergy seem to capitalize on this to appeal to families of children and adolescents. It is an empirical fact that religiously involved youth generally do better in life than youth not religiously involved, for various reasons. This can be heartening for religious believers. But making this into religion's key legitimating focus easily degenerates into a church-is-good-because-it-will-help-keep-my-kid-off-drugs-and-increase-their-seatbelt-use mentality. This obviously undermines larger and deeper questions of truth, tradition, discipleship, and peoplehood that matter to communities of faith. We have no simple answers. But we think religious leaders need to be more aware of and grapple better with the fact that an instrumentalist, public health justification model of faith as producing healthy and good citizens (instead of, say, committed believers) may increase congregational attendance, but comes at a long-term cultural cost: faith and practice get redefined as instrumental therapeutic mechanisms to achieve personal goals which themselves may or may not be formed by religious faith and practice.

Finally, and most generally, we repeat what we said in the conclusion: adults of all sorts in religious communities should be taught to stop thinking about teenagers as aliens or others. Any generation gap that exists between teens and adults today is superficial compared with and far outweighed by generational continuities. Contemporary teenagers are almost entirely bought into the mainstream system, anxious to succeed on the system's terms, and well socialized to want to enjoy the consumerist and experiential benefits of U.S. society as much as they are able. Most problems and issues that adults typically consider teenage problems are in fact closely linked to adult-world problems. Furthermore, most teens appreciate their relationships with adults and most of those who lack them wish they had such ties. Moreover, the traditional "storm and stress" model of adolescence accurately depicts only a minority of teens and, in our view, is a counterproductive lens through which adults in faith communities (and beyond) view youth. That lens unnecessarily and unhelpfully creates distance when what is badly needed is connection. Adults need alternative ways of thinking and talking that emphasize adult similarities, ties to, and common futures with youth.

No doubt there are other useful implications of the NSYR findings that we have not mentioned or do not have the perspective to see. In any case, many of the suggested implications center on the general observation of frequent misplaced concerns and misguided perceptions among adults in religious communities concerning youth and what seems to us to be the need to refocus and recommit to certain good practices around youth ministry and, more broadly, congregational life. Some of these implications—for example, dealing with competition with schools and the media—are quite challenging. But others are within the realistic possibilities of many religious denominations and congregations to act on. Which of the above ideas, if any, apply to which religious communities is for the religious communities themselves to determine. Whatever diverse communities of faith decide about their work with youth, however, it is clear to us that much more attention to and discussion about the lives of teenagers is warranted if such communities desire to be faithful and effective in their work of faith engagement, formation, and education. We hope this book provides a useful step to that end. This may be only a beginning. More extended, soul-searching conversations will have to continue well beyond what we offer here. But this, we trust, is a helpful start.

Appendix A. Race, Class, Gender, Etcetera
Demographic Differences in U.S. Teenage Religiosity

The primary analytical approach we use in this book to examine NSYR survey data on U.S. teenage religion and spirituality has been to separate out teens into the six major U.S. religious traditions of conservative, mainline, and black Protestantism, Catholicism, Judaism, and Mormonism, and the category nonreligious. A second analytical approach we employ to categorize teenage religiosity is the four ideal religious types used to explore teenage outcomes described in chapter 7. We think these categories provide an illuminating comparative perspective on adolescent religious differences in the United States today. However, these are not the only ways one might view variance in teenage religion. A more standard sociological approach to making sense of distinctions in people's lives is to examine differences associated with what are thought of as key demographic characteristics. What some call the "holy trinity" of these sociological variables are race, social class, and gender. We briefly examine teen religious difference in light of these demographic distinctions in this appendix. In addition, we consider how adolescent religion may differ by age of teen, structure of teen's family, rural-urban residence, regional location, and supply of religious congregations per county. During the process of writing this book, we received many inquiries about how such demographic variables distinguished religious outcomes, indicating an apparent demand for such demographic analyses of the teen religion data. Any book aspiring to present a general overview of the results of such an inclusive study of national teen religiosity, yet lacking an analysis using these kinds of demographic variables, would be incomplete. Therefore, here we examine bivariate relationships in cross-tabulations between the demographic and religiosity variables. Then we enter all of the demographic variables examined in this appendix into multivariate ordered logit and binary logistic regression models to determine the independent effects of each variable while controlling for the possible effects of the other variables included. These findings contribute to our basic stock of knowledge about variances in U.S. teenage religious and spiritual practices and experiences.

TEEN RACE

Race is a major social factor differentiating many people's identity, life experiences, and outcomes in the United States. Do racial differences also associate with variance in religious practices and experiences among U.S. youth? Table A.1 examines differences in religious service attendance, importance of religious faith in everyday life, personal commitment to God, current involvement in a religious youth group, frequency of personal prayer, and feelings of closeness to God according to the racial categories of white, black, Hispanic, and Asian (the numbers of Native American, Pacific Islander, mixed, and other races were too small to include in this comparison). According to the findings presented in table A.1, racial differences do indeed associate with adolescent religious differences. Surveying our six religiosity variables, we see, for example, that, with many measures of religiosity, black teenagers tend to be more religious than white teenagers: 19 percent more black than white teens say religious faith is very or extremely important in their daily lives, 14 percent more have made a commitment to live their lives for God, 17 percent more pray alone daily or more often, and 15 percent more feel very or extremely close to God. Black teens are less likely than white teens, however, to belong to a religious youth group. On many, but not all, measures, Hispanic teenagers also appear to be somewhat more religious than whites. Hispanic youth are more likely to feel close to God and to engage in personal prayer, but are also much less likely to attend youth groups and to have made a commitment to live life for God. Asian teens generally reflect somewhat lower levels of religiosity than white teens, especially in the 18 percentage point difference between them in having committed to live for God. Results of multivariate regression analyses for these race categories controlling for all of the other variables addressed in this appendix are examined below.

SOCIAL CLASS

U.S. society is characterized by a distinct social class system of inequality that separates underclass, working poor, lower-middle-class, middle-class, upper-middle-class, and upper-class Americans.[1] Such class differences are defined by multiple factors, including education, income, and occupational status. Here we use three social class variables—family income, parental education, and median county family income—to explore possible differences in teenage religiosity with which they may associate. Are U.S. teenagers in higher- or lower-class families and counties more or less likely to be religious?

Table A.2 presents differences in our six adolescent religiosity measures according to differences in the incomes of the teens' families. We have grouped family income into three broad categories. Those families earning less than $30,000 per year are counted as low income (23 percent of the sample); those earning $80,000 or more per year in family income are counted as high income

Table A.1. Religiosity by Race of U.S. Adolescents, Ages 13–17 (Percentages)

	U.S.	Teen Race			
		White	Black	Hispanic	Asian
Religious service attendance					
More than once a week	16	16	20	12	9
Once a week	24	26	16	25	30
2–3 times a month	12	11	16	11	12
Once a month	7	7	4	7	4
Many times a year	8	6	16	9	6
A few times a year	14	15	11	17	17
Never	18	18	17	17	23
Importance of religious faith shaping daily life					
Extremely important	20	19	31	14	10
Very important	31	29	36	35	33
Somewhat important	31	30	27	38	33
Not very important	11	13	4	7	13
Not important at all	7	8	3	5	12
Has made a personal commitment to live life for God	55	55	69	46	37
Currently involved in a religious youth group	38	41	33	25	28
Frequency of teen praying alone					
Many times a day	16	13	28	17	10
About once a day	22	21	22	24	11
A few times a week	15	15	16	16	21
About once a week	12	12	12	9	18
1–2 times a month	13	14	12	13	16
Less than once a month	7	8	3	7	5
Never	15	17	7	12	19
How close teen feels to God					
Extremely close	11	9	20	13	10
Very close	25	25	29	22	19
Somewhat close	35	34	34	43	36
Somewhat distant	17	20	12	15	9
Very distant	5	5	4	3	5
Extremely distant	3	3	2	2	12
Does not believe in God	3	4	~	3	9

Source: National Survey of Youth and Religion, 2002–3.

Note: Percentages may not add to 100 due to rounding and unreported don't know and refused answers; cells of <1 are reported as ~.

(27 percent); those earning between $30,000 and $80,000 are counted as middle income (44 percent, with the percentage balance being "don't know" and refused answers on the family income question). These are somewhat crude categories, but they aid in ease of presentation for present purposes. Table A.2 shows only fairly minor differences between the three family income groups. The only broad generalizations one might venture based on the findings are that teens in low-income families appear to be less religiously involved in organizational aspects of religion (service attendance and youth group), and teenagers in high-income families are less likely to score higher on subjective and personal religiosity measures

Table A.2. Religiosity by Family Income of U.S. Adolescents, Ages 13–17
(Percentages)

	U.S.	Family Income		
		Low	Middle	High
Religious service attendance				
More than once a week	16	14	18	16
Once a week	24	16	25	29
2–3 times a month	12	13	12	10
Once a month	7	7	6	7
Many times a year	8	10	8	6
A few times a year	14	13	14	16
Never	18	26	16	15
Importance of religious faith shaping daily life				
Extremely important	20	20	21	18
Very important	31	34	32	27
Somewhat important	31	33	31	31
Not very important	11	8	11	14
Not important at all	7	5	6	10
Has made a personal commitment to live life for God	55	54	57	52
Currently involved in a religious youth group	38	27	41	40
Frequency of teen praying alone				
Many times a day	16	19	17	11
About once a day	22	21	23	20
A few times a week	15	16	15	16
About once a week	12	11	12	12
1–2 times a month	13	11	12	17
Less than once a month	7	5	8	8
Never	15	16	13	16
How close teen feels to God				
Extremely close	11	14	12	7
Very close	25	23	26	26
Somewhat close	35	36	35	34
Somewhat distant	17	16	17	19
Very distant	5	4	5	6
Extremely distant	3	3	3	2
Does not believe in God	3	3	2	5

Source: National Survey of Youth and Religion, 2002–3.

Note: Percentages may not add to 100 due to rounding and unreported don't know and refused answers.

(importance of faith, personal prayer, closeness to God). But any such differences are not large.

What about the education levels of parents of U.S. teenagers? Does variation in parental education associate with differences in teen religiosity? Table A.3 addresses these questions, not by breaking out parental education into the twelve different possible levels measured by the NSYR parent education survey question, but by focusing on three very different ideal types of parental education. Table A.3 compares the levels of teenage religiosity between those teens whose parents both have only high school degrees or less (N = 455), whose parents both have

Table A.3. Religiosity by Parents' Education of U.S. Adolescents, Ages 13–17, Two-parent Households Only (Percentages)

	U.S.	Parents' Education		
		Both Have High School Degrees or Less	Both At Least Some College and At Least One a College Degree	Both Graduate School Experience or Degree(s)
Religious service attendance				
More than once a week	16	17	16	15
Once a week	24	21	33	24
2–3 times a month	12	11	11	15
Once a month	7	7	6	9
Many times a year	8	9	7	7
A few times a year	14	18	14	14
Never	18	18	14	17
Importance of religious faith shaping daily life				
Extremely important	20	18	21	16
Very important	31	36	30	19
Somewhat important	31	34	30	31
Not very important	11	7	13	21
Not important at all	7	4	6	14
Has made a personal commitment to live life for God	55	57	60	44
Currently involved in a religious youth group	38	32	44	35
Frequency of teen praying alone				
Many times a day	16	20	16	12
About once a day	22	24	20	18
A few times a week	15	15	15	11
About once a week	12	13	13	10
1–2 times a month	13	10	15	13
Less than once a month	7	6	10	13
Never	15	12	11	22
How close teen feels to God				
Extremely close	11	13	11	6
Very close	25	26	24	18
Somewhat close	35	39	37	33
Somewhat distant	17	15	18	22
Very distant	5	2	3	10
Extremely distant	3	2	3	6
Does not believe in God	3	2	4	5

Source: National Survey of Youth and Religion, 2002–3.

Note: Percentages may not add to 100 due to rounding and unreported don't know and refused answers.

at least some college education and at least one parent has a bachelor's degree (N = 367), and whose parents both have done some work in graduate school if not earned graduate degrees (N = 191). Again, these are not all-inclusive categories but ideal types that do not include all U.S. teenagers and parents but do have the virtue of identifying clear, comparative categorical differences. The findings in table A.3, nonetheless, do not reveal any major parental education differences in teenage religiosity. Teens whose parents earned bachelor's degrees appear somewhat more likely than the others to attend religious services weekly or more often and to be involved in a religious youth group, and teens whose parents have a graduate degree seem less likely than the others to report that religious faith is important in their lives or that they have made personal commitments to live their lives for God. But such differences are not major. Below we will explore results of multivariate regression analyses for family income and parental education which control for the other variables examined in this appendix.

Social class influences on people's lives do not always operate at the individual or family level. People of similar social class tend to group or be grouped together socially and geographically for various reasons, creating possible social class effects at the community level, net of the individual level. Is U.S. teenage religiousness shaped by such community-level social class influences? To address this possibility, we used U.S. Census 2000 data to group counties into quartiles by the median family income of county and cross-tabulated those county income quartiles with our six teenage religiosity measures. The results, shown in table A.4, show that the highest levels of religiosity are among teens living in the poorest median family income counties and that teen religiosity generally drops off as the median family income of counties increases. The least religious teens are those living in the highest median family income counties. In other words, U.S. adolescent religiousness appears to be associated with social class at the county level, such that the higher the county family incomes, the less religious the teens who live in those counties tend to be.

TEEN GENDER

Are there gender differences in religiosity among U.S. teenagers? According to the findings presented in table A.5, there are. On each of the six religiosity variables examined, girls score higher than boys. The differences are not enormous but, as we will see below, they are statistically significant for all religion variables. On most religiosity indicators, although we can observe only a handful of percentage point differences between girls and boys across the answer categories given, after controlling for other demographic variables in multivariate regression models, teen gender remains statistically significant for all six religiosity measures. We therefore observe that teenage girls in the United States are a bit more religious than teenage boys. This finding is consistent with similar gender differences in religiosity observed among adults in the United States and in most other societies.[2]

TEEN AGE

The years that comprise teenage status in U.S. culture actually involve major differences in maturity, experience, mobility, and independence. The life of a 13-year-old is often vastly different from the life of a 17-year-old, even though only

Table A.4. Religiosity by Median Family Income of County of Residence (Grouped by Quartiles) of U.S. Adolescents, Ages 13–17 (Percentages)

	U.S.	Median Family Income of County			
		Lowest Quartile	Second to Lowest Quartile	Next Highest Quartile	Highest Quartile
Religious service attendance					
More than once a week	16	21	17	16	10
Once a week	24	23	25	27	23
2–3 times a month	12	13	12	10	13
Once a month	7	6	7	6	7
Many times a year	8	8	8	9	7
A few times a year	14	12	13	15	18
Never	18	17	18	17	20
Importance of religious faith shaping daily life					
Extremely important	20	26	20	17	15
Very important	31	34	33	32	25
Somewhat important	31	28	31	33	33
Not very important	11	8	10	10	16
Not important at all	7	4	6	8	11
Has made a personal commitment to live life for God	55	62	58	55	46
Currently involved in a religious youth group	38	43	39	39	29
Frequency of teen praying alone					
Many times a day	16	21	16	17	10
About once a day	22	24	22	24	17
A few times a week	15	15	19	14	14
About once a week	12	13	10	12	13
1–2 times a month	13	11	14	12	16
Less than once a month	7	5	6	8	10
Never	15	11	13	14	20
How close teen feels to God					
Extremely close	11	15	11	12	7
Very close	25	26	26	26	23
Somewhat close	35	35	36	34	35
Somewhat distant	17	15	17	17	21
Very distant	5	3	4	4	7
Extremely distant	3	3	2	3	4
Does not believe in God	3	2	3	4	4

Source: National Survey of Youth and Religion, 2002–3.

Note: Percentages may not add to 100 due to rounding and unreported don't know and refused answers.

four years separate them. One may imagine that religious identification, participation, and commitment could drop off in the later teenage years, particularly after the age of 16, when many teens begin to drive cars, become more sexually active, and establish greater autonomy from their parents. Are American 16- and 17-year-olds that much less religious than 14- and 15-year-olds or even 13-year-olds? According to the findings presented in table A.6, not especially so. Exam-

Table A.5. Religiosity by Gender of U.S. Adolescents, Ages 13–17 (Percentages)

	U.S.	Teen Gender	
		Male	Female
Religious service attendance			
More than once a week	16	13	19
Once a week	24	24	25
2–3 times a month	12	12	12
Once a month	7	6	7
Many times a year	8	8	8
A few times a year	14	16	13
Never	18	20	16
Importance of religious faith shaping daily life			
Extremely important	20	16	23
Very important	31	31	31
Somewhat important	31	32	30
Not very important	11	13	9
Not important at all	7	9	6
Has made a personal commitment to live life for God	55	52	59
Currently involved in a religious youth group	38	35	40
Frequency of teen praying alone			
Many times a day	16	12	20
About once a day	22	19	25
A few times a week	15	15	16
About once a week	12	12	11
1–2 times a month	13	15	11
Less than once a month	7	8	6
Never	15	19	10
How close teen feels to God			
Extremely close	11	9	14
Very close	25	24	27
Somewhat close	35	35	35
Somewhat distant	17	19	16
Very distant	5	5	4
Extremely distant	3	4	2
Does not believe in God	3	4	2

Source: National Survey of Youth and Religion, 2002–3.

Note: Percentages may not add to 100 due to rounding and unreported don't know and refused answers.

ining differences among the three age groups across our six religiosity variables, we observe only minor if any decreases in the religious involvements of 16- and 17-year-olds compared to the younger teens. The 16- to 17-year-olds, for instance, attend religious services weekly or more often only two percentage points less than the 13-year-olds. The same comparison shows only a 2 percent drop from the 13-year-olds to the 16- to 17-year-olds in the number who say that religious faith is very or extremely important in their lives. Furthermore, only 4 percent fewer of older U.S. teens are involved in religious youth groups than younger teens. We also see little change in the total percentage who pray once a day or more often between the younger and older age categories of U.S. teens. The most noticeable change across the age groups is evident in feeling close to

Table A.6. Religiosity by Age Group of U.S. Adolescents, Ages 13–17 (Percentages)

	U.S.	Teen Age Group		
		13	14–15	16–17
Religious service attendance				
More than once a week	16	18	17	15
Once a week	24	23	26	24
2–3 times a month	12	13	12	12
Once a month	7	6	6	7
Many times a year	8	9	8	8
A few times a year	14	14	14	15
Never	18	17	17	20
Importance of religious faith shaping daily life				
Extremely important	20	17	22	19
Very important	31	34	30	30
Somewhat important	31	32	31	31
Not very important	11	12	10	11
Not important at all	7	5	6	9
Has made a personal commitment to live life for God	55	56	57	54
Currently involved in a religious youth group	38	39	39	35
Frequency of teen praying alone				
Many times a day	16	16	17	15
About once a day	22	23	20	23
A few times a week	15	13	15	16
About once a week	12	13	12	12
1–2 times a month	13	13	16	10
Less than once a month	7	7	7	8
Never	15	14	13	16
How close teen feels to God				
Extremely close	11	16	12	9
Very close	25	26	26	24
Somewhat close	35	36	35	35
Somewhat distant	17	15	17	19
Very distant	5	4	5	5
Extremely distant	3	2	2	4
Does not believe in God	3	1	3	4

Source: National Survey of Youth and Religion, 2002–3.

Note: Percentages may not add to 100 due to rounding and unreported don't know and refused answers.

God, but even there the change is not enormous. In other words, older U.S. teenagers, at least through 16 and 17 years of age, appear not to be dramatically less religiously engaged than younger U.S. teenagers. We do witness modest drops in religiosity between the ages of 13 and 17 for most measures. And the religiosity of teenagers *older* than 17 may drop significantly. But the evidence does not suggest that teenage religiousness drops off precipitously when teens come to enjoy more independence—wheels, jobs, and real girlfriends and boyfriends. Older high school–age teenagers seem to be less religious than younger teenagers by only a handful of percentage points.

FAMILY STRUCTURE

Compared to prior years, the structure of the American family has become noticeably more complicated in recent decades. The rise in rates of marital separation, divorce, remarriage, single parenthood, and cohabitation of unmarried partners has created significant numbers of American teenagers living in family forms other than nuclear families involving two married parents of children.[3] Do family structure variations make any difference in levels of teenage religiosity? Are adolescent youth in certain family types more or less likely to be religiously involved? According to the findings presented in table A.7, yes. In most cases, the U.S. teenagers who are most likely to be more highly religious are those whose residential parents, mostly both biological parents but also including stepparents, are married. As with teen age, the differences are not enormous, but they are noticeable. The reasons explaining any family structure association with religiosity are not hard to imagine. Parental separation and divorce are disruptive life course events that usually restructure relational networks and generally depress religious participation. Divorce and the death of a parent can also precipitate emotional crises for parents and children alike, which can be expressed as resentment or anger toward God. Many U.S. religious traditions also oppose cohabitation, birth out of wedlock, and divorce, and so, intentionally or not, likely raise the discomfort level for potential adherents in those life situations who are religiously involved. Furthermore, as a matter of parental attention and family resources, it is generally more difficult for one parent to mobilize and sustain family congregational religious involvements than it is for two parents. Finally, it may be that some religious traditions exert ongoing moral and ideological influences on their adherents that actually reduce their readiness personally to consider cohabitation, separation, divorce, and birth out of wedlock. One particularly complicating factor when it comes to family structure and religiosity, however, is race: black teenagers are both more likely than whites to have parents who are not married and are more likely to be more religious than whites. Below we use multivariate regression models to remove that race effect and perhaps other relevant associations in order to isolate the possible independent associations of family structure per se, net of race.

REGIONAL LOCATION

The United States is notably divided into culturally distinctive regions of the country: the urban Northeast, the South, the Midwestern heartland, and the Rocky Mountain and Pacific Coast regions. Many people associate these regions with different kinds and degrees of religiosity. Do geographic regional differences actually associate with variance in teen religiosity? According to the findings presented in table A.8, they do. These findings confirm those of previous research[4] and show that teenagers resident in the Northeast are the least religious among the compared regions, teens who are residents of the South are the most religious, and teenagers living in the Midwest and West generally fall between these two extremes. Below we examine results of multivariate regression analyses for these regional differences that control for all the other demographic variables addressed in this appendix to see if the region variables remain statistically significant.

Table A.7. Religiosity by Family Structure of U.S. Adolescents, Ages 13–17
(Percentages)

	U.S.	Current Family Structure					
	All	Currently Married	Cohabiting	Separated	Divorced	Never Married	Widowed
Religious service attendance							
More than once a week	16	17	12	17	14	11	8
Once a week	24	28	14	17	19	17	19
2–3 times a month	12	11	12	15	15	14	16
Once a month	7	6	12	5	5	9	9
Many times a year	8	8	6	6	8	14	9
A few times a year	14	14	22	14	16	15	8
Never	18	16	21	26	24	22	32
Importance of religious faith shaping daily life							
Extremely important	20	20	15	19	17	22	12
Very important	31	31	25	35	32	33	30
Somewhat important	31	30	41	31	30	33	43
Not very important	11	11	10	10	12	5	11
Not important at all	7	7	8	5	9	6	4
Has made a personal commitment to live life for God	55	56	46	54	53	57	57
Currently involved in a religious youth group	38	41	34	31	34	23	24
Frequency of teen praying alone							
Many times a day	16	16	17	15	17	17	20
About once a day	22	23	18	22	17	23	23
A few times a week	15	15	12	21	14	18	14
About once a week	12	11	11	11	14	14	7
1–2 times a month	13	13	15	11	14	11	15
Less than once a month	7	7	8	5	8	5	9
Never	15	14	18	14	17	12	11
How close teen feels to God							
Extremely close	11	11	11	12	10	18	15
Very close	25	26	17	23	25	20	29
Somewhat close	35	35	39	43	32	34	29
Somewhat distant	17	17	23	14	19	18	19
Very distant	5	5	4	2	6	6	5
Extremely distant	3	3	2	2	5	3	1
Does not believe in God	3	3	5	3	4	1	3

Source: National Survey of Youth and Religion, 2002–3

Note: Percentages may not add to 100 due to rounding and unreported don't know and refused answers.

Table A.8. Religiosity by Regional Location of U.S. Adolescents, Ages 13–17
(Percentages)

	U.S.	Northeast	South	Midwest	West
		Teen Region			
Religious service attendance					
More than once a week	16	9	22	13	15
Once a week	24	25	23	29	23
2–3 times a month	12	12	12	14	11
Once a month	7	7	7	6	7
Many times a year	8	6	12	6	6
A few times a year	14	18	12	16	14
Never	18	24	12	16	25
Importance of religious faith shaping daily life					
Extremely important	20	15	26	15	17
Very important	31	26	36	29	29
Somewhat important	31	33	27	35	32
Not very important	11	15	7	13	11
Not important at all	7	10	3	8	10
Has made a personal commitment to live life for God	55	40	66	53	52
Currently involved in a religious youth group	38	22	45	37	36
Frequency of teen praying alone					
Many times a day	16	10	20	13	17
About once a day	22	18	25	21	20
A few times a week	15	14	16	14	16
About once a week	12	13	12	13	9
1–2 times a month	13	15	13	14	12
Less than once a month	7	9	5	9	7
Never	15	20	9	16	19
How close teen feels to God					
Extremely close	11	7	14	10	11
Very close	25	20	30	25	22
Somewhat close	35	39	34	35	34
Somewhat distant	17	21	14	19	18
Very distant	5	5	4	5	6
Extremely distant	3	3	2	3	4
Does not believe in God	3	4	1	3	5

Source: National Survey of Youth and Religion, 2002–3.

Note: Percentages may not add to 100 due to rounding and unreported don't know and refused answers.

URBAN-RURAL DIFFERENCES

Next we examine differences in the residential locations of teenagers along rural-urban lines, measured as population of county of residence. Are teens who live in sparsely populated counties, that is, in rural counties, more or less religious than those who reside in high-population counties? We address these questions by grouping the NSYR sample of teenagers into four categories by county population, ranging from counties with populations of fewer than 40,000 residents to counties with more than 1 million residents. We then cross-tabulate these four county population categories with our six religiosity measures. Table A.9 reports the results. There we find that U.S. teenage religiosity is indeed negatively associated with the population of counties. Teens who live in sparsely populated, rural counties score higher on our six religiosity measures than teens from more densely populated, urban counties. Comparing teens who live in the least populated group of counties with those who live in the most populated group of counties, we see,

Table A.9. Religiosity by Urban or Rural Residence (County Population) of U.S. Adolescents, Ages 13–17 (Percentages)

	U.S.	Teen Residential County Population			
		Fewer than 40,000	40,000– 200,000	200,000– 1,000,000	1,000,000+
Religious service attendance					
More than once a week	16	25	18	13	14
Once a week	24	25	27	24	21
2–3 times a month	12	13	11	13	12
Once a month	7	6	6	7	7
Many times a year	8	6	7	10	7
A few times a year	14	11	14	17	13
Never	18	14	16	17	25
Importance of religious faith shaping daily life					
Extremely important	20	24	20	19	17
Very important	31	33	33	29	30
Somewhat important	31	29	29	33	32
Not very important	11	9	11	11	11
Not important at all	7	4	6	8	9
Has made a personal commitment to live life for God	55	61	61	52	49
Currently involved in a religious youth group	38	48	42	35	28
Frequency of teen praying alone					
Many times a day	16	20	17	15	14
About once a day	22	24	24	19	21
A few times a week	15	14	16	14	18
About once a week	12	14	11	12	12
1–2 times a month	13	10	12	15	14
Less than once a month	7	4	8	9	5
Never	15	14	13	15	15
How close teen feels to God					
Extremely close	11	13	12	10	12
Very close	25	30	26	23	24
Somewhat close	35	37	34	36	33
Somewhat distant	17	13	18	18	19
Very distant	5	4	5	5	6
Extremely distant	3	2	3	3	3
Does not believe in God	3	1	2	4	3

Source: National Survey of Youth and Religion, 2002–3.

Note: Percentages may not add to 100 due to rounding and unreported don't know and refused answers.

for example, a 15 percent difference in weekly religious service attendance, a 12 percent difference in commitment to live for God, and a 20 percent difference in youth group involvement. It appears, then, that adolescent religiosity is higher in rural areas and lower in urbanized areas. We will test below whether these differences remain statistically significant in multivariate regression models after controlling for other demographic variables.

SUPPLY OF RELIGIOUS CONGREGATIONS IN COUNTY

Finally, we examine one social contextual religion effect at the county level on individual teenage religiosity: the religious supply-side factor of the number of religious congregations per capita in counties in which teenagers reside. The idea here is that individual religiosity may not simply reflect the desire to be religious but may also reflect the supply of religious organizations available. Clearly, religious demand and supply influence each other. But we might wish to know simply whether greater supply of religious congregations per capita is associated with variance in teen religiosity. Using data on the number of religious congregations per county in the United States and the population of counties, we calculated the number of religious congregations per capita for all counties and multiplied those numbers by 10,000. We then grouped counties into four categories, ranging from fewer than seven congregations on the low end to 20 or more on the high end. The results of those four categories cross-tabulated with our six religiosity variables are presented in table A.10. There we see that supply of religious congregations at the county level and teenage religiosity appear positively related. Comparing the lowest and highest categories of congregation per capita (fewer than seven compared to 20 or more), we see, for example, a 20 percent difference in religious service attendance weekly or more often, a 17 percent difference in faith being very or extremely important, a 17 percent difference in commitment to live for God, and a 27 percent difference in youth group involvement. To what extent supply of religion helps to promote teenage religious practice and experience, as opposed to simply reflecting a larger historical demand for religion in a county population that teen religiosity indicates, we cannot say with precision. We can, however, observe that supply of congregations and religiosity do seem, in fact, to be positively associated. Whether this association is statistically significant after controlling for other variables, however, we are about to see.

MULTIVARIATE REGRESSION ANALYSES

To determine which of the above demographic variables are statistically significantly associated as independent variables with variance in U.S. adolescent religiosity, we ran ordered logit and binary logistic regression models including all of the demographic variables.[5] The results of these multivariate regressions are presented in table A.11, which names only the statistically significant variables, indicated in the positive or negative direction. Insignificant variables are left blank. (For now, differences between boldface and nonboldface positives and negatives should be ignored.) In table A.11 we see that, with regard to race, net of all other factors, black teenagers in the United States are significantly more religious on five of the six religiosity measures than white teenagers, the one exception being youth group participation, which they are significantly less involved with com-

Table A.10. Religiosity by Congregations per Capita of County of Residence of U.S. Adolescents, Ages 13–17 (Percentages)

	U.S.	Congregations per Capita of County (×10,000)			
		<7	7–14	15–19	20+
Religious service attendance					
More than once a week	16	13	17	20	28
Once a week	24	23	24	30	28
2–3 times a month	12	12	13	13	11
Once a month	7	7	7	5	4
Many times a year	8	8	8	8	8
A few times a year	14	16	14	11	10
Never	18	21	18	13	10
Importance of religious faith shaping daily life					
Extremely important	20	17	20	23	26
Very important	31	29	31	38	37
Somewhat important	31	33	31	26	27
Not very important	11	12	12	7	7
Not important at all	7	9	6	6	2
Has made a personal commitment to live life for God	55	49	58	68	66
Currently involved in a religious youth group	38	30	40	49	57
Frequency of teen praying alone					
Many times a day	16	14	16	19	22
About once a day	22	20	21	30	25
A few times a week	15	15	16	17	12
About once a week	12	12	10	9	17
1–2 times a month	13	14	14	8	10
Less than once a month	7	8	8	7	3
Never	15	17	14	10	10
How close teen feels to God					
Extremely close	11	10	12	14	14
Very close	25	24	25	26	32
Somewhat close	35	34	35	36	37
Somewhat distant	17	19	18	15	12
Very distant	5	5	5	3	2
Extremely distant	3	3	2	4	2
Does not believe in God	3	4	3	1	1

Source: National Survey of Youth and Religion, 2002–3.

Note: Percentages may not add to 100 due to rounding and unreported don't know and refused answers.

pared to white teens. Hispanic teenagers, controlling for all other variables, score significantly lower than whites on the commitment to God and youth group measures, but higher on the personal prayer and closeness to God measures. Asian teenagers are only significantly different from white teens in their fewer numbers committed to live their lives for God. Thus, racial categories help to differentiate levels of religiosity among teens in the United States. These findings largely comport with those of previously published analyses,[6] confirming our knowledge of significant racial differences in religiosity and raising ongoing research questions about how such racial differences are generated and sustained.

Social class variables show mixed results in table A.11. As also evident in the bivariate tables earlier, teenager's family income (entered here as a single, 12-point, continuous variable) and parental education (entered here as a 15-point ordered scale)[7] are not significantly associated with teenage religiosity, with the one exception that teens of more highly educated parents are significantly less

Table A.11. Statistically Significant Variables in Ordered Logit and Binary Logistic Regressions of Demographic Variables on Religiosity Measures, U.S. Adolescents, Ages 13–17

	Teenage Religiosity Measures					
	Attendance	Importance of Faith	Commitment to God	Youth Group	Personal Prayer	Close to God
Race						
Black	Positive	Positive	Positive	Negative[1]	Positive	Positive
Hispanic			Negative	Negative	Positive	Positive
Asian			Negative			
White[3]						
Family income						
Parental education			Negative			
Median family income of county		Negative	Negative	Negative	Negative	Negative
Female teen	Positive	Positive	Positive	Positive	Positive	Positive
Teen age (older)	Negative	Negative	Negative	Negative	Negative	Negative
Family structure						
Married[3]						
Unmarried partner	Negative	Negative	Negative	Negative	Negative[2]	Negative
Separated	Negative		Negative[2]	Negative	Negative	
Divorced	Negative	Negative	Negative[2]	Negative[2]	Negative	Negative
Widowed	Negative	Negative		Negative[2]		
Never married	Negative		Negative	Negative	Negative	Negative
Region						
Northeast	Negative		Negative	Negative		
South	Positive	Positive	Positive	Positive	Positive	Positive
West						
Midwest[3]						
County population (higher)						
Religious congregations per capita of county	Positive	Positive	Positive	Positive	Positive	Positive

Source: National Survey of Youth and Religion, 2002–3.

Notes:
[1]Black is negatively associated with youth group (without religious tradition controls) at the p=0.058 level and becomes insignificant with religious tradition controls entered.
[2]These variables are significant at the p.<0.05 levels in models without religious tradition entered and at the p=0.07 level in models with religious tradition variables entered.
[3]Reference group.

likely to have committed to live their lives for God. The social class variable that *does* significantly associate with all of the religiosity variables except religious service attendance, however, is median family income of county. And this effect is net of county population and religious congregations per capita of the county. Teenagers who are residents of counties where families tend to earn higher incomes tend to score significantly lower on five of our six religiosity measures. Why or how things work this way we are not certain, but it appears that increased wealth at the community level is correlated with lower levels of teenage religious practices and experiences.

Teen sex and age are also significantly associated with all of the religiosity measures, even when controlling for the effects of the other variables in the models. On all variables, girls are more religious than boys. For whatever reason, religious practice and experience among U.S. teenagers are clearly gendered. For reasons more explicable, on all measures older teens are less religious than younger teens. The numbers themselves in table A.6 show these age differences are not large, but they are statistically significant.

Family structure is also clearly associated with variance in teenage religiosity. Across all six measures, teens in families with currently married residential parents, including both biological parents and stepparents, are more religious than teens in other types of families. After controlling for race, class, and numerous other factors here, with a few exceptions, U.S. adolescents with cohabiting or unmarried parents score significantly lower on these measures of religious practice and experience than those with residential parents who are married. There are probably multiple influences at work here. The experience of marital breakup itself likely reduces religious involvement of parents and teens, for various reasons. It could also be that families that are more religiously involved are also more capable of avoiding marital breakup, for other sundry reasons. And it could be that adults who are prone to relational and family instability also tend to select themselves out of religious involvements. Sorting through these possibilities to better understand how these processes work will require more research.

Regional variables perform in the multivariate models as the findings in the bivariate table A.8 suggest they would. In these models, teenagers living in the South are consistently more religious than those living in the Midwest. The Bible Belt effect continues to exert its influence in the lives of U.S. teens. By contrast, teenagers living in the Northeast are often less religious than those living in the Midwest. Teens living in Western states are not statistically significantly different in religiosity from those living in the Midwest. Finally, after controlling for all demographic variables in multivariate models, any rural-urban differences as measured by county population that were evident in the bivariate table A.9 become statistically insignificant. Teens living in rural counties are not significantly more or less religious than those in urban counties, net of other demographic effects. However, the supply-side factor of religious congregations per capita at the county level is significantly related to teenage religiosity. In these models, the greater supply of religious congregations available in a county, the more personally religious are teenagers who live in those counties, net of the other demographic controls.

Before concluding, we subject these demographic analyses to a more rigorous test by entering controls for the religious traditions of teenagers. We do this because religious tradition is correlated with some of these demographic variables, as evident in table A.12, and with adolescent religiosity (table B.4 likewise shows the demographic characteristics of the four religious ideal types used in chapter 7's analysis). For example, certain religious traditions that correlate with different levels of teen religiosity are also geographically concentrated. Religious traditions also vary by race, both of which are associated with teenage religiosity. So it is possible that some of the regional and racial differences observed in table A.11, for example, are actually the result of religious tradition differences, which, once accounted for, would reduce or eliminate the regional, racial, or other differences. We test for this possibility by adding to our regression models variables control-

Table A.12. Demographic Traits of Religious Types of U.S. Adolescents, Ages 13–17 (Percentages)

	U.S.	Religious Tradition						
		CP	MP	BP	RC	J	LDS	NR
Age								
13	19	21	18	20	17	25	9	17
14	20	21	19	18	20	24	24	18
15	21	21	19	22	23	16	29	18
16	21	20	23	17	20	21	18	24
17	20	17	21	23	20	14	20	23
Female	49	51	51	55	49	48	49	42
Race								
White	66	83	87	3	62	93	89	69
Black	17	5	6	93	4	2	~	14
Hispanic	12	7	2	1	28	~	5	10
Other race	5	5	5	3	6	5	6	7
Region								
Northeast	17	9	14	11	27	37	4	23
Midwest	22	20	31	17	24	15	6	24
South	37	51	39	60	24	21	12	22
Mountain/Pacific	24	20	17	12	25	28	79	31
Parent marital status								
Married	70	76	78	47	72	88	79	61
Living with unmarried partner	4	4	1	6	5	~	3	5
Widowed	2	2	1	3	1	~	~	3
Divorced	13	11	14	14	10	9	17	17
Separated	5	4	3	10	5	1	1	7
Never married	6	3	2	20	8	3	~	7
School type attending								
Public	87	85	91	91	86	87	92	87
Catholic	4	~	2	1	10	2	2	2
Private other Christian	2	8	2	2	~	~	~	1
Jewish	~	~	~	~	~	1	~	~
Private nonreligious	1	2	3	2	1	5	~	2
Home-schooled	2	4	1	2	1	~	5	4
Other	2	~	~	1	~	5	~	~
Not going to school	1	1	~	1	2	~	~	2

Source: National Survey of Youth and Religion, 2002–3.

Note: Percentages may not add to 100 due to rounding; cells of <1 are reported as ~.

ling for teenage affiliation with evangelical, mainline, and black Protestantism, Catholicism, Judaism, Mormonism, and other religious traditions. Previously significant variables that remain statistically significant after controlling for teen religious tradition are in boldface in table A.11, and variables that become statistically insignificant are in roman.

In table A.11, we see that, net of teen religious tradition differences, many but not all of the previously significant variables remain statistically significant. All of the teen gender and most of the black teen, median family income of county, nonmarried family structure, and South region variables remain statistically significant. The supply of religious congregations per capita by county, however, becomes statistically insignificant, along with two of the three Northeast region variables. Most likely, those counties with more congregations per capita also have concentrations of religious traditions, conservative and black Protestantism and Mormonism, with typically higher levels of teen religiosity. Furthermore, although not noted in the table, after controlling for religious tradition, Hispanic teens become significantly higher in importance of faith compared to white teens, and larger county population becomes significantly positively associated with closeness to God. Finally, we note, first, that all of the religious tradition dummy variables are statistically significant for all models (using nonreligious as the reference group) and, second, that the Pseudo-R^2s for all of the models are increased by two to 10 times the magnitude with the inclusion of the religious tradition variables. This suggests that religious tradition differences explain more of the variance in teen religiosity than do the demographic variables, which is in part why most of the tables in this book use religious tradition differences rather than demographic differences to analyze the data.

CONCLUSION

What have we learned from this appendix's analysis? In general, we see that the religiosity of adolescents in the United States is somewhat socially patterned. Sociocultural factors such as racial identity, gender, place in the adolescent life course, parental marital situation, and regional location of residence appear somewhat to influence the extent of teenagers' subjective religious experiences and commitments and organizational practices and ties. In many cases, being black, female, younger, in a family with married parents, and from the South associate with higher levels of religiosity. On the other hand, social class differences at the family level do not seem to associate with differences in teenage religiosity. U.S. adolescent religiousness appears fairly evenly spread across the range of family incomes and parental education. Social class measured at the community level as median family income of county, however, does appear correlated with teenage religiosity, even net of religious tradition differences, with teens living in higher-income counties scoring lower on the subjective religiosity measures of importance of faith, closeness to God, and frequency of personal prayer. Furthermore, very much in keeping with this book's emphasis on significant parental and adult influences in the religious and spiritual lives of teenagers, we have seen that higher levels of teen religiosity are positively associated with growing up in married parent households. For various reasons, teens whose parents are not married tend to be personally less religious themselves. Beyond these findings, we observe a significant regional difference in the religiosity of teenagers living in the South versus the Northeast. Stereotypical images of differences between the secular, urban Northeast and the Southern Bible Belt are borne out in the religious lives of adolescents, illustrating the sociological observation that people's lives are, net of many personal factors, significantly shaped by features of their social environment. Finally, the most significant factor differentiating levels of teenage religiosity appears to be teen religious affiliations: differences in religious traditions, themselves shaped by their own theological differences, community histories, and organizational practices, seem to best explain differences in teenage religious practices and beliefs.

Appendix B. Survey Methodology

The National Survey of Youth and Religion (NSYR) is a nationally representative telephone survey of 3,290 English- and Spanish-speaking teenagers between 13 and 17, and of their parents. The NSYR also includes 80 oversampled Jewish households, not nationally representative (described below), bringing the total number of completed NSYR cases to 3,370. The survey was conducted from July 2002 to April 2003 by researchers at the University of North Carolina at Chapel Hill using a random-digit-dial (RDD) method, employing a sample of randomly generated telephone numbers representative of all household telephones in the 50 United States, including Alaska and Hawaii. The national survey sample was arranged in replicates based on the proportion of working household telephone exchanges nationwide. This RDD method ensures equal representation of listed, unlisted, and not-yet-listed household telephone numbers. Eligible households included at least one teenager between 13 and 17 living in the household for at least six months of the year.[1] To randomize responses within households, and so help attain representativeness of age and gender, interviewers asked to conduct the survey with the teenager in the household who had the most recent birthday. Parent interviews were conducted with either a mother or father, as available, although the survey asked to speak with mothers first, believing that they may be better qualified to answer questions about their family and teenager. Stepparents, resident grandparents, resident partners of parents, and other resident parent-like figures were also eligible to complete the parent portion of the survey.

An RDD telephone survey sampling method was chosen for this study because of the advantages it offers compared to alternative survey sampling methods. Unlike school-based sampling, for example, our RDD telephone method was able to survey not only school-attending youth, but also school dropouts, home-schooled youth, and students frequently absent from school. Using RDD, we were also able to ask numerous religion questions which many school principals and school boards often disallow on surveys administered in school. Explicit informed consent from parents also proved more feasible using RDD than school-based sampling. And the verbal reading of survey questions by trained interviewers facilitated question-and-answer clarifications that increased the validity of answers, compared to paper-and-pencil questionnaires administered en masse in school classrooms. Also, given the relatively low incidence rate (14 percent) of American households with teenagers 13 to 17 years old, the NSYR's RDD telephone survey method was much more cost-effective than an in-home survey, which would have been cost-prohibitive. The NSYR's RDD telephone method also eliminated potential design effect problems associated with sampling from a limited number of geographic or school clusters. Furthermore, the greater anonymity of an RDD survey interviewer on the telephone, compared to an in-person interviewer in the home, may have also increased the validity of teenagers' answers to sensitive questions and reduced possible biasing effects of in-person interviewers' sex, race, and age.[2] No good sampling frames exist with which the NSYR might have conducted a mail survey, which typically garners extremely low cooperation and response rates in any case. Finally, superior Internet-based methods of sampling and surveying were not sufficiently developed and tested by the time of this survey's fielding to have been useful for the NSYR.[3]

Prior to conducting this survey, the researchers conducted 35 in-depth pilot interviews with teenagers to help inform the construction of the survey instrument. The researchers also conducted additional survey-focused interviews and focus groups with a variety of types of teenagers to improve question wording and comprehension. Prior to the survey, researchers also conducted modest (N=175) pretests of the survey instrument using both nationally representative and convenience samples. Based on pretest results, the researchers revised questions and answer categories to enhance survey clarity and validity. The final survey instrument is available by Internet download at the project Web site: www.youthandreligion.org/publications/docs/survey.pdf.

The NSYR survey was conducted with members of both English- and Spanish-speaking households. The English version of the survey was translated into Spanish by a professional translation service. That translation was then closely reviewed, evaluated, and revised by four separate native Spanish-speaking translation consultants and six Spanish-speaking survey interviewers to ensure the best translation for Spanish-speaking respondents. The final Spanish-language version was then programmed into the computer-assisted telephone interview (CATI) system for calls to Spanish-speaking households. Surveys with Spanish-speaking households were conducted by native Spanish-speaking interviewers who are fluent in both English and Spanish and who had extensive experience conducting the survey in English before conducting the Spanish version. The parent and teen respondents from households could each choose the language with which to complete the survey, so that a parent might use the Spanish version, for example, while the teen used the English version. Spanish-speaking household numbers are included in the calculations of the national sample cooperation, completion, and response rates below.[4]

All survey interviewers received two days of project-specific training in the significance and purpose of the survey, the meaning of all survey questions and their answer categories, the proper pronunciation of religious terms, and the ethical treatment of human subjects. They also completed an Internet-based Human Participant Protections Education for Research Teams course offered by the National Institutes of Health, U.S. Department of Health and Human Services (www.cme.nci.nih.gov). Immediately prior to conducting all surveys, interviewers obtained respondents' verbal informed consent and provided respondents with information about the confidentiality of their answers and their right to refuse to answer questions. Household eligibility was determined through the use of an initial screening question about resident teenagers. Incentives of $20 to parent respondents and $20 to teenage respondents were offered to complete the survey, for a total of $40 to completing households.[5] Survey respondents were also able to complete the survey at their convenience by calling a toll-free number that linked to their sample record. Throughout the fielding of the survey, interviewers were monitored by project staff (primarily the authors) using remote technology to ensure data quality, and the interviewers, monitors, and researchers were routinely debriefed about survey performance. Upon completing the survey, all respondents were given contact information for the researchers, the research firm, and the university Institutional Review Board to verify the survey's authenticity or ask any questions about the survey or their rights as respondents. This information was also included in written form in thank-you letters accompanying the mailed incentives.

To help protect the privacy of survey respondents, the NSYR obtained a Federal Certificate of Confidentiality from the National Institutes of Health. With this certificate, researchers with the NSYR could not be forced to disclose information that might identify respondents, even by a court subpoena, in any federal, state, or local civil, criminal, administrative, legislative, or other proceedings. The certificate was thus useful for resisting any potential demands for information that would identify respondents (with the following exceptions: a Certificate of Confidentiality does not prevent respondents or members of their families from voluntarily releasing information about themselves or their involvement in the NSYR; if and when an insurer, employer, or other person were to obtain respondent's own voluntary written consent to receive research information, the NSYR could not use the certificate to withhold that information; neither does the Certificate of Confidentiality prevent the researchers from disclosing without respondents' consent information that would identify them as a participant in the research project in stated cases of child abuse or intent to hurt self or others; if teen respondents disclosed evidence of neglect or abuse, the NSYR had an obligation to inform the appropriate authorities).

The NSYR survey was conducted over nine months, between the end of July 2002 and the beginning of April 2003. All randomly generated telephone numbers were dialed a minimum of 20 times over a minimum of five months per number, spread out over varying hours during weekdays, weeknights, and weekends. The calling design included at least two telephone-based attempts to convert refusals. Households refusing to cooperate with the survey yet established by initial screening to have children age 13 to 17 in residence and with telephone numbers able to be matched to mailing addresses were also sent information by mail about the survey, contact information for researchers, and a request from the principal investigator to cooperate and complete the survey; those records were then called back for possible refusal conversions.[6] Most cell phone numbers were screened out of the initial sample through the identification of unique cell phone exchange numbers. All other nonhousehold numbers (business, government, nonprofit, payphones, remaining cell phones, etc.) were screened out of the sample through direct calling dispositions and ascription of contact and noncontact telephone numbers for noncompletes based on proportions of household numbers among working telephone numbers.[7] Of the sample producing only voice-mail or answering machine, 34 percent were dialed more than 99 separate times; 23 percent of those voice-mail numbers were dialed between 50 and 99 times, and 43 percent of those voice-mail numbers were dialed between 25 and 49 times.

The NSYR survey itself took a mean of 30 minutes to complete the parent portion and 52 minutes to complete the teen portion of the instrument, for a mean parent-teen combined survey length of 82 minutes. A total of 3,370 respondent households completed our full survey, 3,290 of which were RDD national sample respondents and 80 of which were Jewish oversample respondents. The overall cooperation rate of our national sample was 81 percent. Ninety-six percent of parent complete households also achieved teen completes. Using the American Association for Public Opinion Research (AAPOR) RR4 calculator, the final NSYR national sample survey response rate was 57 percent.[8] For descriptive purposes, a weight was created ("weight2") to adjust for number of teenagers in household, number of household phone numbers, census region of residence, and household income.[9]

Diagnostic analyses demonstrate that the NSYR provides a nationally representative and unbiased sample of U.S. households with resident teenagers age 13–17. Comparative tests were run for the national representation of or potential sampling biases in the NSYR sample employing known population characteristics on key variables from 2002 U.S. Census data. Table B.1 shows that the NSYR provides a nearly perfectly representative sample of 13- to 17-year-olds living in U.S. households by the comparable variables of gender, age, race/ethnicity, and household type. The region and household income variables also demonstrate a very close representation by NSYR data of the known national population, which is nearly entirely corrected for when weights are applied.[10]

Comparisons are also made in table B.2 between weighted NSYR data and 1999 National Household Education Survey (NHES) data, 1996 Monitoring the Future survey data, 1994 National Longitudinal Survey of Adolescent Health (Add Health) data, and 1999 Survey of Adults and Youth data on key comparable variables. Table B.2 reveals only minor differences between the NSYR and other samples on these variables. The percentage in the NSYR sample who never drink alcohol, never used marijuana, and who smoke cigarettes regularly is similar to the percentages found in the Monitoring the Future and Add Health surveys. Based on these interdataset analyses, we can say with some confidence that findings from the NSYR appear to offer a reasonably unbiased representation of the sampled population and so, particularly when region and income are weighted, might be assumed to accurately describe the population of U.S. teenagers age 13–17 and their parents living in residential households.

These between-dataset comparisons were supplemented with analyses in the NSYR dataset comparing key demographic and behavioral traits of respondents who initially cooperated (90 percent of the sample) with respondents who were initial refusals but subsequently cooperated after successful attempts at refusal

Table B.1. Demographic Characteristics Comparing Unweighted and Weighted NSYR Samples and the 2002 U.S. Census Population, Households with 13- to 17-Year-Olds in Residence, 2002–3 (Percentages)

	NSYR (Unweighted)	2002 Census	NSYR (Weighted)
Census Region			
Northeast	15	17	17
Midwest	23	22	22
South	42	37	37
West	20	24	24
Gender			
Male	50	51	50
Female	50	49	50
Age			
13	19	20	19
14	19	20	20
15	21	20	21
16	20	20	21
17	20	20	20
Teen race/ethnicity			
White/Hispanic	77	78	78
Black	17	16	16
Asian/Pacific Islander/American Indian/ mixed/other	5	7	5
Household type			
Married couple	67	68	70
Income			
Less than $10K	4	6	5
$10K–$20K	7	9	10
$20K–$30K	13	10	10
$30K–$40K	14	11	11
$40K–$50K	14	11	11
$50K–$60K	12	8	8
$60K–$70K	8	8	9
$70K–$80K	7	7	8
$80K–$90K	5	6	6
$90K–$100K	4	5	5
More than $100K	13	19	19

Note: Percentages may not add to 100 due to rounding.

conversion (10 percent of the final sample).[11] Results, displayed in table B.3, reveal that the refusal-conversion respondents in the sample disproportionately are somewhat more Midwestern (and less Southern), involve more male parent and teen respondents, involve more 15- and 16-year-old teen respondents (and fewer 13- and 14-year-old respondents), are white (and not black), represent more married parent households, represent higher-income families, and represent more regular religious service–attending parents. Most of these differences are quite modest, however, typically representing less than 10 percentage point spreads. Nevertheless, most of these differences remain statistically significant when considered together in logistic regression analyses predicting refusal-conversion versus

Table B.2. Comparison of Weighted NSYR Results with Parallel National Survey Results on Selected Lifestyle Variables, U.S. Adolescents, Ages 13–17 (Percentages, unless otherwise noted)

	NSYR (N=3,290) (2002–3)	Monitoring the Future (N=45,173) (1996)	Add Health (N=15,084) (1996)	Survey of Adults and Youth (N=874) (1999)	NHES (N=6,569) (1996)
Never drinks alcohol	63	62	61	—	—
Never uses marijuana	75	64	74	—	—
Smokes cigarettes regularly	7	9[a]	9	—	—
Nights per week eats dinner with one parent (mean)	5	—	5	5	—
School type attending					
Public	87	—	—	—	90
Private religious	7	—	—	—	7
Private secular	2	—	—	—	2
Home-schooled	2	—	—	—	2
Attends religious services weekly or more	41	33	39	45	47
Never attends religious services	18	15	14	11	13

Note: [a]=data from 2002 Monitoring the Future (N=43,700); percentages may not add to 100 due to rounding.

initial-cooperator survey respondents (results not shown). These modest differences suggest that, when conceptualizing a survey respondent continuum from easy cooperators to serious noncooperators—and differences between potential respondents who lie on that continuum—successful researcher efforts to convert initial refusals for inclusion in the final dataset increase the full representation of different types of respondents in the final sample, reducing possible sampling biases that would be found in surveys with less rigorous refusal-conversion methods. Because the NSYR successfully employed multiple, extensive, sustained measures to convert initial refusals into cooperators—who represent fully 10 percent of the final sample—it significantly reduced possible biases affecting measured variables potentially associated with respondents' propensity to cooperate with surveys, rendering its sample data more accurately representative. This assurance, together with the between-dataset analyses presented above, corroborates this methodological report's general conclusion that the NSYR provides a satisfactorily unbiased, nationally representative sample of the target population of U.S. teenagers age 13–17 living in households.

In addition to a main national sample of 3,290 cases, the NSYR conducted surveys with a modest oversample of Jewish households, 80 completes in all, to help obtain a large enough number of cases with which to conduct meaningful statistical analyses of Jewish youth. A national RDD sampling method screening out all but eligible Jewish households with teenagers would, theoretically, have been ideal, insofar as it would have provided a true probability sample yielding a genuinely nationally representative oversample of Jewish teenagers in propor-

Table B.3. Comparison of Weighted NSYR Initially Cooperating and Refusal-conversion Respondents (Percentages)

	Initial Cooperators (N=3,030)	Refusal Conversions (N=340)
Census region		
Northeast	17	17
Midwest	21	28
South	38	32
West	24	23
Male parent	18	26
Male teen	50	54
Teen age		
13	19	15
14	20	16
15	21	23
16	20	26
17	20	20
Race/ethnicity		
White/Hispanic	78	81
Black	16	13
Asian/Pacific Islander/ American Indian/ mixed/other	6	7
Household type		
Married Couple	69	77
Income		
Less than $10K	5	3
$10K–$20K	10	4
$20K–$30K	9	8
$30K–$40K	11	9
$40K–$50K	10	9
$50K–$60K	8	7
$60K–$70K	9	9
$70K–$80K	7	6
$80K–$90K	5	7
$90K–$100K	4	7
More than $100K	16	27
Parental religious service attendance		
Parent attends weekly or more	44	50
Parent never attends	15	13

Note: Percentage may not add to 100 due to rounding.

tion to their actual geographic and social locations in the United States. However, because Jewish households with resident teenagers age 13–17 represent only about 1 in every 400 U.S. households (approximately 0.25 percent of all households), this method would have been unreasonably time-consuming and cost-prohibitive. As a more efficient alternative, the NSYR employed another standard survey method for obtaining a Jewish oversample, by calling a set of telephone numbers listed with one of 200 "Jewish" surnames agreed on by the National Jewish Technical Advisory Committee and selected from White pages listings throughout the United States on a population-proportional basis. These numbers were obtained from the survey sampling firm Genysis, Inc., and screened in calling for eligible households with resident 13- to 17-year-olds. Compared to yet a third alternative oversampling method—namely, the high-density Jewish sampling frame method of RDD calling of replicates of telephone numbers within geographic areas containing defined minimum Jewish residency rates, which, by definition, samples areas with higher concentrations of Jewish inhabitants, schools, synagogues, and other Jewish institutions and produces all of the associated sampling biases—the listed Jewish surname method employed by the NSYR has the distinct advantage of sampling Jewish youth from all social and geographic locations in the country. Nevertheless, the listed surnames sample method employed is by no means a nationally representative probability sample, because it systematically excludes both Jewish households with unlisted telephone numbers and Jewish households with surnames not considered by the survey sampling firm to be "Jewish-sounding."

To estimate any possible sampling bias involved in this nonprobability oversampling method, analyses compared key characteristics of the Jewish cases drawn from the nationally representative sample to those drawn from the Jewish oversample on a variety of key demographic and religious measures. Cross-tabular comparisons of the unweighted Jewish national sample and oversample cases reveal no statistically significant differences with regard to the following variables: teen gender, age, race, religious service attendance, religious youth group participation, belief in God, importance of religious faith, type of school attending, household income, family debt or savings, family home ownership, parental marital status, parental religious service attendance, parental importance of faith, and father's education.[12] The two differently sampled groups, then, are remarkably similar along important dimensions of analysis. Therefore, it is deemed not necessary to construct or use special weights to compensate for any religious or demographic differences generated by the nonprobability oversampling method used here.

In sum, the National Survey of Youth and Religion may be taken as providing a nationally representative RDD telephone survey of 3,290 English- and Spanish-speaking teenagers living in households in all 50 U.S. states in the years 2002 and 2003, between the ages of 13 and 17, and of their parents; the survey also includes 80 oversampled Jewish households (not nationally representative), bringing the total number of completed NSYR cases to 3,370. Every effort was made in project design, instrument construction, interviewer training, and survey fielding to produce the best possible results. Multiple diagnostic analyses demonstrate that the NSYR appears to provide a reasonably unbiased representative sample of its target population and so, when weights are applied, can be taken to accurately describe the population of U.S. teenagers age 13–17 and their parents living in residential households.

Table B.4. Demographic and Religious Traits of Religious Ideal Types of U.S. Adolescents, Ages 13–17 (Percentages)

	U.S.	Religious Type			
		Devoted	Regulars	Sporadics	Disengaged
Age					
13	19	16	20	18	16
14	20	23	21	22	19
15	21	21	21	19	18
16	21	24	20	18	24
17	20	17	18	23	24
Female	49	63	46	45	40
Race					
White	66	78	67	69	80
Black	17	10	13	10	5
Hispanic	12	9	12	14	7
Other race	5	3	8	7	8
Region					
Northeast	17	10	17	22	21
Midwest	22	19	28	24	23
South	37	46	33	28	21
Mountain/Pacific	24	25	23	26	35
Parent marital status					
Married	70	81	74	70	67
Living with unmarried partner	4	4	3	6	7
Widowed	2	2	2	2	3
Divorced	13	9	12	12	16
Separated	5	2	5	3	3
Never married	6	3	5	7	4
School type attending					
Public	87	80	89	90	88
Catholic	4	1	6	4	2
Private other Christian	3	12	3	1	~
Jewish	~	~	~	~	~
Private nonreligious	2	2	1	2	3
Home-schooled	2	4	1	1	4
Other or not going to school	2	~	1	3	2
Religious type					
Conservative Protestant	30	59	30	23	6
Mainline Protestant	11	14	14	13	5
Black Protestant	11	8	10	8	1
Catholic	27	4	37	39	16
Jewish	2	~	1	5	3
Mormon	3	12	3	2	2
Other religion	5	4	5	7	3
Not religious	12	~	~	3	65

Source: National Survey of Youth and Religion, 2002–3.

Note: Percentage may not add to 100 due to rounding; cells of <1 are reported as ~.

Table B.4 shows the demographic characteristics of the four religious ideal-type categories used in the analysis of chapter 7.

Appendix C. Interviews Methodology

The second phase of the data collection of the National Study of Youth and Religion (NSYR) involved in-depth personal interviews with 267 teens. The purpose of the interviews was to provide extended follow-up discussions about teens' religious, spiritual, family, and social lives. The questionnaire followed closely and expanded on the topics that were included on the NSYR telephone survey. All interviews were conducted in person and were digitally recorded (except in three cases in which the interviews ran long and because of schedule constraints had to be completed over the phone; two other interviews were conducted over the phone in their entirety). Interviews lasted an average of two hours each and ranged from about 1.5 to 3 hours long. Teens were given a $30 cash incentive to complete the interviews. The majority of the in-person interviews were conducted between March 2003 and August 2003, with a final few completed as late as January 2004. All interview subjects were selected from among the 3,370 teens who completed the NSYR telephone survey. At the conclusion of that survey, teens were asked if we could contact them again in the future. More than 98 percent of the survey respondents agreed to be contacted again in the future.

The interviewees were selected from the telephone survey respondents using a stratified quota sample. Rather than a nationally representative sample, we wanted interviewed teens to represent a range of demographic and religious characteristics in order for us to be able to draw substantive conclusions about the variety of teen experiences in the United States. Therefore, the interview sample was drawn taking into account the following demographic characteristics: region, urban/suburban/rural, age, sex, race, household income, religion, and school type. We attempted to achieve a balance in each of these areas. We also oversampled home-schooled teens and those who attend private school because these are relatively understudied portions of the teen population, given that many surveys of teens are conducted in public school settings. The original telephone survey was conducted with teens between the age of 13 and 17. The time lapse between a teen completing the telephone survey and completing a personal interview could range from three months to more than a year. Therefore, the personal interviews included teens between the age of 13 and 18. The ages listed in table C.1 reflect the age of the teen at the time of the personal interview.

Table C.1. NSYR Personal Interview Demographics

	N		N
Gender		Region	
Male	142	West	87
Female	125	South	81
Age		Northeast	44
13	17	Midwest	55
14	53	Religion	
15	54	Protestant	131
16	54	*Adventist*	3
17	58	*Assemblies of God*	1
18	31	*Baptist*	41
Race		*Bible Church*	1
White	174	*Brethren*	1
Hispanic	39	*Christian of Just Christian*	36
Black	37	*Church of Christ*	2
Asian	8	*Church of the Nazarene*	1
Native American	3	*Congregationalist*	3
Islander	1	*Episcopalian*	1
Mixed	2	*Evangelical*	1
Other	3	*Lutheran*	8
School type		*Methodist*	14
Public	196	*Nondenominational*	6
Private	47	*Pentecostal*	3
Home-schooled	20	*Presbyterian*	9
Magnet or charter school	2	Catholic	41
Not going to school/dropped out	2	Mormon	21
Household income		Jewish	18
Less than $10K	6	Buddhist	3
$10K–$20K	15	Muslim	2
$20K–$30K	19	Jehovah's Witness	2
$30K–$40K	28	Hindu	2
$40K–$50K	41	Christian Science	1
$50K–$60K	25	Eastern Orthodox	1
$60K–$70K	32	Native American	1
$70K–$80K	19	Pagan or Wiccan	1
$80K–$90K	15	Don't know	4
$90K–$100K	13	Not religious	39
More than $100K	42	Language of interview	
Don't know	5	English	263
Refused	7	Spanish	4
		Total interviews	267

Seventeen interviewers conducted interviews in 45 states, each interviewer conducting between 10 and 20 interviews. Preliminary research and consultation with other youth scholars suggested the importance of matching interviewers and interviewees on race whenever possible. The majority of the 267 NSYR interviews conducted were matched on gender and race. All of the black teens in the sample were interviewed by black interviewers. Because of the sensitive nature of the interview questions asked of teens, prior to interview data collection, the NSYR obtained a Certificate of Confidentiality from the U.S. NICHD to protect the data from subpoena.

All 17 interviewers participated in a two-day training. The training covered the logistics of the interview process, procedural requirements, Institutional Review Board (IRB) concerns, the protection of human participants, safety and liability concerns, a review and discussion of the interview questionnaire, keys to interview success, and the proper use of the digital recording equipment. In addition to that training, all interviewers were required to obtain a Human Participants Training Certificate through the U.S. NIH Web site.

The 17 project interviewers were assigned to sets of specific geographic locations around the United States. Each interviewer was provided with groups of contact sheets for teens in their assigned geographic areas. The contact sheets included teen name, teen nickname (if known), parent name, address, phone number, date of telephone survey, teen age, teen gender, teen race, household income, school type, religious affiliation, and religious denomination or tradition. Also included was a place to note any changes to the contact information provided (new phone number, additional e-mail address, etc.) and a call record. Interviewers recorded each household contact, noting the date, time, who they talked with, and the outcome of each contact. Along with the contact sheets, interviewers received instruction sheets indicating which of the teens were considered high-priority contacts. High-priority contacts were those with characteristics that were more difficult to complete, such as minority religions, lower incomes, non-public school, and minority race. As the project progressed through the interviews, the priorities shifted somewhat according to what types of teen interviews were still needed. In this way, we filled in the cells of the quota sample.

Interviewers were also provided with a survey information sheet for each teen. This sheet contained a list of answers to selected questions from the telephone survey. It included information from the parent about family background, parent religion, family stress, and parent education and work status. It also included answers from the teen about importance of faith, moral beliefs, youth group participation, and some risk behaviors. These answers were not referred to specifically in the interviews, but were often useful in providing interviewers some background on the teens they were interviewing.

Using a standard call script provided by NSYR, interviewers made contact with potential interviewee households. Interviewers identified themselves as researchers with the "National Youth Study." The full name of the research project was not used because we did not want to introduce any bias by identifying religion as a key focus of the study. It was often helpful for interviewers to explain their connection with the project as graduate student, coinvestigator, or other. When possible, interviewers also tried to establish a personal connection to the geographic area. For example, an interviewer might have mentioned that he or she grew up or went to school in the area. This seemed to help put some people at ease and reduced the sense that interviewers were total strangers from a far-away university. However, because much of the interview was about religion and we did not want to bias the answers of the teens, interviewers were instructed to avoid divulging information about their own personal beliefs and commitments (about which there was considerable diversity on the interviewing team).

Interviewers were required to obtain verbal consent to conduct the interview from both a parent and the teen. If parents or teens seemed hesitant about participating, an additional script provided more information about the project and offered the phone number for the principal investigator, whom they could (and sometimes did) call with questions or concerns. In addition, interviewers offered to mail to hesitant respondents written information about the project and then call back in a few days. Interviewers worked hard to obtain consent from the parents. However, when teens refused to participate even after being offered additional information, interviewers made no further attempts to convert those who refused.

Upon receiving verbal consent from both parent and teen and scheduling an interview time, interviewers mailed packets of information to households. The packet contained a cover letter from the principal investigator, multiple copies of the parent and teen written consent forms, and an appointment card including a portrait photo of the interviewer. Teens were required to bring the written consent forms with them to their interviews, signed by both the teen and parent. Interviewers also called the teens at least one week prior to the interview and again the day before the interview to confirm that they were still planning to participate in the interview.

Interviews were conducted in public settings that nevertheless provided confidentiality for the teen. The ideal location for these interviews was in study rooms at local libraries. However, when these were not available, interviews were conducted in restaurants, coffee shops, mall food courts, public parks, and school cafeterias, classrooms, and libraries. Interviewers were given guidelines for how to present themselves during the interviews as well as appropriate attire to ensure consistency in the presentation of interviewers across the interviews. Specifically, interviewers did not attempt to relate to teens by dressing down or dressing in a more trendy fashion. Instead, they built rapport by presenting themselves as professional researchers with a sincere interest in teenagers' lives.

At the close of the interview, teens were given a $30 cash incentive for their participation and in appreciation of their time and effort. Interviewers also followed up interviews with hand-written thank-you notes mailed to teens. Because these interviews were with minors, a protected population, it was particularly crucial that all interviewers were aware of their responsibilities and obligations concerning the protection of interview participants and mindful of the potential safety and liability issues involved. There were three main human participant protection concerns with these interviews:

1. HANDLING SENSITIVE INFORMATION DIVULGED BY TEENS

Given the personal nature of the interviews, it was necessary to be prepared for the possibility of troubled teens revealing information about personal crises and dangers during the interviews. All interviewers were instructed about mandatory reporting and how properly to handle cases of abuse, harm to self or others, or other serious issues. In addition, all interviewers had in their possession at all times copies of a Teen Hotlines resource sheet. This sheet was prepared by NSYR staff and contained national phone numbers for a wide range of potential teen crises. It included toll-free hotlines for suicide, mental health problems, eating disorders, family violence, and other issues that might arise during interviews. Interviewers provided this resource sheet to any teen who appeared to be struggling with any of these issues, even cases that did not technically require mandatory reporting.

2. INFORMED CONSENT OF BOTH PARENT AND TEEN

Interviewers were required to obtain verbal and written informed consent from both parent and teen before conducting interviews. In the initial phone contact to set up the interview, interviewers obtained verbal consent from both parent and teen. Both were also informed that the teen would have the right to skip any question and to terminate the interview at any time for whatever reason. Prior to actually conducting interviews, interviewers had to collect written consent forms signed by both parents and teens; in cases where teens were 18 years old or older, parental written consent was not required. All teens were also reminded at the start of interviews and again in the middle of interviews that they were free to skip any question they were not comfortable answering.

3. PROTECTING CONFIDENTIALITY
A. *Protecting Confidentiality of Teens' Answers with Respect to Parents*

Some parents were interested in what the interviewers were discussing with their teens. In addition, it seemed that for some teens the presence of parents or an environment that triggered concerns about their parents could have had the effect of making them more reserved and less candid in their responses during interviews. To ensure that teens were able to speak openly and honestly, interviewers took a number of precautions. First, they made sure to be very clear with parents ahead of time that parents may not listen to the interview or be in close proximity while an interview was taking place. Often, the parents brought the teens to the interview location and planned to wait for them. In these cases, interviewers made sure that the parents were well out of earshot and out of the teen's line of vision during the interviews. In restaurants, this meant choosing a table as far away from the parents as possible; in libraries, this involved trying to conduct interviews in a separate room or on a separate floor from where parents were waiting.

B. *Protecting Confidentiality of Teens with Respect to Unknown Others*

During interviews, it was important to protect teens from having other people listening to their responses. Interviewers did their best to select locations that were confidential settings yet in public places. Interviewers also remained aware of potential eavesdroppers when locating interviews and throughout the process of interviews. Interviewers were also trained to rearrange question orderings or postpone sensitive questions if and when there were other people nearby who may overhear them.

Before and after actual interviews, interviewers followed strict procedures for handling all data and paperwork related to the interviews. The protocol was designed to prevent any of the data files from being linked to the contact information of the teen participants. Interviewers were trained to treat all documentation and audio files as confidential and to handle them so as to minimize any risk of teens having their interview responses identified by others.

In addition to concerns about the protection of human research participants, other basic safety and liability concerns related to the conduct of interviews with teens. Interviewers took steps to ensure their own safety during interviews, to not take unnecessary risks. It was also important to keep interviewers from getting into situations where they could be held responsible for harm (real or fabricated) to the teenager. Given these concerns, interviewers were provided with the following guidelines:

1. Always conduct interviews in a public place.
2. Never conduct interviews inside a teenager's home (very rare exceptions had to be arranged with the principal investigator, who talked with parents about particular situations beforehand).
3. Behave in such a way as to not invite suspicion or leave open the possibility of misinterpreted intentions or actions.
4. When unsure about a given neighborhood in which you may be traveling, research the area ahead of time to assess the safety factors.
5. Always let someone know where you are going and when you expect to return, and always give someone your cell phone or other contact number. Interviewers were asked to consider carrying a safety device to interviews (e.g., whistle, pepper spray). These were optional, but were not provided by the project.
6. There were some cases where teens needed transportation to or from an interview. Interviewers were not obligated to provide this, but were allowed to choose to provide such transportation if they were comfortable doing so.

Appendix D. Teen Religious Denominational Category Codings

We categorized NSYR teen respondents into major religious types for analysis using a procedure very similar to the RELTRAD method.[1] We assigned respondents to religious categories based on information about teen and family religion obtained from a variety of religious attendance and identity variables in the teen and parent surveys. The key variable used was the religious tradition of the congregation the teen most attends, following the coding scheme specified below. Note that teens who say they are not religious may still be categorized into one of the religious categories if they attend religious services at a congregation with an identifiable religious tradition occasionally or more often with their parents; likewise, teens who say they never attend religious services still may be categorized into one of the religious categories if they say that they nevertheless identify with some religious tradition. In 2.2 percent of all teen cases, this religion information from all relevant survey variables was insufficient to make a conclusive categorization; these teens were categorized as indeterminate.

CONSERVATIVE PROTESTANT (CP): Adventist/Seventh Day Adventist; Assemblies of God (Assembly of God); Bible Church/Bible Believing; Charismatic; Christian and Missionary Alliance; Church of Christ (Churches of Christ); Church of the Nazarene; Calvary Chapel; Evangelical; Evangelical Covenant Church; Evangelical Free Church; Four Square; Fundamentalist; Independent; Mennonite; Missionary Church; Nazarene; Vineyard Fellowship; Wesleyan Church; Baptist Missionary Association; Charismatic Baptist; Conservative Baptist Association of America; Free Will Baptist; Fundamentalist Baptist; General Association of Regular Baptists; North American Baptist Conference; Free Methodist; Wesleyan

Methodist; Evangelical Presbyterian Church; Presbyterian Church in America; Reformed Presbyterian Churches of North America; Other Presbyterian; Missouri Synod; Wisconsin Synod; Other Lutheran; Christian Reformed Church; Church of the Brethren; Grace Brethren Church; Plymouth Brethren; Other Brethren; Church of God, General Conference; Church of God of Anderson, Indiana; Church of God of Cleveland, Tennessee; Church of God of Prophecy; Just Church of God; Worldwide Church of God; Other Church of God; Don't know type of Church of God; Just Church/Churches of Christ; Other Churches of Christ; Don't know type of Church of Christ; Full Gospel; Just Pentecostal; Pentecostal Church of God; Pentecostal Holiness Church; Spanish Pentecostal; United Pentecostal Church International; Other Pentecostal; Just Christian or Just Protestant if self-identified evangelical or fundamentalist. The following denominations when respondents were white: Holiness, Interdenominational Protestant, Nondenominational, American Baptist Association, American Baptist Churches in the U.S.A., General Baptist, Independent Baptist, Just Baptist, Missionary Baptist, National Missionary Baptist Convention, Southern Baptist Convention, Other Baptist, Don't know type of Baptist, Other Methodist, Church of God International, Churches of Christ, Don't know type of Pentecostal.

MAINLINE PROTESTANT (MP): Congregationalist; Disciples of Christ; Episcopalian; Evangelical Lutheran Church in America; Just Lutheran; Don't know type of Lutheran; Moravian; Northern Baptist; Quaker or Friends; United Brethren in Christ; United Church of Christ; United Methodist Church; Just Methodist; Don't know type of Methodist; Presbyterian Churches of the U.S.A.; Just Presbyterian; Don't know type of Presbyterian; Reformed Church in America; Refused type of Lutheran; Just Christian or Just Protestant if self-identified mainline or theologically liberal Protestant; Just Christian or Just Protestant if parent is religiously liberal or very liberal and not self-identified as an evangelical or fundamentalist.

BLACK PROTESTANT (BP): African Methodist Episcopal Church; African Methodist Episcopal Zion; Christian Methodist Episcopal; National Baptist Convention, U.S.A., Inc.; National Baptist Convention of America; United Baptist; Church of God, Holiness; Church of God in Christ; Church of God in the Apostolic Faith. The following denominations when respondents were African American: Apostolic Pentecostal, Holiness, Interdenominational Protestant, Nondenominational, American Baptist Association, American Baptist Churches in the U.S.A., General Baptist, Independent Baptist, Just Baptist, Missionary Baptist, National Missionary Baptist Convention, Southern Baptist Convention, Other Baptist, Don't know type of Baptist, Just Methodist, Other Methodist, Don't know type of Methodist, Church of God International, Churches of Christ, Don't know type of Pentecostal.

CATHOLIC (RC): Catholic.

JEWISH (J): Jewish.

MORMON (LDS): Mormon, Church of Jesus Christ of Latter-day Saints.

OTHER RELIGION (OR): Association of Unity; Buddhist; Christian Science; Hindu; Jehovah's Witness; Native American; Unitarian-Universalist; Unity Church; Wiccan.

NOT RELIGIOUS (NR): No religious affiliation named.

Notes

INTRODUCTION

1. One major 1995 Carnegie Council report on adolescents, *Great Transitions: Preparing Adolescents for a New Century* (New York: Carnegie Council on Adolescent Development), for instance, only sporadically alludes to religious organizations as one among many kinds of community institutions that may help youth. Otherwise, religion in this report is invisible. S. Shirley Feldman and Glenn Elliott's important 1990 overview of adolescent life, *At the Threshold: The Developing Adolescent* (Cambridge, MA: Harvard University Press), mentions religious influences a mere three times in its 642 pages, one of which is a reference to life in the seventeenth and eighteenth centuries. Similarly, in Jeylan Mortimer and Reed Larson's 2002 survey, *The Changing Adolescent Experience: Societal Trends and the Transition to Adulthood* (Cambridge, UK: Cambridge University Press), the word "religion" is found on one page, and that in reference to a survey of *adult* uses of the Internet. One also searches in vain many special issues of professional journals on adolescence for any significant discussions of the role of religion in youth's lives. See, for example, "The Mass Media and Adolescent Health," *Journal of Adolescent Health* 27 (2000); "Adolescents' Preparation for the Future: Perils and Promises," *Journal of Research on Adolescence* 12 (2002). Also see Carnegie Council on Adolescent Development, *Turning Points: Preparing American Youth for the 21st Century* (New York: Carnegie Corporation of New York, 1989). There does exist an extensive body of literature about teenage religion that is journalistic and impressionistic (for example, Tom Beaudoin, *Virtual Faith: The Irreverent Spiritual Quest of Generation X* (San Francisco: Jossey-Bass, 1998); Jon Sweeney, ed., *God Within: Our Spiritual Future—As Told by Today's New Adults* (Woodstock, VT: Skylight Paths, 2001); Kristoffer Cox, *GenX*

and God: A GenX Perspective (Kearney, NE: Teckna Books, 1998); Patricia Davis, *Beyond Nice: The Spiritual Wisdom of Adolescent Girls* (Minneapolis: Fortress Press, 2001); David Lewis, Carley Dodd, and Darryl Tippens, *The Gospel According to Generation X* (Abilene, TX: Abilene Christian University Press, 1995); William Mahedy and Janet Bernardi, *A Generation Alone: Xers Making a Place in the World* (Downers Grove, IL: InterVarsity Press, 1994); Dawson McAllister, *Saving the Millennial Generation* (Nashville: Thomas Nelson, 1999); Steve Rabey, *In Search of Authentic Faith: How Emerging Generations Are Transforming the Church* (Colorado Springs: Waterbrook Press, 2001); Wendy Zoba, *Generation 2K: What Parents Need to Know about the Millennials* (Downers Grove, IL: InterVarsity Press, 1999). But little of it provides reliable social scientific knowledge. There also exists a handful of interesting sociological ethnographies of teenage religion. See Richard Flory and Donald Miller, eds., *GenX Religion* (New York: Routledge, 2000); Lynn Schofield Clark, *From Angels to Aliens: Teenagers, the Media, and the Supernatural* (Oxford: Oxford University Press, 2003); Carol Lytch, *Choosing Church* (Louisville: Westminster John Knox Press, 2004); William Myers, *Black and White Styles of Youth Ministry: Two Congregations in America* (New York: Pilgrim Press, 1991). But, as valuable as these are, it is impossible to say exactly who their findings can be generalized as representing. So we continue to lack reliable, nationally representative knowledge about and understanding of the religious and spiritual lives of American youth.

2. See, for example, Diana Eck, *A New Religious America: How a "Christian Country" Has Become the World's Most Religiously Diverse Nation* (New York: HarperCollins, 2001).

3. See, for example, Wade Clark Roof, *Spiritual Marketplace: Baby Boomers and the Remaking of American Religion* (Princeton: Princeton University Press, 1999); Wade Clark Roof, *A Generation of Seekers: The Spiritual Journeys of the Baby Boom Generation* (New York: HarperCollins, 1993); James Davison Hunter, *Evangelicalism: The Coming Generation* (Chicago: University of Chicago Press, 1987); Jeffrey Arnett and Lene Jensen, "A Congregation of One: Individualized Religious Beliefs among Emerging Adults," *Journal of Adolescent Research* 17, no. 5 (2002): 451–467; George Barna, *Generation Next: What You Need to Know about Today's Youth* (Ventura, CA: Regal Books, 1995); also see Alan Wolfe, *Moral Freedom: The Search for Virtue in a World of Choice* (New York: Norton, 2001).

4. Tom Beaudoin, *Virtual Faith: The Irreverent Spiritual Quest of Generation X* (San Francisco: Jossey-Bass, 1998); Steve Rabey, *In Search of Authentic Faith: How Emerging Generations Are Transforming the Church* (Colorado Springs: Waterbrook Press, 2001); George Barna, *Baby Busters: The Disillusioned Generation* (Chicago: Northfield, 1994).

5. Robert Fuller, *Spiritual but Not Religious* (New York: Oxford University Press, 2001); Robert Wuthnow, *After Heaven: Spirituality in America Since the 1950s* (Berkeley: University of California Press, 1998); Conrad Cherry, Betty DeBerg, and Amanda Porterfield, *Religion on Campus: What Religion Really Means to Today's Undergraduates* (Chapel Hill: University of North Carolina Press, 2001); Paul Heelas, Linda Woodhead, Benjamin Seel, Bronislaw Szerszynski, and Karin Tusting, *The Spiritual Revolution: Why Religion Is Giving Way to Spirituality* (Malden, MA: Blackwell, 2004); Bruce Greer and Wade Clark Roof, " 'Desperately Seeking Sheila': Locating Religious Privatism in American Society," *Journal for the Scientific Study of Religion* 31, no. 3 (1992): 346–352; also see Lynn Schofield Clark, *From Angels to Aliens: Teenagers, the Media, and the Supernatural* (New York: Oxford University Press, 2003).

6. This is the distinct impression conveyed, for example, in Patricia Hersch, *A Tribe Apart: A Journey into the Heart of American Adolescence* (New York: Ballantine Books, 1998); also see Charles Kadushin, Shaul Kelner, and Leonard Saxe, "Being a Jewish Teenager in America: Trying to Make It," research report, Cohen Center for Modern Jewish Studies, Brandeis University, 2000.

7. Colleen Carroll, *The New Faithful: Why Young Adults Are Embracing Christian Orthodoxy* (Chicago: Loyola Press, 2002).

8. Richard Flory and Donald Miller, eds., *GenX Religion* (New York: Routledge, 2000).

9. See, for example, Jimmy Long, *Generating Hope: A Strategy for Reaching the Postmodern Generation* (Downers Grove, IL: InterVarsity Press, 1997); Tony Jones, *Postmodern Youth Ministry* (Grand Rapids, MI: Zondervan, 2001).

10. See, for example, Dean Hoge, William Dinges, Mary Johnson, and Juan Gonzales, *Young Adult Catholics: Religion in the Culture of Choice* (Notre Dame, IN: University of Notre Dame Press, 2001).

11. See, for example, Peter Zollow, *Getting Wiser to Teens: More Insights into Marketing to Teenagers* (Ithaca, NY: New Strategist Publications, 2004); Alissa Quart, *Branded: The Buying and Selling of Teenagers* (New York: Perseus, 2003).

12. Specifically, as of the time of this writing, Dr. John Bartkowski of Mississippi State University is writing a book on U.S. Mormon teenagers; Dr. Philip Schwadel, an NSYR postdoctoral research fellow, is writing a book on U.S. Jewish teenagers; the NSYR is publishing a report on large Protestant denominations, *Portraits of Protestant Teens: A Report on Teenagers in Major U.S. Denominations*; and Dr. Mark Regnerus of the University of Texas at Austin is writing a book on adolescent religion and youth life outcomes.

CHAPTER 1

1. Both of the interview subjects described here are real, specific teens that I (Smith) interviewed. Some of the personal information about the interview respondents described here and in other chapters, including names and states, has been changed to protect the confidentiality of their identities. Furthermore, many of the interview quotes throughout the book have been streamlined or edited for readability and clarity, though always to reflect the apparent intended meaning of the original quotations.

2. Five recent books in agreement with this observation are Terri Apter, *The Myth of Maturity: What Teenagers Need from Parents to Become Adults* (New York: Norton, 2001); Robert Shaw, *The Epidemic: The Rot of American Culture, Absentee and Permissive Parenting, and the Resultant Plague of Joyless, Selfish Children* (New York: HarperCollins, 2003); Kay S. Hymowitz, *Ready or Not: What Happens When We Treat Children as Small Adults* (San Francisco: Encounter Books, 2000); Kay S. Hymowitz, *Liberation's Children: Parents and Kids in a Postmodern Age* (Chicago: Ivan R. Dee, 2003); David Elkind, *All Grown Up and No Place to Go* (Cambridge, MA: Perseus Press, 1998). Also see Institute for American Values, *Hardwired to Connect: A New Scientific Case for Authoritative Communities. A Report to the Nation from the Commission on Children at Risk* (New York: Institute for American Values, 2003).

CHAPTER 2

1. In trying to make sense of the findings of this book, it is essential that readers be aware of the qualifications and limitations of our research data and therefore of

the conclusions we can draw from them. The findings of our telephone survey, for example, represent only teenage households with telephones, not the few percent of definitely poorer and more transient families who do not have household telephones. Our survey findings also represent only teen households where one parent and the eligible teen speak either English or Spanish; those families who speak other languages exclusively are omitted from our sample. Furthermore, survey questions themselves involve some amount of inevitable superficiality and misrepresentation. Forced-choice survey questions written to be useful for an entire population of respondents are limited, for example, in their ability to measure the ambivalences, contradictions, and complexities of people's beliefs, experiences, and feelings. To better get at these, we employed personal, in-depth, face-to-face interviews with a sample of teenage survey respondents. Yet even the most honest and in-depth interviews have limits in their ability to comprehend and represent a person's life in its fullness. An ideal research project would also bring in significant linked elements of ethnographic participant observation, but this was beyond the scope of our project. Some of the limitations inherent in our research methods and subject matter we cannot fully assess. For instance, it may be that some teen interview respondents refrained from fully elaborating on their religious and spiritual beliefs and experiences because they viewed us as academic researchers from a secular state university and felt the need to be circumspect or polite in company whose religious commitments they did not know. We can know none of this with certainty precisely because of the very limitations intrinsic to such academic social research. Readers must recognize, therefore, the bounded value of our findings, which we think are rich and informative but know are not flawless, exhaustive, or absolutely definitive. More research using alternative methods from different perspectives is needed to move us closer to an even more complete understanding of the issue at hand.

2. Diana Eck, *A New Religious America: How a "Christian Country" Has Become the World's Most Religiously Diverse Nation* (New York: HarperCollins, 2001).

3. It is possible that we slightly undersampled certain Asian minority religions by not offering our survey in various Asian languages, but, given the relatively minuscule size of only-Asian-language-speaking minority religion U.S. residents, the marginal differences here are extremely slight.

4. Many Latter-day Saints consider themselves Christians. But for purposes of clear analytical distinctions, in this book we refer to Catholic and Protestant groups as Christian and Mormons distinctly as Mormons.

5. We do not disaggregate all of the many specific denominations under the Baptist, Methodist, and Lutheran umbrellas. Statistics on many specific major U.S. denominations, however, can be found in the 2005 NSYR-published report, *Portraits of Protestant Teens: A Report on Teenagers in Major U.S. Denominations*, by Phil Schwadel and Christian Smith (Chapel Hill, NC: National Study of Youth and Religion). See www.youthandreligion.org for more information.

6. For teens, "not religious" is a self-identity measure, but for parents is an affiliation measure equivalent to "not religiously affiliated."

7. We recognize that there is no generic way of asking this question that works equally well across all religious traditions; some, for instance, use the phrase "born again," others clearly do not. "Personally committed to live life for God" is the most general phrasing we could devise. Interpretations of the particular numbers on this question must be especially cautious.

8. See, for example, Dorothy Bass, ed., *Practicing Our Faith: A Way of Life for a Searching People* (San Francisco: Jossey-Bass, 1997); Dorothy Bass and Don Rich-

ter, eds., *Way to Live: Christian Practices for Teens* (Nashville: Upper Room Books, 2002). Also see Craig Dykstra, *Vision and Character* (New York: Paulist Press, 1981).

9. Note that we cannot assume these teens are definitely attending Catholic churches; most but not all are.

10. But also see Charles Kadushin, Shaul Kelner, and Leonard Saxe, *Being a Jewish Teenager in America: Trying to Make It* (Waltham, MA: Cohen Center for Modern Jewish Studies, Brandeis University, 2000).

The NSYR also sampled 12 Muslim parents of U.S. teenagers, 14 first-religion U.S. Muslim teenagers, and one second-religion Muslim teen (whose first religion is Christian). Nine of the 12 Muslim parents' teenagers (75 percent) were also Muslim, two were not religious, and one was Protestant. Nine of the 15 Muslim teens' parents were Muslim, three were Christian, one did not know, and one parent refused to answer the religion question. Table N.1 reports on certain Islamic religious practices for our sampled Muslim teens or teens with a Muslim parent. The sample size, 18, is too small to place much significance on these findings, but lacking another good national sample of U.S. Muslim adolescents, this small national sample might serve as a starting point for reflection and future studies. According to table N.1, 50 percent of this Muslim parent and Muslim teen sample fasts during Ramadan, but only 5 percent regularly attend Friday prayers at mosque. Smaller minorities (17 and 11 percent, respectively) offer Muslim prayers five times a day and give alms to the poor. Three percent of this sample have already made a pilgrimage to Mecca, 65 percent plan to make such a pilgrimage, and 24 percent do not plan to. Finally, 48 percent of this sample report that their religious faith is very or extremely important in their daily lives. When the sample is narrowed down to the 14 sampled U.S. Muslim teens (i.e., excluding the four non-Muslim teens with Muslim parents), most of these numbers increase, suggesting, unsurprisingly, that actual Muslim teens are more serious about Muslim practices than non-Muslim teens with a Muslim parent. To the extent that we can rely on these small samples to tell us anything suggestive about U.S. Muslim teenagers and teens with Muslim parents, we might observe that a minority of these teens appear to practice their Islamic faith in a serious manner, by regularly fasting, praying, attending mosque, and giving alms to the poor. These serious adolescent Muslims are by no means a minuscule proportion among their Muslim peers, but neither are they the large majority. Any more definitive findings about Muslim youth in the United States beyond these tentative observations will require a focused study dedicated to that particular religious and age population. Our findings can serve only as suggestive possibilities.

Twelve parents in the NSYR sample identified themselves as Buddhists. Of their 12 teens, only three also consider themselves Buddhist; seven reported that they are not religious and two said they are Protestant. To the extent that we can trust this small sample, the most likely apparent outcome for teenage children of Buddhist parents in the United States appears to be becoming nonreligious. Thus, although these numbers are very small and must be interpreted with great caution, unless there is a systematic sampling bias influencing our cases, these results do not suggest that Buddhist parents in the United States are transmitting their religious identities to their teenage children at high rates. Eight teens identified Buddhism as their first religion, two as their second religion, and one as a third religion. Of the eight teenagers who claimed Buddhism as their first religion, three had a Buddhist parent, two had parents who are Episcopalian, and one each had a Catholic, Lutheran, and nonreligious parent. Of the two teens who claimed Buddhism as their second religion, both said their

Table N.1. Religious Faith and Practices of U.S. Muslim and Buddhist Adolescents, Ages 13–17 (Percentages)

	All	Muslim Teen (N=14)
Muslim Practices (N=18)		
Practices Sawm (fasting during Ramadan) usually or always	50	57
Attends Friday prayers at mosque usually or always	5	7
Practices Salat (prayers five times a day) usually or always	17	22
Practices Zakat (giving alms to the poor) usually or always	11	14
Pilgrimage to Mecca:		
Has made pilgrimage to Mecca	3	4
Plans to make pilgrimage to Mecca	65	70
Does not plan to make pilgrimage to Mecca	24	26
Refused	7	—
Religious faith is very or extremely important	48	51
Buddhist Faith and Practices (N=10)		
Attends religious services 2–3 times a month or more often (Buddhism first or second teen religion)	30	
Prays once a week or more (Buddhism first or second teen religion	31	
Religious faith is very or extremely important (Buddhism first or second teen religion)	8	
Have religious altars in homes (includes non-Buddhist teens with Buddhist parents, N=23)	25	

Source: National Survey of Youth and Religion, 2002–3.

Note: Low Ns for Muslim and Buddhist teens require circumspection in interpreting percentages, and for Buddhist teens prevent subset comparisons.

first religion was Christian. The one teen who said that Buddhism was a third religion was by first and second religion Catholic and Jewish, respectively. Thus, of the 11 teens who associated themselves with Buddhism, three appear to come from Buddhist families, seven from Christian families, and one has a nonreligious parent. Putting all this together, we might observe that Buddhism in families of teenagers in the United States appears to be a somewhat transitory religious identity, in that most teens of Buddhist parents have not become Buddhist themselves and most parents of teens who report themselves as Buddhist are not Buddhist. U.S. teens seem to move in and out of Buddhism from and to one or another religious tradition or to being not religious.

But what of the U.S. teens who do identify as Buddhist? Can we say anything about the shape of their religious faith? Only 10 NSYR teenagers identified Buddhism as their first or second religion, hardly enough to say anything reliable. Still, in the absence of any other good sample of U.S. adolescent Buddhists, some readers may be interested in what a national sample of even only 10 tells us. According to the findings presented in table N.1, about three out of ten U.S. teenage Buddhists attend some kind of religious services two to three times a month or more often and pray alone once a week or more. Fewer than one out of ten, however, report that their religious faith is very or extremely important in their daily lives. Finally, expanding to all Buddhist teens and teens with Buddhist parents, one in four have religious altars in their homes (only about one in ten of the first and second religion Buddhists have altars in their homes). In short, to the extent that we may draw any tentative ideas from these small samples, we might observe that only a minority of the small number of teenage Buddhists in the United States practice their faith through regular prayer and temple visits; far fewer report that faith is very important in their lives or have religious altars in their homes. It could very well be that Buddhism in the lives of its U.S. adolescent adherents plays a less significant role than the faith of other kinds of U.S. religious teenagers. But, again, only a dedicated and focused study of U.S. teenage Buddhists can verify any of these tentative observations based on the NSYR's small Buddhist sample.

The NSYR sampled only five parents who considered themselves Hindus, of whom three had teenagers who also considered themselves Hindu and two who considered themselves not religious. These numbers were too small to report in a table. However, we note a few observations about this handful of cases. Our survey asked those five teens whether they regularly observe traditional Hindu cleansing rituals before prayer or not. All five said no. Of the three teens identifying as Hindu, one each said their religious faith was extremely important, very important, and somewhat important. Of the three teens identifying as Hindu, one reported attending religious services once a week and two reported attending a few times a year. And of the same three teens, one reported praying alone about once a day, one a few times a week, and one teen one or two times a month. It is clearly impossible to represent all Hindu teens in the United States with five sampled teenagers who are Hindu or have Hindu parents. However, observers prepared to venture onto methodologically very thin ice—rather than to forswear any observations about Hindus at all—might observe that our available unreliable and inconclusive evidence does not clearly suggest that teens of Hindu parents in the United States are obviously carrying on the practices of the Hindu faith with great consistency. The evidence is hardly conclusive, but it does not suggest great religious dedication among U.S. teenagers from Hindu families. Again, a dedicated study of U.S. Hindu teens is called for.

11. This confirms what a significant body of research literature on religious retention has shown. See, for instance, Scott Myers, "An Interactive Model of Religiosity Inheritance: The Importance of Family Context," *American Sociological Review* 61 (October 1996): 858–866; Dianne Kieren and Brenda Munro, "Following the Leaders: Parents' Influence on Adolescent Religious Activity," *Journal for the Scientific Study of Religion* 26, no. 2 (1987): 249–255; Hart Nelson, "Religious Transmission versus Religious Formation: Preadolescent-Parent Interaction," *Sociological Quarterly* 21 (spring 1980): 207–218; Elizabeth Weiss Ozorak, "Social and Cognitive Influences on the Development of Religious Beliefs and Commitment in Adolescence," *Journal for the Scientific Study of Religion* 28, no. 4 (1989): 448–463; Gerald Stott, "Familial Influence on Religious Involvement," *The Religion and Family Connection: Social Science Perspectives* 3 (1988): 258–271. For a larger review and analysis, see Christian Smith and David Sikkink, "Social Predictors of Retention in and Switching from the Religious Faith of Family of Origin," *Review of Religious Research* 45, no. 2 (2003): 188–206.

12. The differences for Jewish teens are a mathematical outcome of minority status largely surrounded by teens of other faiths, although the Mormon teens appear to have surmounted that situation, perhaps through high geographic concentrations of Mormons in Utah and high in-group solidarity among Mormon communities elsewhere.

13. Note the very low numbers in this cell, however, which must be interpreted with circumspection: only two Jewish teens did not have adults in their congregations to relate to, and both of them (100 percent) reported wanting to have such relationships.

14. See, for instance, Christian Smith, with Michael Emerson, Sally Gallagher, Paul

Kennedy, and David Sikkink, *American Evangelicalism: Embattled and Thriving* (Chicago: University of Chicago Press, 1998); Rodney Stark and Roger Finke, *Acts of Faith: Explaining the Human Side of Religion* (Berkeley: University of California Press, 2000).

CHAPTER 3

1. See, for example, Robert Fuller, *Spiritual but Not Religious* (New York: Oxford University Press, 2001); Wade Clark Roof, *Spiritual Marketplace: Baby Boomers and the Remaking of American Religion* (Princeton: Princeton University Press, 1999); Robert Wuthnow, *After Heaven: Spirituality in America Since the 1950s* (Berkeley: University of California Press, 1998); Conrad Cherry, Betty DeBerg, and Amanda Porterfield, *Religion on Campus: What Religion Really Means to Today's Undergraduates* (Chapel Hill: University of North Carolina Press, 2001); Jeffrey Arnett and Lene Jensen, "A Congregation of One: Individualized Religious Beliefs among Emerging Adults," *Journal of Adolescent Research* 17, no. 5 (2002): 451–467; Paul Heelas, Linda Woodhead, Benjamin Seel, Bronislaw Szerszynski, and Karin Tusting, *The Spiritual Revolution: Why Religion Is Giving Way to Spirituality* (Malden, MA: Blackwell, 2004); Bruce Greer and Wade Clark Roof, " 'Desperately Seeking Sheila': Locating Religious Privatism in American Society," *Journal for the Scientific Study of Religion* 31, no. 3 (1992): 346–352; Phillip E. Hammond, *Religion and Personal Autonomy: The Third Disestablishment in America* (Columbia: University of South Carolina Press, 1992); Amanda Porterfield, *The Transformation of American Religion: The Story of a Late Twentieth-Century Awakening* (New York: Oxford University Press, 2001); Phyllis A. Tickle, *Re-Discovering the Sacred: Spirituality in America* (New York: Crossroad, 1995); also see Penny Long Marler and C. Kirk Hadaway, " 'Being Religious' or 'Being Spiritual' in America: A Zero-Sum Proposition?" *Journal for the Scientific Study of Religion* 41 (2002): 289–300; Kelly Besecke, "Speaking of Meaning in Modernity: Reflexive Spirituality as a Cultural Resource," *Sociology of Religion* 62 (2001): 365.

2. Wade Clark Roof, *A Generation of Seekers: The Spiritual Journeys of the Baby Boom Generation* (New York: HarperCollins, 1993).

3. Conrad Cherry, Betty DeBerg, and Amanda Porterfield, *Religion on Campus: What Religion Really Means to Today's Undergraduates* (Chapel Hill: University of North Carolina Press, 2001); Jeffrey Arnett and Lene Jensen, "A Congregation of One: Individualized Religious Beliefs among Emerging Adults," *Journal of Adolescent Research* 17, no. 5 (2002): 451–467; Mark Healy, *Spiritualized: A Look inside the Teenage Soul* (New York: Alloy Books, 2000).

4. Throughout this book, we rely heavily on the language of religious "traditions," which we mean in the sense defined by Alasdair MacIntyre in *After Virtue* (Notre Dame, IN: University of Notre Dame Press, 1984) and *Three Rival Versions of Moral Enquiry: Encylopaedia, Genealogy, and Tradition* (Notre Dame, IN: University of Notre Dame Press, 1990), or more simply as suggested by Jaroslav Pelikan's phrase, "Tradition is the living faith of the dead, [as opposed to] traditionalism [which] is the dead faith of the living." *The Vindication of Tradition* (New Haven: Yale University Press, 1984), p. 65. In this we take an inescapably normative position which, the reader will see, informs this book's interpretations, particularly its criticisms of religious individualism and inarticulacy.

5. Nathan Hatch, *The Democratization of American Christianity* (New Haven: Yale University Press, 1991).

6. Fritz Ridenour, *How to Be a Christian without Being Religious* (Ventura, CA: Regal Books, 2002).

7. Ordered logit regression analyses separating the three answer categories produce almost identical results. Regression models included the following variables: teen age, gender, race, religious tradition, attendance, desired attendance, importance of faith, religious ties to friends, parental religiosity, teen participation in organized activities, quality of teen relationship with parents, degree of autonomy parent grants teen, parental education, parental marital status, family income, family debt, number of teen siblings, residential regional location, urban-suburban-rural residence, and parent political orientation.

8. For a complement to the analysis below, see Carol Lytch, *Choosing Church: What Makes a Difference for Teens* (Louisville, KY: Westminster John Knox Press, 2004). Also see Merton Strommen and Richard Hardel, *Passing on the Faith* (Winona, MN: Saint Mary's Press, 2000). For a history of religious youth groups, see Jon Pahl, *Youth Ministry in Modern America: 1930 to the Present* (Peabody, MA: Hendrickson, 2000).

9. The results show a negative association between black Protestant denominations and youth group participation, net of the general black race effect. See chapter 2, n. 12.

10. Many otherwise religiously serious black teenagers were probably screened out of this highly devoted group by black youth's relatively lower participation in religious youth groups.

11. Only the category of divorced parents was statistically significant among the parent marital status variables, largely because of the low size of the other nonmarried parent types; but all nonmarried parents (with the exception of widowed) were quite negatively associated, even if not always significantly, with teen religious devotion, compared to married parents.

CHAPTER 4

1. Anna Freud, "Adolescence," in *Psychoanalytic Study of the Child*, vol. 13 (New York: International Universities Press, 1958), p. 275; also see G. Stanley Hall, *Adolescence* (New York: Appleton, 1904); Peter Blos, *On Adolescence: A Psychoanalytic Interpretation* (New York: Free Press, 1962). A number of recent popular books on youth reflect the same sampling bias, such that their subjects are hardly representative of the average or typical youth. For example, see Mary Pipher, *Reviving Ophelia: Saving the Selves of Adolescent Girls* (New York: Ballantine Books, 1994); William Pollack, *Real Boys: Rescuing Our Sons from the Myths of Boyhood* (New York: Henry Holt, 1998); Daniel Kindlon and Michael Thompson, *Raising Cain: Protecting the Emotional Life of Boys* (New York: Ballantine Books, 2000).

2. This standard account of contemporary youth religion has roots going back at least to concerns in the 1960s and 1970s about how the generation gap was undermining the religion of youth. See, for instance, C. Ellis Nelson, "Symposium on Our Divided Society, a Challenge to Religious Education: Can Protestantism Make It with the 'Now' Generation?," *Religious Education* 64 (1969): 376–383; James Kimball, "A Generation Apart: The Gap and the Church," *Dialogue* 5 (1970): 35–39.

3. See, for example, Elinor Burkett, *Another Planet: A Year in the Life of a Suburban High School* (New York: HarperCollins, 2001); Marcel Danesi, *My Son Is an Alien: A Cultural Portrait of Today's Youth* (Lanham, MD: Rowman and Littlefield, 2003); Donna Gaines, *Teenage Wasteland: Suburbia's Dead End Kids* (Chicago: Uni-

versity of Chicago Press, 1990); Ron Powers, "The Apocalypse of Adolescence," *Atlantic Monthly* 289, no. 3 (March 2002): 58–74; Newton Minow, *Abandoned in the Wasteland* (New York: Hill and Wang, 1995); Alexandra Parsons and Iain Parsons, *Making It from 12 to 20: How to Survive Your Teens* (London: Judy Piatkus, 1991); James Gardner, *The Turbulent Teens: Understanding, Helping, Surviving* (Carson, CA: Jalmar Press, 1993); Cheryl Dellasega, *Surviving Ophelia: Mothers Share Their Wisdom in Navigating the Tumultuous Teenage Years* (New York: Perseus Books, 2001).

4. Hence the felt need for the book by Sabrina Solin Weil, *We're Not Monsters: Teens Speak Out about Teens in Trouble* (New York: HarperCollins, 2002). See also Ron Powers, "The Apocalypse of Adolescence," *Atlantic Monthly* 289, no. 3 (March 2002): 58–74; Cliff Linedecker, *Killer Kids* (New York: St. Martin's Press, 1993); Charles Ewing, *Kids Who Kill* (New York: Avon, 1992).

5. In recent decades, many more solid studies of nonclinical adolescent populations have cast doubt on the storm and stress stereotype, emphasizing instead the diversity of adolescents' experiences, the lack of inevitability in any youth outcome, and the relative low levels of intense turmoil in teenagers' lives. See, for example, S. I. Powers, Stuart Hauser, and L. A. Kilner, "Adolescent Mental Health," *American Psychologist* 44 (1989): 200–208; M. P. Rutter, P. Graham, O. Chadwick, and W. Yule, "Adolescent Turmoil: Fact or Fiction?," *Journal of Child Psychology and Psychiatry* 17 (1976): 35–56. According to Stuart Hauser and Mary Kay Bowlds, only about 10 to 20 percent of adolescents manifest severe emotional disturbance, approximately the same percentage as in the adult population. "Stress, Coping, and Adaptation," in S. Shirley Feldman and Glen Elliott, eds., *At the Threshold: The Developing Adolescent* (Cambridge, MA: Harvard University Press, 1990). Laurence Steinberg writes that only between 5 and 10 percent of families experience dramatic decline in the quality of parent-child relationships during the teenage years. "Autonomy, Conflict, and Harmony in the Family Relationship," in S. Shirley Feldman and Glen Elliott, eds., *At the Threshold: The Developing Adolescent* (Cambridge, MA: Harvard University Press, 1990), p. 260. A scholarly consensus has emerged, therefore, that most American youth and their families do not experience adolescence as an unavoidably distressing period of intense psychosocial turmoil. Adolescence does involve major changes for youth and their families, but most negotiate these changes fairly successfully. Sustained teenage rebellion against, conflict with, and alienation from parents and traditional social institutions are not only not inevitable, they are not the adolescent norm.

6. See, for instance, Steve Rabey, *In Search of Authentic Faith: How Emerging Generations Are Transforming the Church* (Colorado Springs: Waterbrook Press, 2001); Tom Beaudoin, *Virtual Faith: The Irreverent Spiritual Quest of Generation X* (San Francisco: Jossey-Bass, 2000); William Mahedy and Janet Bernardi, *A Generation Alone: Xers Making a Place in the World* (Downers Grove, IL: InterVarsity Press, 1994); George Barna, *Baby Busters: The Disillusioned Generation* (Chicago: Northfield, 1994); Tony Jones, *Postmodern Youth Ministry* (Grand Rapids, MI: Zondervan, 2001); Jimmy Long, *Generating Hope: A Strategy for Reaching the Postmodern Generation* (Downers Grove, IL: InterVarsity Press, 1997).

7. Pierre Bourdieu, *Outline of a Theory of Praxis* (Cambridge, UK: Cambridge University Press, 1997).

8. Thanks to Kenda Dean for first putting this point to us in these terms.

9. Many observers, in our view, unhelpfully confuse a belief that one religion is true and others are less true or untrue with intolerance per se. It is possible to be a

religious particularist theologically and remain behaviorally very tolerant of differences, just as it is possible to be a religious pluralist or relativist and relate quite intolerantly toward those who disagree. For elaboration regarding conservative Protestants, see Christian Smith, *Christian America? What Evangelicals Really Want* (Berkeley: University of California Press, 2000).

10. Nicholas Townsend, *The Package Deal: Marriage, Work, and Fatherhood in Men's Lives* (Philadelphia: Temple University Press, 2002), pp. 66–67.

11. Despite all of this, see Robert Lane, *The Loss of Happiness in Market Democracies* (New Haven: Yale University Press, 2000).

12. In David Brooks, *Bobos in Paradise* (New York: Simon and Schuster, 2000). For example, Brooks writes, "Bobos are uncomfortable with universal moral laws that purport to regulate pleasure. Bobos prefer more prosaic self-control regimes. The things that are forbidden are unhealthy and unsafe. The things that are encouraged are enriching and calorie burning. In other words, [they] regulate [their] carnal desires with health codes instead of moral codes" (p. 216).

13. See, for a somewhat related analysis, Douglas Porpora, *Landscapes of the Soul: The Loss of Moral Meaning in American Life* (New York: Oxford University Press, 2001).

14. For a larger theoretical framework, see Glen H. Elder, "The Life Course and Human Development," in Richard M. Lerner, ed., *Handbook of Child Psychology, Volume 1: Theoretical Models of Human Development* (New York: Wiley, 2000), pp. 939–991; G. O. Hagestad and B. L. Neugarten, "Age and the Life Course," in Robert Binstock and Ethel Shanas, eds., *Handbook of Aging and the Social Sciences* (New York: Van Nostrand Reinhold, 1985), pp. 46–61; Linda George, "Sociological Perspectives on Life Transitions," *Annual Review of Sociology* 19 (1993): 353–373. For an interesting comparative case study of cultural scripts informing the role of the self in adolescent education, see Gerald Letendre, *Learning to Be Adolescent: Growing Up in U.S. and Japanese Middle Schools* (New Haven: Yale University Press, 2000).

15. There is a strong connection between this vision of morality and the "emotivism" described by Alasdair MacIntyre in his 1982 book, *After Virtue* (Notre Dame, IN: University of Notre Dame Press). Note, too, the parallels with Nancy Ammerman's "Golden Rule Christianity" (in David Hall, ed., *Lived Religion in America* [Princeton: Princeton University Press, 1997], pp. 196–216).

16. For more on the therapeutic in culture, see James Nolan, *The Therapeutic State: Justifying Government at Century's End* (New York: New York University Press, 1998); Philip Rieff, *The Triumph of the Therapeutic* (Chicago: University of Chicago Press, 1966); Christopher Lasch, *The Culture of Narcissism* (New York: Warner Books, 1979); James Hunter, *The Death of Character: Moral Education in an Age without Good or Evil* (New York: Basic Books, 2000); Joel Shuman and Keith Meador, *Heal Thyself: Spirituality, Medicine, and the Distortion of Christianity* (Oxford: Oxford University Press, 2003); Andrew Polsky, *The Rise of the Therapeutic State* (Princeton: Princeton University Press, 1991); John S. Rice, *A Disease of One's Own: Psychotherapy, Addiction, and the Emergence of Co-Dependency* (New Brunswick, NJ: Transaction Publishers, 1996); Ronald Dworkin, *The Rise of the Imperial Self* (Lanham, MD: Rowman and Littlefield, 1996); Robert Bellah et al., *Habits of the Heart* (Berkeley: University of California Press, 1985); Daniel Bell, *The Cultural Contradictions of Capitalism* (New York: Basic Books, 1976); Daniel Yankelovich, *New Rules: Searching for Self-Fulfillment in a World Turned Upside Down* (New York: Bantam Books, 1981); James Nolan, *Reinventing Justice: The American Drug Court Movement* (Princeton: Princeton University Press, 2003).

17. Four other Jewish teenagers mentioned Sabbath specifically to say that they do not keep or observe the Sabbath. Three Jewish teens mentioned keeping Kosher to say that they do not.

18. Robert Bellah, "Civil Religion in America," *Daedalus* (winter 1967): 1–21.

19. See, for example, David Hall, *Lived Religion in America* (Princeton: Princeton University Press, 1997); Erling Jorstad, *Popular Religion in America* (Westport, CT: Greenwood Press, 1993).

20. For an explanation about how such status differentiations and cultural constructions of difference are essential to the making of human identities, see Christian Smith et al., *American Evangelicalism: Embattled and Thriving* (Chicago: University of Chicago Press, 1998).

21. As specified by numerous, defining historical creeds and confessions, including the Apostle's Creed, the Nicene Creed, the Chalcedonian Creed, the Athanasian Creed, Canons of the Council of Orange, the Belgic Confession, the Westminster Confessions, the Heidelberg Catechism, the Augsburg Confession, the Canons of Dort, the Scots Confession, the Thirty-Nine Articles of the Church of England, the First London Confession of Faith, the Schleitheim Articles, the Articles of Religion of the Methodist Church, Documents of the Second Vatican Council, and the Catechism of the Catholic Church.

CHAPTER 5

1. See chapter 4, note 16. Therapeutic individualism is quite different from the self-mastering, production-oriented, rugged individualism of nineteenth-century Victorian American culture, which stressed self-control, hard work, sobriety, character improvement, dependability, and the deferral of immediate gratification. See Daniel Rogers, *The Work Ethic and Industrial America, 1850–1920* (Chicago: University of Chicago Press, 1974); Stanley Coben, *Rebellion against Victorianism: The Impetus for Cultural Change in 1920s America* (New York: Oxford University Press, 1991).

2. James Nolan, *The Therapeutic State: Justifying Government at Century's End* (New York: New York University Press, 1998), p. 3.

3. See Christian Smith, ed., *The Secular Revolution: Power, Interests, and Conflict in the Secularization of American Public Life* (Berkeley: University of California Press, 2003).

4. Peter Berger, *The Sacred Canopy* (Garden City, NY: Anchor Books, 1969).

5. See, for example, James Nolan, *Reinventing Justice: The American Drug Court Movement* (Princeton: Princeton University Press, 2003); James Hunter, *The Death of Character: Moral Education in an Age without Good or Evil* (New York: Basic Books, 2000); Joel Shuman and Keith Meador, *Heal Thyself: Spirituality, Medicine, and the Distortion of Christianity* (Oxford: Oxford University Press, 2003); James Nolan, *The Therapeutic State: Justifying Government at Century's End* (New York: New York University Press, 1998); Philip Rieff, *The Triumph of the Therapeutic* (Chicago: University of Chicago Press, 1966); Andrew Polsky, *The Rise of the Therapeutic State* (Princeton: Princeton University Press, 1991); John S. Rice, *A Disease of One's Own: Psychotherapy, Addiction, and the Emergence of Co-Dependency* (New Brunswick, NJ: Transaction Publishers, 1996); Daniel Bell, *The Cultural Contradictions of Capitalism* (New York: Basic Books, 1976).

6. See Patrick McNamara, *Conscience First, Tradition Second: A Study of Young American Catholics* (Albany: State University of New York Press, 1992); Dean Hoge, William Dinges, Mary Johnson, and Juan Gonzales, *Young Adult Catholics: Religion*

in the Culture of Choice (Notre Dame, IN: University of Notre Dame Press, 2001); Keith Meador, " 'My Own Salvation': The *Christian Century* and Psychology's Secularizing of American Protestantism," in Christian Smith, ed., *The Secular Revolution* (Berkeley: University of California Press, 2003); Wade Clark Roof, *A Generation of Seekers: The Spiritual Journeys of the Baby Boom Generation* (New York: HarperCollins, 1993); James Davison Hunter, *Evangelicalism: The Coming Generation* (Chicago: University of Chicago Press, 1987); Marsha Witten, *All Is Forgiven: The Secular Message in American Protestantism* (Princeton: Princeton University Press, 1995); Jeffrey Arnett and Lene Jensen, "A Congregation of One: Individualized Religious Beliefs among Emerging Adults," *Journal of Adolescent Research* 17, no. 5 (2002): 451–467; Joel Shuman and Keith Meador, *Heal Thyself: Spirituality, Medicine, and the Distortion of Christianity* (Oxford: Oxford University Press, 2003); Robert Bellah et al., *Habits of the Heart* (Berkeley: University of California Press, 1985).

7. See Christian Smith, *Moral, Believing Animals: Personhood and Culture* (New York: Oxford University Press, 2003).

8. See, for example, Patrick McNamara, *Conscience First, Tradition Second* (Albany: State University of New York Press, 1992); Phillip Hammond, *Religion and Personal Autonomy* (Columbia: University of South Carolina Press, 1992); Wade Clark Roof, *Spiritual Marketplace* (Princeton: Princeton University Press, 1999).

9. For historical perspective, see Roland Marchand, *Advertising the American Dream* (Berkeley: University of California Press, 1985).

10. For an analysis on how consumerism shapes status systems and hierarchies in schools, see Murray Milner, *Freaks, Geeks, and Cool Kids: American Teenagers, Schools, and the Culture of Consumption* (New York: Routledge, 2004).

11. Teenage Research Unlimited, "Teens Spent $170 Billion in 2002," press release, February 17, 2003; Rosalind Bentley and Terry Collins, "Teens: The Lifeblood and Headache of the Mall," *Minneapolis Star-Tribune*, August 5, 2002.

12. See, for example, Alissa Quart, *Branded: The Buying and Selling of Teenagers* (New York: Perseus, 2003); Peter Zollow, *Getting Wiser to Teens: More Insights into Marketing to Teenagers* (Ithaca, NY: New Strategist Publications, 2004). This helps to explain the disproportionately adolescent character of so much contemporary television programming and movie offerings: the advertising industry driving television and movies is especially interested in gathering and shaping adolescent markets, whose loyalties they are more likely to win over than middle-aged and elderly Americans, whose brand loyalties are more firmly established.

13. See the 2001 Public Broadcasting System documentary, *Merchants of Cool*, www.pbs.org/wgbh/pages/frontline/shows/cool/.

14. Nielsen Media Research, *1998 Report on Television* (New York: Nielsen Media Research, 1998); V. C. Strasburger, "Children, Adolescents, and Television, 1989, II: The Role of Pediatricians," *Pediatrics* 83 (1989): 446–448; D. F. Roberts, U. Foehr, V. Rideout, and M. Brody, *Kids and Media at the New Millennium* (Menlo Park, CA: Henry J. Kaiser Family Foundation, 1999).

15. Note, however, that although the logic of the technologies themselves tend toward decentralization and diffuse networks, property ownership of much hardware and programming in the communications industry that controls technologies is simultaneously moving toward greater concentration, with distinct other consequences for content. See David Croteau and William Hoynes, *Media Society: Industries, Images, and Audiences* (Thousand Oaks, CA: Pine Forge Press, 2000).

16. By unregulated we do not mean controlled by state regulation, but lacking an

institutional gatekeeping authority, such as news or magazine editor, book publisher, professional peer reviewers, television producer, who has reviewed its quality and approved its public dissemination.

17. See George Landow, *Hypertext 2.0* (Baltimore: Johns Hopkins University Press, 1997); Ananda Mitra, "Diasporic Web Sites: Ingroup and Outgroup Discourse," *Critical Studies in Mass Communication* 14 (1997): 158–181; Ananda Mitra and E. Cohen, "Analyzing the Web: Directions and Challenges," in Steve Jones, ed., *Doing Internet Research* (Newbury Park, CA: Sage, 1998); Don Tapscott, *Growing Up Digital* (New York: McGraw-Hill, 1998); Lynn Owen, "Ideology in Utopia: Anarchism on the World Wide Web" (MA thesis, University of North Carolina at Chapel Hill, 2001); Douglas Rushkoff, *Cyberia* (Manchester, UK: Clinamen Press, 2002); Mitchell Stephens, *The Rise of the Image, the Fall of the Word* (New York: Oxford University Press, 1998); Roger Fidler, *Mediamorphosis* (Thousand Oaks, CA: Pine Forge Press, 1997).

18. See Neil Postman, *Amusing Ourselves to Death: Public Discourse in the Age of Show Business* (New York: Penguin Books, 1985).

19. That is, logic and experience themselves could never verify the tenets of logical positivism, which requires presuppositions and belief commitments beyond what pure logic and experience could provide, making logical positivism itself internally incoherent. See, for starters, William Alston, *The Reliability of Sense Perception* (Ithaca, NY: Cornell University Press, 1993); Alasdair MacIntyre, *Three Rival Versions of Moral Enquiry* (Notre Dame, IN: University of Notre Dame Press, 1988); Alasdair MacIntyre, *After Virtue: A Study in Moral Theory* (Notre Dame, IN: University of Notre Dame Press, 1981); Nicholas Wolterstorff, *Reason within the Bounds of Religion* (Grand Rapids, MI: Eerdmans, 1976); C. A. J. Coady, *Testimony: A Philosophical Study* (New York: Oxford University Press, 1992); Richard Rorty, *Philosophy and the Mirror of Nature* (Princeton: Princeton University Press, 1979); Alvin Plantinga, *Warrant and Proper Function* (Oxford: Oxford University Press, 1993); William Alston, "Knowledge of God," in Marcus Hester, ed., *Faith, Reason, and Skepticism* (Philadelphia: Temple University Press, 1992); William Alston, *Perceiving God* (Ithaca, NY: Cornell University Press, 1991); Alvin Plantinga, *Warranted Christian Belief* (Oxford: Oxford University Press, 2000); Alvin Plantinga, *Warrant: The Current Debate* (Oxford: Oxford University Press, 1993); Alvin Plantinga and Nicholas Wolterstorff, eds., *Faith and Rationality* (Notre Dame, IN: University of Notre Dame Press, 1983); Thomas Kuhn, *The Structure of Scientific Revolutions* (Chicago: University of Chicago Press, 1962); Sergio Sismondo, *Science without Myth: On Construction, Reality, and Social Knowledge* (Albany: State University of New York Press, 1996); Michael Polanyi, *Science, Faith, and Society* (London: Oxford University Press, 1948); Michael Polanyi, *The Tacit Dimension* (Garden City, NY: Doubleday, 1983).

20. The following discussion draws on Thomas Hine, *The Rise and Fall of the American Teenager* (New York: Avon Books, 1999); Grace Palladino, *Teenagers: An American History* (New York: Basic Books, 1996); Harvey Graff, *Conflicting Paths: Growing Up in America* (Cambridge, MA: Harvard University Press, 1995); Joseph Kett, *Rites of Passage: Adolescents in America, 1790 to the Present* (New York: Basic Books, 1977); John Modell, *Into One's Own: From Youth to Adulthood in the United States, 1920–1975* (Berkeley: University of California Press, 1989); Philippe Ariès, *Centuries of Childhood* (New York: Vintage Books, 1962); C. John Sommerville, *The Rise and Fall of Childhood* (New York: Vintage Books, 1990).

21. Lenore Weitzman, *The Divorce Revolution* (New York: Free Press, 1985).

22. See Terrie Moffitt, "Adolescent-limited and Life-course-persistent Antisocial Behavior: A Developmental Taxonomy," *Psychological Review* 100 (1993): 674–701.

23. In 2000, the estimated median age at first marriage for women was 25.1 years and for men was 26.8 years, compared to 20.3 years for women and 22.8 years for men in 1950. U.S. Bureau of the Census, "America's Families and Living Arrangements: March 2000," *Current Population Reports*, Series P20–537, and earlier Census reports.

24. See, for instance, Jane Brown, Jeanne Steele, and Kim Walsh-Childers, *Sexual Teens, Sexual Media: Investigating Media's Influence on Adolescent Sexuality* (Mahwah, NJ: Lawrence Erlbaum, 2002); Paula Kamen, *Her Way: Young Women Remake the Sexual Revolution* (New York: Broadway Books, 2000); Naomi Wolf, *Promiscuities: The Secret Struggle for Womanhood* (New York: Fawcett Columbine, 1997); Sharon Thompson, *Going All the Way: Teenage Girls' Tales of Sex, Romance, and Pregnancy* (New York: Hill and Wang, 1995).

25. Added to these are many other mixed signals embedded in social age limits, such that certain teenagers may be old enough to drive but not to vote, old enough to have a baby and fight in a war but not old enough to buy cigarettes or to buy or drink alcohol.

26. For example, in 1998, 19.1 percent of 12- to 17-year-olds compared to 60.9 percent of 26- to 34-year-olds consumed alcohol at least once a month; 18 percent of 12- to 17-year-olds compared to 32.5 percent of 26- to 34-year-olds smoked cigarettes; 0.8 percent of 12- to 17-year-olds compared to 1.2 percent of 26- to 34-year-olds did cocaine at least once a month; and 9.7 percent of clients of U.S. substance abuse treatment facilities in 1998 were under 18 years old, compared to 72.7 percent that were 25 and older. *Statistical Abstract of the United States: 2000*, p. 141. In 1993, the rate of drug overdose deaths in California for 13- to 19-year-olds was 9 per million, compared to 211 per million for 35- to 49-year-olds, a rate 23 times larger for the adults. Mike Males, *The Scapegoat Generation* (Monroe, ME: Common Courage Press, 1996), p. 174. In 2001, 7,963 drivers age 16–20 were involved in fatal drunk driving accidents, compared to 49,517 for those 21 and over. National Highway Traffic Safety Administration, *Traffic Safety Facts, 2001* (Washington, DC: U.S. Department of Transportation, 2001), figure 1 and table 3. In 1999, American 10- to 19-year-olds represented 17.6 percent of all suicide deaths, while 20- to 54-year-olds represented more than twice that number at 36.4 percent. National Center for Health Statistics, *National Vital Statistics Report, 1999, Vol. 49, No. 11, Oct. 12, 2001* (Washington, DC: U.S. Department of Health and Human Services, 2001), table 1. In 1999, 90.3 percent of all murder and nonnegligent manslaughter arrests were made of Americans 18 years old or older; in 1999, 83.4 percent of all arrests were made of Americans 18 years old or older, compared to 16.6 percent of arrests of Americans under 18 years old. U.S. Census Bureau, 2001, *Statistical Abstract of the United States: 2001*, tables 308. Only 1.5 percent of all AIDS cases in the United States in 2001 involved teenagers. Center for Disease Control and Prevention, *HIV/AIDS Surveillance Report, 2001*, vol. 13, no. 2. According to the 1999–2000 National Health and Nutrition Examination Survey, 15 percent of 12- to 19-year-olds are overweight (Body Mass Index of 25.0–29.9), compared to 34 percent of adults. U.S. Department of Health and Human Services, Centers for Disease Control and Prevention, National Center for Health Statistics. In 1999, 80.6 percent of legal abortions involved women 20 or older; in 1995, the abortion rate for girls less than 15 years old was two per 1,000; for 15- to 19-year-olds was 22 per 1,000; and for 25- to 29-year-

olds was 24 per 1,000 women of the same age. Centers for Disease Control and
Prevention, 1999, *Morbidity and Mortality Weekly Report Surveillance Summaries:
Abortion Surveillance—United States, 1999*, table 1 and figure 2; U.S. Department of
Health and Human Services, Centers for Disease Control and Prevention, National
Center for Health Statistics, 1995. According to the 1996 and 1998 General Social
Survey, 25 percent of American adults had viewed an X-rated movie in the previous
year. *General Social Surveys, 1972–1998: Cumulative Codebook* (Chicago: NORC,
January 1999), p. 238. Fully 10.9 percent of American women over the age of 59
(2.8 million) abuse or are addicted to psychoactive prescription drugs, and 7 percent
(1.8 million) abuse or are addicted to alcohol—a "hidden epidemic," according to
the National Center on Addiction and Substance Abuse at Columbia University. *Under the Rug: Substance Abuse and the Mature Woman* (New York: Center on Addiction and Substance Abuse, 1998). Also see Mike Males, *Framing Youth* (Monroe,
ME: Common Courage Press, 1999); Laurence Steinberg, "Autonomy, Conflict, and
Harmony in the Family Relationship," in S. Shirley Feldman and Glen Elliott, eds.,
At the Threshold: The Developing Adolescent (Cambridge, MA: Harvard University
Press, 1990).

    27. Robert Bellah, "Is There a Common American Culture?" *Journal of the American Academy of Religion* 66, no. 3 (1998): 613–625.

    28. Juliet Schor, *The Overspent American: Upscaling, Downshifting, and the New
Consumer* (New York: Basic Books, 1998).

    29. Nielsen Media Research, *2000 Report on Television* (New York: Nielsen Media Research, 2000).

    30. According to nationally representative 1998 Survey of Parents and Youth data,
for instance, 26.4 percent of teens age 13–17 eat dinner with one or both of their
parents between zero and three nights per week; another 13.5 percent eat dinner with
one or both of their parents four nights a week; only 35.2 percent of teens age 13–
17 report eating dinner with one or both of their parents seven days a week.

    31. C. Wright Mills, *The Sociological Imagination* (New York: Oxford University
Press, 1959).

CHAPTER 6

Bob McCarty, Mark Moitoza, Kathy Carver, and Jim Heft, S.M., all read and critiqued an earlier version of this chapter and offered very helpful comments; none,
however, shares any culpability for any of this chapter's possible shortcomings.

    1. "I" being Christian Smith, Reliant Stadium being the venue where three months
after this Catholic conference, Super Bowl XXXVIII was played.

    2. See, for example, *Catechism of the Catholic Church* (Washington, DC: United
States Catholic Conference, 2000).

    3. Two of the three cases, for instance, have religiously mixed parents, far above
the national average for Catholic teenagers, which tends to associate with lower levels
of religiosity.

    4. For example, in this case, for Catholic parents who report that their faith is
extremely important in their lives, 58 percent of their teenage children report that
their own faith is extremely or very important, while only 7 percent say that their
faith is somewhat important, not very important, or not important at all. By comparison, for Catholic parents who report that faith is not very important or not at all
important in their lives, only 18 percent of their teenage children report that their

own faith is extremely or very important, while 33 percent say that their faith is only somewhat important, not very important, or not important at all. Teen religion tends to track parental religion fairly closely.

5. Andrew Greeley, *Religious Change in America* (Cambridge, MA: Harvard University Press, 1989), pp. 42–56; Ronald Johnstone, *Religion in Society* (Upper Saddle River, NJ: Prentice-Hall, 2004), pp. 352–362.

6. See, for example, Christian Smith, *American Evangelicalism* (Chicago: University of Chicago Press, 1998), pp. 27, 34.

7. The Catholic teen effect remains statistically significant even when controlling for all four parental religiosity variables when conservative Protestant teens instead of mainline Protestant teens are used as the reference group because conservative Protestant teens attend church more than mainline Protestant teens, and so set the bar of difference at a higher level. Even so, the Catholic teen coefficient is more than cut in half with the parental religiosity controls entered (from −0.936 to −0.378).

8. Not all Catholic youth ministry programs are called youth groups, which might have brought this Catholic percentage down; on the other hand, Catholic respondents may well have included CCD, religious education, Confirmation programs, youth ministry/peer counseling programs, and so on as "religious youth groups" as they answered this survey question.

9. Although Catholic parishes often do have other designated ministry personnel working with youth, such as CCD teachers, religious educators, and Confirmation leaders, who might not have counted in survey answers as youth ministers.

10. One way to consider the situation of Catholic youth ministry at the national level is by examining the apparent organizational and symbolic position of youth in the overall priorities and structure of the United States Conference of Catholic Bishops (USCCB) as represented on its Web site at the time of this writing: www.usccb.org/. The Catholic Youth Ministry "Projects and Topics" page, it turns out, is buried there four layers deep below the USCCB home page, under the Subcommittee on Youth and Young Adults, which is a subsidiary of the Committee on the Laity, whose information is found on the "Family, Laity, Women, and Youth" page, which is one of 43 USCCB departments and associated offices, the list of which can be accessed by a click on the USCCB home page. Youth evangelization, ministry, and formation, in other words, does not appear to figure prominently in the USCCB system. At least symbolically, then, if not in actual fact, viewed sociologically in this one possible way, Catholic youth appear to be situated near the bottom of the USCCB priority list— this despite official pronouncements about the importance of youth in the Church, such as National Conference of Catholic Bishops, *Renewing the Vision: A Framework for Catholic Youth Ministry* (Washington, DC: United States Catholic Conference, 1997). On the other hand, the USCCB is only one level of the Catholic Church. Other organizations, such as the National Federation of Catholic Youth Ministry, appears to be doing an excellent job in fostering effective youth ministry.

11. Anecdotal evidence suggests that a number of Catholic dioceses have closed down their youth ministry offices in recent years due to financial constraints, likely resulting from a weak economy and perhaps priest abuse payouts. At least some frustrated Catholic youth ministry workers with whom we have communicated interpret this as a sign of the relatively low priority of youth ministry in some sectors of the Church, and that youth ministry is often seen as a luxury, not a necessity.

12. The Sacred Congregation of the Council was the Church entity that was later renamed by Pope Paul VI as the Congregation for the Clergy in the Apostolic Constitution Regimini Ecclesiae Universae, dated August 15, 1967.

13. See Michael Warren, ed., *Sourcebook for Modern Catechetics* (Winona, MN: Saint Mary's Press, 1983).

14. Fraser Field, "How Catholic Are Our Catholic Schools?" *Catholic Exchange*, December 26, 2001.

15. David Baker and Cornelius Riordan, "The 'Eliting' of the Common American Catholic School and the National Educational Crisis," *Phi Delta Kappan* (September 1998): 16–24. Also see James Heft, S.M., and James Davidson, "The Mission of Catholic High Schools and Today's Millennials," *Catholic Education*, 6, no. 4 (June 2002): 410–422; Terence McLaughlin, Joseph O'Keefe, and Bernadette O'Keefe, eds., *The Contemporary Catholic School: Context, Identity, and Diversity* (London: Routledge Falmer, 1996).

16. David Baker and Cornelius Riordan, "The 'Eliting' of the Common American Catholic School and the National Educational Crisis," *Phi Delta Kappan* (September 1998): 16–24. Also see James Youniss and John Convey, eds., *Catholic Schools at the Crossroads: Survival and Transformation* (New York: Teachers College Press, 2000).

17. Dale McDonald, *United States Catholic Elementary and Secondary Schools 2003–2004: The Annual Statistical Report on Schools, Enrollment, and Staffing* (Washington, DC: National Catholic Education Association, 2004). Also see Anthony Bryk, *Catholic Schools and the Common Good* (Cambridge, MA: Harvard University Press, 1993).

18. Bernard Marthaler, "The Rise and Decline of the CCD," *Chicago Studies* 29 (1990): 3–15.

19. David Baker and Cornelius Riordan, "The 'Eliting' of the Common American Catholic School and the National Educational Crisis," *Phi Delta Kappan* (September 1998): 16–24. Recent research suggests that number may have dropped to as low as 10 percent.

20. See, for instance, R. A. Billington, "Tentative Bibliography of Anti-Catholic Propaganda," *Catholic Historical Review* 18 (1932): 492–513; John McGreevey, "Thinking on One's Own: Catholicism in the American Intellectual Imagination, 1928–1960," *Journal of American History* (June 1997): 97–131; James D. Hunter, *Culture Wars* (New York: Basic Books, 1991), pp. 36–37.

21. Jay Dolan, *The American Catholic Experience: A History from Colonial Times to the Present* (Garden City, NJ: Doubleday, 1985); James Davidson et al., *The Search for Common Ground: What Unites and Divides Catholic Americans* (Huntington, IN: Our Sunday Visitor Press, 1997); Andrew Greeley, *The American Catholic: A Social Portrait* (New York: Basic Books, 1977); Norval Glenn and Ruth Hyland, "Religious Preference and Worldly Success," *American Sociological Review* 32 (1967): 73–85.

22. Twentieth-century American liberalism included a significant anti-Catholic attitude expressed, among other ways, in its concern about "Catholic power." See John McGreevey, "Thinking on One's Own: Catholicism in the American Intellectual Imagination, 1928–1960," *Journal of American History* (June 1997): 97–131; Timothy Walch, *Catholicism in America: A Social History* (Malabar, FL: Robert E. Krieger, 1989). Also see Philip Jenkins, *The New Anti-Catholicism: The Last Acceptable Prejudice* (New York: Oxford University Press, 2003).

23. James D. Davidson, "American Catholics and American Catholicism: An Inventory of Facts, Trends, and Influences," paper presented at "The Church in America: The Way Forward in the 21st Century. A Dialogue," July 7, 2003, Washington, DC, sponsored by the Boisi Center for Religion and American Public Life at Boston College.

24. Ernst Troeltsch, *The Social Teachings of the Christian Church* (1912; New York: Macmillan, 1931); Rodney Stark and Roger Finke, *Acts of Faith: Explaining the Human Side of Religion* (Berkeley: University of California Press, 2000); Christian Smith, *American Evangelicalism: Embattled and Thriving* (Chicago: University of Chicago Press, 1998).

25. Patrick McNamara, *Conscience First, Tradition Second: A Study of Young American Catholics* (Albany: State University of New York Press, 1992); William D'Antonio et al., *American Catholics* (Walnut Creek, CA: Alta Mira Press, 2001); Dean Hoge et al., *Young Adult Catholics: Religion in the Culture of Choice* (Notre Dame, IN: Notre Dame University Press, 2001), pp. 5–18.

CHAPTER 7

1. In any case, the pattern of findings we see below does hold when the individual religion variables composing the ideal types are used independently in this way; the findings are not an artifact of the particular construction of the ideal types. We do recognize that these ideal types are somewhat Christiancentric, particularly leaning toward some Protestant ideals. There is simply no way to construct a religion-neutral, one-size-fits-all ideal-type system. This categorization, however, ought not to exaggerate differences between types, as highly religious teens in non-Protestant and non-Christian traditions who were screened into less religious categories because of the criteria used would normally have the effect of *reducing*, not increasing, differences between the category types.

2. Also see Barbara Dafoe Whitehead, Brian Wilcox, and Sharon Scales Rostosky, *Keeping the Faith: The Role of Religion and Faith Communities in Preventing Teen Pregnancy* (Washington, DC: National Campaign to Prevent Teen Pregnancy, 2001).

3. See, for example, Christian Smith, "Religious Participation and Network Closure among American Adolescents," *Journal for the Scientific Study of Religion* 42, no. 2 (2003): 259–267; William Carbonaro, "A Little Help from My Friend's Parents: Intergenerational Closure and Educational Outcomes," *Sociology of Education* 71 (1998): 295–313; A. Fletcher, D. Newsome, P. Nickerson, and R. Bazley, "Social Network Closure and Child Adjustment," *Merrill–Palmer Quarterly* 47, no. 4 (2001): 500–532; S. L. Morgan, and A. Sorensen, "Parental Networks, Social Closure, and Mathematics Learning," *American Sociological Review* 64 (1999): 661–681; James Coleman, "Social Capital in the Creation of Human Capital," *American Journal of Sociology* 94 (1988): 95–120.

4. The alternative options were either to choose to follow the advice of parents, teachers, or other adult authorities; or to do what God or the scriptures say is right.

5. Robert Putnam, *Bowling Alone* (New York: Simon and Schuster, 2000).

6. Also see Independent Sector, *Volunteering and Giving among Teenagers 12 to 17 Years of Age* (Washington, DC: Independent Sector, 1997), pp. 55–69; Elizabeth Weiss Ozorak, "Love of God and Neighbor: Religion and Volunteer Service among College Students," *Review of Religious Research* 44, no. 3 (2003): 285–299.

7. This confirms the findings of prior studies of teen religiosity and life outcomes using older survey datasets. See, for example, Christian Smith and Phillip Kim, *Family Religious Involvement and the Quality of Parental Relationships for Families with Early Adolescents* (Chapel Hill, NC: National Study of Youth and Religion, 2003); Christian Smith and Phillip Kim, *Family Religious Involvement and the Quality of Family Relationships for Early Adolescents* (Chapel Hill, NC: National Study of Youth and Religion, 2003); Christian Smith and Robert Faris, *Religion and American*

Adolescent Delinquency, Risk Behaviors, and Constructive Social Activities (Chapel Hill, NC: National Study of Youth and Religion, 2002); Christian Smith and Robert Faris, *Religion and the Life Attitudes and Self-Images of American Adolescents* (Chapel Hill, NC: National Study of Youth and Religion, 2002); Mark Regnerus, Christian Smith, and Melissa Fritsch, *Religion in the Lives of American Adolescents: A Review of the Literature* (Chapel Hill, NC: National Study of Youth and Religion, 2002).

8. Christian Smith, *Moral, Believing Animals: Human Personhood and Culture* (New York: Oxford University Press, 2003).

9. When other assorted scholars have paid attention to religion, it has often also predicted many important positive adolescent outcomes. Scattered journal articles and research reports suggest that religion in youth's lives is statistically associated with positive outcomes in avoiding drug, alcohol, and tobacco use, delinquency, suicide, depression, and risky sexual behaviors, and achieving hopefulness, healthy behaviors, life satisfaction, involvement with families, skills in solving health-related problems, emotional coping, academic achievement, political and civic involvement, and participation in community service. See, for example, D. Balk, "Sibling Death, Adolescent Bereavement, and Religion," *Death Studies* 15 (1991): 1–20; G. Brody, Z. Stoneman, and D. Flor, "Parental Religiosity, Family Processes, and Youth Competence in Rural, Two–parent African American Families," *Developmental Psychology* 32 (1996): 696–706; J. Cochran, "The Variable Effects of Religiosity and Denomination on Adolescent Self–Reported Alcohol Use by Beverage Type," *Journal of Drug Issues* 23 (1993): 479–491; J. Cochran and R. Akers, "Beyond Hellfire: An Exploration of the Variable Effects of Religiosity on Adolescent Marijuana and Alcohol Use," *Journal of Research in Crime and Delinquency* 26 (1989): 198–225; M. Donahue, "Religion and the Well–being of Adolescents," *Journal of Social Issues* 51 (1995): 145–160; T. D. Evans, F. Cullen, R. G. Dunaway, and V. Burton Jr., "Religion and Crime Reexamined: The Impact of Religion, Secular Controls, and Social Ecology on Adult Criminality," *Criminology* 33 (1995): 195–217; R. Jessor, M. Turbin, and F. Costa, "Risk and Protection in Successful Outcomes among Disadvantaged Adolescents," *Applied Developmental Science* 2 (1998): 194–208; N. Krause, C. Ellison, B. Shaw, J. Marcum, and J. Boardman, "Church-based Social Support and Religious Coping," *Journal for the Scientific Study of Religion* 40, no. 4 (2001): 637–657; C. Lammers, M. Ireland, M. Resnick, and R. Blum, "Influences on Adolescents' Decision to Postpone Onset of Sexual Intercourse: A Survival Analysis of Virginity among Youths Aged 13 to 18 Years," *Journal of Adolescent Health* 26 (1999): 42–48; C. Muller and C. Ellison, "Religious Involvement, Social Capital, and Adolescents' Academic Progress: Evidence from the National Longitudinal Study of 1988," *Sociological Focus* 34 (2001): 155–183; V. Murry, "Black Adolescent Females: A Comparison of Early versus Late Coital Initiators," *Family Relations* 43 (1994): 342–348; R. Pawlak and J. Defronzo, "Social Bonds, Early Trauma and Smoking: Evidence of the Group-Specific Relevance of Control-Theory," *Journal of Drug Education* 23 (1993): 201–214; M. Regnerus, "Shaping Schooling Success: Religious Socialization and Educational Outcomes in Urban Public Schools," *Journal for the Scientific Study of Religion* 39 (2000): 363–370; A. Scharf, "Environmental Stress, Potential Protective Factors, and Adolescent Risk–taking" (PhD diss., Fordham University, 1998); R. Serow and J. Dreyden, "Community Service among College and University Students: Individual and Institutional Relationships," *Adolescence* 25 (1990): 553–566; J. Shortz and E. Worthington Jr., "Young Adults' Recall of Religiosity, Attributions, and Coping in Parental Divorce," *Journal for the Scientific Study of Religion* 33 (1994): 172–179; Christian Smith and Robert

Faris, "Religion and American Adolescent Delinquency, Risk Behaviors, and Constructive Social Activities," in *Research Report of the National Study of Youth and Religion*, University of North Carolina at Chapel Hill, 2002; Christian Smith and Robert Faris, *Religion and the Life Attitudes and Self-Images of American Adolescents* (Chapel Hill, NC: National Study of Youth and Religion, 2002); E. S. Smith, "The Effects of Investments in the Social Capital of Youth on Political and Civic Behavior in Young Adulthood: A Longitudinal Analysis," *Political Psychology* 20 (1999): 553–580; V. Stuart and A. Riley, "Relationship between Maternal Church Attendance and Adolescent Mental Health and Social Functioning," *Psychiatric Services* 50 (1999): 799–805; A. Thornton and D. Camburn, "Religious Participation and Adolescent Sexual Behavior and Attitudes," *Journal of Marriage and the Family* 51 (1989): 641–653; J. Wallace Jr. and T. Forman, "Religion's Role in Promoting Health and Reducing Risk among American Youth," *Health Education and Behavior* 25 (1998): 721–741; L. Wright, C. Frost, and S. Wisecarver, "Church Attendance, Meaningfulness of Religion, and Depressive Symptomatology among Adolescents," *Journal of Youth and Adolescence* 22 (1993): 559–568; J. Youniss, J. McLellan, and M. Yates, "Religion, Community Service, and Identity in American Youth," *Journal of Adolescence* 22 (1999): 243–253; Lisa Bridges and Kristin Anderson Moore, "Religious Involvement and Children's Well-Being: What Research Tells Us (and What It Doesn't)," *Trends in Child Research Brief* (Washington, DC: Child Trends, 2002).

10. One philosophical sidebar on religious influences to consider here: sociology has a long history of reductionistic thinking and analysis. With regard to religion, this reductionism has often expressed itself in claims that what appear to be religious phenomena on the surface are in fact revealed by serious analyses to *really* only be about other things quite unrelated to religion. Thus, what appears to be divine or spiritual or transcendent or pious or sacred are *really only* about social class, race, gender, ethnicity, nationalism, solidarity, social control, and so on. We number ourselves among those, however, who believe that both this general tendency toward such reductionism and many (though not all) of the specific cases of analytical reductionism are intellectually parochial and simplistic. We will do far better instead to understand the realities we study as multidimensional and multilevel and involving emergent properties and supervenient processes. Such a nonreductionistic mentality has at least two intellectual consequences, one epistemological and one substantive. First, epistemologically, this approach recognizes the analytical limits of sociology. Thus, this chapter's attempt at a somewhat integrated sociological explanation of religious effects among adolescents self-consciously focuses on a range of human, social factors that may be involved. It makes no disconfirming or affirming claims about possible divine (or biological) influences involved, nor denies that these human, social effects are ones through which divine (or biological) influences might in theory potentially operate. These matters are simply beyond sociology to make claims about. Second, a nonreductionistic sociological approach to religion is interested in understanding how the distinctively religious dimensions of the phenomenon "religion" exert significant social influences. That is, this approach assumes that there is something particularly *religious* in religion, which is not reducible to nonreligious explanations, and that these religious elements can exert causal influence in forming cultural practices and motivating action. For example, something particular about belief in a divine being or some distinctive element in the content of a particular religious moral tradition may produce some specific social outcome. By contrast, reductionistic approaches tend to look for significant influences in factors that happen to be found in religious contexts but which themselves are not particularly religious in any sense. Thus, for in-

stance, religious influences may be reduced to the generic resources or social networks or organizational capacities or memberships that just so happen to be found in religious groups in particular cases. But there is nothing significantly religious about any of it. The factors that *really* matter only just so happen in certain instances to be located in religious contexts. Taken to its extreme, this approach would completely dissolve the sociology of religion as a distinctive field and divide up its component parts into the fields of culture, organizations, race and ethnicity, collective behavior and social movements, and so on. Against this approach, we suggest that religion exerts influences in the lives of youth not by happenstance or generic social process, but precisely as an outcome of American religions' theological, moral, and spiritual substance. The distinctively religious dimensions of American religions, in other words, are necessary conditions for the explanatory factors examined in this chapter to emerge as social influences in the lives of youth.

11. Steven Reiss, "Why People Turn to Religion: A Motivational Analysis," *Journal for the Scientific Study of Religion* 39 (2000): 47–52; Steven Reiss and S. M. Havercamp, "Toward a Comprehensive Assessment of Fundamental Motivation: Factor Structure of the Reiss Profiles," *Psychological Assessment* 10 (1998): 97–106; Mark Regnerus and Christian Smith, "Selection Effects and Social Desirability Bias in Studies of Religious Influences," paper presented at the 2004 annual meeting of the Society for the Scientific Study of Religion; Alan S. Miller and John P. Hoffmann, "Risk and Religion: An Explanation of Gender Differences in Religiosity," *Journal for the Scientific Study of Religion* 34 (1995): 63–75; Alan S. Miller and Rodney Stark, "Gender and Religiousness: Can Socialization Explanations Be Saved?" *American Journal of Sociology* 107 (2002): 1399–1423; Laurence R. Iannaccone, "Risk, Rationality, and Religious Portfolios," *Economic Inquiry* 38 (1995): 285–295; James E. Curtis, Douglas Baer, and Edward Grabb, "Nations of Joiners: Explaining Voluntary Association Membership in Democratic Societies," *American Sociological Review* 66, no. 6 (2001): 783–806. Note, however, that Bernard Spilka, Ralph Hood, and Richard Gorsuch found few significant associations between religion and standardized personality tests in *The Psychology of Religion: An Empirical Approach* (Englewood Cliffs, NJ: Prentice-Hall, 1985).

12. Mark Regnerus and Christian Smith, "Selection Effects and Social Desirability Bias in Studies of Religious Influences," paper presented at the 2004 annual meeting of the Society for the Scientific Study of Religion.

13. Brent Benda and Robert Corwyn, "A Test of a Model with Reciprocal Effects between Religiosity and Various Forms of Delinquency Using 2-State Least Squares Regression," *Journal for Social Service Research* 22 (1997): 27–52; also see Brent Benda and Nancy Toombs, "Religion and Drug Use among Inmates in Boot Camps: Testing a Theoretical Model with Reciprocal Relationships," *Journal of Offender Rehabilitation* 35 (2002): 161–183; Arland Thornton, William Axinn, and Daniel Hill, "Reciprocal Effects of Religiosity, Cohabitation, and Marriage," *American Journal of Sociology* 98 (1992): 628–651; Ann Meier, "Adolescents' Transition to First Intercourse, Religiosity, and Attitudes about Sex," *Social Forces* 81, no. 3 (2003): 1031–1052; Steven Burkett, "Perceived Parents' Religiosity, Friends' Drinking, and Hellfire: A Panel Study of Adolescent Drinking," *Review of Religious Research* 35, no. 2 (1993): 134–154; Mark Regnerus and Christian Smith, "Selection Effects and Social Desirability Bias in Studies of Religious Influences," paper presented at the 2004 annual meeting of the Society for the Scientific Study of Religion. Note that Burkett's sample was drawn from two public high schools in a medium-size city in the Pacific Northwest, and no sample size or attrition rate is reported. Also note that Benda's

study of 1,093 adolescents from six public high schools in Arkansas, Oklahoma, and Maryland—which suggests that alcohol and drug use and crime do reduce teenage religiosity—is based on cross-sectional data and so, despite its reliance on two-stage least squares regression, is, in our view, unable to establish the sequential order of that observed relationship.

14. For one more in-depth exploration of these issues, see Mark Regnerus and Christian Smith, "Selection Effects and Social Desirability Bias in Studies of Religious Influences," paper presented at the 2004 annual meeting of the Society for the Scientific Study of Religion.

15. Clearly, then, we are not persuaded by claims of spuriousness, the suggestion that higher religious involvement and more positive youth outcomes are both independently the effects or outcomes of some other, prior causal factor that produced them, such that there exists no causal relationship whatsoever between religion and outcomes. Such a spurious association hypothesis suggests that *some other unknown independent factor influences certain youth both to be religious and to hold more positive attitudes and engage in more positive practices.* We know that the number of fire engines at a fire and the damage caused by the fire tend to be highly correlated, but not because fire engines cause fire damage; rather, a third factor, the intensity of the fire, produces both of them. Similarly, the apparent association between religion and positive youth outcomes may have nothing to do with religion's causal influence, but instead may result from some other nonreligious factor that influences both independently. The spurious association hypothesis is difficult to reject. In principle, it is perpetually unfalsifiable, as there may always be an as yet unidentified, unknown, other factor out there that could explain away what would then be a spurious association between religion and youth outcomes. In theory, we cannot be sure that tomorrow somebody will not identify an antecedent factor that explains both religious practices and positive youth outcomes, removes significant associations between religion and outcomes, and thus shows the previous correlation to be spurious. Even longitudinal data cannot necessarily address this problem if those data do not contain measures of possible third, independent variables demonstrating spuriousness. Thus, scholars who believe that religion could not or does not exert a causal influence on youth outcomes can maintain the spurious association hypothesis as an alternative to the other causal processes discussed above.

There are a number of reasons, however, why the spurious association hypothesis's challenge to the idea of religious influence is limited. Note, first, as a point of background, that the spurious association hypothesis is not applicable merely to the youth religion-outcomes question, or even to claims about religion's possible causal effects generally. It is a relevant challenge to *every* research claim about causal influences among studied variables. Every time a researcher interprets causal relations and directions among factors under study, however plausible that interpretation might be, there is always the possibility that some other as yet unspecified factor explains away the observed associations, showing the correlations between them to be spurious. Yet, despite this ever present possibility, this does not paralyze interpretations of research findings generally. For the deadening paralysis of utter skepticism is far less reasonable than advancing the most plausible interpretations of findings, even knowing theoretically that the claimed associations may be potentially spurious. Thus, in practice, scholars generally still use their best available insights and information to develop and sustain their best understandings of the workings of the social world. The fact that the spurious associations hypothesis is theoretically always waiting in the wings of any analysis does not stop researchers from making and defending reasonable causal influence claims about thousands of other associations involving race, gender, education, income, age, family structure, crime, fertility, civic participation, voting, work, aging, public opinions, and everything else social scientists study. Unless there is something especially suspect about the idea of religion causally influencing life outcomes—and we do not believe that there is reasonable basis for thinking so—there is no justifiable reason why the spurious associations hypothesis should be a *particularly* troubling or neutralizing possibility when it comes to interpreting youth religion-outcomes findings. Even so, that argument itself does not resolve the issue in question but merely puts it into larger perspective.

Furthermore, note that all of the many good studies showing positive associations between youth's religious practices and positive outcomes are multivariate analyses controlling for the possible influencing effects of many other variables. The analyses presented in this chapter likewise are multivariate. In their findings, the associations between the religion and outcome variables are statistically significant even when controlling for the possible influences of factors such as youth respondents' age, sex, race, number of siblings, neighborhood type, residential region of the country, family structure, parental work status, family income, and parental education. If there is some other independent variable demonstrating the many observed religion-outcome associations to be spurious, it has to be something besides these factors. At some point in the discussion, the burden shifts to proponents of the spurious association hypothesis to produce a specific variable as this unknown explanatory factor and to demonstrate empirically that this variable does in fact eliminate the many observed statistical associations between religion and youth outcomes. Unless and until this is done, practically speaking, the spurious association hypothesis inevitably increasingly becomes an interesting hypothetical possibility for researchers to keep in mind, but one lacking much practical importance for interpreting findings well.

16. See, for example, the promise of "fuzzy set" analysis: Charles Ragin, *Fuzzy Set Social Science* (Chicago: University of Chicago Press, 2000).

17. This section first appeared as part of an article in the *Journal for the Scientific Study of Religion*: Christian Smith, "Theorizing Religious Effects among American Adolescents," *Journal for the Scientific Study of Religion* 42, no. 1 (2003): 17–30.

18. See Charles Taylor, *Human Agency and Language* (Cambridge, UK: Cambridge University Press, 1985); Charles Taylor, *Sources of the Self* (Cambridge, MA: Harvard University Press, 1989); Amatai Etzioni, *The Moral Dimension* (New York: Free Press, 1988); Robert Wuthnow, *Meaning and Moral Order* (Cambridge, MA: Harvard University Press, 1987); Alasdair MacIntyre, *After Virtue* (Notre Dame, IN: University of Notre Dame Press, 1984).

19. James Hunter, *The Death of Character: Moral Education in an Age without Good or Evil* (New York: Basic Books, 2000). In this we take a clearly *normative* approach to human culture, and not merely instrumental, even though that is unfashionable among culture scholars recently. See, for example, Ann Swidler, "Culture in Action: Symbols and Strategies," *American Sociological Review* 51 (1986): 273–286.

20. Robert Wuthnow, *Meaning and Moral Order* (Cambridge, MA: Harvard University Press, 1987).

21. Robert Wuthnow, *Learning to Care* (New York: Oxford University Press, 1995).

22. Peter Berger, *The Sacred Canopy* (New York: Anchor Books, 1967).

23. Laurence Iannaccone, "Religious Practice: A Human Capital Approach," *Journal for the Scientific Study of Religion* 29, no. 3 (September 1990): 297–315.

24. Alexis de Tocqueville, *Democracy in America* (Garden City, NJ: Doubleday, 1969).

25. Kenneth Pargament, Bruce Smith, Harold Koenig, and Lisa Perez, "Patterns of Positive and Negative Religious Coping with Major Life Stressors," *Journal for the Scientific Study of Religion* 37, no. 4: (December 1998): 710–711; Christopher Ellison, "Religious Involvement and Subjective Well-Being," *Journal of Health and Social Behavior* 32, no. 1 (March 1991): 80–100; Harold Koenig, Linda George, and Ilene Siegler, "The Use of Religion and Other Emotion–Regulating Coping Strategies among Older Adults," *The Gerontologist* 28, no. 3 (June 1988): 303–311. Also see Evelyn Parker, *Trouble Don't Last Always: Emancipatory Hope among African American Adolescents* (Cleveland: Pilgrim Press, 2003).

26. Everett Worthington, Jack Berry, and Les Parrott, "Unforgiveness, Forgiveness, Religion, and Health," in T. G. Plante and A. C. Sherman, eds., *Faith and Health: Psychological Perspectives* (New York: Guilford, 2001), pp. 107–138; Robert Joseph Taylor, Christopher Ellison, Linda Chatters, Jeffrey Levin, and Karen Lincoln, "Mental Health Services in Faith Communities: The Role of Clergy in Black Churches," *Social Work* 45, no. 1 (January 2000): 73–87.

27. Robert Wuthnow, *Meaning and Moral Order* (Cambridge, MA: Harvard University Press, 1987); James Hunter, *The Death of Character: Moral Education in an Age without Good or Evil* (New York: Basic Books, 2000).

28. Pierre Bourdieu, *Distinction: A Social Critique of the Judgment of Taste* (Cambridge, MA: Harvard University Press, 1984); Ralph McNeal, "Parental Involvement as Social Capital: Differential Effectiveness on Science Achievement, Truancy, and Dropping Out," *Social Forces* 78, no. 1 (September 1999): 117–144; Paul DiMaggio, "Cultural Capital and School Success: The Impact of Status Culture Participation on the Grades of U.S. High School Students," *American Sociological Review* 47 (1982): 189–201.

29. Douglas Holt, "Does Cultural Capital Structure American Consumption?," *Journal of Consumer Research* 25, no. 1 (1998): 1–25.

30. Laurence Iannaccone, "Religious Practice: A Human Capital Approach," *Journal for the Scientific Study of Religion* 29, no. 3 (September 1990): 297–315.

31. Mark Regnerus, "Shaping Schooling Success: Religious Socialization and Educational Outcomes in Urban Public Schools," *Journal for the Scientific Study of Religion* 39 (2000): 363–370; David Sikkink and Edwin Hernandez, "Religion Matters: Predicting Schooling Success among Latino Youth," Institute for Latino Studies, University of Notre Dame, 2003; also see Milbrey McLaughlin, Merita Irby, and Juliet Langman, *Urban Sanctuaries* (San Francisco: Jossey-Bass, 1994); Dean Borgman, *Hear My Story: Understanding the Cries of Troubled Youth* (Peabody, MA: Hendrickson, 2003).

32. Carnegie Council on Adolescent Development, *A Matter of Time: Risk and Opportunity in the Nonschool Hours* (New York: Carnegie Council on Adolescent Development, 1992).

33. Christian Smith, Melinda Lundquist Denton, Robert Faris, and Mark Regnerus, "Mapping American Adolescent Religious Participation," *Journal for the Scientific Study of Religion* 41, no. 4 (2003): 597–612; Robert Putnam, *Bowling Alone* (New York: Simon and Schuster, 2000); Corwin Smidt, "Religion and Civic Engagement: A Comparative Analysis," *Annals of the American Academy of Political and Social Science* 565 (September 1999): 176–177.

34. See Pamela King, "Adolescent Religiousness and Moral Behavior: A Proposed

Model of Social Capital Resources and Moral Outcomes" (PhD diss., School of Psychology, Fuller Theological Seminary, 2000).

35. James Coleman, "Social Capital in the Creation of Human Capital," *American Journal of Sociology* 94 (1988): 95–120; James Coleman and T. Hoffer, *Public and Private Communities: The Impact of Communities* (New York: Basic Books, 1987).

36. Anne Fletcher, Deborah Newsome, Pamela Nickerson, and Ronda Bazley, "Social Network Closure and Child Adjustment," *Merrill–Palmer Quarterly* 47, no. 4 (2001): 500–532 (also see for child adjustment). For closure and community integration, see N. Darling, L. Steinberg, M. Gringlas, and S. M. Dombusch, "Community Integration and Value Consensus as Forces for Socialization: A Test of Functional Community Hypothesis," paper presented at the meetings of the Society of Research on Child Development, New Orleans, 1993. For educational outcomes, see W. J. Carbonaro, "A Little Help from My Friend's Parents: Intergenerational Closure and Educational Outcomes," *Sociology of Education* 71 (1998): 295–313; S. L. Morgan and A. B. Sorensen, "Parental Networks, Social Closure, and Mathematics Learning," *American Sociological Review* 64 (1999): 661–681; Neal Krause, Christopher Ellison, Benjamin Shaw, John Marcum, and Jason Boardman, "Church-based Social Support and Religious Coping," *Journal for the Scientific Study of Religion* 40, no. 4 (2001): 637–657. For studies examining religious social networks using samples of adults, see James Cavendish, Michael Welch, and David Leege, "Social Network Theory and Predictors of Religiosity for Black and White Catholics," *Journal for the Scientific Study of Religion* 37, no. 3 (1998): 397–411.

37. Elsewhere, we have tried to show how this might be done: Christian Smith, "Religious Participation and Network Closure among American Adolescents," *Journal for the Scientific Study of Religion* 42, no. 2 (2003): 259–267; Christian Smith, "Research Note: Religious Participation and Parental Moral Expectations and Supervision of American Youth," *Review of Religious Research* 44, no. 4 (2003): 414–424.

38. For example, see Anson Shupe, William Stacey, and Susan Darnell, eds., *Bad Pastors: Clergy Misconduct in Modern America* (New York: New York University Press, 2000); "Sex Abuse by Priests," *America* 186, no. 5 (February 18, 2002): 3.

39. Jerald Belitz and Anita Schacht, "Satanism as a Response to Abuse: The Dynamics and Treatment of Satanic Involvement in Male Youths," *Adolescence* 27, no. 108 (winter 1992): 855–873. Also see Roger Levesque, *Not by Faith Alone: Religion, Law, and Adolescence* (New York: New York University Press, 2002).

40. Alfred Darnell and Darren Sherkat, "The Impact of Protestant Fundamentalism on Educational Attainment," *American Sociological Review* 62, no. 2 (1997): 306–316; Christopher Ellison and Darren Shekat, "Conservative Protestantism and Support for Corporal Punishment," *American Sociological Review* 58, no. 1 (1993): 131–145. But see Kraig Beyerlein, "Specifying the Impact of Conservative Protestantism on Educational Attainment," *Journal for the Scientific Study of Religion*, 43, no. 4 (2004): 505–518.

41. See Michael Emerson and Christian Smith, *Divided by Faith: Evangelical Religion and the Problem of Race in America* (New York: Oxford University Press, 2000), pp. 3–19; Glen Loury, *One by One from the Inside Out* (New York: Free Press, 1995); Eduardo Bonilla-Silva, *White Supremacy and Racism in the Post–Civil Rights Era* (Boulder, CO: Lynne Rienner, 2001).

CONCLUSION

1. For a popular anecdotal account of this, see David Brooks, "The Organization Kid," *Atlantic Monthly* (April 2001): 40–54.

POSTSCRIPT

1. Charles Taylor, *Sources of the Self* (Cambridge, MA: Harvard University Press, 1989); Charles Taylor, "Self-Interpreting Animals," in *Human Agency and Language* (Cambridge, UK: Cambridge University Press, 1985).

APPENDIX A

1. Gilbert Dennis and Joseph Kahl, *The American Class Structure: A New Synthesis* (Belmont, CA: Wadsworth, 1998).

2. See, for instance, Rodney Stark, "Physiology and Faith: Addressing the 'Universal' Gender Difference in Religious Commitment," *Journal for the Scientific Study of Religion* 41, no. 3 (September 2002): 395–507; Christian Smith, Robert Faris, Melinda Lundquist Denton, and Mark Regnerus, "Mapping American Adolescent Subjective Religiosity and Attitudes of Alienation toward Religion: A Research Report," *Sociology of Religion* 64, no. 1 (2003): 111–123; Christian Smith, Melinda Lundquist Denton, Robert Faris, and Mark Regnerus, "Mapping American Adolescent Religious Participation," *Journal for the Scientific Study of Religion* 41, no. 4 (December 2002): 597–612.

3. See, for example, Andrew Cherlin, *Marriage, Divorce, Remarriage* (Cambridge, MA: Harvard University Press, 1992); Steve Mintz and Susan Kellogg, *Domestic Revolutions: A Social History of American Family Life* (New York: Free Press, 1989).

4. For example, see Christian Smith, David Sikkink, and Jason Bailey, "Devotion in Dixie and Beyond: A Test of the 'Shibley Thesis' on the Effects of Regional Origin and Migration on Individual Religiosity," *Journal for the Scientific Study of Religion* 37, no. 3 (September 1998): 494–506.

5. NSYR data show relatively little clustering of respondents in counties, indicating the lack of need to run these as multilevel regressions in a Hierarchical Linear Modeling program, as they include contextual variables.

6. See, for instance, Christian Smith, Robert Faris, Melinda Lundquist Denton, and Mark Regnerus, "Mapping American Adolescent Subjective Religiosity and Attitudes of Alienation toward Religion: A Research Report," *Sociology of Religion* 64, no. 1 (2003): 111–123; Christian Smith, Melinda Lundquist Denton, Robert Faris, and Mark Regnerus, "Mapping American Adolescent Religious Participation," *Journal for the Scientific Study of Religion* 41, no. 4 (December 2002): 597–612.

7. Scale construction combines both mother's and father's education and yet properly accounts for single-parent family situations.

APPENDIX B

1. Another survey conducted using similar methods is the 1998–99 Survey of Parents and Youth (SPY, later renamed the Survey of Adults and Youth [SAY]), which was designed by Princeton University's Center for Research on Child Wellbeing in conjunction with the National Evaluation Team for the Urban Health Initiative at the

Center for Health and Public Service at New York University's Robert F. Wagner Graduate School, and was funded by the Robert Wood Johnson Foundation. SPY was designed to monitor trends in youth's access to parental and community resources and included interviews with parents and youth. SPY was administered as an RDD telephone survey to a nationally representative sample of youth age 10–18 and to oversamples of youth in five selected cities (Philadelphia, Baltimore, Detroit, Oakland, Richmond, and Chicago). Parents were screened and then interviewed, after which point the interviewers asked permission to interview the youth. SPY was conducted in English, Spanish, or Chinese, and lasted an average of 30 minutes for youth and 20 minutes for parents.

2. For some teenagers, to be sure, the anonymity of a telephone survey may have increased their level of discomfort with sensitive questions; we cannot know with certainty.

3. See Melinda Lundquist Denton and Christian Smith, *Methodological Issues and Challenges in the Study of American Youth and Religion*, project report (Chapel Hill, NC: National Study of Youth and Religion, 2001). One disadvantage of an RDD-sampled survey is that it does not include the approximately 4 percent of U.S. households without telephones at any given time. This concern, however, is somewhat alleviated by the fact that the majority of households without telephone service are not permanently so, but typically fluctuate in and out of having service over time, thus increasing their chances of inclusion in this survey insofar as it was conducted over seven months, and by the likelihood that households with teenagers in residence are underrepresented among households lacking telephone service. Neither does the NSYR represent those households with teenagers 13–17 whose telephone service consists only of cell phones, of which we would expect there to be very few.

4. See Leo Morales, "Cross-Cultural Adaptation of Survey Instruments," in *Assessing Patient Experiences with Assessing Healthcare in Multi–Cultural Settings* (Santa Monica, CA: Rand Corporation, 2001); R. W. Brislin, "The Wording and Translation of Research Instruments," in W. J. Lonner and J. W. Berry, eds., *Field Methods in Cross-Cultural Research* (Beverly Hills, CA: Sage, 1986).

5. Such incentives increase response rates without appearing to distort the quality of responses. See Eleanor Singer, "The Use of Incentives to Reduce Nonresponse in Household Surveys," in Robert Groves, Don Dillman, John Eltinge, and Roderick Little, eds., *Survey Nonresponse* (New York: Wiley, 2002). In the case of our (mean) 82-minute-long survey, such incentives seemed particularly important.

6. Such extensive and persistent contact efforts are expected significantly to reduce nonresponse bias. See Peter Lynn, Paul Clarke, Jean Martin, and Patrick Sturgis, "The Effects of Extended Interviewer Efforts on Nonresponse Bias," in Robert Groves, Don Dillman, John Eltinge, and Roderick Little, eds., *Survey Nonresponse* (New York: Wiley, 2002).

7. See Federal Communications Commission, *Statistics of Communications Common Carriers* (Washington, DC: Federal Communications Commission, 2000); J. Michael Brick, Jill Montaquila, and Fritz Scheuren, "Estimating Residency Rates for Undetermined Telephone Numbers," *Public Opinion Quarterly* 66 (2002): 18–39. Survey noncooperators are also known to have a relatively higher incidence of single-person and elderly households and of households without children in residence. See Robert Groves and Mick Couper, *Nonresponse in Household Interview Surveys* (New York: Wiley, 1998), pp. 119–154.

8. AAPOR RR4 is calculated thus: $(I+P)/(I+P)+(R+NC+O)+e(UH+UO)$, where

I = completed interview, P = partial interview, R = refusal and breakoffs, NC = noncontacts, O = other contacts, e = estimated proportion of cases of unknown eligibility that are eligible, UH = unknown if household occupied, and UO = other unknown; see www.aapor.org under "Survey Methods: Response Rate Calculator." A 90 percent household rate is ascribed for voice mail, unknown qualification callback, and unknown qualification refusal sample; among households, a 4 percent teen qualified incidence rate is ascribed for voice mail, unknown qualification callback, and unknown qualification refusal sample. Calculated with no adjustments for teen qualification incidence rates (e), thus more conservatively, the response rate is 48 percent. Comparative studies show an annual negative trend in survey response rates across Western nations due to increased difficulties with respondent contact and cooperation. See Edith de Leeuw and Wim de Heer, "Trends in Household Survey Nonresponse: A Longitudinal and International Comparison," in Robert Groves, Don Dillman, John Eltinge, and Roderick Little, eds., *Survey Nonresponse* (New York: Wiley, 2002). While a higher response rate is always desirable, the NSYR's final response rate represents among the highest possible given the methodology employed and prevailing social conditions and available technologies. Findings of extensive comparative analyses of the data (described in the next paragraph) document the NSYR's lack of sampling bias and national representation of U.S. teenagers 13–17, significantly mitigating response rate concerns.

9. See Jelke Bethlehem, "Weighting Nonresponse Adjustments Based on Auxiliary Information," in Robert Groves, Don Dillman, John Eltinge, and Roderick Little, eds., *Survey Nonresponse* (New York: Wiley, 2002); Judith Lessler and William Kalsbeek, *Nonsampling Error in Surveys* (New York: Wiley, 1992), pp. 183–193; C. H. Fuller, "Weighting to Adjust for Survey Nonresponse," *Public Opinion Quarterly* 38 (1974): 239–246. The 6 percent of cases with missing data on income, a much lower number than is typical of survey income data, were imputed using these variables in the following order of assigned importance: resident father's and mother's education, parental marital status, family home ownership status, and family race.

10. The South was overrepresented and the Northeast underrepresented by 5 and 2 percentage points, respectively; incomes greater than $100,000 were underrepresented by 6 percent.

11. Here we follow a similar procedure employed with success by the Survey of American Attitudes and Friendships; see Michael O. Emerson, "Report on the Lilly Survey of American Attitudes and Friendships," Department of Sociology, Rice University, Houston, 2000; also see Michael O. Emerson, George Yancey, and Karen J. Chai, "Does Race Matter in Residential Segregation? Exploring the Preferences of White Americans," *American Sociological Review* 66, no. 6 (2001): 922–935.

12. On only two measures tested were the two groups different: (1) the parent respondent for the oversample cases was 6 percent more likely to be a mother than a father; and (2) the educational attainment of the mothers of the oversample respondents was greater (only 5 percent of them had not attended any college, compared to 14 percent of the national Jewish sample mothers).

APPENDIX D

1. Described in B. Steensland, J. Z. Park, M. D. Regnerus, L. D. Robinson, W. B. Wilcox, and R. D. Woodberry, "The Measure of American Religion: Toward Improving the State of the Art," *Social Forces* 79, no. 1 (2000): 291–318.

Index